WHEN POLICE BECOME PREY

The Cold, Hard Facts of
Neil Stonechild's Freezing Death

By Candis McLean

Book Cover Design: Marla Thompson
Editor: Angelika Harvey
Typeset: Greg Salisbury
Portrait Photographer: Sean Phillips, Riverwood Photography

WHEN POLICE
BECOME PREY

To Aniya & Neema
Neema —

From your dyslexic
friend —
Lots of love
Candis

McLean, Candis, 1949-, author
    When police become prey : the cold, hard facts about Neil
Stonechild's freezing death / Candis McLean.

Issued in print and electronic formats.
ISBN 978-1-77141-146-2 (paperback).--ISBN 978-1-77141-147-9 (pdf)

    1. Police--Complaints against--Saskatchewan--Saskatoon. 2. Police
misconduct--Saskatchewan--Saskatoon. 3. Saskatoon (Sask.). Saskatoon
Police Service. 4. Stonechild, Neil, 1973-1990--Death and burial. 5. Indians
of North America--Crimes against--Saskatchewan--Saskatoon. 6. Race
relations--Saskatchewan--Saskatoon. I. Title.

HV8160.S27M35 2015   363.2'09712425   C2015-906946-7
                                                    C2015-906947-5

Dedicated to
Const. Larry Lockwood (SPS 1977–2004)

"I would like to speak directly to our First Nations people. I'm a cop; I have racist and bigoted tendencies; however, I'm doing my best to deal with these shortcomings," wrote Sr. Const. Larry Lockwood in a letter to the editor after a Saskatchewan Aboriginal leader made unfounded and hateful remarks about Jewish people. His letter continued:

"What I want to say is: As disturbing as [Saskatchewan First Nations politician] David Ahenakew's racist remarks have been, I will not let his remarks reinforce those feelings within me that may influence my thinking. On the contrary, I find I have more empathy for your struggle because of his remarks. His insensitivity highlights mine, making me much more aware of the need for understanding and tolerance.

I know that, as a people, you feel ashamed that a person such as Ahenakew would say such things, and that his words reflect badly on all you are trying to achieve. You are not alone; we all have these people among us. Words that hurt today will hopefully help us heal tomorrow. …Together we are going to make this world a better place, despite our prejudices – our stupid, unthinking, hurtful prejudices.

In a backhanded sort of way, what a great opportunity Ahenakew has provided us. Together, we will, despite his remarks, strengthen our resolve to better our communities. Ahenakew's heart may not be in the right place, but I know yours is. Be proud of who you are, and I will be proud with you. Larry Lockwood, Saskatoon" [1]

The following year, Const. Lockwood had a two-part letter published, this one headlined "McNab Park proves community policing works":

"Community policing is not rocket science; it's not some wishy-washy philosophy, although some would complicate it beyond all recognition. It's simple – give people the opportunity to participate in reducing crime in their neighbourhoods and they will reduce crime.

… McNab Park was one of those communities where the futility and frustration for cops was overwhelming. It had a staggering amount of crime for its size. It would have been easy for police just to throw up our hands in defeat. …

It didn't take long to realize that the root of 75 percent of the community's crime problems could be traced back to the kids having nothing to occupy their time. There was no community centre. Most, if not all, of the playground equipment was dilapidated or broken. How do you have a game of pick-up baseball if you're poor and don't have a bat and ball? ...

In the two years the McNab Park Youth Project – a community policing initiative -- has been operational, there has been nearly a 78-percent decrease in crime – to 60 offences against persons and property in 2002-03 from 270 in 2000-01." [2]

Jim McLaren is a mentally-ill street person befriended by Const. Lockwood. He writes:

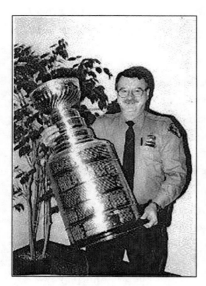

Larry Lockwood guarding the Stanley Cup. Photo courtesy of Mrs. Sharon Lockwood

"It took a long time to get my schizophrenia under control but Larry still stood by me. It was a funny thing – a schizophrenic and a police officer; usually everybody is afraid of both of us, so we were quite the scary pair. We'd talk about stuff. He told me one time that National Geographic did a big study and found that everyone in the world is 99.9% the same in their chromosomes and stuff. He had that understanding about people; I operated accordingly and so did he. He never talked to me about religion, but I said once, when I was gabbing with him, 'Love conquers all.' He said, 'Yes it does, Jim.'"

Const. Lockwood was one of the Saskatoon police officers this writer tarred with the brush of "Racist Cops" in my first news story about so-called "starlight tours." In 2004, he retired earlier than planned, to fight for fellow officers he believed wronged by the justice system: Constables Ken Munson, Dan Hatchen, Larry Hartwig and Brad Senger. I interviewed him as he led a march in front of his police station, carrying a sign reading "Wright inquest is a witch-hunt! McCarthyism!" Much research later, I realized he had identified the social phenomenon behind an extraordinary time in Saskatchewan when a few citizens lost touch with reason and common sense, and those in authority permitted dangerous lapses in due judicial process.

Having contributed significantly to this book, Const. Lockwood died of cancer in 2010. His work as both a crime and anti-apartheid fighter is part of this story about a dramatic on-going search for justice.

In November 1990, Saskatoon teenager Neil Stonechild froze to death. Eleven years later, his body was disinterred for forensic testing. The RCMP and a public inquiry pointed fingers at two police officers as having been involved, in some mysterious way, in his death. This is the story of these two cops.

"The only perfect crime is not the one that remains unsolved, but the one which is solved with the wrong culprit."
– **2008 film, The Oxford Murders**

"The good guys became the bad guys in this one. Many involved in this process manufactured evidence, suppressed evidence, concealed evidence, edited evidence, took evidence out of context, and/or did not weigh the evidence properly. This is corruption at its worst."
– **Larry Hartwig, disgraced and fired Saskatoon police officer**

"The story is so much bigger than a few alleged incidents of conflict between Natives and police. The story involves a racially biased and politically corrupted justice system. The story is how political interference in our judicial system is a blight on our country, making a mockery of our so-called 'Just Society.'"
– **Mike Ritchie, retired Royal Canadian Air Force fighter pilot**

"Every day the injustice flashes back into my heart and mind and I so wish it had never happened. I grieve over the officers I left on the battlefield. I hope and pray that God will mercifully clear them someday."
- **Dave Scott, Saskatoon Police Chief, retired**

"The witches they were presumed to be were little more than fantasies conjured by a mixture of fear, ambition, frustration, jealousy, and perverted pride."
– **Professor Christopher Bigsby analysing the Salem witch-hunt.**
He might have been describing Saskatchewan's own *"Crucible."*

Acknowledgements:
Deconstructing the Labyrinth

This is the true story of a house of cards the size of a city. Built lie upon lie, this house contains multiple horrors, which makes opening each door intriguing in a disturbing sort of way. All it will take now is the collapse of one card to set the entire fabrication toppling.

The house of lies was built by a few people with tunnel vision, unaware they were ruining *innocent* lives and causing excruciating pain to so many more. What appalls me is how many others had to have known the truth, and pretend they didn't.

I want to thank the many who deconstructed the skillfully built labyrinth, and those who contributed in other ways to the writing of this book.

First, my husband, Ross McLean, who kept me going when months turned into years, and one book grew into three. I could not have done it without you, it's that simple. To my sons, Stuart and Steven, and wives, Adelheide and Irina, thank you for your astute advice and support when I needed it most. Stuart, thank you for writing and performing the stirring music for my documentary, *When Police Become Prey*, teaching yourself how to edit film, and then putting it all together in an award-winning format. A tour de force for which I will always be grateful.

Stan Goertzen, president of the Saskatoon Police Association, worked unceasingly to prove the innocence of his fellow officers, even years after he retired. The level of stress on him has been brutal. Yet, as one officer says in the book, "Stan is the rock that kept everyone going through the hell of the first decade of the twenty-first century."

Sandy Hartwig, Larry Hartwig's wife, was one inspiration for writing the book. A diminutive Saskatchewan farm girl, she is the dynamo who kept her husband and family together through one devastating emotional blow after another, all while working as a devoted registered nurse.

Thanks to Darrell Connell of the prodigious memory, and to dozens of other Saskatoon police officers who gave unstintingly of their time to help me sort out cold, hard facts from hot, malleable lies.

Colleen and Dave Scott were there the whole time, full of ideas and encouragement, toiling daily to write up information and answers to my barrage of questions. After I was caught in the Great Alberta Flood of 2013, their words got me drying out soggy research and starting in again. To this day, Dave's dedication to the officers he feels he "left on the battlefield" is undying.

My editor Angelika Harvey, fact-checker Gail Radford-Ross, legal mind Danielle Rondeau, proof-readers Jeri Pearce and Trijnie Mulder, and publisher Julie Salisbury all kept me on-track and upbeat. Friends Birgitte Michie and Marian Mann lent me their homes and their coffee to get the job done. Brothers, Dave and George Hart, and their wives Sharon and Shirley, contributed to my book and my life. Judge Wallace Gilby Craig researched the case relentlessly, and contributed many learned thoughts about the case. John Reilly, Calvin Helin and Dennis Watlington kindly read and endorsed the book. Thank you to the many citizens and police officers who gave me their evidence in an effort to "speak truth to power," particularly the three key witnesses who should have been called to testify at the Stonechild Inquiry, but, for some mysterious reason, were not. Thank you to Saskatoon *StarPhoenix* editor Heather Persson for permission to reprint articles. Finally, I acknowledge three University of Saskatchewan professors: Dr. Keith Johnstone, Dr. Lew Horne, and Dr. L. J. Morrissey, whose inspiration to "write fearlessly" echoes down the years.

You are heroes, every one.

Contents

FOREWORD by Judge Craig:
'Suspiciously Murky Story'

Investigative journalist Candis McLean analyzes the circumstances surrounding the hypothermic death in November 1990 of Neil Christopher Stonechild, 17, a First Nations youth. Initially, Saskatoon police – and the coroner – determined no foul play was involved in his death. Using a historian's approach, McLean unravels the complicated and suspiciously murky story that arose 10 years later. In 2000, suspicions that police were somehow involved in Aboriginal freezing deaths ignited a firestorm of controversy, as tabloid-like media coverage fanned out, worldwide. McLean reveals that it became a *cause célèbre* rife with venomous muckrakers characterizing the Saskatoon Police Service as racist.

Faced with this out-of-control controversy, the Government of Saskatchewan created a Commission of Inquiry and appointed Justice David H. Wright as its commissioner to conduct an inquiry "into the circumstances that resulted in the death of Neil Stonechild, and the conduct of an investigation into the death of Neil Stonechild, for the purpose of making findings and recommendations with respect to the administration of criminal justice in the Province of Saskatchewan." It was an inquiry merely to determine facts.

McLean takes dead aim at the commissioner's conclusion, open to the inference that two Saskatoon police officers transported Stonechild to the outskirts of Saskatoon and abandoned him to the peril of hypothermia. In the Afterword to this book, I analyze that devastating report.

– Wallace Gilby Craig served 26 years as judge in Vancouver's Provincial Criminal Court, followed by six years as adjudicator with the federal Human Rights Tribunal

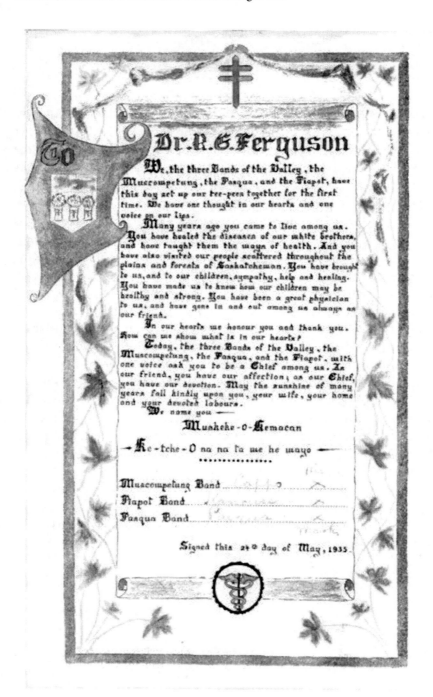

NOTE FROM THE AUTHOR:
Into the Land of Myth

Covering the hearing into the wrongful dismissal of two Saskatoon police officers, I was embarrassed. A hard-nosed investigative journalist of many years, as I sat taking notes, I found tears rolling down my cheeks. I could not make them stop. The 2004 hearing was examining the officers' firing over concerns they might have been involved, in some unknown way, in the freezing death of Neil Stonechild. That day, photos of Neil's body were projected onto a huge screen for those in attendance to study. He was 17 at the time of his death; my own sons were not much older. The tragedy was heartbreaking. I wanted to learn how his death might have been prevented.

The lad was Aboriginal. At that point in my life, my sister-in-law was my only Native friend (researching this book, I've made more Native friends), but I was brought up with great respect for their culture. A favourite childhood story starred the aged Chief Towweeaka who, every Christmas, walked miles from his reserve to my grandparents' home near Fort Qu'Appelle, Saskatchewan.

"His visit was fascinating because the chief and Father spoke two very different languages," my elderly aunt told me. "Mother would serve them tea by the fire, my grey-haired father with his bowtie always a little crooked, and this dignified old man with a feather in his braid who sat so straight and looked so wise. Mostly they discussed the health of Towweeaka's people. There would be much waving of hands, nodding of heads, sign language, and, now and then, laughter. It took a while, but the two would come to understand one another. Finally they would sit in silence, smoking their pipes. The silence was important; it was almost as though they could feel what the other was feeling.

"When the chief was ready to leave, Dad would offer him a ride, but he would shake his head, 'No.' And he would walk [six miles][3] home! One Christmas Towweeaka did not appear. My father went to the reserve and they had one last visit together."

Why did the aged chief make that long, cold walk year after year? My aunt says it was to say, "Thank you." My grandfather, Dr. George Ferguson, was for many years medical-director of the three tuberculosis sanatoria in Saskatchewan. Many patients were Aboriginal, since they were drastically over-represented in contracting the frequently deadly disease. In Manitoba, for example, although Aboriginal people were then only two percent of the population, they made up 45 percent of TB victims.[4] Chief Towweeaka probably remembered the terrible 1880s when, across the country, *one Aboriginal person in 10 died of TB.*[5] In a rare photo of the time, renowned Blackfoot Chief Crowfoot smiles proudly, surrounded by six robust children. The caption reads: "Crowfoot and his family in 1884. All the children in the picture had died of tuberculosis within two years."[6]

Because so many on reserves suffered from undiagnosed TB, they unwittingly infected others. Recognizing this, sanatoria staff devised a plan to detect pulmonary tuberculosis before symptoms became apparent, while treatment was still effective and their family uninfected. Devising a portable lung X-ray machine, the staff loaded it and a gas-powered generator onto a truck and visited remote reserves from one end of the province to the other – three times. Meanwhile, glandular TB was treated by local surgeons including Dr. Maurice Seymour who did "extensive resections of glands ... on an acutely ill schoolboy. That boy recovered and became Canada's famous Marathon runner, Paul Acoose."[7]

With early detection, immunization, and, in 1929, Saskatchewan pioneering free TB treatment, death rates plummeted. In 1936, the death rate for Native infants in their first year was 1,603 per 100,000; by 1948, it was down to 17 per 100,000[8] – a nearly 100% improvement. As my grandfather wrote, "Resistance [to the 'White man's disease'], therefore, guaranteed the survival of the tribes."[9]

My grandfather was also the North American pioneer in desegregating sanatoria pavilions where patients stayed. "He just couldn't see any reason why races should be separated," says my aunt. His greatest tribute, he said, was being named, in 1935, honourary Indian Chief *Muskeke-O-Kemacan* – Great White Physician. Along with a ceremonial headdress, the bands gave him a plaque inscribed:

"We, the three Bands of the Valley, the Muscowpetung, the Pasqua and the Piapot, have this day set up our tee-pees together for the first time. We have one thought in our hearts and one voice on our lips. Many years ago you came to live among us. You have healed the diseases of our white brothers and have taught us the ways of health. And you have also visited our people scattered throughout the plains and forests of Saskatchewan. You have brought to us, and to our children, sympathy, help and healing.

...You have been a great physician to us and have gone in and out among us, always as our friend."

Knowing a few of the thousands who, to this very day, supported by citizens and government, worked and still work themselves to exhaustion battling the disease once decimating Aboriginal peoples – the reverse of genocide! – we find it hurtful that some educators today fill young Aboriginal minds with hate. Why suppress truth about all the caring, life-saving work done in various fields on behalf of Native people? This suppression promotes hostility, and encourages separation.

The Aboriginal and Caucasian communities are more alike today than at any time in the past because we live in the same cities. Yet many Aboriginal politicians seek separation – even apartheid – by demanding changes such as a separate justice system. What divisive system, creating more "apartness," will be demanded tomorrow?

Someone is benefiting by fomenting hostility between races, but our country is not. I believe that if, like Towweeaka and my grandfather, Aboriginal and White people worked together sincerely, "The two would come to understand one another." To appreciate one another. On the other hand, we can only be driven disastrously apart by chicanery and guile, such as the deceit behind alleged "starlight tours" revealed in this book.

As the author, this is my background. As a journalist writing my initial story about Aboriginal freezing deaths in Saskatoon, like many others, I accepted the line fed the public: White police were somehow responsible. Digging deeper, I followed my grandfather's words: "Constantly struggle for the truth!" *When Police Become Prey* documents my journey of discovery into the land of myth, followed by efforts to learn how the disastrous lie – *the snow-job!* – could possibly have been foisted upon the intelligent peoples of my home province.

TIMELINE:
Saskatoon Freezing Deaths

Nov. 24, 1990: Neil Stonechild, 17, of Saskatoon, goes missing. Last known sighting: a disturbance at Snowberry Downs apartment complex.

Nov. 29, 1990: Stonechild's frozen body found in the vicinity of the 800 block 58th Street.

Dec. 1, 1990: Saskatoon *StarPhoenix* quotes Coroner Dr. Brian Fern: "We have excluded obvious foul play, as he didn't have an injury of any kind."

Dec. 5, 1990: Sgt. Keith Jarvis closes SPS investigation into death of Neil Stonechild without interviewing any suspects alleged by family and friends to have been involved in his death or determining how he got out to the industrial north end.

Ten years later, January 19, 2000: Lloyd Joseph Dustyhorn, 53, found frozen to death outside a locked apartment building. Three hours earlier, following time spent in custody, police had driven him home to his own apartment, two blocks from where he was found.

Fri. Jan. 28, 2000: Darrell Night, 33, dropped off by police near Queen Elizabeth power plant at approximately 5 a.m. Arrives home safely.

Sat. Jan. 29: Rodney Hank Naistus, 25, found frozen to death several km from power plant, and five blocks (.8 km) from residential area.

Sun. Jan. 30: Lawrence Kim Wegner, 30, goes missing.

Tues. Feb. 1: Night spends 21 recorded minutes calling police 911 line. He does not complain about his drop-off by police four days earlier, or any mistreatment by police.

Thurs. Feb. 3: Wegner found frozen to death near power plant.

Thurs. Feb. 3: Saskatoon police officer Const. Bruce Ehalt stops Night in car; Night tells him police had dropped him off near power plant.

Fri. Feb. 4: Ehalt drives to home where Night is staying, invites him to make a report, and drives him into the station to do it. Night gives first statement. Police chief asks deputy chief to work all weekend investigating allegation.

Mon. Feb. 7: Night invited to return to station to provide more details. He gives very different second statement, including, for the first time, a claim that police made racial slurs. The Federation of Saskatchewan Indian Nations later claimed it had intervened: "Darrell Night came out and the police were looking for him, okay? They wanted to interview him, they wanted to talk to him and sweep this incident under the rug. But no, fortunately he came to us and this is basically where this whole process started."[10]

Mon. Feb. 7, 2000: Munson and Hatchen voluntarily step forward to say they had dropped Night off. Waiving their right to lawyers, they give self-condemning Warned Statements and demand polygraphs regarding any involvement in Naistus' death. They were not on duty the night Wegner went missing. (For complete Munson/Hatchen story, see *When Police Become Prey: Book 2: Darrell Night Walked and Justice Died.*)

Thurs. Feb. 10: Police chief tells Munson and Hatchen that Sask Justice has decided not to proceed with charges. They are suspended pending internal police investigation.

February: Previously unreleased to the public, FSIN's Lawrence Joseph has admitted that during this time, Aboriginal chiefs held meetings in which they put pressure on RCMP, Sask Justice and the premier. "And I think eventually the minister of justice decided to go ahead with this," Lawrence said.

Wed. Feb. 16: Sask Justice decides to move investigation of possible police involvement in freezing deaths from local police to RCMP, even though there is neither indication of bias nor support in law to bypass normal procedure without clear evidence of bias. Operation Ferric launches. RCMP task force is to investigate circumstances of freezing deaths of Wegner and Naistus, as well as Night's allegation that Saskatoon police had dropped him near the outskirts of the city. 1990 freezing death of Neil Stonechild later added to investigation.

Thurs. Feb. 17: Front-page story in Saskatoon newspaper with error-laden lead: "Darrell Night says he remembers the racial slurs, the blue-and-white police cruiser, and having his jacket stripped off by the uniformed officers who drove him outside the city and abandoned him." On page three, a columnist writes: "The worst thing in the world is a police state. To have police torturing and killing people they don't like is as bad as it gets. After this, it is only a question of how many. How many people were driven out of town in a police cruiser and left to freeze to death? How many more will turn up in spring when the snow melts? How many others were thrown into the river to turn up downstream, days or weeks later? How many officers are involved? How many looked the other way?"[11]

Fri. Feb. 18: *StarPhoenix* buries correction, that police did not remove Night's jacket, 27 paragraphs down in its follow-up story. Other media miss the correction and spread the lie, suggesting police are attempting to murder Aboriginal people, around the world.

Fri. Feb. 18, 2000: RCMP sets up a 1-800 tip line for those complaining about unwanted drop-offs; results are to be sent to Sask. Dept. of Justice for decision on charges.

Fri. Feb. 18: FSIN justice commission meets in Prince Albert, demanding public inquiry into police treatment of First Nations, stating that if the Province does not yield to its demand, FSIN will organize its own inquiry.

Sat. Feb. 19: Darcy Dean Ironchild, 33, found dead in his bedroom by relatives after being sent home by taxi from police custody four hours earlier. Police Chief Dave Scott immediately reports his death to task force, which adds his death to four already being investigated. Aboriginal leaders call for public inquiry into Aboriginal peoples and the justice system.

Feb. 19: Media coverage includes headline in London, Ont. *Free Press*: "First Nations Chief [Phil Fontaine] fears police racism rampant in Canada."

Feb. 22: *StarPhoenix* story in which Jason Roy makes his first public allegation that Neil Stonechild was in police custody 10 years before, and he heard Stonechild yell, "They're gonna kill me!"

Feb. 22: Métis politician overheard recommending that what was needed was "a commission that would take sworn statements, so that the justice system could be bypassed."

February: Rodney Wailing, 29, comes forward with allegation that three years earlier, two police officers picked him up while he was high on lacquer thinner. Claims they drove him to riverbank near power plant, where they tried to drown him. Wailing's lawyer launches lawsuit. RCMP investigates, finds no evidence. Lawsuit quietly dropped.

February: Two marches to the police station staged, complete with police escorts. People carry signs including: "Police to serve and protect, yeah right!" "I am Scared to Walk at Night!" and "Two Dead Natives = 30 Day Holiday with Pay!"

Feb. 29: FSIN justice commission recommends pressing for justice inquiry to address all First Nations justice issues rather than merely conduct of SPS.

March 1, 2000: Saskatchewan Justice Minister Chris Axworthy calls on federal justice minister to become involved in potentially explosive issue of race relations in Saskatchewan; hints province will continue to meet with FSIN to explore possible Native justice system in province.

March: Munson and Hatchen undergo three-hour polygraph tests. RCMP officer in charge tells this writer, "There was no implication as a result of the polygraph that either Ken Munson or Dan Hatchen was involved in either death." Yet RCMP does not announce this publicly. Night never polygraphed.
Mar. 4: Darrell Night stabbed in a bar. Called to scene, police officers keep him alive until ambulance arrives. Night hospitalized, but will not allow police investigation; no charges laid.

March: RCMP tipped off to plot to attack homes of Munson and Hatchen with homemade pipe bombs. Panic buttons directly linked to police station installed in their homes.

Mar. 13: First Nations community calls for public inquiry when RCMP investigation is complete because "without a public inquiry, Native politicians say, no one will be at fault for the deaths of the four Aboriginal men, including the 1990 death of Neil Stonechild."[12]

Mar. 20: RCMP announces completion of investigation regarding Night. Munson and Hatchen are shocked since investigators have not interviewed them about their statements, thereby missing crucial information. Investigation into other freezing deaths continues.

Mar. 21: FSIN announces it will hire private investigators to shadow RCMP task force and "investigate the investigators." Declares Vice Chief Joseph, "The RCMP have their marching orders and that's all."

Mar. 31: RCMP shuts down 1-800 tip line after six weeks. Eighty percent (141 out of 179) of complaints received are against RCMP, including allegations of abandonments. RCMP will investigate allegations under Operations Faculty and Forest, but never release findings.

Apr. 2000: Amnesty International joins fray, writing Justice Minister in support of Aboriginal politicians' calls for inquiry into freezing deaths.

Apr. 11: After earlier deciding against charges for Munson and Hatchen, Saskatchewan Justice charges them with assault and unlawful confinement. FSIN wants them charged with attempted murder.

May 2000: FSIN commits money from gaming revenues to investigate how police treat Sask Native people. A year later, FSIN asks province to pick up its future tab.

May 18: RCMP investigators accuse Constables Larry Hartwig, 41, and Brad Senger, 36, of having had Neil Stonechild in their custody the night he went missing 10 years earlier.

May 23: FSIN makes presentation to Sask Justice Minister and Aboriginal Affairs Minister, seeking a Truth and Reconciliation Commission, demanding an evaluation by First Nations as to appropriateness of the "Canadian alien system of law."

May 31, 2000: Amnesty International's annual report of Human Rights Abuses, published worldwide, chronicles "torture, killings and persecution," including slavery in Sudan and allegations of "patterns of police abuse against First Nations men in Saskatoon." Report based solely on reporting by journalists before any evidence is produced.

June 7, 2000: FSIN makes presentation to two deputy ministers of justice seeking a forum for Sask people "to tell their truth about the pain, suffering, humility, disrespect or injustice inflicted upon them by law enforcement officials." The chiefs threaten: "Victims will turn on governments if 'the people who are supposed to take care of them' remain on the sidelines."

Sept. 11, 2000: Separate preliminary hearings begin for Constables Munson and Hatchen. Despite Darrell Night admitting to inconsistencies and even lies in his allegations, the judges order the officers to stand trial.

September: Lawyer Donald Worme faxes Operation Ferric about another complainant who claims police picked him up at home in December, 1999, dropped him off north of Saskatoon, "stripped him of his jacket," and then waited outside his home for him to hitchhike back so they could return the jacket and hurl racist remarks. RCMP finds no substantiation. Matter dropped; no one sanctioned over unsubstantiated allegation.

Oct. 26, 2000: Former SPS officer Jim Maddin elected mayor. Police Chief Scott predicts he will be ousted abruptly by the following June.

Dec. 2000: Coroner's inquest into death of Darcy Ironchild finds no police involvement after RCMP had come to same conclusion. Ironchild had collected more than 160 drugs, paid by his federal prescription coverage, including sleeping medication on which he overdosed. He died in his home.

Jan. 27, 2001: Front-page story claims Night's lawyer, Donald Worme, will file civil suit against police officers over alleged dumping, seeking $2-million in damages. Suit later quietly dropped.

Feb. 26, 2001: Front-page story claims Rodney Naistus' mother filing suit against unknown members of Saskatoon Police Service for wrongful death of her son. Suit later quietly dropped.

Mar. 9, 2001: Page 7 *StarPhoenix* story headlined "Mother doesn't blame police for son's death" quotes Mary Wegner suggesting someone (other than police) is responsible: "Whoever does this, they don't know how many people they're hurting."[13]

Mar. 24, 2001: Sask Justice agrees to review of justice system and its treatment of Aboriginal peoples.

Apr. 24, 2001: Eleven years after Neil Stonechild's freezing death, his body is disinterred for second autopsy. Alberta Chief Medical Examiner reports: "… there is no evidence of any injury or other natural disease process to refute the original [1990] autopsy findings and conclusions."

May 8-10, 2001: Lloyd Dustyhorn inquest concludes death accidental, caused by hypothermia.

May 31, 2001: For second year, Amnesty International annual report includes "allegations of patterns of police abuse against First Nations men in Saskatoon."

June 5, 2001: Parliamentary committee addresses issues of First Nations health caused by prescription drug abuse. Lorraine Stonechild, sister of Darcy Ironchild who overdosed in his home, speaks at their Ottawa meeting. Within a year, changes are made to tackle problem which led to Ironchild's death: taxpayer-funded prescription drugs.

June 21, 2001: Chief Scott informed that his contract has been terminated effective immediately. Reason given: insufficient community policing.

Sept. 11, 2001 (9/11): Ten-day trial of Munson and Hatchen begins. Night testifies that (A) his only documented injury resulted from a tight handcuff and, (B) he did not talk to officers about either where he lived or a drop-off point. Jury acquits officers of assault charge but convicts them of unlawful confinement. Both officers fired.

Oct. 27, 2001: Four months after Chief Scott fired for insufficient community policing, SPS wins major international award for community policing under Chief Scott.

Oct. 30: Week-long inquest into freezing death of Rodney Naistus begins. Jury concludes he died of hypothermia with no evidence of police involvement. Jury aims bulk of recommendations at police.

Oct. 30: Munson and Hatchen's sentencing arguments heard. They request sentencing circle; denied.

Nov. 1: Announcement of creation of (Saskatchewan) Commission on First Nations and Métis Peoples and Justice Reform.

Dec. 8, 2001: Munson and Hatchen sentenced to eight months in jail. They appeal both conviction and sentence.

Jan. 14, 2002: Month-long inquest into freezing death of Lawrence Wegner begins. Jury concludes Wegner died of hypothermia, no evidence of police involvement, and aims eight of 22 recommendations at police. Despite Mrs. Wegner's publicized statement a year earlier that she "doesn't blame police," at inquest she blames police. Wegner family lawyer Gregory Curtis, a member of Worme's firm, says, "I suspect a lawsuit is going to be in the offing."[14] Threatened lawsuit later quietly dropped.

Feb. 8, 2002: Sask Justice decides not to lay charges in death of Neil Stonechild.

Mar. 5, 2002: Darrell Night, who, at Munson/Hatchen trial five months earlier testified he was "scared of the cops," pleads guilty to spitting all over interior of locked police car in which he is sole occupant.

May, 2002: According to SPS officer, Aboriginal man tells him and several police staff outside on break that he works for FSIN and FSIN is paying witnesses to tell their stories about police involvement in their cases.

Jan. 2003: A first for Canada, Beardy's and Okemasis First Nation opens own justice building to host court and other justice services. Minister of justice hopes Saskatchewan's Aboriginal Justice Commission will help set path to build Aboriginal justice system.

Feb. 20, 2003: Justice Minister Eric Cline announces public inquiry into Stonechild's death

Mar. 13, 2003: Court of Appeal upholds provincial court decisions re: Munson and Hatchen; they turn themselves in for sentence of eight months in Saskatoon Correctional Centre. Hatchen says staff discovered knives and five prisoners hidden in yard in plot to harm Munson.

Sept. 8, 2003: Inquest into Death of Neil Stonechild begins. Scheduled for six weeks, it extends to eight months.

Jan. 31, 2004: Memorial Round Dance for Lawrence Wegner. Aboriginal man, Russell Charles, freezes to death after being turned out by Aboriginal security. Newspaper reports story briefly before dropping it. Charles' uncle later contacts this writer to disclose story.

Mar. 26, 2004: New evidence brought to light indicating Munson and Hatchen were telling truth and did exactly as they claimed: released Night at his request 3.2 km from Clancy Village apartment he had recently shared with his cousin, Lorna Night, who still lived there. RCMP investigates reopening Munson/Hatchen case, but in August announces decision against it.

June 21, 2004: Report issued by $3-million Commission on First Nations and Métis Peoples and Justice Reform. Addressing the high incarceration rate, FSIN's Joseph does not say it demonstrates a need for Native leaders to help their people. Instead, he says, it demonstrates the need to create a separate Native justice system.

Oct. 26, 2004: Province releases report of Stonechild Inquiry. On the basis of inconsistent testimony by one man with lengthy criminal record and despite documented contradicting evidence, judge effectively imposes responsibility for Stonechild's death on Constables Hartwig and Senger when he finds: "Stonechild was probably last seen in the custody of the two officers," and "finds" officers had time to take Stonechild out where his body was found.

Oct. 26, 2004: FSIN media release: "The findings of Commissioner David H. Wright in the Inquiry into the Death of Neil Stonechild undeniably proves the need for a First Nations developed, implemented and administered Justice system."

Nov. 12, 2004: Hartwig and Senger fired for not having written in their 1990 notebooks what Commissioner Wright had decided at Stonechild Inquiry: that they had Stonechild in their custody the last night he was seen alive.

July 2005: Stonechild family lawyer gives Police Commission October deadline to pay a six-figure settlement to Stonechild's family to compensate for his death and police handling of the investigation, or face a lawsuit. Money not paid; threatened lawsuit quietly dropped.

May 2 – Nov. 1, 2005: Hearing under Police Act into firing of Hartwig and Senger. Decision handed down a year later, Nov. 1, 2006, upholds police chief's decision (itself based on the inquiry) to fire the officers.

Nov. 1, 2005: Front-page *StarPhoenix* story announces Stonechild family lawyer, Worme, to sue police service and several officers, including Hartwig, Senger, Jarvis, Scott and Wiks. Plaintiffs seek $30-million for alleged negligence, deception and misinformation.

Nov. 2, 2005: *StarPhoenix* story on page eight quotes officers' lawyers saying Stonechild lawsuit is baseless. Following publicity, lawsuit is quietly dropped, in same manner lawsuits for Night, Naistus and Wailing were filed (and for Wegner as well as Stonechild against the police commission, threatened), given wide publicity and dropped.

Aug. 2006: Hartwig, Senger and Saskatoon Police Association independently apply to Sask Court of Appeal to throw out results of Public Inquiry. They seek to quash Justice Wright's conclusion that Stonechild had been in the officers' custody, maintaining Wright exceeded his jurisdiction when "he effectively imposed criminal and/or civil responsibility" for Stonechild's death upon the officers.

June 19, 2008: Court of Appeal dismisses applications.

July, 2008: Former officers seek to have case heard by Supreme Court. Denied

PROLOGUE:
Dawn

Sunday, Nov. 25, 1990. First light was brightening the sky to pewter-grey when Larry Hartwig jumped from his car and ran up the walk, his breath a steaming trail of vapour. "Sandy!" he called, bursting through the door. "Where are you?"

"In the kitchen, coffee's on!" his wife called. The petite blond, a Saskatchewan farm girl, could have been a model, but she preferred the gruelling work of an RN. In addition to the toll extracted by shift work, she was six months pregnant with their first child, and exhausted.

"How are you two feelin'?" he asked, pulling a chair up to the gleaming pine table.

"We're a little tired," she said, lazily stretching her arms out to him. "Busy shift? Gosh, Honey, what's wrong?"

"Got to tell you," he said. "Worst thing I've ever done."

"Oh, no! What happened?" During their two-and-a-half years of marriage, Sandy had become accustomed to trading stories-without-names with her police officer husband. She had seldom seen him so upset.

"Just one of those crazy, crazy Saturday nights where we were going from call to call to call and then my partner and I – tonight I was partnered with a guy named Brad Senger, brand new constable, still on probation – we had to um ...." Pressing his lips together, he blinked rapidly.

"Horrible!" Sandy murmured, pouring his coffee, squeezing his hand, stirring in cream.

"RCMP asked us to notify a woman that her estranged husband, when he took their boys out for a visitation ... he actually ... he shot their sons. Murdered them both."

"Oh Larry!"

"Can you imagine telling that to their mom? Both sons dead? She was so distraught and I felt so useless ...."

Sandy let him talk. "Not only that, the father was going to kill himself, too, but then he flinched when the gun went off and he wounded himself. He was found outside his house, alive but ...."

After she calmed him down, Larry went to bed but couldn't sleep, so she listened some more. He went over what he had said trying to assist the traumatized woman and he asked what he could have done better.

Neither of them would ever forget the conversation. But it was a completely different call that Larry, 31, and Brad, 26, had taken that same bitterly cold 1990 night – a routine call that Larry hadn't even mentioned to her because nothing happened since he and his partner had been unable to find the youth they were dispatched to look for – that 10 years later would somehow, impossibly, transform their vital young lives.

Sometime that same night, a strikingly handsome teenager with shiny, coal-black hair had gone missing. He later found himself miles from the detention home to which he had been sentenced, stumbling through knee-deep snow in an empty lot in Saskatoon's industrial north end. His cheeks white with frostbite, faculties numbed with cold, bare hands pulled up into the sleeves of his unzipped jacket, he felt like a hot iron was pressing his skin. Somewhere he had lost a running shoe, but he kept on going. An indentation in a snow-filled ditch revealed where he had fallen earlier. Urged on by all the life-seeking instincts in his strong young body, he crawled out of the ditch, but was unable to return to his feet. Finally, he could move not one inch further. The snow was a cool, clean sheet. Sinking onto it face-first, he pulled his arms up against his chest, breathed a quiet sigh, and drifted off to sleep.

Discovered later in a pocket of his faded jeans, a creased and worn clue may help solve, finally, the decades-old mystery: why was that youth out in that part of the city? And how did he get there – miles from home, miles from anywhere?

~ ~ ~

The notice of identification of the youth, Neil Stonechild, appeared in the Dec. 1, 1990 edition of the Saskatoon *StarPhoenix*. Above it was the report of the murders:[15]

■■■ City Briefs ■■■

)ad charged with shooting sons

Saskatoon RCMP have charged Tom Seesequasis with two counts of first-degree murder in the shooting deaths of his two sons.

The charges were laid following an RCMP investigation this week into the deaths. DEC 1 1990

The bodies of Marc, 16, and Joey, 8, were found in a house on the Beardy's Okemasis Indian Reserve about 3 a.m. Sunday morning. Seesequasis was found nearby, suffering from an apparent self-inflicted gunshot wound to the head.

Royal University Hospital has upgraded the 41-year-old man's condition to fair from critical.

The boys' parents are separated and their mother, Blanche, lives in Saskatoon, where she attends university.

Body found in city field identified

Saskatoon police have identified Neil Christopher Stonechild, 17, as the person whose body was found Thursday in a field in the city's north industrial area. DEC 1 1990

An autopsy is expected to be conducted in the next few days to determine the cause of death.

CHAPTER 1 - Blindsided!
RCMP Level an Accusation

'I thought, "Well, I have nothing to hide, so why be rude about it?"'
— **Const. Bradley Senger**

Ten years later: Thursday, May 18, 2000. Brad Senger was in his element. Now a 36-year-old constable in his eleventh year on the Saskatoon Police Service with several policing awards to his credit, he was off-duty and babysitting his boys. Four and five years old, they were often mistaken for twins. The morning was warm, already 15 degrees; summer was on its way. Tousling the two heads intent on a puzzle, Senger asked, "You two hungry? It's almost noon."

"First finish the dinosaur. Puh-leease?" asked one.

"Peanut butter samiches!" said the other.

The doorbell rang. Fitting in the horned nose to whoops of triumph, the lithe young officer hopped up, laughing, to answer it. Standing stiffly on the doorstep was a tall, meticulously groomed, balding-blond man in his mid-fifties. "Hello, Brad," he said. "Jack Warner. I'm the one who interviewed you before."

"Hi. How's it going?" Senger smiled, trying to remember this particular Mountie. As a law enforcement colleague, he had spoken sometime over the previous two months to members of the RCMP task force, Operation Ferric, helping them reinvestigate the 1990 freezing death of Neil Stonechild. Senger had only been able to tell them the name of another officer who said he had "done a track" at the time the youth's body was discovered. The tracker was trying to establish where Stonechild came from, and where he lost one of his runners. Stonechild was one of several Aboriginal freezing deaths that the task force was now investigating.

"I wonder if we could discuss some of those cases we discussed earlier at the eighth street police station," Warner said. "I need a little more information." *[Most quotes in this chapter are taken verbatim from notes obtained through Access to Information legislation.]*

"Sure," Senger said. "You'll have to come in because I'm watching the kids."

"Boys, this is Constable Warner," Senger said, entering the kitchen. "He's a Mountie and I'm helping him solve a case." The boys' smiles faded when their father moved their puzzle to a nearby coffee table so he and the Mountie could talk at the kitchen table.

"What can I help you with, Jack?"

Warner looked at him soberly. "Larry Hartwig is being interviewed at our office right now concerning the death of Neil Stonechild. Our investigations have focused on you and Larry for a number of reasons. We have eyewitness accounts of Neil being in the back of a police car, and that information suggested that it was you two." *[Whatever the intent for claiming more than one eyewitness, Warner's statement was inaccurate. Only one person claimed to have seen Stonechild in a police car. That was Jason Roy who, in 1990, had been 16 and already had convictions for robbery, possession of stolen property over $1,000 and attempt to obstruct justice. By 2000, when the RCMP began investigating, Jason Roy had been in conflict with the law more than 50 times over a seven-year period, and had four known aliases – meaning that the sole witness had been caught lying to police, using four different names on at least four different occasions.]*

"Gee, I don't recall a thing about that," Senger replied. "I'd have to look at my notes."

"Where are they?" Warner asked.

"Downstairs. I'll go get them." Turning to the children, he asked, "You boys all right?"

"I'm hungry, Daddy."

"Have one of these good bananas! I'll get lunch in a minute, okay?"

Within minutes, Senger was back with a Tupperware box full of black police notebooks. "What was the date of occurrence?"

"Saturday, November twenty-fourth, 1990."

Pulling out a notebook, Senger leafed through it and stopped. "I have Stonechild's name in my notebook. Here's what I wrote … '23:55: 10-25 @ apartment 306 – 3308 33rd Street West. Neil Stonechild to be removed.'" Turning the page, he read, "'Checked out AA' – that means Above Address. 'GOA,' meaning Gone on Arrival, the person sought had already left the scene. '00:17. Clear. No report.'"

"And a 10-25 is …?" Warner asked. Many RCMP terms and practices vary widely from those of city police, a fact that some blame for confusion in the investigation.

"An 'intoxicated person' complaint from an apartment on thirty-third. 3308 would be Snowberry Downs apartment. We were dispatched at five to midnight. We must have gone there and found Stonechild GOA. Then, because he was gone, he was no longer causing a problem, so we cleared the call at 17 minutes after midnight. We didn't have to write a report because nothing happened. Two minutes later, at 00:19, we were dispatched to another complaint at O'Regan Crescent... that would be just a few blocks away. Notes say 'A male looking into garages.' We pushed the on-scene button, indicating we were at O'Regan at 00:24, looked for that person but he was GOA, too, so we went on with the rest of our shift."

Brad flipped to previous pages. "I started out working alone, then joined Larry Hartwig at 10:43. Our first dispatch was ten minutes later at 10:53 to a guy in a suspicious vehicle. Says we drove him home. Then looked for Stonechild, then to O'Regan Crescent. We had nine ... ten ... eleven dispatches in the eight hours we worked together. Busy night, looks like."

"What can you recall about the Stonechild dispatch?"

"I don't recall anything," Senger said. "He was Gone on Arrival."

Slowly, momentously, Const. Warner shifted in his chair, made eye contact with his host, and said: "Brad, I have no doubt in my mind that you and Larry Hartwig had Neil Stonechild in your police car that night." Senger glanced at his sons, hoping they weren't feeling the sudden jolt of tension. Within earshot of his sons, a lead RCMP investigator in Operation Ferric had seemingly accused him of having had a high-profile sudden-death victim in his custody the night he went missing.

The media had been all over this for weeks. Operation Ferric was the largest RCMP investigation ever undertaken in the history of the province, and the largest investigation into alleged police misconduct in Canadian history. It was examining possible police involvement in freezing deaths of several Aboriginal males including Neil Stonechild.

Ten years after Stonechild died, someone had come forward in February of this year, 2000, claiming he'd seen Stonechild in a police car the last night he was seen alive. If that were true – that Brad and his partner had had Stonechild in their vehicle – it meant that Brad hadn't noted that fact in his notebook. That, in turn, would mean that he had failed to disclose important information about someone who later died under unknown circumstances. This could be serious.

Const. Warner, heading up the Stonechild section within the larger freezing death investigation, was speaking again, reiterating the allegations. A man had recently disclosed he and Stonechild had been drinking together when Stonechild decided he wanted to look for a former girlfriend who was babysitting at Snowberry Downs. The two walked the six blocks over there, even though it was a bitter night. At Snowberry Downs, Stonechild rang some doorbells, looking for the girl. A resident disturbed by the random doorbell-ringing called police.

Later, following an argument, the friend left Stonechild and returned to the house where they'd been drinking. That friend, Jason Roy, now, all these years later, suddenly publicly claimed that, on the way back, he had been stopped by two policemen in a vehicle who asked him his name. Roy claimed that, because he might have a warrant out for his arrest, he lied about his name, address and date of birth, providing instead, those of his cousin, Tracy Lee Horse. Roy was now claiming that, 10 years earlier, while the officers were checking that name on their computer, he had seen Stonechild handcuffed in the back seat of their car, bleeding from the face and screaming, "Help me Jay, they're going to kill me!" Roy was the last person claiming to see Stonechild alive.

Warner again looked at Senger and said, "Brad, the police badge that queried Tracy Lee Horse on CPIC [Canadian Police Information Centre, a criminal database] that night was yours. You also queried Neil Stonechild twice." *[Again untrue. According to CPIC records, Stonechild was queried once; Tracy Horse twice.]*

"I just can't recall," Brad said, going through his notes. "There's a Next of Kin notification here that I recall. Like yesterday. We had to tell a mother that her husband had murdered their sons. But that's the only thing I can recall from that night."

"Brad, there is no doubt in my mind that you had Neil Stonechild in your car that night. What I can't understand is why you can't recall that."

"Like I said, Jack, he was Gone on Arrival. How can I recall a GOA from ten years ago? We couldn't find him. You can see in my notes that we had two Gone on Arrivals that night alone. Do you have any idea how many GOAs I've had in the past ten years? People I couldn't find, didn't even see? How am I supposed to remember those? I remember things that actually happened. Like notifying that mother."

Warner touched the notebook. "Do you mind if I hang onto this, as long as I give it back to you, in time?"

"Sure, take it!"

"I guess you know it looks very bad for you and Hartwig, Brad, and if you don't tell the truth about matters, it's gonna cause you real problems."

"I agree that it looks very bad."

"I apologize for having to do this."

"I understand," Brad said. "I would think the same way if I were in your shoes."

"But I also want to caution you that if you were to cover for someone it would be a terrible mistake."

"I'm not covering for anyone. I just don't recall."

"I don't believe that your actions were anything but a bad choice. There was probably no intent to injure anyone."

Brad thought a moment and then asked, "What time were the CPIC queries made relative to our being dispatched and arriving?"

"I'm quite certain the queries were made after your arrival, but I'm not positive."

"It would be helpful to know."

"If you and Larry got together, perhaps you could assist one another to recall the matter."

"I don't want to do that."

"Don't you two get along well?"

"Oh yeah. He's a good guy."

"Larry mentioned that he wanted to talk with you about it...."

"Did he? Well then, maybe I will."

"Would you be willing to take a polygraph?"

"Of course."

"Good. We'll try to arrange that as soon as possible, but it may take a while. Probably not within the next couple of days."

"Okay."

"It may be the only way of convincing anyone of your innocence."

"I agree. I'd like to do that."

At the door, Senger turned to Warner. "I just wanted to say, Jack, you came to my home to talk to me about this with my kids around. I think this was kind of inappropriate, don't you?"

"Well, if you thought it was inappropriate, you should have asked me to leave," Warner replied, stepping out the door. "I'll copy your notes and return them along with the times you CPICed the name, 'Stonechild.'"

~ ~ ~

Later that afternoon, Larry Hartwig arrived at the door, agitated. He had just left the RCMP detachment where he also had been accused of having had Stonechild in his custody. "Brad, they just told me that you and me had Neil Stonechild in our custody and we let him go!" Larry said. "Boy, did I drop the ball! I was the senior officer, I should have known better. I believed him when he gave us an alias and I let him go and if I hadn't done that, he might be alive today!"

"Come on in, Larry," Brad said. "They'll figure out it's baseless. Have a chair." But Larry was in fight or flight mode, adrenaline pumping, and he had to keep moving. They went over Brad's notes, but they were no help jogging Larry's memory, and he left to pick up his kids from school.

Soon after, Brad's wife returned from work. A dark-haired woman with empathetic eyes and an air of strength, she had met Brad years before when they were both psychiatric nurses. "The weirdest thing happened today," he said, shaking his head. "An RCMP showed up at the door and told me I was going to be under investigation for the freezing death of Neil Stonechild."

"Under investigation for – Honey, you're kidding, right?"

"No! He came on the pretence that he wanted to discuss some of the other freezing deaths because I had talked to him about them before. I welcomed him into the house. Then all of a sudden he turns it into more of an interview. With the boys sitting right there! So as he was leaving, I said, 'I think it was kind of inappropriate.' Warner said, 'If you thought it was inappropriate, you should have asked me to leave.' He was right, I should have, but I had thought, 'Well, I have nothing to hide, so why be rude about it?'"

Later, Warner returned to the Senger home with a towering, six-foot-five RCMP officer with the face of a benevolent grandfather. "Brad, this is Sergeant Ken Lyons who works with me in the Regina Major Crimes Unit." This time, Senger did not welcome his accusers into his home. Still, he politely allowed them inside the front door. "Here's the copy of your notes I promised, Brad," Warner said, "and also the times of the CPIC query. It was after you were dispatched to find Stonechild." (In other words, standard procedure.) "Brad, just so there's no misunderstanding between us, I'm going to charter and warn you." There it was. As good as an accusation. Police charter a person only if they believe there is a probability they are responsible for whatever is being investigated, and therefore may be charged.

"Okay, but you don't have to," Brad said.

"You are not obliged to say anything. Anything you do say may be given in evidence. You have the right to retain and instruct counsel without delay." From now on, everything Senger said would be admissible in court.

"Okay. And I'd like to take the polygraph tomorrow."

"Unfortunately we are unable to do that until next Friday. Nine-thirty a.m."

"You can't do it any sooner?"

"Unfortunately not."

Unfortunate indeed, because in the end, the polygraph would not be done until December, seven months later. In those months, Senger would hear various allegations tossed around, some true, some false, but all contaminating his memory of that night.

Within a month, says a source, Warner told another RCMP investigator that their ultimate goal was a confession from Hartwig and Senger. None of the other suspects, many with violent criminal records, were apparently of interest.

Was Warner correct? Were Hartwig and Senger a pair of cops gone bad? Or were the RCMP so convinced that they had engaged in misconduct that they would attempt to prove it regardless of evidence to the contrary? Is it possible that, because an Aboriginal youth had frozen to death, and an activist organization of elected chiefs called the Federation of Saskatchewan Indian Nations was trying to find someone other than themselves to blame, they must be appeased at all cost? Therefore, two officers must pay with their careers, their reputations, their health? If any of this is true, both the Royal Canadian Mounted Police and the Saskatchewan Department of Justice would go to shocking lengths to support lies.

But why? Is it possible the sole motivation was chillingly cold, cynical and calculated – to shape the outcome to be publicly and politically acceptable?

CHAPTER 2 - 'Terrified!'
Kidnapped at Knifepoint by Jason Roy

'Throughout the entire ordeal, Jason Roy had his knife aimed at my ribs!'
– Saskatonian Blair Pischak

"Three men suddenly materialized out of the dark!" says Saskatoon businessman, Blair Pischak. "One guy growled, 'Let's get going!' while Jason Roy pulled out a knife." An inauspicious start to the New Year, it was 10 p.m. in the freezing fog of January 2, 1996 when Pischak met Jason Roy, then 22, the only person who would claim to have seen Neil Stonechild in a police car the night he went missing. Pischak, 33, was at a phone box on Avenue P and 20th Street. "'Get in your car!' one of them barked.

"I was terrified, and just did as they said!" Pischak recounts. All four got into his car. Pischak drove; Jason Roy sat in the passenger seat, his knifepoint quivering a foot from Pischak's ribcage. A man, later identified as Elton Dustyhorn, sat behind Pischak; the third man beside Dustyhorn. "They just told me to drive, as if they hadn't figured out where they wanted to go," Pischak says.

"As we drove, they asked, 'What are you doing out here?' I explained that I had been a drug addictions counsellor for eight years at Calder Centre, but that I had recently relapsed and now was back doing drugs. I kept trying to say, 'You want drugs? Maybe I can help you!' But they started calling me 'Racist!' and 'White trash!' and, as I drove, every few minutes Dustyhorn would clout me across the back of my head and yell, 'Shut up!' I asked them what they wanted and they said, 'We want you to drive us somewhere!'

"They made me drive them around for about twenty minutes. Their exact words, which I will never forget because I was so terrified, were: 'We're going to give it to you if you don't do what we want! You're going to get it! We're taking your car!' I thought I was going to get beaten up.

"Then there was talk amongst the three of them about what they were going to do with me. I don't remember the exact words, but it was along the lines of, 'Where do we get rid of this guy?' Now I'm not saying they were going to kill me, but that thought was likely a big part of my motivation to do what I did. I think they wanted my car but not me, and they were kind of stuck with me, as they had kidnapped me.

"Finally, they said they wanted to 'make a plan' and told me to pull over in front of the Lucky Horseshoe Bingo Hall on Avenue G. I stopped the car, ripped open the door and I just ran! Security in the bingo hall phoned police; we went back outside and my car was gone. Within four minutes, police were there! They said, 'We have retrieved your car and have three people in custody. Please come with us to identify them.'

"By then I had become part of the street culture, and in that world you just don't go to the police! So as they drove me, brewing in the back of my mind was: 'This isn't going to look good for me.' But I wanted my damn car back! They took me over to Avenue D and 27th where the police pulled up beside my car; the kidnappers had got it stuck in the snow. I looked in the car and it was kind of a weird moment because just a few minutes before, I'd been their captive. The guy in the back was furious; the feeling I got was: 'If looks could kill!' Jason Roy just looked scared.

"I identified the three guys. The next day we went to court where the charges were read: kidnapping, unlawful confinement, and robbery. A week later I was driving with Jimmy Naytowhow when I spotted Roy and Dustyhorn. They were already out on the street! I was shocked they had been released so fast! We tried to confront them, but they ran away. When all was said and done, there was a plea bargain that saw the charges for kidnapping and robbery dropped. The legal system needs to figure out a way to include justice in it!"

On June 18, 1996, Roy was given a stay of proceedings on charges of Kidnapping and Robbery with Violence, but sentenced to 40 months in jail for two charges of Possession of Property Obtained by Crime over $5,000, Driving while Disqualified, Failure to Attend Court, and Failure to Comply with Recognizance.

"What did I think of the Stonechild investigation and inquiry?" asks the soft-spoken Pischak. "I followed the investigation closely and attended the inquiry. I think it was a political bullshit cover-up! Believing the word of a punk over two good, caring, honest officers like Hartwig and Senger – it's a farce! The RCMP hanging their entire case on the ever-changing uncorroborated word of a convicted felon! What were they thinking?

"I knew Brad Senger from years earlier and he was always a caring, gentle, honest sort of fellow. I knew his wife, and knew the kind of people they both were. Regarding Mr. Hartwig, I had met him a few times when I worked at Calder Centre starting in the late eighties, and found him to be a caring police officer. He was unlike the few 'rough and tumble' kind of police that I had met in Saskatoon at that time. He seemed genuinely interested in helping people that were down and out rather than 'throwing the book' at them.

"Jason Roy was the only one to claim he had seen Stonechild in their cruiser. Why didn't they get him to take a polygraph? I believe he's lying, as do many people. I recall some of his BS testimony at the inquiry, and his claim then that he had been a trouble-maker in the years preceding the inquiry, but he had turned his life around quite a lot since. Trying to paint a better picture of himself. The whole thing stinks!"

Blair Pischak has been living a sober lifestyle since 1999, running his own business, Professional Home Detailing. Elton Dustyhorn was stabbed to death in 1998. Jason Roy went on racking up run-ins with the law into the 2000s.

At the officers' appeal of their firing in 2005, Roy's police record up to the beginning of the 2000 RCMP Investigation was entered into evidence. It included:

Jason Edward Roy; DOB Dec 22, 1973.

Aliases: Jason Frank, Jason George, Tracey Lee Horse, Dayton William Kinney.

Identifying Marks: slash marks left forearm, two scars right forearm, tattoo left upper arm: skull with top hat, tattoo 'PS' right base thumb."

Offenses included: four Shoplifting Under $1,000, four Possession of Stolen Property, Theft from Vehicle under $1,000, Robbery, Stealing a Vehicle, Fraud, being Unlawfully at Large, Trespassing at Night, two Breaking-and-Entering Residences, Escaping Custody, two Breach of Probation, a Bail Violation, a Break, Enter and Theft, Damage over $1,000, Driving without Due Care or Attention, Accomplice to Kidnapping/Unlawful Confinement and Robbery.[16] He also had convictions for Obstructing Police (for example, lying to police about who you are) as well as the much more serious Obstructing Justice (for example, threatening or intimating to prevent their testifying against you).

In 2000, four years after kidnapping and robbing a citizen at knifepoint, and with 50 known run-ins with the law including a conviction for Obstructing Justice, Jason Roy became the RCMP's star witness – indeed, the only witness claiming to have seen police involvement – in their investigation implicating two reputable police officers in the freezing death of Neil Stonechild.

CHAPTER 3 - Growing Uproar:
Darrell Night's Drop-off

'I view the world through the eyes of a fighter pilot. I flew dangerous missions and was willing to risk my life because I love people and feel a deep obligation to protect them. I think most young men and women join the police force for the same reason: "To serve and protect." The September eleventh, 2001 attack on our society from abroad was not unlike the attack on Dan and Ken in that courtroom on 9/11. My faith in the "justice" or "legal" system has been shaken.'
– **Mike Ritchie, airline pilot and Dan Hatchen's brother-in-law**

Neil Stonechild's body might never have been disinterred and his death reinvestigated had it not been for two officers who raised the frightening spectre of police involvement in Aboriginal freezing deaths. The mere possibility created uproar in the normally sedate "City of Bridges."

The controversy which became a full-blown international incident began about 5:30 in the morning of Friday, January 28, 2000. Two officers arrested a 33-year-old man, Darrell Night, for causing a disturbance. Because rank and file officers could not speak to the media, the public was told only that, instead of taking the Cree man to jail, police dropped him off near the southern outskirts of town on a frigid winter morning. Night walked to the Queen Elizabeth II power plant where he knocked on the door until someone answered and phoned him a taxi. The cab driver who drove him to his sister's apartment several miles away later testified Night arrived home ready to "party" with the people who hired the taxi after him.

Night got home safely. But in a tragic "perfect storm" of events, within six days of his drop-off, two Aboriginal men were found frozen to death in the same southeast industrial area of the city. The body of Lawrence Wegner was found near the power plant; Rodney Naistus' body was found several kilometres away in an industrial area of the city, five blocks from a residential area. Both were partially clothed and frozen solid in the shallow snow. Although Night suffered no injury from the cold, the officers were tried and found guilty of unlawful confinement and sentenced to eight months in jail.

Initially this journalist wrote an article sticking to the accepted view of the incident. The sub-headline on the Oct. 22, 2001 *Report* newsmagazine

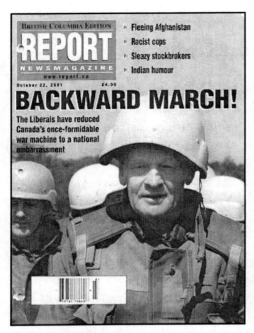

BRITISH COLUMBIA EDITION

REPORT

NEWSMAGAZINE

www.report.ca

October 22, 2001 $4.50

▸ Fleeing Afghanistan
▸ Racist cops
▸ Sleazy stockbrokers
▸ Indian humour

BACKWARD MARCH!

The Liberals have reduced Canada's once-formidable war machine to a national embarrassment

read: "Racist Cops." There was no question mark. The article was headlined "Canada's Ugly Side: The findings of a Saskatchewan probe into racism against Indians may be horrifying indeed." While researching, I had phoned Ken Munson to obtain his side of the story, but he replied that he and Dan Hatchen were not permitted to speak to the media. I asked if I might contact him when legalities were concluded; he agreed. It was August 2003 before that happened: Munson and Hatchen's case went to the Saskatchewan Court of Appeal, it was upheld, they served the standard three-quarters of their sentence in jail and were released. Soon after, I contacted them. Now working for the *Western Standard* newsmagazine, I wanted to tell their side of the story as honestly as I could. I did not mention I also wanted to learn whatever useful lessons society could glean from their sick, twisted, perverted racist minds.

A few years earlier, I had attended a Prairie university graduation ceremony. The audience was seated in rows of steeply-descending seats, absorbed in the ceremony. You could have heard a pin drop when a Caucasian man near me put his foot on the shoulder of an Aboriginal woman sitting in the row below and said in a low voice, "What are you doing here?" She had given him a look of utter disgust and returned her attention to the stage.

I was still mortified, still mad, and wanted to make amends for my race. Smarten people up! Munson, however, declined, saying he and his family were recovering from the ordeal, and did not wish to relive it. I understood. He did not want a nosy reporter digging up uncomfortable truths. So I was surprised, several months later, when he emailed that, because of the ongoing injustice against Constables Hartwig and Senger, he wanted to set the record straight about his own so-called "starlight tour."

Travelling to Saskatoon to meet monsters, I took my husband as bodyguard.

What I did not know was that Munson felt the same degree of trust for media. He brought his wife as witness. My impression upon meeting the couple? Serious mismatch! What was a classy lady like her doing with a thug? The first time my satisfying sense of righteousness and revenge wobbled was an hour into the interview. Munson was describing how, as an officer, he had saved some kids a criminal charge by organizing them (on his own time, it emerged) to repaint the school fence they had defaced. "We had a grea' time of it," he started to laugh. "And we ended up decidin' it was more fun to fix than to wreck!"

"Were um ... any of those kids Aboriginal?" I ventured.

"All of 'em," he replied. "It was an Aboriginal school."

"Why didn't you mention that?"

"What difference does it make? I just like to get cre-a-'ive [his British midlands way of pronouncing 'creative'] abou' avoidin' criminal charges and gettin' some good to come ou' of it."

"Well, it just wrecks my theory totally about you, that's all!" I thought, trying to be pleased. I'd had the article half-written in my head. It would have been so easy.

After interviewing Dan Hatchen and numerous others, most of them First Nations, I filed a story for the April 12, 2004 issue of *The Western Standard*. I already knew I'd do more. The evidence was so intriguing, I couldn't quit. I'd spoken to an officer who said he had proof of evidence, exculpatory to the officers, repressed by the RCMP, and I'd spoken to a young Aboriginal man who said of Ken Munson, "I love that man with all my heart!" This was a living, breathing puzzle – that kept growing pieces. If it was a travesty of justice, how was it pulled off? Who was involved? How high did it go? At the same time, with every fragment of evidence, another piece of my cherished vision of our justice system was being shot down in flames.

Learning that the officers were, in fact, dedicated men of conscience, I investigated further, discovering new evidence that supported Munson and Hatchen's innocence (and poor judgment) in listening to a man who asked to be dropped off rather than go to jail. A man who got home safely, and who changed his story about the drop-off several times when talking to authorities, and changed it again dramatically when I interviewed him. The evidence pointed, instead, to a rigid determination by RCMP and Sask Justice to convict the officers to placate old angers of some Aboriginal leaders.

The firestorm of racism allegations were all superimposed on the grim reality of our winter climate. Freezing to death while "under the effects" has long been a fact of Canadian life, but one that our increasingly urban populace seems to have forgotten. What I discovered to be troubling in this case, however, was confabulating racist violence as the cause.

CHAPTER 4 - RCMP Task Force Launches, and so does FSIN

'At that meeting, 19 chiefs sat together and in turn pointed their fingers at these [senior RCMP] officers....'
– FSIN Vice Chief Lawrence Joseph admitting to applying political pressure (Material obtained under Access to Information legislation)

Wednesday, Feb. 16, 2000 was the day everything changed for the Saskatoon Police Service. After Chief Dave Scott had launched an investigation into police involvement in freezing deaths "regardless of how many resources it takes," Sask Justice decided to move the investigation from the police to RCMP, even though there was no indication of bias, and no support in law to bypass normal procedure *without* clear evidence of such bias. It was an extraordinary action, apparently taken only on the spur of extraordinary press and possibly, behind-the-scenes pressure by the Federation of Saskatchewan Indian Nations (FSIN). Yet to be discovered: on what basis was it assumed SPS could not investigate its own?

That same day, Minister of Justice Axworthy wrote the Assistant Commissioner of Saskatchewan RCMP, Harper Boucher, requesting an investigation into the deaths of Randy Naistus and Lawrence Wegner, "and to review the related allegations that members of the Saskatoon Police Service had engaged in the practice of transporting and abandoning individuals at the outskirts of the city as reported in a complaint from Darryl Night." The requested task force, Operation Ferric, was struck that same afternoon.

Previously unrevealed to the public, FSIN Vice Chief Lawrence Joseph has admitted that Saskatchewan Aboriginal chiefs (who did not have all the facts at the time) applied focused, direct political pressure – some might call it threats and intimidation – on the government. "What I did right after the discovery of the dead bodies and Darrell Night came out," Joseph said in the National Film Board (NFB) interview never broadcast, "was I called a meeting of the chiefs that sit on the Justice Commission in Saskatchewan First Nations. And also the senior officers of the RCMP were invited. And at that meeting, *19 chiefs sat together and in turn pointed their fingers at these officers* and basically told them, 'We do not trust you to do the right thing! We don't want to deal with you people anymore, the way you're doing this thing!'

… And from there, our meetings with not only the premier of Saskatchewan, justice minister of Saskatchewan, but other people, we were really on track, saying that we're not going to sway from this. And I think eventually the minister of justice decided to go ahead with this."[17]

Several years before I obtained the information about the FSIN meeting with the premier and Sask Justice, Dave Scott had told me that such a conversation must have occurred:

"All of a sudden, things started to turn around. I had been confident that the Minister of Justice [Chris Axworthy] would support my action to discipline them [Munson and Hatchen] under the Police Act, which he did, until reneging. I never in my wildest dreams thought they would be charged criminally. It's sad that people count on the justice system to be objective and unemotional and address a case from a factual point of view, but there was a lot of political motivation to satisfy the FSIN. They had to pacify them for whatever reason – political? We may never know. But I would love to find out the conversation between the justice department and the FSIN. What would motivate them to do a 180? Was it intimidation?

By that time, it was explosive, as the media believed they were onto something that ultimately was not there. They never once wanted to hear the other side or to do any investigation. It was one-sided. I had hoped, after my contract was bought out [to be replaced by Chief Russ Sabo], that the courts would abide by the evidence. Now we realize they denied key evidence and were part of the firestorm!"

The day after Sask Justice took over the investigation, the StarPhoenix did "explode" with stories about SPS. These were eight headlines on Feb. 17, 2000:

Police chief under siege: Dave Scott reverses stance, calls for outside investigation (Page A1/FRONT)

Saskatoon under microscope: Man who sparked internal probe tells horror story (A1/FRONT)

Retracing Rodney Naistus's footprints up to the day he died (A1/FRONT)

Deaths heighten tension between Natives, police (A1/FRONT)

Deeds too dark to dismiss (A2) (Columnist Randy Burton wrote: "It may well be that police will be cleared of any suspicion of racism. But under the circumstances, the notion of Saskatchewan as 'Mississippi North' no longer seems quite so far-fetched.")

[Mayor] Dayday backs outside probe of deaths: Seriousness of allegations against police officers warrants outside investigation (A3)

How many other frozen bodies will turn up? (A3)

Students to hold vigil in memory of classmate (A8)

Operation Ferric launched immediately. February 17, 2000, a core team of five Mounties rolled into Saskatoon from across the province. Their opening meeting established the rhythm of the investigation. The Mounties would be fed spectacular rumour and innuendo, only to find, in the end, nothing but hot air. Yet the tempo of insinuations presumably had a purpose. Was it to encourage the Mounties that they were after something big and that the "something big" involved police?

For example, at the team's first meeting, 4:15 pm at the Sandman Inn, they were fed this block buster: "Rumours of prostitutes being taken out in similar fashion." No source was given, but earlier that day Sgt. Ken Lyons had written in his notes, obtained under Access to Information legislation: "Darrel McFadyen … will call when done at FSIN." Is this the origin of the prostitute rumour, which investigation would find completely unfounded – the FSIN?

Destined to become the largest task force the province had ever seen, Operation Ferric would involve 16 investigators, including two First Nations officers, and six support staff. It would run 18 months, and come with a price tag of millions. The code name, Ferric, was chosen, according to RCMP tradition, not because the case had anything to do with the element, iron, but because the RCMP's Saskatchewan "F" Division always uses code names, chosen at random, beginning with the letter F.

Saskatoon RCMP Major Crimes had been expected to do the investigation. However, to ensure independence, Sgt. Colin Crocker who headed the division asked to have the task assigned to officers outside the area. The now-retired Sgt. Crocker explains:

"We said to Regina [RCMP] that we thought it wouldn't be fair to us as investigators, so Regina Major Crimes investigated while we looked after major crimes in the entire rest of the province. The four of us put in lots of 18-hour days for three or four months. It would have been easier for us to do the investigation ourselves, but we were too close to SPS members. There could have been hard feelings and animosity, and we were all one family.

Dave Scott was a super guy to work with. We called on him often when we had a homicide case dumped outside city limits. For example, a girl was found murdered. I'd say, 'Dave, we'd like to have a couple of your guys working on this.' Dave would say, 'Sure, take two major crimes guys for as long as you want.' In that murder case, the SPS officers said, 'We know this girl; she lived in this area and her brother lives at this address and her sisters at these addresses.' SPS officers have a world of knowledge. Other police forces who work on cases with RCMP draw up Memos of Understanding, but we didn't even need that. It was perfect."

By February 18, RCMP had established a toll-free number for anyone to call with allegations of improper police drop-offs. The Federation of Saskatchewan Indian Nations immediately set up its own number, 1-877-353-FSIN, to document police "misconduct and brutality" and establishes its own investigation to the tune of nearly $300,000 of gaming revenues. Joseph said, "This is a clear message to the provincial government and also the federal government that the First Nations of Saskatchewan are together in this and that they speak not only politically but with their wallets." A year later, when no charges regarding improper drop-offs had been laid beyond those against Munson and Hatchen (and none ever were), FSIN asked the provincial government to take over financing another five years of its shadow investigation of the RCMP. Asking price: $1,500,000. This was not approved.

One justification Lawrence Joseph cited for government funding, with no shred of evidence provided, was a claimed 35 complaints against SPS withdrawn – hinting at police wrong-doing. "Our follow-up investigations indicate," his February 2001 written media release alleged, "3 primary reasons that complainants choose not to pursue their cases:

1. *Complainants were allegedly threatened or intimidated by police officers*
2. *They were subject to numerous interviews – so many, in fact, that they felt harassed*
3. *They were too uncomfortable when the FSIN Special Investigations Unit turned over their files to a police investigator, as the unit was required to do.*
...Finally, I want to conclude with the announcement that I will, in the next week or so, be petitioning the Attorney General for some kind

of a review of 3 specific cases involving serious police misconduct. All 3 cases are, I believe, morally outrageous. I am sorry, but I CANNOT COMMENT FURTHER on these cases at this time."

Nothing further was heard of the "morally outrageous" cases. *StarPhoenix* columnist Randy Burton was one of the few daring to challenge Joseph:

"From the outset, the Night affair has been about more than just cleaning house at the Saskatoon Police Service. It's also about pushing the FSIN's agenda for a parallel justice system run by and for Native people.
Joseph has described Native-run courts and a separate police system as the only solution to the current unfairness of the system. Even though the province has rejected this idea outright, it won't go away anytime soon.
But if Joseph's pronouncements on his idea of justice are any indication of how such a thing would work, we should be very worried indeed. For example, in spite of the emotional atmosphere surrounding the case, he opposes the idea of Munson and Hatchen being tried anywhere other than Saskatoon in the interests of a fair trial.
Joseph argues they should be tried where the crime took place but there's also an element of theatre to this. It's a lot tougher to get television coverage of demonstrations in Melfort, say, than it is in Saskatoon where a crowd can be convened outside the courthouse at a moment's notice.
Nor is Joseph's campaign against police chief Dave Scott particularly encouraging. He holds Scott personally responsible for the frozen bodies of Rodney Naistus and Lawrence Wegner and has demanded the chief's resignation for it. This is an amazing double standard, especially for a man who can spot one so easily."[18]

Regarding that parallel justice system, the FSIN website reveals the issue had been on their agenda for years before the developments of 2000: "In 1996 the Chiefs-in-Assembly mandated the FSIN to deal with outstanding Treaty issues, justice being one of them. The Treaty Governance Processes were established to develop a renewed government-to-government relationship with the Crown and Saskatchewan." Next, the FSIN website details finances sought: "ensuring that the Crown finance the establishment of First Nations Just Relations processes including resources to undertake development, research, executive management, professional services, contractual arrangements with other governments, administration, and capital requirements."[19] The Night incident may indeed have been seen as an opportunity to forward FSIN's several goals.

On February 18, FSIN goaded the province to hold a public inquiry, stating at a Prince Albert meeting that they might hold their own inquiry into the way First Nations people were treated by police and the justice system if the province did not soon commit to doing it. Vice Chief Joseph told the media that the FSIN chiefs expressed "pain, anger, frustration and a lack of trust not only with the police but also with the government."

FSIN soon announced it would hire private investigators to monitor the RCMP investigation, and "investigate the investigators…. The RCMP have their marching orders and that's all." Asked by the media if the month-long probe was proceeding quickly enough for him, Vice Chief Joseph replied, "I don't think it's expedient. It feels like a lifetime for 19 investigators to investigate something that has already been admitted."[20]

In April, Amnesty International jumped in, writing the justice minister in support of calls for an independent inquiry into freezing deaths despite the fact that it had already begun, while in its May *Annual Report on Human Rights* Abuses around the world, it included theatrically false allegations based solely on media reports, and in complete contradiction to RCMP determinations, that Saskatoon police had dumped three Native men outside the city.[21]

Rather than remind citizens that Amnesty International's claim was based merely on suspicion, that there was nothing to indicate police had been involved with Naistus and Wegner and people are considered innocent until proved guilty, Axworthy spoke as though he had prejudged allegations to be true and in need of redress. He told *The StarPhoenix*: "This is not the kind of international image you want to convey. It's a pretty serious matter. Our hope, of course, is that next year there will be a different story as we *begin some kind of reform-oriented process.*"[22] And this was the justice minister.

In May 2000, FSIN Chief Perry Bellegarde told Canadian Press that Munson and Hatchen should face tougher charges, "possibly attempted murder," while Donald Worme commented: "One needs only to harken to the death squads that are out and about, particularly in Central America. This situation is only one step away from that. It is deeply disturbing. It is that level of fear."[23] In 2001, the NFB went searching for terrified grassroots

Aboriginal people for their documentary, *Two Worlds Colliding*, and found the truth to be quite the reverse. All seven youths interviewed, for example, said they personally had no problems with police but *had heard stories* about someone, somewhere, treated badly. Four samples:

Youth #1: "Me? Scared of the cops? No, I ain't scared of the cops. Why be scared of the cops? They're out there to serve and protect. It's just that, you know, cops can be a--holes sometimes. I'm sure they can be, but you know, you just give them the attitude, they can treat you like dirt right back."

Youth #2: "Well, about a month ago, I think, a policeman came in here. I'm actually going through charges right now; like I'm charging someone. And throughout that, that officer has been very nice, you know, and understanding, listening and I respected him for that."

Youth #3: "Like, back where I'm from, you know, you phone the cops about a complaint or something, it takes them about half an hour to get there. You know, here it's snap of the fingers, they're here. And yeah, just helpful. They usually catch the criminals, basically, so they're good at that, I noticed."

Youth #4: "There'd be less violence right now if we just put more trust in the police these days. Like shootings and stuff and violence and people getting robbed, like. People do report these things now, but there's the, like, getting jumped. I live in Meadow Green, I've seen a lot of people get jumped in my neighbourhood – like this one time it was back and forth, back and forth for about a month."

Not one of the young men made it into *Two Worlds Colliding*. Perhaps because, at this point, the film-maker was realizing she should retitle her doc: *Two Worlds Cooperating*.

A former street kid who knew Stonechild told me: **"I didn't find the cops racist, I found them tired. Tired of having to deal with the same crap over and over and over again. I think they were fed up, and they did their jobs. No matter what, they did their jobs. They were fair."**

In May, too, FSIN would make a presentation to two deputy ministers of justice, titled "Proposed Formal Review of the Relationship between First Nations and the Saskatchewan Justice System," threatening: "Victims will turn on governments if 'the people who are supposed to take care of them' remain on the sidelines." A few weeks later, the FSIN would meet with the Ministers of Justice and Aboriginal Affairs seeking a Truth and Reconciliation Commission, as well as "an evaluation by First Nations as to the appropriateness of the Canadian alien system of law."[25]

Axworthy even called on the federal justice minister to get involved in the issue of race relations in Saskatchewan, implying that the province would continue to meet with FSIN to explore establishing a parallel Native justice system in the province.[26]

As for the police service, "We cooperated fully in giving the RCMP evidence, whatever they wanted," Scott says:

"And I informed our people: we will provide everything. So then it started to go from there, and I think actually what happened then is, people started to form an intent, to develop a theory, and I don't know where it came from. I don't know whether it came from Sask Justice, whether it came from FSIN, whether it came from the media, I have no idea, and I'll never know, but I think someone started to develop the theory that, 'Okay, we need to deal with this quick, expeditiously, so who is gonna be the fall guy? Who is gonna be the organization that's gonna be held responsible?'

And I'm going to tell you something! The RCMP and some of the Native organizations have a long-standing relationship, and I think they need to separate, to distance themselves more. I think it is something that happens in some policing organizations and I refused to allow it to happen in our organization – where members and especially the police chief becomes politicized, and begins to look at a political means of maintaining law and order rather than a legal means. That's what took place with Operation Ferric: the RCMP became politicized, and they looked at a political answer, political resolution, a political means of maintaining law and order, rather than using the due process of law.

Due process of law would have meant standard investigative techniques and investigative know-how: 'Let's stick with the facts.' It would have meant maintaining law and order without fear or favour: without fear of politicians or repercussions, and doing it without favour.

In other words, you don't twist the evidence in some way to cause favour to be reflected on someone who is not deserving, which is what happened here. It is, without doubt, the biggest injustice this province has ever seen!"

24

Is it possible that the decision by Sask Justice was changed, and the officers charged, because behind the scenes, pressure was being exerted on the justice system by FSIN? Were some RCMP and police leaders influenced by those with political clout?

Two months before the Mounties' Task Force launched in Saskatoon, I had written a story with retired RCMP Deputy Commissioner Robert Head about political interference hobbling the Mounties. Head, who spent years in Ottawa, said:

> "The next step in politicizing the force was the revision of the RCMP Act in the early 1980s, giving the RCMP commissioner a position in government of deputy Solicitor General. This puts him or her in some conflict of interest. Too often, the thinking of the commissioner and the force can be diverted from law enforcement to social policy issues. …Due to the commissioner's position as deputy-minister in government, there have been instances of government interference into policing decisions. In the past, the RCMP was even reporting to the ministry about crimes under investigation…. If significant changes are not made to the RCMP, the management will continue to drift further into the malleable hands of politicians."[27]

In a 2005 interview with Commissioner Giuliano Zaccardelli, head of the RCMP from 2000 to 2006, I explained my concerns about Operation Ferric. I then asked the question: Is it possible that RCMP members could be told by others within the RCMP or justice department, which side of an investigation to support?

> "Zaccardelli: The fact that officers may or may not make a mistake does not mean that they are being influenced. I know of no case and no chief or constable who would accept being politically directed or influenced when it comes to the independent issue of criminal investigation. I mean, it is so ingrained in our system that to try to influence somebody is not acceptable, and our men and women are taught from the very beginning: 'You are independent. When you act under the law, your authority under the law cannot be in any way diluted or influenced by anybody when it comes to who you investigate, who you arrest, or who you interview.' I can tell you, of everybody I know, if anyone even dared to try that, they would

either resign, or they would go public, and the person who tried to exert that influence would be in very serious problems.

Q: Now, you are Deputy Solicitor General of Canada. Does that ministerial role compromise your independence as commissioner of the RCMP?

A: I have three roles to play. First: head of the RCMP and policing in general under our British Common Law system. When I'm asked as the commissioner to deal with criminal investigations that are carried out through the men and women who work for the RCMP, I'm independent in the sense that I take no direction from anyone as to, for example, who to investigate, who to interview, who to arrest, and so on. In that capacity I answer to the law itself. The Supreme Court has pronounced itself on that very clearly. So it means that no government official, no politician, nobody including the highest official can direct me or ask me to do things in that area.

My second role: protective operations. For example, for the G-8 summit or APEC conference, we have to provide the security. If the government of Canada decides they're going to have a G-8 summit in a particular location, they obviously come to me and consult with me, I give them my opinion, but ultimately it is their decision. But how I provide that security and the number of people that I deploy is up to me. So in that sense I am less independent.

My third role: head of the department or 'The Agency' as we call it. In that role, I really am part of the government structure. For example, the RCMP has close to a $3 billion budget [$2.6 billion for 2015]. So when I'm playing that role, I'm obviously not independent, I have to answer to the minister and Parliament for that because I'm a public official. So when I get involved from the administrative side in terms of the managing public funds or the policy advisor dealing with my colleagues in other departments, I have a relationship with them and an interplay with them, but that never touches upon my independence in terms of my criminal investigative capacities.

Q: Have you ever had anyone in government attempt to influence your decisions?

A: Henry Jensen [RCMP deputy commissioner from 1981-89 under both Liberal and Conservative governments] told me that he had ministers come and try to influence him. But I have never had anyone try to

*influence my decisions. As a matter of fact, when it comes to the area
of criminal investigation, and who to investigate, who not to investigate,
most people I talk to will often say: 'Look, whenever we're talking,
whatever I'm saying, in no way should be interpreted to mean as in any
way trying to influence you in your area of independence.' The reason we
discuss it is that we want to make sure that the question of independence
is not misunderstood.*

*Q: Do you see any need for changes to the commissioner's position as a
deputy minister?*

*A: I believe the system works very well the way it is right now, but if the
courts or the authorities deem it necessary to make some changes, it's up
to them. I would not be the one to make those decisions."*

Police Association President Sgt. Stan Goertzen is probably the best-informed authority regarding facts and details of the Stonechild investigation. He believes one of the problems the Mounties faced was not understanding SPS procedures regarding querying names and the normal use of the MDTs (in-car computers) when dealing with street checks. The RCMP did not have in-car computers when Operation Ferric was taking place; they were still using only radio or phones to query people while they were in the field. Goertzen believes that lack of first-hand working knowledge about the way Saskatoon police routinely handled calls appears to have left Warner and other Ferric investigators suspicious of routine activities such as their method of checking individuals on CPIC.

However, he believes the RCMP were neither guided by outside officials, nor corrupt in terms of believing SPS officers innocent but implicating them anyway. Goertzen says, "I believe lead investigator Warner bought into the FSIN assertion that Saskatoon officers were routinely dropping off First Nations people. This was the furthest thing from the truth. In my 32 years in Saskatoon, the only drop-off that I'm aware of was Darrell Night's. *I think Warner put those blinders on early in the process and, because he was lead investigator, influenced other members of the RCMP."*

CHAPTER 5 - Two Freezing Deaths: 'Witnesses' Cash in

'For nearly two decades, thought has been that Saskatoon's freezing deaths were the result of a racist police department. Little consideration has ever focused on the inquiry's cheerleaders – native leaderships, various levels of government and academics – that have collectively failed to work together with the billions allocated annually to First Nations, and turn around the plight of a population that has been downtrodden for centuries.'
– Robert Marshall, police detective turned columnist[28]

What was known about the death of 25-year-old Rodney Naistus at this point, early in 2000, was that on Friday, January 28, the young man had been released from jail after serving seven months for Break-and-Enter. His life had been tough; much of his youth spent in foster homes, much of his adult life in jail. The government provided him with a bus ticket home to Onion Lake Cree Nation, but he cashed it in and went out celebrating with relatives. Around midnight, he and another man left the relatives. They tried to stop Naistus but, as one relative explained: "He said, 'No, I'm gonna go find myself a woman,' and we couldn't stop him." His last confirmed sighting was in downtown Saskatoon a few hours later, in front of Winston's Pub at two a.m. closing time. Toxicology reports found evidence of alcohol and marijuana in his body.

Later that day, MLA Pat Lorje, out for her Saturday morning jog, discovered his body. It was a few blocks from a residential area and several km from where Night had been released. "The police were very serious and respectful of the dead. It was my impression that they really cared about what had happened to this person," Lorje told *The StarPhoenix*.[29]

The only information on the second freezing victim, Lawrence Wegner, 30, was that sometime between 11 p.m. and midnight on Sunday, January 30, he had pounded on the door of a home not far from St. Paul's hospital, yelling, "Pizza! Pizza!" When the occupants refused to let him in, the man who they said was wearing no jacket in -20 weather, ran toward St. Paul's Hospital while the homeowner, Eliza Whitecap, phoned police. Their conversation was recorded:

"Policeman: Police Communication, may I help you?
Woman: Yes, there is a guy who just came to my door ...
Policeman: Yeah.
Woman: ... and he was trying to imitate the pizza guy ...
Policeman: Uh-huh.
Woman: ... and I guess he must have came running from downtown or
whatever, but he is knocking on the door yelling, 'Pizza! Pizza!'" ...

His body was found five days later by workers fixing railcars in the area. It was in a field east of the power plant, six km from Whitecap's home. Although two RCMP investigations and two inquests would show clearly there was no police involvement in the deaths of either Wegner or Naistus, lawyer Donald Worme tried hard to suggest one. "He's a courageous one," Worme told the Toronto *Sun* in February 2000. "Mr. Night stepped up to the plate and he made these disclosures. It is not an easy thing to do. Would we have known about the others if he had not?" A breath-taking question! Worme, one of the province's foremost unelected Aboriginal leaders, was suggesting, prior to any investigation, that Wegner and Naistus had also been dropped off by police. "Sadly, I suspect not," Worme's quote continued. "Looking back, the news reports said 'no foul play suspected' and that may very well have been his headline as well."[30]

Two days after the Mounties set up their task force to investigate the freezing deaths, a front-page story headlined "Witness recalls Native man struggling with police," claimed that police had committed violence in front of a hospital with people and vehicles constantly visiting the busy emergency department: Albert Chatsis, retired, was driving near St. Paul's Hospital when he saw a man wearing only jeans and a t-shirt talking to police officers in their parked car. Suddenly "... the officer [got out of the cruiser,] opened the back door, grabbed the man by the head and shoved him in the car." This permitted Chatsis to see he was wearing only socks. This was near midnight, yet Chatsis was later able to recognize him from a picture in the paper as Lawrence Wegner.

In a coroner's inquest into Wegner's death three years later, Chatsis would add to his story. Not only had he seen the police throw a man who looked like Wegner into a police car in front of the hospital but then Chatsis, with double knee-transplants, said he took a walk in Diefenbaker Park – several miles away, at midnight in January in -20 C weather – and climbed up onto a train bridge, and from there said he saw, nearly a mile across the river, through the trees, police throwing someone out of their cruiser near the power plant.

Asked, under cross-examination, how he could see these were police if it was dark, Chatsis said that he could see them when their cruiser's door opened, automatically turning on the interior light. Advised that police cars' interior lights had long been factory-altered specifically so they did *not* automatically turn on when doors opened, Chatsis sat silently in the stand, apparently at a loss for words. He then admitted that he had asked the RCMP if he'd be able to collect a financial reward under Crime Stoppers for his story. Finally, asked why, in the intervening three years, he had never before told anyone about that sighting from the train bridge, Chatsis revealed he "wanted to make a surprise."

Finding Chatsis' claim far-fetched, the six-member jury took two walks in Diefenbaker Park at night, even venturing onto the train bridge to discover what they could see across the river and through the trees, subsequently throwing out the claim as not credible. But it was 2003 when the inquest discredited the story. During those years, some media such as CBC's *The National* repeated his story. It is impossible to calculate what effect the repeated disinformation had on jury members in the Munson and Hatchen trial, since it concluded *before* reports about Wegner's "starlight tour" were revealed as a snow-job. (Some media members, such as two CBC employees writing the book, *Starlight Tour*, even retold the story two years *after* Chatsis had been rejected as a witness!)

Two years after the inquest, Saskatonian Dorothy Zoorkan had a memorable experience. On Feb. 8, 2005, a man in her doctor's office asked her to read some letters for him. The kindergarten teacher tells the story in the soft voice she has learned holds students' attention:

> "I asked him if he was sure that he wanted me to read these as they looked like they contained personal information. He assured me he did, so I began to read. He wanted to know what was at the beginning of each letter and who the letter was from. I thought that maybe he was illiterate or had difficulty seeing. The letters were all written to the Human Rights Commission, complaining about some lady, and they were all signed: Albert Chatsis. As I read each of the three or four letters, he placed them in different pockets inside his jacket.
> Then the nurse came out and presented him with another letter which

he also gave me to read. I once again asked if he wanted me to read personal information; he said yes. The information stated that Albert had severe arthritis and was unable to walk any great distance, that he needed special transportation.

When I got home, I told my husband what had happened. He asked if I knew who I had been talking to, and I said, 'No, the name doesn't mean anything to me.' He then told me what Albert Chatsis had said at a public inquest [three years earlier]. I found that odd because I had just read this information that he had severe arthritis and needed special transportation. So my first thought was that, when he talked about going for that midnight walk, he was lying."

Another Native man, Rodney Wailing, 29, came forward in February with an allegation that two police officers had picked him up five years earlier, in the summer of 1995, while he was high on lacquer thinner. He said the police first dumped the remainder of the stinking, intoxicating chemical onto the back seat of their police vehicle and then drove him to the riverbank near the Queen Elizabeth power plant. In a national CTV interview, he claimed that the police had not said "much of anything" in the vehicle:

"Like, they didn't tell me I was under arrest. I just figured I was just going in for intox. ...But that's not the way it went. They literally took me to the water with one cop on each side holding my arms and took me to the water and stuck my head under the water. ...When I was down there the second time, my arms came free and I got underneath and I pushed like I was in a push-up and I got my head up and I tried to back up and I still couldn't back up. So I went forward into the water and they weren't ready for that and that's how I got away."

The RCMP had added his allegation to their list of investigations, while a lawyer launched a civil suit against unspecified police officers for loss of short-term memory and income, head and soft tissue injuries, headaches, and interruption of sleep patterns. The RCMP task force investigated the complaint and found no evidence whatsoever. (What they did learn was that SPS Const. David Malanovich had pulled Wailing out of a dumpster one cold night in 1996, possibly saving his life.) Soon Wailing, who already had a long criminal rap sheet, faced two new charges of assault causing bodily harm against his girlfriend's sons, ages nine and 14. Released from custody pending trial, he was found by police in a back alley. An officer testified that Wailing smelled strongly of alcohol, was wearing only one shoe and bumping into walls. Charged with public intoxication, he was taken to the police station where a hypodermic needle was discovered in his back pocket. On the stand, Wailing said he had not been drinking that night. Instead he had been walking to the hospital, without telling his family, to get his stomach pumped because he feared he had overdosed on sleeping pills. His reason for requiring sleeping pills? Nightmares about the near-drowning experience five years earlier. Declared Judge Ron Bell: "I don't believe anything this gentleman said at this trial."

In September, 2000, unbeknownst to the public until now, lawyer Donald Worme faxed the RCMP investigation team about a third complainant:

"We write to bring to your attention another matter which, in our opinion, warrants investigation by your office. Mr. Joe Abel Halkett has contacted our office with respect to an incident which occurred on or about December 30, 1999. At such time, Mr. Halkett was picked up at 1514 - 1st Ave. N. by two Saskatoon Police Service officers, transported north of Saskatoon near the chemical plant, stripped of his winter jacket and abandoned. Mr. Halkett flagged down a passing vehicle and hitched a ride back to the noted address. Upon his arrival, the two officers were waiting outside of the residence, at which time Mr. Halkett was subjected to repeated racist remarks before the officers returned his winter jacket. Mr. Halkett notes that this was the second such incident, as the same officers had subjected him to similar conduct in 1995 or 1996. We would be pleased to discuss this matter in greater detail with you and, accordingly, look forward to hearing from you."

One of the many difficulties with that claim, in addition to the improbability of officers hanging onto the damning evidence of a man's jacket and then spending an impossible-to-predict amount of time (which they would have to explain to their sergeants) waiting outside his home for his arrival to return the jacket – without the neighbours noticing men in uniforms loitering, or Halkett complaining to the authorities – *twice!* – and all this risk for the presumed reward of flinging racist epithets – was that Munson and Hatchen had not been working December 30, or several days before and after. When no confirmation whatsoever was unearthed supporting Worme's submission, the matter was quietly dropped with no repercussion to anyone, despite expenditure of RCMP time and taxpayer dollar.

These were only some of the frenzied, far-fetched accusations against police with which citizens were being inundated in the free-for-all that was Saskatoon, 2000. There were a record-breaking 60 that year, as retired Sgt. Darrell Connell recalls:

> *"The number of complaints against the police in Saskatoon skyrocketed and, in my opinion, it was to beat a charge, lessen any penalties and/or to solicit lawsuits for monetary gain. One example of a complaint happened when an Aboriginal female walked by a police vehicle which was stopped at a red light and the two officers inside were reading the computer. She said they refused to make eye contact with her because they were racists. It was investigated, even though the officers never looked up or even saw her. Now tell me we aren't bordering on the ridiculous!"*

However outrageous, complaints took time to disprove, resulting in many fake complaints being used – in fact, still used today – to bolster allegations against cops.

No charges of mischief for "laying false complaints against police" were ever laid against Halkett, Wailing, Chatsis or others. What is the effect of not laying a well-publicized charge against such culprits? Retired Const. Ed Singbeil explains:

> *"It seems that just about every day someone is filing a complaint against the police, and the unfortunate thing is that the greatest percentage of complaints against police are proven to be false complaints.*
>
> *The consequence to the individual that lays that complaint is nothing. Personally, when I've had complaints filed against me that were false, I was very angry that they could run me through the mill and nothing would happen to the individuals that falsely accused me of wrongdoing. It puts your entire life in an uproar, it upsets your family, it upsets co-workers. And yet the person that causes all this turmoil suffers no penalty whatsoever. That is fundamentally wrong.*
>
> *If people have a legitimate complaint against police, absolutely make the complaint. It will be investigated, it will be dealt with. But don't make complaints just for the sake of getting even. If you think you were wronged,*

you have your day in court. It's that simple. But don't twist peoples' lives for no apparent reason!"

Saskatoon's police association now wanted those making false complaints – at a rate of several per week – charged. "Where before, if a complaint was unfounded – meaning a total fabrication – I don't recall the police department ever pursuing a charge," says Association President Goertzen. "After the Night incident, however, the association encouraged members who were lied about to make a formal criminal complaint in order to have it investigated. Then, if it led to grounds for a charge of public mischief, it could be exposed. We thought people needed to know what we were facing, and there were some convictions where people were found guilty because they made false allegations against Saskatoon police officers."

Goertzen sent an email during this time: "We had two more young people resign this week. One went to another police force and one will be working in the oil industry. Their dream of being police officers and having a positive effect on their community has turned into a surreal nightmare."

More apparent moral entrepreneurship was discussed by Const. Larry Lockwood in the documentary, *When Police Become Prey: What Lies Behind "Starlight Tours":*

"The day that all this information broke about Munson and Hatchen, there was going to be all these investigations and that sort of thing, I was working in the station, working plain-clothes. I go over to Mulberry's restaurant to have lunch. Sitting directly across from me were some Métis politicians. One was extremely well-known within the justice system.

While they were having lunch, sitting right across from me – they don't recognize me as a cop – they were laughing about this whole incident with the Natives freezing to death. And what really got me, what really drove me crazy about that, was they're joking to the waitress about it, and she was shocked!

After lunch I went back to the station, I got a witness statement, and came back and took a witness statement and passed that all on to Chief Scott at that time. I was shocked by their statement, that this was going to make them lots of money. It was just incredible. So here was just another issue...

Q: A cash cow to be milked?

Lockwood: Yes, exactly. Not that, you know, peoples' lives were involved here and peoples' feelings – the families of the frozen victims and that – no, they weren't looking at it in that tone at all. You know, I think there are ulterior motives here, big time!"

In the statement submitted to Chief Scott on Feb. 22, 2000, Lockwood wrote: "At approx. 1220 hrs the table conversation returned to incidents involving the police and natives being taken for rides, with the described person stating in a loud voice … **that what is needed now is a commission that would take sworn statements, so that the justice system could be bypassed.**"

The Aboriginal community called for just that – a public inquiry, as *Saskatchewan Sage* wrote:

"This whole drama is like a movie that is so predictable. Everybody has strong reason to believe [although no reasons are given] that it was the two senior officers, Munson and Hatchen, who drove Wagner [sic] and Naistus out of town, their bodies were later found frozen to death. However, the police will always deny the fact that the deaths of Wagner and Naistus have any direct connection to the complaint filed by Darrel Knight [sic], which told the exact same story. As for the two other Aboriginal men whose bodies were found at their apartment after being driven home from the police station...no one knows who to connect their deaths to.

Since the controversy began, every two weeks in Saskatoon there has been a vigil by the Aboriginal community calling for a public inquiry and organizers won't stop the vigils until a public inquiry is held. **My advice is to stop having vigils and start having riots.** *If not, hold a vigil on 8th Street and upset the thousands of non-Aboriginal drivers who are on their way to work. [The publication, apparently, was never charged for counselling people to commit crimes.] The Aboriginal community is calling for a public inquiry when the RCMP investigation is complete;* **without a public inquiry, Native leaders say, no one will be at fault for the deaths of the four Aboriginal men, including the 1990 death of Neil Stonechild.**" [32]

And someone, apparently, must be found at fault. That final sentence was prophetic. As though knowing in advance there would be no evidence to support any charges, that newspaper was recommending a public inquiry. In fact, an inquiry would be called with no rules other than "assign no blame," yet still manage to leave the pubic with no conclusion other than: two officers were to blame for Stonechild's death.

Fanned by the media, the city was soon aflame. A textbook example of the classic sociological phenomenon, "moral panic," an emotional frenzy which leads to "frantic persecution of perceived enemies" and, worse, "*lapse of due legal process.*" In fact, in years to come, the years 2000-2005 in Saskatoon undoubtedly will be studied to prevent other communities – and its scapegoats – having to endure the "surreal nightmare" of another Great Canadian Witch-hunt.

CHAPTER 6 - Moral Panic in the Streets!

'The entire nation was looking at us as a rogue bunch of killers. The RCMP looked at 12 or 13 deaths – some had been in custody many hours before – as though we had put some kind of time-pill in the body. They were stacking up bodies at our feet like cordwood!'
– Saskatoon police officer

Like all perfect storms, it seemed too much for coincidence. The shocking timing of three events – Night's allegation about police dropping him off against his will and the nearly simultaneous discovery of two frozen Aboriginal bodies within a few kilometres of that drop-off point – led to "moral panic." Moral panic is to human nature what a tornado is to nature: a convergence of events which escalate off one another, spiralling into a deadly tempest. Where such squalls randomly touch down, lives lie ruined. Desecrated.

Moral panic is an explosion of outrage. Intense emotions fuel a fiery controversy which can lead to a witch-hunt. The emotion stems from the issue "at stake" being so frightening that it seems to threaten the social order and everything people believe in. Moral panics can, but seldom do, result in positive social changes. Resolution of the social tension is extremely difficult because, importantly, the central issue around which the whirlwind cycles is banned from discussion! The subject is taboo. Sacrosanct. Unmentionable.

Sociologist Stanley Cohen, who introduced the term, explains:

"Societies appear to be subject, every now and then, to periods of moral panic. A condition, episode, person or group of persons emerges to become defined as a threat to societal values and interests; its nature is presented in a stylized and stereotypical fashion by the mass media; the moral barricades are manned by editors, bishops, politicians and other right-thinking people...."[33]

"During the moral panic," social scientists explain, "the behaviour of some members of a society is thought to be so problematic to others, the evil they do or are thought to do, is felt to be so wounding to the substance and fabric of the body social, that serious steps must be taken to control the behaviour, punish the perpetrators, and repair the damage. The threat this evil presumably poses is felt to represent a crisis for that society: something must be done about it, *and that something must be done now*; if steps are not taken immediately, or soon, we will suffer even graver consequences. The sentiment generated or stirred up by this threat can be referred to as a kind of fever; it can be characterized by heightened emotion, fear, dread, anxiety, hostility, and a strong feeling of righteousness."[34]

The phenomenon of heightened collective emotion is immortalized in the folk tale, "The Sky is Falling!" Chicken Little, beaned by an acorn, starts to fear monger, shouting warnings like the Saskatoon columnist: "After this, it is only a question of how many!" Scaring the other animals who then run around aimlessly until eaten by the wily fox. The ancient fable was devised to teach children the old folks' hard-earned wisdom: "Do not believe everything you're told! And, whatever you do, do not panic! You'll lose your head!"

In the midst of the moral panic, SPS Const. Ernie Louttit offered this calming wisdom in an interview with me: "Sometimes in the enthusiasm to do the right thing, things go off a bit to the right or left. And somewhere in the middle always lies the truth. And if we take a neutral stance always in the administration of justice, and in race relations between the police and Native people if we *always* take a step back when the fire gets hot and take a look, we'll find the right solution. If I could speak to everybody, that's what I would say: 'Let's take a step back! The sky's not falling! Life goes on and the truth always plays out in the end.'"

During a moral panic, "A category of people becomes defined as a likely causal agent in producing current social misfortunes."[35] A witch-hunt can follow: a form of "tunnel vision." People develop a theory and go fishing for facts to support it, even *targeting* certain people in order to support it. Soberingly, the federal Department of Justice has identified "tunnel vision as a *leading cause* for wrongful conviction in Canada and elsewhere" and made recommendations for preventing it, including "regular training for Crown [prosecutors] and police on the dangers and prevention of tunnel vision."[36]

Those who start the panic when they fear a threat are called moral crusaders or entrepreneurs because they *stand to gain from the situation*. To be successful, they must be vocal. They "have to gain the media's attention and attempt to secure legitimization for their definition of the reality of the condition being addressed. They do this by painting their issue in terms of good versus evil, and using the language of moral indignation."[37] Conversely, those who know the truth must be silenced. "Racist!" is one label frequently flung to light the fiery torch of indignation. With the Saskatoon screening of my documentary, *When Police Become Prey: What Lies behind "Starlight Tours,"* the message was silenced by activists shrouding the theatre entrance in canvas, requiring potential attendees to run the gauntlet of protesters. Attendance shrank from the first night's "standing room only" to a handful that second night. Imagine the uproar if non-Aboriginal activists suppressed the screening of an Aboriginal person's documentary. Is this fair? How can equality be restored?

"It is widely acknowledged that this is the age of the moral panic," wrote sociologist Kenneth Thompson in 1998. "The concept of 'moral panic' can be useful in spotlighting a form of behaviour and pattern of events that is increasingly common in our media-saturated (or media-rich) modern society."[38] One wonders, "What is the connection between media and moral crusades?"

Are many journalists closet crusaders? "I think journalists have always regarded themselves as moral guardians," says Yorkton, SK journalist Ann Harvey. "We are out-of-the-closet crusaders with cheap cars for Batmobiles!"

Perhaps journalists have learned that appeals to "Mount the moral barricades!" sell, penning what Thompson describes as "dramatic narratives and spectacles with a strong moral content."[39] Do those who once attended church now seek direction about underdogs and crusades in the Sunday papers? Is it easier for us as a society to run in circles and squawk than correct issues at the heart of social breakdown?

Sociologist Cohen writes, "The media have long operated as agents of moral indignation, even when they are not self-consciously engaged in crusading or muckraking. Simply reporting the facts can be enough to generate concern, anxiety or panic."[40] And, of course, in any moral panic, many journalists act in good faith, convinced the allegation is true. Plus, people make mistakes. Concerning his powerful role in creating the "Starlight Tour Panic," a *StarPhoenix* reporter privately admitted to Larry Hartwig, "I probably took the received wisdom, the information that was presented, more than I should have, instead of going to all the witnesses themselves. ...But as I get older and I look back, I can see that, regardless of what I concluded, **somebody was going to be sacrificed for the sins of white police**. I think that is clear." By 2006, Const. Mathew Bradford in a letter to the editor of the *StarPhoenix* would demand a novel solution to "biased" coverage:

"In light of what is apparently partisan and guerilla journalism in our print media monopoly, would it not be reasonable to dismantle the entire corrupt and dysfunctional organization and replace it with reporters from the Regina Leader Post?"[41]

"By means of the Stonechild Inquiry," Const. Lockwood said, "the Saskatchewan government was able – in one fell swoop and with the appearance of taking action – to remove suspicion from the RCMP, and temporarily pacify the Aboriginal community. This was all at the expense of two completely innocent officers. They were conveniently caught up, and then served up, in the *whirlwind of elements that intensified one another:* political correctness, Aboriginal activism, provincial politics, and what looks like RCMP investigative corruption."

Retired SPS officer Ron Frazer: "I had a feeling of helplessness because I knew these two deaths had nothing to do with police other than one other guy had been dropped off and got home safely. The agenda was fuelled by Aboriginal politicians. They've got a good thing going, making lots of money in salaries. The best way to draw attention away from 'I'm not spending money on housing!' is a diversion: 'Police are bad!' All things came together – the newspaper was biased, and it had no competition to print the other side."

Perhaps surprisingly, the intense coverage of freezing deaths increased *StarPhoenix* sales only 1.3 percent for the year 2000. In 2001, sales dropped back below 1999 levels. Is it possible Saskatonians became suspicious of allegations against police and no longer "bought the story"?[42]

Sociologist Thompson explains: "If social changes provided the grounds for anxiety, and the media gave those fears publicity, in each panic [sociologist] Jenkins found a number of influential claims-makers, each with a set of interests, or a political agenda [the wily foxes]. It seemed that a crucial role was played by various types of moral entrepreneurs and interest groups: individuals, pressure groups, and bureaucratic agencies, each with a complex and often shifting pattern of alliances between them."[43]

Sociopaths often view weakness as opportunity to prey upon another's misfortune, so some of those leap on the bandwagon. A colloquial description of moral entrepreneurial thinking: "Someone's down? Let's kick 'em and then see what's in this for us." Common terms for such people? Bullies. Predators.

On the other hand, people who supposedly threaten the social order are called "folk devils" or scapegoats. The term, "scapegoat," stems from a Biblical ritual thousands of years ago. According to *The Oxford English Dictionary (OED)*: "a goat was [completely arbitrarily] chosen by lot to be sent out into the wilderness, after the chief priest had symbolically laid the sins of the people on it." The meaning evolved to: "A person or thing blamed or punished for a mistake, fault, etc. of another or others." Other terms include whipping boy, fall guy, patsy.

The scapegoats become the prey – grievously wounded, totally bewildered and frantically protesting as they are randomly chosen as the ones to be blamed, shamed and "thrown out" into the desert. Maybe now the terrible problem plaguing the community will go away! But it does not. The only thing changed is the *scapegoats'* world. Overnight, they are in unknown and extremely dangerous territory, trusted friends unfathomably turned foe.

Larry Hartwig described the process to me long before I learned about moral panics:

"My whole career just went down the tubes. We are simply the scapegoats for this, and that's the way history will write it. We've been stonewalled,

not charged so we can't defend ourselves. The whole process so far is just to drain us dry financially so we can't fight. Thank God Stan Goertzen and the Police Association and every police officer across this country that has any ounce of sense is backing us up!

This affects the democracy of our country. People cannot be held accountable for what 'may' have happened or a 'perceived' offense. You have to have rules of evidence, which did not apply here, and you can't hold someone responsible and punish them for something that didn't happen 'just because people think it might have happened.' We have been denied due process under the law. We have not had a fair hearing since day one. We've been denied the ability to produce exculpatory evidence, and we've been denied the opportunity to prove our innocence. That should never have happened in the first place. In Canada you're innocent until proven guilty. In this case, we were guilty until proven innocent – but then we didn't even have an opportunity to do that – prove our innocence!"

In the 2000s, a higher than usual number of homeless people in Nome, Alaska, disappeared. Many were eventually found frozen, the result of what FBI specialists later attributed to a lethal mixing of alcohol and winter. But first! Hollywood rushed out a movie, *The Fourth Kind* (as in "Encounters of"). Rather than scapegoat police for disappearances, it blamed … alien abductions! Noted a Saskatonian: "If we decided to scapegoat aliens instead of police, we could change the mythical term 'starlight tours' to 'Star Trek tours!'"

In short, during moral panic, certain segments of the community lose touch, for a short, extraordinary time, with reality and common sense. No speculation is too outlandish, no allegation too bizarre. It is an irrational time which, for some journalists, is "very heaven." They participate in the process by which a mythology, or illusion, is created, and stereotypes about folk devils take hold.

All four fired officers say their miscalculation was in trusting that justice would be served through the Saskatchewan justice system; instead, they should have spoken out publicly and fought back aggressively against what they deemed false allegations.

A final truth about humanity which applies to all witch-hunts:

"Witches in the abstract were not hanged in Salem; but one by one were

brought to the gallows such diverse personalities as a decent grandmother grown too hard of hearing to understand a crucial question from the jurors, a rakish, pipe-smoking female tramp, a plain farmer who thought only to save his wife from molestation.... By grasping the local, the parochial even, it is possible to make a beginning at understanding the universal."[44]

So it was with the variety of officers and their chief; each so different, yet all roasted, writhing, over the same bonfire. One who wrote in 2015: "As a society, we have become lazy, shallow thinkers with knee-jerk overreactions to surprisingly small stimuli. Everything is to distract us from the obvious fact that we are failing. We are not what our fathers and grandfathers were. Everyone takes and nobody wants to give or pay the dues. When one is the whole world, it is really a pitiful little existence. Without God nothing else is enough...." His son is training to enter the priesthood. One who continues to wear an Aboriginal symbol of truth-speaking, "in the hope that it one day will be spoken." One who, for years, did not tell his children about the stress he was undergoing "in the hope they would not be too terribly affected. I got screwed over but look around the world – lots of people go through worse. It's not nice, but what can you do? I can't control the judge, but I can be the best person I can be: raise my kids and be a good husband." One whose son went on to become a police officer but refuses to serve in Saskatoon. One whose teenaged son said the events "stole my childhood and stole my dad from me!" He believed his father must be guilty, he finally revealed in a flood of tears after years of silence, because "so many people said you were!"

CHAPTER 7 - Accused!
RCMP Inform Constable Hartwig he is Suspect

*'Before Brad and Larry were wrongfully tarred and feathered, I
never understood how normal, decent, intelligent people could get
brainwashed to support what amounted to a witch-hunt.'*
– Sgt. Stan Goertzen, President, Saskatoon City Police Assn.

Life for Const. Larry Hartwig and family had been humming
along smoothly, he and Sandy working hard in their professions and their two
sons doing well in school, when, on Thursday, May 18, 2000, two powerful
men forced all their lives off the rails. Today, the Hartwigs cannot look at
family photos or videos of "before" days: "It reminds us of the lives we used
to have, and how close we used to be," Hartwig says.

Like Const. Brad Senger, who was also formally informed that day (in the
presence of his small sons) that he was a suspect in the Stonechild freezing
death, Hartwig, 41, had spoken previously to the RCMP to assist them in
any way he could. The two officers were tied to the case by the fact that in
1990, they had been dispatched to look for the 17-year-old Stonechild. An
acquaintance of Stonechild, along with other tenants in Snowberry Downs
apartment complex, had called 911, complaining that he was disturbing
residents by randomly ringing doorbells late at night.

In preceding weeks, RCMP had spoken to both Senger and Hartwig
under the pretext of questioning them about their knowledge of the deaths of
Wegner and Naistus, while actually observing whether they would volunteer
information about the Stonechild case. Senger did not recall ever meeting
Stonechild, but Hartwig knew both Neil and his family, as Neil and his
brothers were involved in crime. Hartwig shared all that he remembered with
RCMP Sgt. Ken Lyons.

Hartwig says Lyons brought up a recent *StarPhoenix* story, "Decades-old
death resurfaces," and asked Hartwig if he had read it. Hartwig said he'd read
all the recent "Starlight Tour" stories, and they had created uproar within SPS.

Despite Lyons having arranged for Hartwig to come in, he did not tape
record their interview. Instead, he later wrote this garbled account of what he
could recall Hartwig saying: "All I know is *the guys* arrested him [Stonechild]

in the 3300 block 33rd Street; they were going to a call of a suspicious person or a B & E in progress. *They* found Neil, who was drunk at the time, and arrested him for intox." Hartwig paused and asked in a questioning tone, "Why would they have driven him around trying to find out who he was?" He concluded, "Then they found some guy and asked him who he was. Then some guys are saying things like they are going to kill me or they are going to beat me up all the time."

RCMP investigators believed this to have been a "near confession," which seems to indicate serious bias. Asked about it today, Hartwig says, "I really cannot interpret this, and since Lyons was not called to testify, I have no idea what this is referring to – just like I testified at the public inquiry."

Lyons asked Hartwig if he had been working in November 1990, and who he would have been working with. Hartwig stated he didn't know, that he would check his notebooks from 10 years ago, and provide that information. Thinking Lyons was just being thorough, Hartwig also volunteered to search the SPS database for any incidents in which he'd been involved with Stonechild. Finding three incidents, he provided the information to Lyons, and volunteered there should have been more. Lyons then asked Hartwig if he had been working November 24, 1990; Hartwig said he'd check.

The following day Hartwig located the notebook, turned to November 24, 1990 and discovered that *he* had taken the call to Snowberry Downs where it was alleged that Neil had been in the back of a patrol car! He says, first he said, "*Holy Shit! I was there!*" Then he wondered, "How could that be?" He had clearly stated in his notes that Neil was GOA, Gone on Arrival. Hartwig immediately phoned Lyons to tell him of the discovery. "I knew I had to sit down with the RCMP ASAP to eliminate myself as a 'suspect,'" Hartwig explains today.

Lyons, however, already knew Hartwig had taken that dispatch, and was zeroing in on his target.

In the meantime, Hartwig contacted Ernie Louttit, because he recalled Ernie had been involved in the case years ago. He asked Ernie if there was ever a rumour about police involvement in Neil's death. "Ernie laughed and said, 'No,'" Hartwig says. He also contacted a Police Association representative to determine if he should continue to speak with the RCMP. She echoed what Hartwig believed: "If you have nothing to hide, you have nothing to fear!"

On May 18th, while on days off, Hartwig went into the police station first thing, to photocopy the pages from his notebook, intending to fax them to Lyons. What he didn't realize was that Lyons had already planned on calling him in that day to move forward on the Operation Ferric investigation. Therefore, when Hartwig phoned Lyons to let him know the notes were on the way, Lyons asked if, instead of faxing them, he could deliver them. Hartwig said, "Sure." (Lyons made a note that Hartwig delivered them without asking why.)

Just before Hartwig left the police station, Staff Sgt. Jim Cox advised Hartwig, "If anyone 'cautions' you [as a suspect], you should get up and leave." Hartwig could not even comprehend the possibility of someone believing he had anything to do with Stonechild's death. He knew that, since he had taken the call, he would be considered "a suspect," but expected to be cleared soon. After all, surely the RCMP would have thoroughly checked his background before assuming he would engage in misconduct, even criminal activity. He was a cop with a long-standing reputation for being honest, compassionate, self-motivated, and eager to assist anyone. His reputation, annual assessments, promotional interviews and service record all reflected that. "For me to be involved in any kind of misconduct would be a breach of everything I hold sacred," he explains.

In fact, everyone the RCMP spoke to, said the same thing. These included Police Chief Scott, who says today: "I know Larry. I know his honesty and integrity. I know his commitment to policing the community. I know his desire to protect all people. I know he would never do something like this"; Hartwig's training officers, Staff Sgt. Lorne Mulder: "Larry was diligent. If he had someone and there were grounds to take him into custody, he would have taken him to jail. That's the kind of police officer Larry was"; and Sgt. Don Yonkman: "Larry was a very gung ho individual and, if I can use the words, he was 'true blue.' He was a policeman and he loved to be a policeman and he took his job really serious. He had a very religious side to him, and he just wanted to do the best job that he could." Sgt. Ron Bezoplenko says about both Hartwig and Senger: "They were just super guys that you would want to work with. At no time did I ever experience a situation where I questioned what they were doing or their character or judgment or their ability to be forthright or honest. They were the kind of guys that you could count on to be there to back you. Dealing with various races, I never saw any situation where they acted in a manner where they would consider somebody less than equal to themselves. They were your role-model policemen." Const. Derick Baule talks about receiving his hard-earned 20-year exemplary service medal, taking it over to Hartwig's house and saying, "You deserve this more than me." With that, the 6' 3" officer goes silent, tears welling.

Retired Sgt. Jerry Boechler remembers the time when Hartwig was off-duty, yet turned up at the Little Chief police station. Boechler asked him, "Why are you here?" Hartwig replied that there was a family in Pleasant Hill that was moving that day, needed help, and he had a truck. "I thought that was typical of Larry from my time supervising him – he took that extra step with people," Boechler says. "He wasn't just worrying about assigned time; there was a human side to him, and he had a genuine desire to help people. For Larry, family and church were a big part of everyday life. He is a real people person, he doesn't just do something because it's the job or required, but because of the type of person he is: very generous and giving. He's a good man. When I first heard the accusations against Larry, I thought, 'This is the complete opposite of how I view him.' I was very sad for him and his family, and it also made me realize the positions sometimes we're placed in, in this line of work, and that this could have happened to any one of us. All of us police are very vulnerable to that kind of accusation by the nature of our job."

Retired Sgt. Lane Cooper adds, "Larry is very honest and trusts everybody else to be honest as him. I said to him, 'Larry be careful what you say and who you say it to. You and I know that what you're saying is the truth, but you could have other people take what you say and twist it!' I said, 'These people are not giving you a fair break! They're after you!' I was judging by the tone of the Mounties I talked to. They had a directed investigation. If you went off of the topic and tried to say 'Neil Stonechild was a drunk and a thief; he hung around with criminals and that's where you should be looking,' they would say, 'I don't want to hear about that. I want to hear about what you guys do when you take these kids out.'"

Hartwig continues with his recollection of the day. "I went down to the RCMP detachment as Lyons requested. According to my notes, I was working by myself. Since I was aware from media reports that two police officers were alleged to have been involved in the Stonechild allegation, I wanted to eliminate myself as a suspect ASAP, so the RCMP could focus on the real officers who took Neil. *Based on everything reported by the media, even I believed the allegation might be possible.*"

Arriving at the RCMP detachment, Hartwig was met by Corporal Nick Hartle, whom he knew fairly well. Hartle's wife was very ill with a life-threatening disease, and Hartwig asked how she was doing. Hartwig noted that Hartle looked as if he, too, were sick. "It wasn't long before I discovered why," he says today.

On the RCMP videotape, Hartwig is first seen at 10:50 a.m. in an interview room, reviewing his notebook with the chuckling, avuncular RCMP Sgt. Lyons. Hartwig concludes that two names in his notes, Tracy Horse and Bruce Genaille, are related to the call to Snowberry Downs apartment. Lyons then gives Hartwig the standard police cautionary warning and rights-to-counsel as a suspect in Neil Stonechild's death. Hartwig tells Lyons, "I don't need a lawyer. I've done nothing wrong," and waives his rights to counsel.

Reading the RCMP transcript, it is interesting to observe: Sgt. Lyons asks Hartwig very few questions about the case. Instead, he makes accusatory statements about what the investigators *believe* to be true: that Neil Stonechild was in Hartwig's custody. Hartwig says today, "This was done to feed me – and later, feed other SPS officers such as Sgt. Jarvis – the information the RCMP believed to be true, based on Jason Roy's confabulation." (A confabulation is "the invention of imaginary experiences to fill gaps in memory.") At the Hartwig/Senger Hearing, Roy would state that he "fills in the blanks" regarding things he cannot remember.)

Hartwig, on the other hand, confused by his inability to remember anything about the call, asks Lyons a series of questions about what was supposed to have occurred that night – according to the story that one person, Roy, gave the RCMP.

"Lyons: And that... that's why I say, Larry that... and also then Larry, while we're doing it, ahm... ah... the police warning. You need not say anything. You have nothing to hope from any promise...
Hartwig: Uhm-hmmm [affirmative].
Lyons:...of favour and nothing to fear from...
Hartwig: Right.
Lyons: ...any threat, whether or not you say anything.
Hartwig: Right.
Lyons: Anything you say can be used as evidence.
Hartwig: Right.
Lyons: Not news to you.
Hartwig: Not exactly.
Lyons: It's almost... it's almost insulting to say it, but...
Hartwig: O no... no. I... I understand... I understand what you have to do. I understand what your job is."

Initially Hartwig asks for a police association representative, but then, wanting to clear up the matter immediately, waives that protection as well:
"Lyons: Larry, ahm... if... you... you'd mentioned representation...
Hartwig: Right.
Lyons: ...from, ah...someone. We can stop right now, if you want...
Hartwig: Okay.
Lyons: ...or you can hear me out.
Hartwig: Okay, I'll hear you out, buddy. Yah!"

Lyons admits that he has not been honest with Hartwig; Hartwig actually has been a suspect right from their first interview, three weeks earlier. Lyons then follows the Chicago-based "Reid" interrogation technique, the primary method taught to the C.I.A., F.B.I. and police officers North America-wide, including SPS. The investigator *accuses* rather than questions, while completely ignoring any denials. The investigator may also lie to the suspect, as RCMP Const. Warner would soon lie to SPS Const. Brad Senger about more than one person having witnessed Stonechild in a police car the last night he was seen alive.

Originating in the 1950s, the Reid interview technique has been criticized because, although effective when dealing with a liar, it has induced false confessions from honest persons, since they tend to believe that the accuser is being honest with them. In fact, of the 311 Americans exonerated by 2013 through DNA testing, a startling number – more than one-quarter! – had given false confessions, presumably most during the Reid-style interviews which have been standard for decades.[45] Hartwig explains: "In the absence of information, a person will adopt erroneous information as fact, especially if that source of information is someone they trust, such as another police officer."

In 2012, Boston University journalism professor Douglas Starr attended basic Reid training. He was taught "the hallmark of lying is anxiety [rather than, as many psychologists claim, taking an inordinate length of time to answer questions], and interviewing therefore involves watching for signs of anxiety and occasionally causing it." Starr summarized his training:

"If the suspect denies the accusation, you bat it away. 'There's absolutely no doubt that this happened,' you say. 'Now let's move forward and see what we can do.' ...Having headed off denials, you steer the subject toward a confession by offering a face-saving alternative [making it easier to

admit to]. The process is called 'minimization' – down-playing the moral consequences of the crime without mentioning the legal ones. ...You might even lie: 'Why were your fingerprints found on that gun?' ... Gregg McCrary, a retired F.B.I. agent, told me that Reid-style training creates a tendency to see lies where they may not exist, with an unhealthy amount of confidence in that judgment. 'They just assume they're interviewing the guilty guy,' he said."⁴⁶

An Alberta judge denounced the technique in 2012, saying it can cause innocent people to make coerced [or "persuaded"] false confessions. Provincial Court Judge Mike Dinkel deemed a daycare worker's confession inadmissible and dismissed charges against her, chastising Calgary police for what seemed "a desperate investigative team bent on extracting a confession at any cost," as the Vancouver *Sun* reported, citing a psychology professor's description of the technique as a "guilt-presumptive, confrontational, psychologically manipulative procedure whose purpose is to extract a confession." ⁴⁷

Reid & Associates claims false confessions are the result of interviewers misusing the Reid technique, rather than the technique itself. They advocate that it be used only when all evidence supports the conclusion of involvement in an offense, and an initial "behavioural analysis interview" has raised suspicions of lying or withholding information.

In Hartwig's case, the RCMP's evidence did not support their assumptions; it supported the position that the officers had not encountered Stonechild, that Hartwig was a "by-the-book" cop with a stellar reputation while, on the other hand, their sole "witness" had a less-than-stellar reputation with more than 30 criminal charges against him – including Lying to Police – yet they accepted whatever the witness said at face value. Some might call this bias.

Despite all this, the RCMP continued with the accusatory interrogation:

"Lyons: Jack [Const. Warner] had determined, and we'll get into how if... if you want to.
Hartwig: Right.
Lyons: That, ah... that you had... that you did, in fact, have Neil in... in custody that night. Ahm... I'll... I'll explain that if... if... if you want me to, after. [Was this an attempt at humour –asking if Hartwig wants him to explain how the word of one convicted felon led to Warner's speculation with the potential to ruin Hartwig's life? Or did Lyons really

expect Hartwig to simply accept the speculation because it came from the Mounties?]
Hartwig: Yah, you betcha!
Lyons: But... but... what I'd... my reason for meeting with you was...
Hartwig: Right.
Lyons: ...ahm... I guess hoping that, ah... there was some reasonable explanation for him having been in your custody.
Hartwig: Right.
Lyons: Ahm... I guess, ah... I guess we were just hoping for some answers that...
Hartwig: Yah.
Lyons: ...made some sense and... and were easily explained.
Hartwig: Right.
Lyons: And, ahm... I guess they weren't there. And that's what brings us... brings us here today.
Hartwig: Well... great. Ahm... how... how do we know that I was the person that had Neil in custody?"

In that segment of the interview, there is only one question and it is Hartwig's. Still believing that he is helping out the RCMP by eliminating himself as a suspect, as indicated by his "how do we know..." he asks how the conclusion was reached that he had Stonechild in his custody.

He also continues to push ahead with questions, despite the fact he has no police association protection. Association President Goertzen says that, had he been called, he would have insisted that Hartwig have his lawyer present.

Goertzen, a polygraphist with extensive training in Reid Technique who taught it to SPS officers for six years, adds that if he had been in Hartwig's shoes, he would have said, "I know what you are trying to do, so get to the issue," and then stated unequivocally, "I didn't do this bloody thing!"

Hartwig agrees that he should have "called Bullshit!" and said, "You are lying to me!" But because he didn't know the details of the investigation, he trusted the RCMP to be competent, honest, and fair. "At that time," he says, "I had a great deal of respect for the RCMP."

"Lyons: Well, do you want to get into it?
Hartwig: Yah, you betcha!
Lyons: Okay.

Hartwig: I wanna find out, buddy!

Lyons: Okay, ahm, I'm just a little concerned that [police association president] Stickney or... or whomever...

Hartwig: Well...

Lyons: ...If... if you wanna do this... if you wanna...

Hartwig: F---!

Lyons: ...I'm...

Hartwig: I wanna take a polygraph. [A form of denial]

Lyons: ...I'm here...

Hartwig: I wanna take a polygraph.

Lyons: Okay.

Hartwig: I wanna take a polygraph. Like...

Lyons: Alright.

Hartwig: ...like... I... this... I've got a damn good memory, eh... and now I've... I've got something here on the go that, ah... apparently I was involved in that I don't recall...

Lyons: Okay.

Hartwig: ...that I was not involved with. [Denial #1]

Lyons: All right.

Hartwig: I'll tell you right now... you know how many times I've abused a prisoner?

Lyons: No.

Hartwig: [Indicates a zero with his hand.] That many times. [Denial #2]

Lyons: That's my concern here, Larry, is...

Hartwig: Right.

Lyons: ...that this is really gotten out of hand, given everything else that's been going on.

Hartwig: Right.

Lyons: If we... if we separate everything else, this isn't... this isn't a... a big thing. Given the... I guess the current political climate and everything and...

Hartwig: Right.

Lyons: ...that makes it, ah... more so.

Hartwig: Yah, makes a mess. Yah.

Lyons: And... and the media has taken this thing

Hartwig: Uhm-hmmm.

Lyons: ...and they've, ah... I suspect, made this thing a whole lot more sinister...

Hartwig: Uhm-hmmm.

Lyons: ...than what it really is. You... you know... you know what they're suggesting, Larry?

Hartwig: Oh, yah!

Lyons: That... that if...

Hartwig: Oh, yah!

Lyons: ...They... they haven't come out and said this but they're basically saying that Neil Stonechild...

Hartwig: Uhm-hmmm.

Lyons: ...got arrested...

Hartwig: Uhm-hmmm.

Lyons: ...ah... beat on and left for dead.

Hartwig: Right.

Lyons: That's what they're saying.

Hartwig: Right.

Lyons: Do I think that that happened? No. I don't. [chuckles]

Hartwig: It didn't happen! [Denial #3]

Lyons: I... I... I...

Hartwig: [pointing to himself]: It didn't happen here, buddy! [Denial #4]"

Here, Lyons asks three questions and answers two himself. Suddenly realizing the gravity of his situation, Hartwig three times demands a polygraph. Remarkably, Lyons introduces "the current political climate" and what "the media ... are suggesting." Yet what has anything outside the RCMP investigation got to do with determining truth? Is this just a method to move the suspect toward confession? Or does it suggest the RCMP are influenced by the media and "current political climate"?

And why would Lyons say that outside of the media and political climate, "if we separate everything else, this isn't a big thing"? Does he mean that a person dying in unknown circumstances is "not a big thing"? And if that person actually died as the result of foul play, that is "not a big thing"? Presumably this is an attempt at "minimization" to obtain further information from Hartwig.

Lyons presses on, uttering the fateful words of the formal accusation that still echo in Hartwig's head during flashbacks: "Larry, after reviewing everything that is known, there's no doubt in my mind... and the other investigators'... that Neil Stonechild was in your custody..."

Hartwig replies, "F---!"

"...for a period of time that night."

The RCMP transcript records: "Const. Hartwig: [Heavy sigh.]"

The interview continues:

"Lyons: Larry...

Hartwig: Geez, I wish I would have...

Lyons: ...I... I have...

Hartwig: Damn it!

Lyons: ...I... I have... before you say anything more, Larry

Hartwig: Uhm-hmmm.

Lyons: I've got a real fear. My fear is this. I know you're in a bad spot.

Hartwig: Um-hmm!

Lyons: I know you're scared. Y... you should be. I would be.

Hartwig: Oh, yah.

Lyons: But... I've been on the other side of the table, too. Ahm... I don't want you saying... I don't want you saying anything that isn't true...

Hartwig: Right.

Lyons: ...because you know what happens when something... says it isn't true.

Hartwig: Oh, have no fear, buddy!

Lyons: And... and it's... and it's proven that...

Hartwig: Yah.

Lyons: ...that that was wrong. Then...

Hartwig: Then have no fear.

Lyons: ...then everything's out the window.

Hartwig: Have no fear.

Lyons: Okay.

Hartwig: If I did something that... if I screwed up, or if I made a mistake, I'm the first guy to admit it. [Denial #5]

Lyons: Larry... I... and I know that. And you know what I think? That's all that this is... is a mistake.

Hartwig: F---!

Lyons: You know what I think happened?

Hartwig: ...Can you... can you answer me a question?
Lyons: Yah.
Hartwig: Was the warrant [for Stonechild's arrest for being AWOL from his group detention home] on the system that night?
Lyons: Yah.
Hartwig: It was? F---!"

It was a former street kid who knew Neil who pointed out to this reporter that the fact there was a Canada-wide warrant out for Stonechild's arrest meant it was highly unlikely the officers had had Stonechild in their custody. In her words, the RCMP theory was insane:

"I don't think police officers of outstanding credit would do something like that to one individual. Apparently Neil had a Canada-wide warrant out for his arrest. Why would they dump him off? When it's a Canada-wide, province-wide, warrant of any kind, bench warrants, they're not going to let you go. That's insanity! If you've got a warrant out, they want you to deal with that warrant. They'll take you in. I had a bench warrant out for my arrest because of failing to appear in court, and when they got me, 'Well okay you got me, and let's deal with this.' Like, if you've got a warrant out for your arrest, they're not going to dump you off some place. They will take you to the city buckets, and that's where you'll either go to court, or you'll be released, depending on what the judge says, but there is no way that any police officer in Saskatoon would have just dumped off a person with a warrant out for their arrest; there is no way! It would have been a huge feather in their hats to bring in someone with a Canada-wide warrant!"

Retired SPS Const. Larry Cook agrees:

"One of the reasons we never ever believed the RCMP, we always believed Larry and Brad, was because they were brand new. When you get an arrest, you bring the arrest in. You're not going to say, 'Let's see what we can do with this arrest.' Those two wanted to bring arrests in. They were not lazy. There's no way they would have done that. Besides, it was a Canada-wide warrant – all of a sudden you can tell your co-workers, 'Hey, I got someone on a Canada-wide!' And that's a really good thing.

All you get out of it is someone saying 'Way ta go!' But you can show them you're doing a good job. There wasn't even any paperwork involved; in 1990, the arresting officer only had to date and sign the warrant.

Also, there's no way those two would have ever done what they were accused of – just because of who they were. They were guys who went out there and worked hard their whole shift. They did everything by the book. The [Police Chief] Sabo administration was all on the side of the RCMP."

RCMP Sgt. Lyons now claims that not only had Hartwig encountered Stonechild, he also encountered his cousin, Bruce Genaille, who said that police stopped him and accused him of being Neil Stonechild.

"Lyons: And do you know what I think, Larry? Ahm...
Hartwig: That if I think if I w... I... I'm quite certain that if I would have dealt with Neil Stonechild that night, I would have recognized him.
Lyons: ...you pulled Bruce Genaille over and you thought he was Neil.
Hartwig: Pulled... pulled him over?
Lyons: He was walking.
Hartwig: Oh, okay.
Lyons: Ahm... he was walking. He's actually Neil's cousin.
Hartwig: Bruce Genaille?
Lyons: Bruce Genaille. And, ahm...
Hartwig: F---!
Lyons: ...you accused him of being Neil.
Hartwig: Uhm-hmmm.
Lyons: And, ah... he produced some I.D. that said he wasn't.
Hartwig: Okay.
Lyons: Ahm... right after that...
Hartwig: Right.
Lyons: ...because... because he knew you were looking for Neil...
Hartwig: Because Neil knew...
Lyons: ...he had some interest in what was going to happen.
Hartwig: Right.
Lyons: And... and actually the other fellows have talked to Bruce and that's where a great deal of the information has come from."

Today Hartwig says, "I was flabbergasted! From that point on, all through the interview and the trip to Snowberry Downs, and then back to the detachment and for the entire next week, I was in shock. Based on what Lyons told me, *I believed that I had encountered Neil Stonechild and had him in custody without knowing it at the time*, because he must have given me the false name of Genaille." (In police terminology, "in custody" includes any time a person is checked by police.)

Hartwig trusted the RCMP to tell the truth. He therefore assumed the confusion was his fault; he must have a faulty memory. "I wasn't going to leave the detachment until I figured out how the hell the RCMP thought that I was a suspect. I was totally and completely confused by what Lyons told me and I was certain that Neil couldn't have fooled me by providing a bogus name because I'd dealt with him the month before, but as Lyons continued to provide details of what they claimed to be true, I was devastated. **I thought I may have let Neil go without realizing who he was, and if only I'd arrested him, he would not have frozen to death.**

"People sometimes lie," Hartwig continues, "and deceive police officers, in spite of officers' training to detect deception. Often, the lies involve a person's identity when they are checked on the street [as Jason Roy had lied to Hartwig and Senger]. A person will lie if they have warrants out for their arrest or court-ordered conditions that they are violating. Sometimes, when officers are deceived by the person's false identity, they will never know they've been fooled. This is what I concluded in this case, based on what I was told by Lyons. **I believed that I must have let Neil go without determining his true identity. I blamed myself, because I thought I should have recognized Neil from having dealt with him in the past, and thought that, if I had spent more time talking to him, I might have figured it out, arrested him, and he would have been safe.**"

What would eventually be determined, based on computer records and Jason Roy's fragmented memory, was that Hartwig and Senger had, indeed, stopped Roy (exiting the area where the officers had been sent to search for Stonechild), and asked him for his name. Roy lied about his name, giving them the name, Tracy Horse. When the RCMP later asked Roy why he had lied to police about his identity, Roy said (repeatedly) that he lied because there was a UAL warrant out for his arrest. This was also untrue, as were all of the circumstances around this disclosure. Despite his admitting to these lies, the RCMP accepted that everything else Roy said was true.

Meanwhile, Lyons continues with his game of "Give the Suspect Shock

Treatment and Let Him Try to Figure Out What is Going On":

"Lyons: Tracy Horse wasn't Tracy Horse.
Hartwig: Oh, f---! Okay. Nobody, nobody, nobody has ever said in my hearing,
or in my range of hearing, "They're going to kill me." I would remember that."

[In the Feb. 22, 2000 front-page *StarPhoenix* story, "Decade-old death resurfaces," Jason Roy had alleged that he heard Stonechild yell, "They're [the police] gonna kill me!" The line had been repeated by The *StarPhoenix* on Feb. 23, *National Post* on Feb. 23 and CBC national television news Mar. 7.]

Lyons suggests Hartwig has simply made a mistake:

"Hartwig: Well, yeah, but hey, I don't like making mistakes, buddy. ...But
I've been fooled before, but now, now I've gotta take it back and find out what
I did with him. He was in my car? (Lyons: Uhm-hmmm.) F---!"

More shock treatment:

"Lyons: And you weren't alone.
Hartwig: And what ... oh, f---! I don't have any notes for that. I don't have
any... and that... and the, ah... the report that I filed after has only me as
the officer...
Lyons: I know.
Hartwig: Who was I working with?
Lyons: Brad.
Hartwig: Brad?
Lyons: Senger.
Hartwig: Senger?
Lyons: Have you talked to him today?
Hartwig: No, I haven't talked to Brad about this at all. I talked to Lorne
Mulder. After I phoned you, I got up... from my nightshift, checked my
notebook. I says, 'Holy shit! I was there!'
Lyons: Okay.
Hartwig: Or I'd... and I phoned Mulder and I says, 'Listen, Lorne,' I says,
'You were my regular partner back then. I... and I have nobody workin' with
me that night. Where... where were you? Where... you know, were you on
holidays or whatnot?' And I says, ah... 'One six... I think it was one-six-seven.'

61

'Ah,' he says, 'well, that's Wally Romanuk.' ...'cause that's who I worked with apparently the night before."

[Remarkably, Lyons would write in his report: "When Lyons told Hartwig that he had a partner that night and he was working with Brad Senger, Hartwig was not surprised." How could Lyons possibly classify Hartwig's reaction that way? *Who was I working with? Brad. Brad? Senger. Senger? Have you talked to him today? No, I haven't talked to Brad about this at all.*]

Lyons says, "Let's get this cleaned up today." Hartwig responds, "I wanna get it done now, buddy, I just have to be home at three forty-five to pick up my kids." Lyons replies that regardless of the outcome of the interview, he will be going home. "Well, damn rights!" Hartwig says. "I've done nothing wrong [chuckles]. [Denial #6] I've made a mistake on my notes, right?"

"More than your notes," Lyons replies quietly, ominously. He continues:

"Lyons: Larry, I have to be honest. I don't completely believe you when you say you don't remember what happened, okay?
Hartwig: Ken, I don't wanna say I don't care, but – [Here Hartwig calls "Bullshit!" without actually using the word.]
Lyons: But you don't, yeah, okay. (Laughs)
Hartwig: If I remembered something, Ken, I'd be the first one to tell ya. [Denial # 7]
Lyons: Okay, how can we determine what happened there?
Hartwig: Don't know, unless you talk to Brad and find out if he's got anything recorded in his notes, eh? I got him down as GOA."
Lyons repeatedly insists on the RCMP theory that Neil Stonechild had been beaten up and left for dead:
"Lyons: The sinister side of things, we've talked about –
Hartwig: Right.
Lyons:...beat him up and left him for dead –
Hartwig: Right.
Lyons: That didn't happen?
Hartwig: No. [Denial #8]
Lyons: What did happen?
Hartwig: F---! I wish I knew now! I'll tell you... I'll tell you... I'll tell you what... well, again I... I better go... I better have a... a repre... re... representative from the association but... I... I can only tell you what I normally do.

Lyons: Larry, that...
Hartwig: I can't tell you what...
Lyons: ...that's something that's gonna stick out in a person's mind...
Hartwig: Right. What?
Lyons: ...if something like that happened.
Hartwig: Oh, of course it would!
Lyons: Oh...
Hartwig: Yah, absolutely!"
Lyons tries another tack. He asks, for the third time, "You wanna know what I think happened?" – more speculation, which Hartwig finds laughable.
"Hartwig: Okay. [chuckles]
Lyons: A variation of this.
Hartwig: Right.
Lyons: You get a call.
Hartwig: Right.
Lyons: We've all been there. You get a call. You're obviously looking for Neil. You know who you're looking for.
Hartwig: Right. Exactly.
Lyons: You dealt with him in the past, ah...
Hartwig: Right.
Lyons: ...within a year or so. You... you th... you've got an idea at least...
Hartwig: Within... less than that 'cause I...
Lyons: ...less than... yah, seven-eight months or whatever.
Hartwig: Yah. Less than that, probably. 'Cause I think that one was... when I dealt with him on the vehicle check.
Lyons: Yah.
Hartwig: That was October, okay? A month before.
Lyons: Right. Ahm... lookin' for him. He's drunk. These kids were all... raisin' hell or whatnot.
Hartwig: Uhm-hmmm.
Lyons: Like they're... some of them...
Hartwig: Allegedly. [Lyons makes assumptions; Hartwig does not.]
Lyons: Some of them are want... ah... wantin' to do... Ahm... You find him. He's causing trouble. He gets... somehow injured. [With all the medical reports, Lyons should know by now that Stonechild was not injured.] How...

Hartwig: Hmm…

Lyons: …I'm not sure.

Hartwig: Didn't happen. [Denial #9]

Lyons: Ahm… okay.

Hartwig: Didn't happen. [Denial #10]

Lyons: Didn't? Okay.

Hartwig: If he was injured, I would have taken him to hospital.

Lyons: Okay. I don't think he was injured that badly, though. The kid mentions some… marks across here. [Sgt. Lyons motions to the facial area.] Ahm… when I…

Hartwig: Who men… who mentioned that?

Lyons: The ah… ah… Horse.

Hartwig: Okay.

Lyons: Ahm.

Hartwig: Did you interview Brad?

Lyons: Pardon me?

Hartwig: Did you guys interview Brad?

Lyons: We'll get into that after.

Hartwig: Okay, good."

Hartwig also says, "If I took Neil anywhere, it would have been home." [Denial #11]

Why did the RCMP not do what this reporter did to help corroborate or dispute Hartwig's statements about his treatment of people in custody? (It was not rocket science.) I checked Hartwig and Senger's notes. Hartwig had written: "[Youth's name] driven home # 96408 22:52 Susp Vehicle 218 Tache Cresc."

Senger had written: "[Name], dob 1973-Mar-03. Took youth home 1001 McCormack Road."

Dispatch had asked them to check on a red Mustang in the 200 block of Tache Crescent. The complainant said a male had been sitting in the vehicle for the past three hours and looked drunk.

Therefore, the first dispatch the two officers ever took together was at 10:59 p.m. to a suspicious vehicle parked in front of a Saskatoon home. They found a young man asleep in the car and woke him up; he was intoxicated and likely very cold; they drove him home.

Reading this information, I had noticed that the person had an unusual name. Hoping there would not be many like it, I called directory assistance, checking for that name anywhere in Saskatchewan. Given a number, I dialed it. A man answered and said yes, that was his name. Introducing myself, I told him I was writing a book about the Saskatoon police, and could he help?

> "A: *If I can...*
>
> Q: *Terrific! In November 1990, did you live at 1001 McCormack Road?*
>
> A: *No.*
>
> Q: *Oh! Well! Sorry to –*
>
> A: *My aunt and uncle did. I stayed with them a lot.*
>
> Q: *No! I mean, wonderful! Now, at that time, did you by any chance drive a Mustang?*
>
> A: *Sure did!*
>
> Q: *Nice! And your date of birth is March third, 1973?*
>
> A: *Yup.*
>
> Q: *So in 1990, you would have been 17?*
>
> A: *Ummm.... Yup!*
>
> Q: *Okay! Now, here's the important question. Do you remember being driven home by two police officers the night of November 24, 1990?*
>
> A: *Nope.*
>
> Q: *Oh. Not what I wanted to hear! Well, could I talk to your aunt and uncle?*
>
> A: *No, they've both died.*
>
> Q: *Hmmm. Well, it's your name and exact birthdate and Mustang car and correct address, so it had to be you.... Were you ever dropped off by police somewhere you didn't ask to be dropped?*
>
> A: *Never.*
>
> Q: *Did the RCMP ever call and ask you, like I just did, about that night, November 24, 1990?*
>
> A: *No.*
>
> Q: *Last question: are you Aboriginal?*
>
> A: *Sure am!"*

That is literally how long it took –perhaps 10 minutes – to track down and interview, 26 years later, the person mentioned in Hartwig and Senger's notes, and to determine that the 17-year-old intoxicated youth they dealt with, perhaps saving his life, immediately before their dispatch to find Stonechild, was Aboriginal. The second point is that the youth was arrestable: sitting behind the wheel for three hours with keys in the car, he could have been arrested for Care and Control of a Motor Vehicle while Impaired by Alcohol. So what did the officers do? Rather than arrest and charge him with a criminal offense, they gave him a break, and *drove him home.*

Therefore, is it logical that in their next, virtually identical, dispatch to look for an intoxicated 17-year-old Aboriginal male, they would have picked him up, beaten him up, driven him far out of their district and dropped him off? (Risking, in the process, being seen by other officers in the two adjoining districts they would have had to pass through, and therefore being asked what they were doing there.) Why wouldn't the RCMP, with far more sophisticated methods of locating people than I, have tracked down and spoken to this man and then told their colleagues, "Whoa, boys! Rein yourselves in! Something isn't adding up here! Two such similar youths – it would be highly inconsistent behaviour to drive one home, and then beat up and dump the next." Yet, apparently no one from the task force bothered to take 10 minutes to find and speak with the very-much-alive Man in the Mustang.

Back in the interview room, Hartwig says that a photo of Jason Roy would help trigger his memory. "I'll just slip out and see if I can find a picture," Lyons says, leaving the room and joining Const. Warner who is covertly observing the interview. Sitting alone, Hartwig looks through his notes and swears. Two minutes later, 11:18 a.m., RCMP Cpl. Hartle enters.

Perhaps because Hartwig was so open with Hartle, the authors of the book, *Starlight Tour,* misrepresented Hartle as the SPS association representative. Without determining the facts, and despite much evidence to the contrary in the videotape, authors Renaud and Reber reported the interview with the spin that Hartle was a fellow SPS officer rather than an investigating RCMP[48] officer. (They even concocted a line, completely false: Lyons "told Hartwig that he'd send in his union rep.") In reality, the interview suggests:

A. Hartwig trusted RCMP Sgt. Lyons to be competent, honest, and fair,

B. he could remember nothing about the incident, and

C. he seemed frank and open with RCMP Cpl. Hartle, as with Lyons.

The *Starlight Tour* authors reported the following. Reinserted in square brackets are significant quotes from the transcript which the authors omitted without indicating they had cut anything:

"Moments later Nick Hartle, the union representative,[sic] knocked on the door and walked in.

'Hi, guy.'

'Man, this is serious stuff,' said Hartwig. 'Frick, I've gotta have something to jog my memory. Obviously now there's something there, because [the guys are saying] I was there, I dealt with Neil that night, I dealt with this other guy who called – said his name was Tracy Horse. And now I gotta remember him. 'Cause obviously there's something there. [There's something there, right?] … And [he's saying] I handcuffed him! [And now I gotta remember him.] And they said he had a – like he was pointing to his eye, had bruises." Hartwig sighed, and cursing again, insisted he remembered none of it. [I've driven so many drunks home it's not even funny. If I dealt with Neil Stonechild, why would I let him go? Sigh] "I gotta talk to Senger. I gotta see if he's got notes on this. This is not good. I dealt with this guy, he's found dead four days later, eh! And I have no notes and I can't remember anything about it. …Talk about getting hit with a baseball bat, eh? I couldn't believe it when he told me that I'd CPICed, that I'd actually dealt with Neil, I had him in handcuffs. He was in my frickin' car. Why didn't this come up ten years ago? Right? I would have been able to remember ten years ago. Right?'

…What bothered Warner most [the authors of the book, Starlight Tour wrote] was that he'd never heard Hartwig lead with outright denials."[49]

[There were 15 denials in the 63-minute interview.]

What those authors also chose to omit, the transcript reveals, is Hartle asking Hartwig if any of the information jogs his memory. Hartwig says it doesn't, and he must find something that does, since there is "something I'm missing." Hartle's approach is the reverse of Lyons' – he asks questions, rather than makes misleading and confusing statements. The actual RCMP interview continues:

Hartle asks Hartwig if he knew Neil. Hartwig replies, "Oh, yeah. Ken [Lyons] called me… [asked] if I was workin' when Naistus and Wegner were found: 'Sorry, guys… don't know anything about it. I'm so far out of the loop bein' in Hit-and-Run that I don't deal with guys on the street anymore… don't hear things anymore, eh.' I says, 'But Neil Stonechild. You wanna talk about Neil Stonechild?' I used to arrest him, eh? I've dealt with him on a B & E and I told Ken all about Neil Stonechild. And I said, 'I dealt with his mom.'

And I said, 'His mom was coming to the realization that, you know, that Neil needs help, eh?' And now this, eh? Now this! (Sigh) Well, I'm glad I was with Senger that night, eh? Cause now he'll be able to back me up. Eh? I hope he kept good notes. …Neil's found under suspicious circumstances in the north end of the city, apparently dumped off by somebody after he'd been… he'd either been beaten up and dumped or beaten up, dumped and froze to death. I don't know, eh? And now, ten years after the fact, I've gotta try to remember what happened ten years ago? I wish I would have kept better f---in' notes. Man, the only thing I can think of… there's only one possible thing I can think of and that's I took him home, eh? But why would I do that if he was on CPIC? Why would I do that? If I did that, there must have been a story. Man, I hope Brad wrote that down. …You know, I don't take that good of notes. Right? But I wish I did that day. …I was telling Ken, I says, 'You know how many prisoners I've abused in fourteen years?' [indicates a zero with his hand.] [Denial #12] I've seen police officers do it, eh? We all have, eh? We've all been there."

Hartle replies, "Yah."

Hartwig: "But that's how many people, eh? Because everybody is a person. I remember one case where somebody committed suicide and one of the people on my shift says, 'Well, good for them. We won't be arresting that person anymore.' And I says, 'That's somebody's son. There's a grieving mother, eh?' Man, that pisses me off."

11:33: Lyons returns to the room; Hartle remains. Hartwig continues to question Lyons. Lyons asks Hartwig if it would be beneficial to go through the witness statement provided by Jason Roy; Hartwig says it would. Lyons insists there is no question of what happened. He repeats the RCMP theory, but, strangely, there are a total of six minutes of audio missing in eight different places from the interview at that point. RCMP claim it was accidental. Lyons completes the Mounties' version of the truth, and leaves.

Hartwig and Hartle continue, Hartwig more concerned that he might have missed a chance to save Stonechild's life than the fact that his own life, as he knew it, was now in jeopardy. Hartwig repeats, "I most certainly… [laugh] I most certainly didn't take somebody out of town. [Denial #13] I most certainly didn't beat somebody up, right? [Denial #14] I most certainly didn't drop somebody off where they didn't wanna go, eh? [Denial #15] And now this guy's dead. F---! If I cut this guy a break and drove him home, I'm partly to blame, eh? **If I had an opportunity to arrest him, Nick, and I didn't** take that opportunity and he shows up dead four days later, he wouldn't be dead if he was in police custody."

He concludes that he wants to go to Snowberry Downs to trigger his memory.

Lyons re-enters. Hartwig discusses the possibility of using anything, including hypnosis, to help him remember, and says he will not be able to sleep with this hanging over his head. He asks if he can speak to Senger and his last recorded words in the interview are: "Good. I wanna fi... Ken, I wanna find out, eh, I wanna remember, eh, what happened."

In those 34 pages of transcript, Hartwig stated repeatedly:
- he had never abused or beaten up a prisoner, and he had never taken anyone out of town or dropped them off where they didn't want to go,
- he had nothing to do with the death of Neil Stonechild, and if he had made a mistake, he would be the first to admit it.
- He wanted a polygraph in order to clear his name.

Sgt. Lyons would write in his report that there were "no denials" by Hartwig. There were 15. **This suggests the RCMP focused not on determining how and why Neil Stonechild died, but on proving Jason Roy's allegation that Stonechild was in their custody.** While Hartwig had said: "*If* you're saying I was there and *if* you are saying there's a witness that put me and Brad there, I was there. *If* I was there, buddy, I'm telling you: I don't remember anything about what happened to Neil Stonechild that night," Lyons would write: "Basically Hartwig said that if the investigation showed that he had Stonechild, then he must have had Stonechild. Hartwig can't recall what he did with Stonechild."

The Mountie's report is not only highly inaccurate, it totally misrepresents events. Presumably to prove a case against Hartwig.

Const. Warner's final report would further twist words by quoting Lyons' *summary* as though it were a quote from Hartwig. For example, Warner claims that Hartwig *stated* that "if the investigation showed he had Neil Stonechild, then he must have had Neil Stonechild." Hartwig had not said that at all. It was merely *Lyons' conclusion* based on Hartwig's self-doubt, which in turn, was based on his believing what he had been told by Lyons.

Both Lyons' notes and Warner's summary were highly inaccurate, and the content manipulated to *manufacture* culpability on Hartwig's part. Worse, Warner's supervisors at every level, including both Lyons and Insp. McFadyen would have had to approve Warner's report. They therefore would have been aware of the intentional manipulation, but did not correct it.

RCMP Cpl. Hartle's report was very different from Lyons'. He noted that Hartwig expressed difficulty remembering what happened the night of November 24, 1990; that Hartwig considered several alternatives, such as he might not have found Neil Stonechild, he might have found him but not recognized him, Neil might have lied about who he was, and maybe he dropped him off at home. Hartle noted that during the interview, Hartwig "denied any wrongdoing whatsoever" and stated he had never hurt, assaulted, or dropped off anyone, ever.

Alarmingly, in the RCMP's final report to Sask Justice, not only were Hartle's notes and observations about Hartwig's interview not included, but the fact that Hartle was present at all was entirely suppressed!

Retired SPS Deputy Chief, Norm Doell, did a statement analysis on the Lyons/Hartwig transcript. He concludes:

"Proper analysis not possible. Hartwig and Lyons were both too eager to talk; neither would let the other finish. I would promptly have told Lyons to pound sand! Lyons painted a picture and used the minimization technique that Hartwig's alleged action was just a "mistake" (p. 10 & 11). The minimization technique is intended to lull the subject into thinking things are not too bad, and then the interviewer steps it up, as Lyons did, to murder! By p. 12 he tells Hartwig what happened! Slowly he builds the framework and, p. 16, says, "They paint a picture of murder." Notes are discussed; how can you have notes of something that did not happen! By p. 28, Hartwig is told, "You are sunk." P. 29 he is told, "You took him some place." One of my biggest frustrations is that no RCMP were called to the stand to testify at the inquiry, so they could be examined on this interview!"

Retired Deputy Chief Wiks analyzes the RCMP approach to both Sgt. Jarvis and Const. Hartwig:

"Jarvis, he couldn't remember the Stonechild file to save his life! And quite frankly, there's some parts of this thing that I wouldn't remember, either. You do that kind of volume and you just can't! And I'm pretty confident that Jarvis, like Hartwig, was just agreeing with what the RCMP were telling them. They took that as, 'That's what they said! Must be right!'
There's ways of interviewing people and you can put suggestions in their head, and all that these guys [Hartwig and Senger] wanted to do was be helpful. The RCMP comes dropping by, and, you know, 'Remember this thing?' 'Uh, well, no, not really,' and that's the way Jarvis started out – 'I

can't remember this thing' – and then all of a sudden, after they kept on talking to him and they were suggesting this, this and this, 'Oh, well, maybe.' It was the same with Hartwig.

One of the things that I thought was very negative as far as Hartwig and Senger were concerned is that Jarvis says that he remembers talking to these guys about Stonechild. I don't believe he remembered that. It was, again, suggested to him, because it's not in the file that he talked to them. It's not in the file! And how would you remember that?"

A few months after that interview, Lyons would review it with an RCMP polygraphist who would later polygraph Senger. The polygraphist would write that in that interview with Lyons, Hartwig "Categorizes as very deceptive" and "interview rehearsed." He did not explain how such an interview could be rehearsed.

Interview over, in a desperate effort to prompt his memory, Hartwig asked Lyons to drive him to Snowberry Downs. Hartwig says that, en route, Lyons told him that Neil Stonechild had been seen in his police car, handcuffed. Hartwig replied that he rarely handcuffed prisoners and if he did, this would always be noted in both his notes and subsequent report. Hartwig's reasoning was that handcuffing takes away an intoxicated person's ability to maintain steady balance and increases their risk of falling and hurting either themselves or him, a 5' 7" officer. This information was not included in Lyons' notes.

When the apartment complex offered no memory cues, Hartwig asked to be taken to Stonechild's residence, but that, too, proved unproductive.

Knowing that his character was in question, and wanting Lyons to know how seriously he took his role as an officer, Hartwig spoke of a call to which he had attended several years earlier. He had been led to a young Asian man lying in bed, near death from an overdose of drugs, ankles bound together with a belt, and a suicide note carved into the headboard. The young man was transported to hospital. Hartwig told Lyons that he later consulted police chaplain Rick Lane, who explained that in the family's culture, suicide, rather than taboo, was considered an acceptable way to die. The belt around the ankles signified self-punishment or a restriction in the afterlife. Hartwig planned to contact the young man later to try to help him, letting him know that someone did care what happened to him, hopefully preventing a recurrence.

Hartwig says he told Lyons during the drive that, from time to time after that call, especially when attending a call to someone suffering from mental health issues, he would think about that young man and be reminded of his intent to speak to him, but was always "too busy." Sometime later, Hartwig learned the young man had again been transported to hospital after attempting suicide. While in the emergency ward, he escaped and was found hanging by the neck in a women's washroom, dead.

Hartwig says he told Lyons he felt bad about not following up with the young man since he may have been able to help him, by telling him that he cared not only for him, but also his spirit. His point with Lyons was that, if he was so concerned about a person's soul, why would he harm a person's body? "I may have to answer to God about that one!" Hartwig told Lyons. It was all wasted on the Mountie, who wrote in his report: "Hartwig once took a call of a suicide and felt bad about it."

Another topic Hartwig says he spoke to Lyons about was his "Why did you do what you did?" story:

> "As I became more experienced as a PO, I realized how substance abuse played a part in the lives of everyone I arrested. I got to the point where, when I arrested someone, had them in the car, and receptive to conversation, I would ask them the "Why did you do what you did?" question. Invariably, the topic would turn to addictions. In many cases, after discussion, the person would tell me that they needed rehab NOW, and I would put that in my report in the notes to prosecutor so the judge would consider this as part of sentencing, so that the person could get the help they needed, in lieu of jail or other penalty."

That information did not appear in Lyons' report. There were other errors, including his claim that Hartwig lived in Bruno, SK. Hartwig believes this indicates that, like other RCMP officers, Lyons submitted to the investigation notes that were not actually made at the time of the interview. "I believe he made rough notes, and then made final notes after the fact and submitted these as his rough notes. This would also account for his inaccurate paraphrasing." Hartwig explains:

> "When police officers make notes on any case, these notes are to be submitted as the actual factual record of what occurred. If a police officer makes notes at the time of an incident or interview, and later rewrites the

notes and submits them instead, there is potential for editing information to suit the officer's point of view. I believe that is what happened here. Lyons took most of what I said out of context and manipulated the content (although I do not believe intentionally, but rather because of confirmation bias [tunnel vision]: favouring information that confirms our beliefs or theories) to suit what the RCMP believed to be true. I do not believe that, at that point, Lyons actually intended to manipulate this evidence, but in the end, this is what happened. In time, however, there are many examples of how the RCMP intentionally manipulated the evidence to bolster Jason Roy's allegation."

After Lyons returned Hartwig to the RCMP office, Hartwig drove to Brad Senger's home where Senger told him he, too, remembered nothing about the Stonechild dispatch, and had also noted him GOA. Senger's notebook indicated their next call was a suspicious person at the 100 block O'Regan Crescent, a few blocks from Snowberry Downs at 3308 - 33rd St. W.

That evening, Hartwig called his RCMP friend, Cpl. Hartle, who later reported that Hartwig felt sick about the whole incident, was in shock over the allegation, believed Lyons had lied to him, and was disappointed with himself for allowing Lyons to manipulate him. If he had encountered Neil Stonechild, Hartwig said, he would have arrested him on the outstanding warrant and taken him to detention. Hartwig said he had spoken to Senger that afternoon, but his notes revealed no new information. Asked about Senger, Hartwig replied: "He's a straight-up guy. No way would Brad ever drop anybody off." Hartwig concluded that Neil Stonechild must have fooled him and he let him go without realizing his true identity. He was not afraid of any criminal investigation but was worried about a civil investigation where the burden of proof is much less than for a criminal case, and stated, "If the media gets hold of this, they will kill me."

Hartwig had no idea who "Tracy" [Horse] was and wanted Hartle to question Lyons for more information because he still couldn't remember anything about the incident. Hartle asked Hartwig straight-out if he did this; Hartwig responded, "Of course not!" Hartwig stated that he "would turn others in if they did something like that." Hartle concluded his report: "He never saw anyone ever drop anyone off like what they're saying he did. He heard about it, he said, by rumour only and then he got into his beliefs in the fifth commandment and, unfortunately I can't off-hand remember what that fifth commandment is." [Hartwig says, "It was actually the sixth commandment, 'Thou shalt not kill,' which includes harming anyone in any way."]

In a written report, Hartwig noted at the time: "I have been deeply hurt and offended by the RCMP and have consulted many friends and colleagues about this incident. I have consulted pastors and fellow active Christians who have been praying for me and my family." Stan Goertzen explains the trauma this way: "When someone's reality suddenly does not match up with their belief system, when their ideas about good and evil, fair and not fair, go up in smoke, the clinical term is 'cognitive dissonance' or contradictory thoughts. What it means is: stress."

Today Hartwig explains:

"By the time I talked to Nick Hartle, I'd had time to think about the misinformation fed to me by Lyons, and the conclusion became even more viable that Neil must have lied to me and I let him go. It wasn't until four days of turmoil that I realized that this was all a lie and Lyons had been trying to set me up by misleading me. He was using trickery and deceit to coax some kind of confession from me.

I lost ALL respect for Lyons when I realized he had manipulated me into admitting that there was a possibility I had Neil Stonechild in custody. I used to have a high opinion of the RCMP. After all, they are the 'premiere' police service in Canada and respected around the world, right? That is all image. The reality is: in my opinion these guys couldn't find the ground if they fell off a horse!

When I spoke to Brad on several occasions afterwards, all of which were recorded in the wiretap, I warned him that what I had told Lyons would be used as ammunition against us. Since I admitted to the possibility of having Neil in custody, given the circumstances I was told and surmised, it provided the physical element of the offense, that is, the issue of 'custody.' All they had to prove next was the mental element of the offense; that is, I had knowledge of who he was. That would have been relatively easy, since I remembered who Neil was.

For lack of a better word, after that interrogation I felt 'raped' by Ken Lyons. I was unable to sleep for months. I would pace the floor at night. When I was able to nap, I had recurring nightmares of the RCMP kicking in my front door in the middle of the night, terrorizing my family and arresting me out of bed, and then placing me in a cell to elicit some sort of 'confession' from me. I would also dream I was in a cell with other prisoners in the same cell block. I was reading scripture and singing hymns out loud. As I walked down the cell block from cell to cell, I would see most prisoners covering their ears and yelling at the top of their voices, trying to drown me out. Some were yelling that if I didn't quit, they would kill me! A very few would sit quietly in their bunks, listening to me. Some would quietly cry to themselves. The nightmares were so bad that I was afraid to go to sleep. I have had sleep problems since, until I was put on medication to put me to sleep.

I had panic attacks on the job and other stress-related issues, but I loved my job, the people I worked with and served, and many people helped me cope, whether they knew it or not. Years later, I was diagnosed with PTSD [Post Traumatic Stress Disorder], took therapy, and was put on medication to help with depression and anxiety. That was before my life really fell apart."

In the weeks afterwards, I was warned by some of my colleges that the RCMP would stop at nothing to prove their case, something I had already concluded. I became so paranoid that the RCMP were listening to my every conversation that I felt I couldn't even speak with my wife about it in our house. I discovered years later that this fear was not unfounded, as when the RCMP didn't get the evidence they were looking, for not only did they have my phones tapped, they even spoke about installing listening devices in private homes.

I became ill and have had physical and mental health problems since but I coped as best I could. I couldn't let anyone know I was ill, even though my colleagues and the RCMP noted my mental health deteriorated. I couldn't let the bastards know I was vulnerable, for fear they would exploit it. They did. The RCMP solicited help from Hartle and my training officers to get me to submit to further interviews and a polygraph. I refused to be a part of this in any fashion. I simply didn't trust them to be competent, honest, and fair.

When my name was released in the media, we had to do a security assessment at our children's school and my wife's place of employment. Anger and hatred were at a fever pitch, and we all feared for our family's safety. My wife was given a panic alarm that would transmit a distress call right to Communications Section. Although we lived out of town and my children went to a rural school, SPS officers would be dispatched, because we couldn't trust a timely response by the RCMP."

(Ken Lyons, retired from the RCMP, did not return calls for an interview.)

Less than a week later, at 8:25 a.m. on May 24, Lyons called Hartwig. Hartwig recalls:

"He asked what I was up to. He stated he wanted to change the polygraph time that had been scheduled for noon May 26th. I told him that I would not speak to him further about these matters on the advice of legal counsel. He said, 'That's a change.'
I said, 'Yep!' and referred him to [lawyer] Robert Borden.
I asked why the change in time. He said the polygrapher had a change in plans. I said, 'I can only guess what that change could be,' and ended the call."

Even knowing that the case against Hartwig and Senger was based entirely on the word of one man with a lengthy criminal record, a faulty memory and ever-changing story (who first lied about who he was, and then lied about why he lied), nevertheless the RCMP carried on, undeterred, with their case against the two reputable officers. Their logic seemed to be: Everything Roy has said so far has proven to be a lie, but he wouldn't lie about the police. Hartwig believes it was worse than that. "It seemed they didn't evaluate each of these alleged 'starlight tour' cases by its own unique evidence, but rather as freezing death committed by someone, most likely the SPS. Each case has to be weighed carefully. Each case has its own evidence. Would you examine a string of armed robberies and look only for the similarities in each case, assuming they were all committed by the same person? Of course not! You examine each case on its own merits. That way you don't miss things and jump to conclusions."

Once they made up their minds that Jason Roy was telling the truth, the RCMP might not actually have set out to prove he was telling the truth, but they "bumped" the evidence to where they wanted it to go, or, in Dave Scott's analogy, "forced the puzzle pieces to fit." As time went on, that ignorance seemed to turn to malice when they had choices on how to evaluate each piece of evidence.

Once they began to interpret the evidence to fit Jason Roy's allegation, it appears they set out simply to prove his allegation, manipulating some evidence to make it inculpatory, and suppressing exculpatory evidence. **This, quite clearly, would constitute criminal misconduct.**

CHAPTER 8 'Arise Saskatoon, Queen of the North!'

'There is less difference between the Aboriginal and Caucasian
communities today than at any time in the past.'
– **Dr. Alan Cairn, Canadian political scientist**

In dramatic contrast to its twenty-first-century furore, Saskatoon's founding principle was temperance – moderation or rational self-restraint. To founding fathers, temperance also meant "total abstinence from alcohol." Methodist minister John Lake journeyed west in 1882 with a small group from the Temperance Colonization Society of Toronto seeking higher moral ground.

The society drew on a Quaker legacy of "doing the right thing." Until two decades earlier, passion for the right thing had led many American Quakers to risk lives and livelihoods illegally helping slaves escape to Canada's "Land of Freedom." Now the Temperance Society was striving to escape enslavement to the twin evils of liquor and urbanization by establishing a "dry" temperance colony in the District of Saskatchewan's scoured and infinite prairie.

At a cost of $1 per acre, Lake and subscribers purchased land from the federal government along both sides of the wide South Saskatchewan River, and in the summer of 1882, arrived. Lake preached a sermon on "the possibility of a new life where only death seemed to reign."[50] Soon after, he had an historic meeting with Chief Whitecap (Wapahaska in his own language) of the Dakota First Nations, an event portrayed in a striking bronze statue erected a century later.[51]

The Dakota, also known as the Sioux, say they have always maintained good relations with their Caucasian neighbours in Canada. When the American Revolution began, more than a century before Lake arrived, the Dakota had allied themselves militarily with the British. Again, in the War of 1812, they were part of a dozen different Nations who, for tactical reasons, helped the British defeat the Americans, fighting against Aboriginal people sympathetic to the American cause.[52]

Now Chief Whitecap, one of Canada's foremost Dakota leaders, guided John Lake to a location within his land grant where, at a bend in the river, both banks were fairly low. While higher moral ground was important, wagon access to a ferry crossing was crucial. Lake declared the picturesque site "the finest we ever had," and within a year, a small, devout colony sprang up.

Residents called it by the lyrical name, Saskatoon, based on the Cree word, "*misâskwatôminihk*," referring to the abundance of a highly-prized royal-purple berry, similar to a blueberry but hinting of almond and cherry. Recognizing its nourishing importance as one of the wind-swept plain's few fruits, tribes became connoisseurs, developing terms to describe its exact colour, taste, seediness and size. Ripened under the prairie sun's brief, dazzling blaze, the berry's burgundy life-blood was mixed with pulverized sun-dried buffalo meat and melted fat, producing the pemmican which sustained people through the worst of winter's grip. So revered was the crop that across the border in Oregon, Klamath Indian legends spoke of the first people being created from saskatoon bushes.[53]

Legend has it that Rev. Lake was inspired with the name for his settlement after he was brought a handful of bright red berries and told they were saskatoons. He proclaimed, "Arise, Saskatoon, Queen of the North!" It may have been a fortunate error, since an historian has determined that, because it was August, past harvest-time for saskatoons whose usual ripe colour is purple, it is "quite possible these fruits were actually choke-cherries!"[54]

In 1885, three years after the colony was established, Métis leaders Louis Riel and Gabriel Dumont led a group of their people in a clash against the North-West Mounted Police at Duck Lake, 90 km north of Saskatoon. "The Métis people were gravely concerned about retaining their language, religion, and their community, as vast areas of the West were being transferred from the Hudson's Bay Company to the Canadian Government."[55]

Since Riel had made threats earlier against the fledgling colony, residents were greatly alarmed about the possibility of attack. Yet, despite considerable pressure from Riel's followers during the North-West uprising, Chief Whitecap resolutely refused to take up arms against Saskatoon. Just how providential he was for the tiny colony is revealed by the fact that several hundred Métis militia, Dominion of Canada soldiers and volunteers were wounded during hostilities. Because, for the first time in the country's history, the Red Cross flag was flown at the battle, the wounded from *both sides* were given equal medical treatment – transported downriver by steamer for doctors' care in Saskatoon.

After the uprising was quelled, three Cree chiefs, Poundmaker, One Arrow and Big Bear, were found guilty of treason and sentenced to three years in a penitentiary. Meanwhile, despite being a member of Riel's council, Chief Whitecap was acquitted of all charges because a Saskatoon merchant's testimony supported him. Whitecap's descendants, based on a reserve bearing his name 30 km south of Saskatoon, refer on their website to continuing trust: "Chief Whitecap, who died in 1889, created a bond with our neighbouring communities that remains firm to this day."[56]

Dave Scott's great grandfather, Bill Scott,
after riding Lary 140 miles with dispatches

When in May, 1885, Major-General Frederick Middleton rushed from Upper Canada to confront Riel and supporters, he hired pony express rider Bill Scott as his chief messenger and scout (whenpolicebecomeprey.com/ Bill Scott). That man, astride "Lary [sic], the fastest horse in the territory," rode 140 miles (225 km) from Prince Albert to Humboldt with dispatches for Middleton – in 23 hours. Pony express rider Bill Scott was great-grandfather to the man who, a century later, would be Saskatoon Police Chief Dave Scott.

The planned temperance colony was soon derailed by fears of possible future Métis unrest as well as lack of transport. The wide river, although 12 percent larger than today, was too shallow for shipping, and a rail link not established until 1890. With the hiss of the steam engine people poured in, and in 1899 settlers succeeded in getting a bar licensed for the first time, only to discover that the spirit of temperance lived on. So many settlers were opposed that, the following year, the licence was cancelled. It remained a society where morality and godliness played an important role. To this day, citizens often use the phrase, "The right thing to do."

Until the 1970s, pubs on the east side of the river could not legally sell beer to be consumed off the premises, a holdover from the Society's influence on the liquor board. Meanwhile, a five-minute drive away on the other side of the river, off-sale had been permitted for decades.

When I interviewed a First Nations Saskatonian about the city's twenty-first-century crime crisis, he replied as though a disciple of John Lake: "I'm amazed at how many bars there are in Saskatoon for as small as it is. They should take Sundays back to the way they used to: no liquor board stores and no off-sales open, and stuff like that. Especially with Saskatoon and surrounding area, there's a lot of religious people, and I remember when I was growing up on Sundays, people were laid back and you could actually go and relax on Sundays and not have to worry about that crime stuff."

In 1906 the city of Saskatoon was incorporated. Two years later it suffered its first shipwreck. A Scottish aristocrat's palatial 130-foot-long flat-bottomed sternwheeler, loaded to the gunwales with summertime merrymakers, was slapping downriver from Medicine Hat toward Winnipeg when it came a cropper. Whether a simple mishap, or the "spirit of temperance" frowning upon the revellers, as their vessel splashed its raucous way toward the very heart of Saskatoon, a telegraph wire strung beneath the newly built traffic bridge lassoed it. As though obeying the many toasts to which it had been a party, the opulent, mahogany-trimmed Titanic-in-miniature S.S. *City of Medicine Hat* went "Bottoms-up!" Before the radio operator could even hammer out a frantic S-O-S, however, partying passengers were providentially saved on the very *brink* of catastrophe by walking ashore. In fact, the sole injuries resulting from the prairie city's only marine disaster were caused by the cattle above which, being herded over the bridge, thought the sky was falling and stampeded.

In earlier history, at different times the Saskatoon area was inhabited by the Assiniboine, the Blackfoot Confederacy, the *Gros-Ventres*, the Plains Cree as well as the Dakota. Today, those bands are based on reserves around the city.[57] But while in 1901, only five percent of Canadian Aboriginal peoples lived in urban areas, by 2006 more than 50% lived in urban areas and more than 20% in rural areas. A remarkable 74% of Aboriginal peoples now live off-reserve; 26% on-reserve.[58]

Importantly this means, as political scientist Alan Cairns points out, there is less difference between the Aboriginal and Caucasian communities today than at any time in the past. This is not to question the uniqueness of Native culture, he says, but rather to point out that each party shares similarities, as well as differences. "Can we be, positively, more than what divides us?" he asks, suggesting that what is required are bonds of mutual obligation, empathy and solidarity between citizens so that we "feel responsible for each other" and thus "our togetherness is moral as well as geographical."[59] Otherwise, he says, we become a society of strangers, fostering indifference or suspicion.

Most of that urban increase occurred in the late twentieth century. In Saskatoon, for example, the Aboriginal population increased an astonishing 500% in the 25 years between 1981 and 2006 (from 4,350 to 21,535, comprising 10% of the city's 210,000 total population).[60] Saskatoon vied with Winnipeg for the highest proportion of Aboriginal people of any major Canadian city.[61] Some believe the move off reserve was prompted by First Nations being "so tired of the factionalism, nepotism and lack of opportunity they see at home."[62] Others claim it part of a world-wide trend toward urbanization, with predictable, universal outcomes.[63]

United Nations figures show that in 2008, for the first time ever, following 200,000 years of living rurally, humankind became a predominantly urban species. Although it took so long to get to the halfway mark, demographers calculate that three-quarters of humanity could be city-dwelling by 2050, which coincides with the expected date of "The Flip," when the First Nations population in Saskatchewan will exceed the white.[64]

For many, as portrayed in the book, *City*, the transition from reserve to urban living is not an easy one. An officer who served as police chief of several Canadian cities describes the "long history of neglect of the plight of urban Aboriginals"[65] which culminated in Winnipeg's tragic 1988 death of Aboriginal leader, J.J. Harper. In 2012, a Regina *Leader Post* columnist wrote about a First Nations leader making a reasonable request for "an orientation program for First Nations people struggling with urban culture and finding work opportunities - a program similar to what the provincial government offers newly arrived immigrants. ...In a very real way," columnist Murray

Mandryk concluded, "our oldest inhabitants have become our newest immigration challenge."[66]

Even the NFB which, in the documentary *Two World's Colliding*, tried to scapegoat cops for what were actually urban problems, admitted the real crisis in a media release:

> "'This is an important time for Canada – it's an ongoing conflict, and at the heart of the conflict is **denial and misunderstanding of the First Nations' urban experience**," said Hubbard, a Cree adopted into a non-Aboriginal family....'"

Saskatchewan has long experience with innovating programs to benefit Aboriginal peoples. In 1929, the Liberal government of James G. Gardiner launched one of the first steps toward Canada's universal publicly-funded medical care when it agreed to become the first jurisdiction in North America to provide free (universally-funded) hospital care for tuberculosis. This tripled the numbers with early-onset TB who presented themselves for hospitalization, increasing their likelihood of survival while decreasing the disease's virulent spread. Aboriginal people in particular benefitted from the move, since they were tragically over-represented in contracting the often-fatal disease.[67]

In 1946, encouraged by Tommy Douglas' CCF government, Cree, Sioux, Saulteaux and Assiniboine tribes convened in Saskatoon to form a united political front under the name Union of Saskatchewan Indians. In 1982, the province-wide organization would be renamed Federation of Saskatchewan Indian Nations (FSIN). In the 1980s, FSIN called for a parallel justice system for Aboriginals. Such a system would require the federal government's involvement because treaty Indians are a federal responsibility. In 1989, federal Justice Minister Doug Lewis rejected the idea because of the expense and precedent it would set for other groups.

By 2012, the activist FSIN, controlled by chiefs representing 74 of the province's 75 First Nations, would have a whopping $19.5-million budget. According to its website, $11.7 M was provided by federal government departments,[68] $1.3 M by the province, with a $6.5 M from unspecified "related parties."[69] At least one columnist would call for funding reform, recommending Ottawa directly fund individual bands since FSIN had "become too far removed from its own people and mostly now exists to benefit the First Nations leadership."[70] Another called for FSIN "to occupy the moral high ground by extending the vote to all treaty and registered First Nations people in the province [because] an oligarchy of chiefs has no place in modern First Nations self-government."[71]

Saskatoon made another historic innovation in 1988, becoming the first city in the country to establish a new urban reserve designed specifically as a First Nation's commercial and economic development project. Regina and Winnipeg soon followed. By 2004, Muskeg Lake urban reserve's 37 Aboriginal and non-Aboriginal businesses were a new commercial hub. Revenues go to the reserve, while the city gains jobs and an annual "municipal service fee" in lieu of property taxes. Although some called it a government-sanctioned tax haven, by most accounts it works very well. Saskatoon Mayor Don Atchison announced at the twentieth anniversary celebration, "Over all these years, we've always been able to work together and come to a consensus that's for the betterment of all."

In Canada, the highest proportion of Aboriginal population lives in Nunavut (85.0% of the population), the Northwest Territories (50.3%), Yukon (25.1%), Manitoba (15.5%) and Saskatchewan (14.9%).[72] Because the majority of Canada's Aboriginal people live on the Prairies, Aboriginal peoples comprise the largest urban minority group in many Prairie cities. Among the large cities, Saskatoon is second only to Winnipeg in its proportion of Aboriginal people: 10% in Winnipeg, 9.3% in Saskatoon, 8.9% in Regina. Other large cities have only a fraction of those percentages: Edmonton, 5; Calgary 2.5; Vancouver, 2; Ottawa-Hull, 2.

Renowned for its sub-Arctic winters, Saskatoon is colder than its northern Prairie counterparts. Between 1971 and 2000, the average extreme minimum temperature for Winnipeg was -41.7° C (-43 F), Edmonton: -45.6 C (-50 F), and Saskatoon: -47.6 C (-54 F).[73]

The important information that no reporters, including this one, discovered at the time of Saskatoon's "starlight tour" panic in 2000, was that **the entire province was vastly over-represented in freezing deaths that year. From 2001 to 2009, Saskatchewan had 3 percent of the Canadian population, but an average 12 percent of the country's freezing deaths.**[74] In 2000, however, that percentage almost doubled; Saskatchewan had *20 percent of freezing deaths.*[75] (The percentage of freezing deaths jumped again in 2004. A common denominator for the years 2000 and 2004 will be divulged in a future book. Few will be amazed.)

When allegations of "starlight tours" began surfacing in February 2000, *The StarPhoenix* had just reported the body of a 58-year-old woman had been found January 31 in the town of La Ronge, 350 km north of Saskatoon. Evelyn Kate Ratt had frozen to death.

Saskatonians had also been reading about a taxi driver who ordered a passenger out of the cab against her wishes in November 1995. Teresa McLeod was transporting passengers from Saskatoon to La Ronge, when a 15-year-old girl apparently began hallucinating and striking an elderly woman in front of her at least twice. McLeod, a former social worker, ordered Becky Charles out of her cab 30 km outside La Ronge. Both taxi driver and passenger were members of the Lac La Ronge Native band; in fact, they were neighbours.

Darkness was falling, the temperature with wind-chill, -28 C, the girl wearing only jeans, dress shoes and a light ski jacket over a blouse. Although the driver notified RCMP upon arrival in town, officers who searched for the girl that night later made the appalling admission that, when they had returned to the isolated junction where Charles was dropped, they never left their car to look for her tracks! Volunteers searched 12 days before finding the girl's body, her shoes and jacket removed, in the bush a mere 90 metres from the drop-off point. Her death was ruled hypothermia. Pleading guilty to failing to provide the necessities of life, the taxi driver was given a one-year conditional sentence. No jail time.

The climate is harsh. Illustrative is *The StarPhoenix's* description of an outdoor function one May 25th, a month short of summer: "Organizers breathed a sigh of relief when Saturday dawned sunny for the second annual Riversdale Rendezvous. There wasn't a winter jacket in sight."[75] Hardy – and witty – citizens take it all in stride. It wasn't until the mid-1950s, for example, that city council finally sprang for the first closed-cab fire truck.[76] Until then, firefighters raced through sleet and snow all winter, in convertibles. Presumably, they rushed to fires to warm up! The publisher of *Saskatchewan Business Magazine* wrote: "I cannot think of anything that would deter people from coming here. Well, maybe the weather – but it has been said for years that it builds character and backbone. I say it builds smarts, backup plans and a market for snow blowers, salt and snow shovels."[77] Saskatchewanites are practical! When something needs fixing, it can be fixed!

The other vital challenge facing the entire province is its alarming crime rate. 2006 Statistics Canada data repeated what it would call "the pattern seen over many decades": eastern provinces with lowest violent crime rates with western provinces higher, territories higher still. Of the provinces, Saskatchewan has the highest violent crime rate.[78]

In an article titled "Canada's Most Dangerous Cities," Maclean's magazine noted the highest crime ratings in Saskatoon, Winnipeg, and Regina:

"The same cities were in a virtual three-way tie last year for the worst crime score. The three cities share several things in common: much of the crime is rooted in poor, inner-city cores and targets its most vulnerable citizens. There is a large gang presence feeding off the drug trade and other illegal activities. Those areas also house a young transient population, with a low level of education, sub-standard housing and high levels of unemployment, broken homes, addictions and psychiatric issues – all risk factors for crime. They have proportionately the highest urban Aboriginal populations among major cities, about 10 percent. This is a predominately young population, burdened with risk factors. 'They are 10 times more likely to be victims and suspects,' says Neil Boyd, a criminologist at Simon Fraser University. 'It's basically a very tragic reality.'"[79]

Of the provinces, the cold, hard fact is that Saskatchewan has the highest crime rate in most classifications.

Crime rate by province, 2007

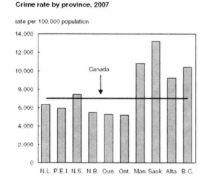
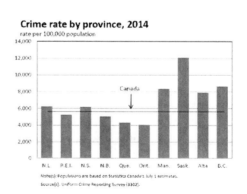

Crime rate by province in 2007 and 2014, according to Statistics Canada:[80, 81]

According to Stats Can, in 2007 Saskatoon had a violent crime rate of 1,376/100,000 people.[82] That is 13% worse than the most dangerous city in the USA. "Detroit is the worst offender on the list of America's most dangerous cities, thanks to a staggering rate of 1,220 violent crimes committed per 100,000 people," wrote Forbes Magazine in a 2009 article titled "America's most dangerous cities":

> "'Detroit has, historically, been one of the more violent cities in the U.S.,' says Megan Wolfram, an analyst at iJet Intelligent Risk Systems, a Maryland-based risk-assessment firm. 'They have a number of local crime syndicates there – a number of small gangs who tend to compete over territory.' Detroit was followed closely on the list by the Greater Memphis, Tenn. and Miami, Fla., metropolitan areas. Those three were the only large cities in America with over 950 violent crimes committed per 100,000 people." [83]

No one looking at the picturesque city of a quarter-million would suspect Saskatoon's secret. "What goes on in the streets of Saskatoon, probably only the cops or EMS or cabbies know," states a man who has worked as both ambulance attendant and taxi driver. He asked not to be identified, but because he reappears in the book, we will call him "Fred Smyth." "As a cabbie, you'd get whacked on the back of the head and have people try to leap out at a red light to jump the fare, so you had to get street-smart real fast. I started demanding to be paid before we went anywhere. And as EMS, you'd go to help someone – they'd be clawing at you, spitting; if they grabbed you, they could seriously hurt you. Other times, people you were taking to hospital because they said they were sick would demand to know where we were and when you'd say, 'Almost to the hospital,' they'd jump out. They'd only wanted to use us as a taxi all along. The general public doesn't want to know about what goes on!"

Cree Saskatonian Lucille Matechuck describes her work at crime-reduction at the apartment complex known as Clancy Village:

> "We initiated city programs for them such as 'Nighthawk.' It was for kids, fifteen to early adulthood, to play sports and then have lunch about ten p.m. and then we sent them home. We ended up with some people who were in their thirties, but mentally in their teens, so we let them play. The program was designed just to keep them occupied and out of trouble, and there was a lot less crime.
>
> Students from the university came out on Saturdays with a reading

tent. Next we started to have volunteers walk the neighbourhood. We would walk at night in groups of four to six, reporting any kind of crime, discouraging the prostitution going on, picking up garbage, and really trying to make the community come together. Our efforts led seven other communities to start walking their neighbourhood. Finally we got to the point where police didn't have to be called in so often.

From there we got after the city to clean up the park here. We got the kids this new jungle gym, and the sand was all raked for needles and debris. From there, we – my husband, Myron and I – joined the Meadow Green Association, and we came up with ideas with them to raise money for a basketball court. We worked bingos, me and my family, and the tenants that lived here. We raised over twenty-nine thousand dollars and the city upgraded our park with a paddling pool and new rink boards for the skating rink. We iced the rink in the winter.

The rink filled up fast with kids, and they started to help us if there was trouble like people coming to the buildings drunk. For example, there were two old people that always came through our parking lot to go home to Appleby Drive; some thugs knocked the old man over and took his apartment keys and the toonie he had in his pocket – all he had! My daughter, Jennifer, and her boyfriend, Ed, heard them yelling and raced down the stairs and out the door to help them. There were about five big, big guys and Jen tackled the one who knocked down the old man. She was going to hold him for the police. The other thugs started trying to get their buddy away from her but she sat on him pretty good. Well, the next thing you know, some big tenants jumped off their first floor balcony and went to help her until the police arrived and the other thugs scattered.

After we started Operation Clean-up, an officer came over here and said he wanted to start a 'Crime-free Multi-housing Program' with the police. That officer was Constable Larry Hartwig. This was way before we heard all the rumours and lies started about him possibly being involved in a freezing death. He wanted a program to get rental properties to add deadbolt locks and patio door locks, and make the site look cared for. Larry did all the work on it, working very hard. We were in the second phase when allegations started to fly against Larry and Brad Senger, and from there it just ended abruptly. It was an awesome program and had it not fallen through, I'm sure we would have been looking at a beautiful area of Saskatoon."

Jennifer Matechuck adds that Larry Hartwig "wouldn't have hurt a fly. I've known him for three years. If he can deal with me when I'm upset – he met me when I was flipping out on another officer, came over and calmed me down. He said, 'Come on Jen, let's go have a talk over here,' and actually listened!"

Another apartment manager who wanted to work with Hartwig on the "Crime-free Multi-housing Program" was Marie Brown:

"I was manager at Golden Oak Apartments on Appleby Drive, and Larry was heading up this program to help keep the kids off the street, trying to do a Neighbourhood Watch-type thing. I went down and asked him if we could get our complex put on his agenda, because we had 240 suites, and, it seemed to me, a million kids that needed supervision. And he was trying to get something constructive done for kids.

Q: Was Larry racist?

A: No, never. Among all the officers I've known, I've never heard them ever say anything derogatory about any nationality. I knew Ken Munson, too, and he was open, honest and calm. Not at all racist. He was dealing with Aboriginal people all the time. When I had to call him and others at three in the morning, they handled it quite professionally. They took care of the situation, there was no yelling or screaming. They just did their job in a respectful way.

Q: When you learned that a judge had decided that Hartwig and Senger had had Neil Stonechild in their custody the night he disappeared, and that they would have had time to drop him off out in the industrial area, what were your thoughts?

A: That it didn't happen. Larry Hartwig who was trying so hard to build a place to keep children off the street, let them play soccer just to keep them busy and occupied? It didn't happen."

Saskatonians are justly proud of their "Paris of the Prairies" with its wide river valley spanned by seven photogenic bridges and overseen by a many-towered castle, the Bessborough Hotel. They are proud of the century-old University of Saskatchewan with its Oxfordian greystone buildings, inspirational professors and ground-breaking nuclear physics research.

With their Quaker legacy of helping other races, Saskatonians embrace diversity. For years, taxpayers have promoted understanding of the Native population with a hefty subsidy to Wanuskewin Heritage Park. Saskatonians, in fact, cheer on fellow citizens wherever possible. Saskatoon's Tribal Council Chief, Glenn Johnston recounted in a 2005 interview:

> *"We had a parade here the other day with a First Nations theme. We hadn't had a float in that parade, I don't think, ever. But, I said, 'This year we're going make a splash!' So we did. We worked hard on our float, got donations and got it together. And I went out there with my headdress; I put my daughter beside me. And I told my wife to curl her hair and all that. We had our staff and we had our young white Buffalo boys' basketball team in uniform, bouncing their basketballs. I told all our people, 'Make sure you wave and smile, and don't fight with one another on this thing.' And we did that, too.*
> *I didn't know what to expect as we turned down Twentieth. We saw all the people. And as soon as we came around the corner, it was like – huge roaring applause! It just surprised us. And as we went through the whole trail we were getting good responses the whole way. People were applauding us and waving at us. Our people were so happy.*
> *And the police officers we met along the way, I always make sure I say hi to them. That's how we're going to do our part. We show that we're mature and that we treat people with dignity. They do the same thing."*

Saskatonians also cheer on individuals such as long-distance runner and elder, Roland Doucette: "In fact, the energy I get from the non-Aboriginal people that greet me, you know, it's so overwhelming, eh, at times," he says. "When I'm running they'll say, 'Good job!' you know, and 'Well done!' And the handshakes that I get from them, it just – it does a real number on me, eh."

Saskatonians are fierce in defense of the underdog. Therefore, when in 2000, an alarming accusation of racism was hurled against their police service, citizens were shocked, they were indignant, and many did not want an investigation. They wanted something done about it – and they wanted it done. Now!

CHAPTER 9 - Dead of Winter:
Freezing Deaths of Rodney Naistus and
Lawrence Wegner

'Why do people keep demanding rational explanations for extraordinarily drunk or stoned people being found in strange places? The term, "under the influence," means the person is not acting either rationally or within the limits of normal human strength.'
– Saskatoon social worker

Following RCMP investigations into the deaths of Darcy Ironchild and Lloyd Dustyhorn, justice officials had determined that, as in the Wegner and Naistus cases, there was no basis for criminal charges.

A coroner's inquest into the death of Ironchild (who did not freeze to death) concluded death was due to an overdose of sleeping medication in his own home. Dustyhorn's inquest concluded that death was accidental, caused by hypothermia, his body discovered outside the locked door of an apartment building. The jury strongly recommended a drop-in detox centre be set up in Saskatoon to solve the long-standing problem of police attempting to care for those found on the street too intoxicated to care for themselves. (These two deaths are investigated more extensively in my second book, *When Police Become Prey: Darrell Night Walked and Justice Died.*)

What about the two men found frozen to death soon after Night was dropped off – were police involved in their deaths? My documentary includes an on-camera interview with the officers first on-scene after 25-year-old Rodney Naistus' body was found on the road in front of a Schuyler Street feed store.

The officers demonstrated how they independently backtracked Naistus' footprints. First to track was Sgt. Leo Daigneault, a Métis officer so proficient at tracking that colleagues nicknamed him "Scout." Mitch Yuzdepski, then a constable, had tracked second.

*"**Sgt. Yuzdepski:** When I arrived, I found the body of Mr. Naistus lying on his back in this area here, with his feet pointed to the west. He had no shirt on, he was bare-chested, had pants on, actually two pairs of pants, and a pair of running shoes. There was a camouflage shirt adjacent to*

him, to the right side of his body, near his right arm. There were some further items of clothing, I believe a ball cap and perhaps another shirt or a light jacket in the snow-covered field just to the west of the building itself.

Q: *How would a person account for his clothing being off?*

Yuzdepski: *It's consistent with someone who's suffering the effects of hypothermia.*

Q: *Because they feel so hot?*

Yuzdepski: *Yes. I mean, that's from what I've read. I'm not an expert on that by any means. I secured the scene, called for a supervisor, who at the time was Sergeant Daigneault; then it took some time. Major Crime investigators were called out to the scene, the coroner was called out to the scene, identification officers were called out to the scene, and that crime scene was processed. We treat all cases of finding a deceased person with the consideration that it is a potential crime scene. And so all those bases were covered with those resources.*

Retired Sgt. Daigneault: *After I arrived at the scene, I sat with the coroner for a while, waiting for the others to arrive. And while we were sitting in the truck, the coroner and I decided, 'Well, let's take a look and see how far we can backtrack.' So then we started. There were a few steps that went into a compounded area this way through the deep snow, and then back out onto the road. It looked like he was staggering as he was walking because the trail went weaving in and back out onto the street a few times."*

(Coroner Douglas DeSchryver confirmed those observations in his Feb. 17, 2000 report: "Mr. Naistus' tracks left the roadway and went out into a field where he vomited. After vomiting, his tracks showed that he walked or crawled to where he was found in the morning deceased. In his last steps before laying down, Mr. Naistus had started to take off articles of his clothing, which follows in line with hypothermia. I called for an autopsy to be performed at the Royal University Hospital." The pathologist also found "no evidence of physical trauma" and concluded death was due to hypothermia.)

(**Daigneault** *continues:) Eventually we [he and the coroner] followed the tracks to the corner of Avenue X, when I got called back to the scene. Mitch later went all the way to Avenue U [the well-trafficked street three blocks further].*

Q: *All right, let's go and trace those footsteps back and relive the experience.*
Daigneault: *As we were driving up here, I had pulled up right in front of a cardboard box which I thought was discarded. Someone had tried to preserve one footprint he had found there from the deceased. And I parked my vehicle there and when I moved it afterwards; I realized I had been parked right on top of the footprint! [Much was made of that in some media.]*
Yuzdepski: *This area here was actually an open field. So there was a portion where it looked like he'd entered the open field and then looped back out. So from this area here, the whole surface was icepack snow-covered surface. The shoulder portion along the curb is not as well-worn with tire tracks as the middle of the road and this is where we could see footprints. That was in the hard-packed snow, frost-covered surface. And those footprints were consistent with the footwear that Mr. Naistus was wearing.*
Daigneault: *And it wasn't just a straight walk like we're doing right now; it weaved back and forth, almost indicating that – I don't know if he was overcome by cold or what, but it wasn't a straight track.*
Yuzdepski: *And I guess we should point out, too, that we didn't do these together. I maintained the scene while Leo and the coroner went. After Mr. Naistus' body was removed from the scene, I then went back and followed the footprints on my own, covering the same tracks.*
Q: *So the direction he came from, it wasn't actually a residential area?*
Yuzdepski: Well, another block past this one, and as you can see a house straight ahead, that is Avenue P. So Q, R, S, T, U, [the body was] five blocks from residential. I just clocked it with my car from the front doors to here; it was eight-tenths of a kilometre [half a mile]. I had been hopeful that I could follow the tracks back to perhaps where he came from. And I was able to follow them as far as this intersection here. I couldn't follow them past this point.
Q: *Did you ever see any evidence of his being dropped off by a car?*
Yuzdepski: *No. I mean there was nothing to suggest in the route that I tracked back anything other than a person walking. I make a habit of calling the weather in the morning, recording in my book often, and I've got a range -- when I called first thing in the morning minus 19 to minus 5 was the high for the day. But, you know, with the wind-chill it certainly could have been a little colder 'cause it was a cool day, I definitely recall*

that. [Environment Canada confirms those temperatures, adding that with the wind-chill, the temperature from 1 a.m. to 6 a.m. on January 29 would have ranged from -19° to -22°.]

Q: *If Mr. Naistus had been dropped off in this area by a police car, where could he have gone for help?*

Daigneault: *The most logical would be to head towards a residential area which is that direction. [The direction opposite to the way he did walk.]*

[In the documentary I concluded]: If police officers were going to drop anyone off at that intersection, busy day and night, they would certainly risk being seen by passers-by. Or did Rodney Naistus walk to that intersection, through it, and keep on walking? The unusual jacket found near Naistus' body was accurately described by the coat check in C-Weeds Nightclub, and a bouncer identified Naistus from a photo as having been in the club that night. Carloads of people had been seen, over the evening, leaving C-Weeds for a house party at 725 Weldon Ave., a kilometre from that intersection. RCMP investigator Sgt. Keyes reported:

"Witnesses interviewed were unable to confirm whether Rodney Naistus was or was not present. A general reluctance was demonstrated by those attending the party to assist in the investigation.... No evidence exists to suggest that Saskatoon city police had any contact with Rodney Naistus during the early morning of 2000-01-29."

Following the RCMP investigation, Justice Department officials decided there was insufficient evidence to lay criminal charges against anyone. A coroner's inquest in the autumn of 2001 also showed there was no evidence of police involvement in Naistus' death. Yet prior to that, his mother, Marvina Sandirson, attempted to sue SPS for his wrongful death. The Naistus family lawyer was Darren Winegarden, Donald Worme's brother who was raised by a different family. The statement of claim alleged that Naistus had been walking with "an unknown companion" near Maxwell Crescent in Confederation Park, heading for Jax Nightclub when he encountered police officers who put him in their cruiser "without lawful reason," drove him to a location south of the city, forced him out of the car "wearing attire that was wholly inadequate for survival in cold weather"[84] even though they must have known that leaving him there would cause his death.

How that information was obtained if the companion was unknown was not explained. Sandirson claimed that she relied on him for financial support and housework. She sought "aggravated damages particularly in light of Mr. Naistus' race and recent disclosure by the Saskatoon Police Service of systemic racism within the police force."

The SPS had, in fact, made no such "disclosure of systemic racism," while it was presumably the lack of any evidence whatsoever regarding police involvement in Naistus' death that led to the lawsuit quietly being dropped. Or was the story someone's clever scheme to get propaganda advertised to the public in advance of the Naistus inquest, without having to pay a cent?

Is the threat of manipulation something that reputable journalists should be wary of when deciding which of the many pre-packaged stories handed to them they will give publicity? In the 2012 book, *Trust Me, I'm Lying: Confessions of a Media Manipulator*, billed as "A playbook for the Dark Arts of exploiting the media," author Ryan Holiday writes that he's "tired of a world where … marketers help write the news, reckless journalists spread lies, and no one is accountable for any of it." Holiday alleges that he "could get the media to 'publish anything.' [The book] was also meant as a wake-up call to show people just how vulnerable the media is to manipulation..."[85]

Subsequently, the fact that lawyers were launching and abandoning lawsuits against police (presumably for fear they would lose) would be turned around and used against the police. During the Wegner inquest, Greg Curtis, a lawyer with Worme's firm, would tell the media that the surprise witnesses against the police had a publication ban on their names because they were afraid of "police retaliation." "I haven't personally witnessed an incident myself but certainly we've had our share of clients that have been suing the police," Curtis said.[86]

Following the Stonechild Inquiry, the lawyer for Stonechild's mother, Greg Curtis issued an ultimatum, giving the Saskatoon Police Commission until October to pay a six-figure settlement to compensate for Stonechild's death and police handling of the investigation, or face a lawsuit. "We're going to be asking for substantially more if *they make us* go to court," Curtis threatened. "We're not going to bring hasty closure to (the claim) if it's unsatisfactory or disrespectful."[87] (The lawyer apparently considered himself entitled, however, to issue disrespectful ultimatums based on hearsay claims made in an out-of-court forum, the Stonechild Inquiry.) Later, the threatened lawsuit against the city was, yes, quietly dropped.

As soon as that October deadline passed, Worme filed a lawsuit, seeking, as his colleague had threatened, "substantially more." On Nov. 1, 2005, a front-page *StarPhoenix* story announced the family of Neil Stonechild was suing the police service and several officers, including Hartwig, Senger, Jarvis, Scott and Wiks. The plaintiffs were now seeking *$30-million* for alleged negligence, deception and misinformation. The following day, Nov. 2, 2005, the newspaper gives the officers' side of the story, but not on the front page. A page eight *StarPhoenix* story quotes officers' lawyers saying Stonechild lawsuit is baseless. Lawyer Aaron Fox says: "As I think we saw at the disciplinary hearing of these two officers, the evidence that we heard there is substantially different from what he (Justice Wright) heard. Had he had the benefit of hearing the evidence and the alterations in the evidence ... maybe he'd come to a different conclusion."[88]

Following publicity, this $30-million lawsuit is quietly dropped, in the same manner lawsuits for Night, Naistus and Wailing had been filed against police officers (while lawsuits had been publicly *threatened* for Wegner against police, as well as for Stonechild against the police commission) before being quietly abandoned.

Typically, the newspaper gave publicity only to the launch of lawsuits, not their abandonment. With the $30-million suit, however, a *StarPhoenix* story followed six months later: "Stonechild suit expires: Mom of teen who froze to death surprised lawsuit against police not acted on." The story divulged that not one of the nine defendants had even been sought out, and quoted a lawyer who asked that his name not be used to protect the identity of his client: "*I think Bignell's lawyers [Worme and Curtis] had no intention of proceeding with this. They just used it to get a lot of media attention and badmouth everyone. I'm truly astounded at this conduct. They took this chance to beat everybody over the head, then left it alone.*"[89]

Should the Law Society discipline lawyers with a high rate of launch-and-drops? Such lawsuits provide lawyers with a one-sided weapon to publicly scourge (or "beat everybody over the head") whenever they wish to strike terror in hearts and wallets, with puny effort and cost to themselves. In addition, many who learn about lawsuits assume the party being sued is guilty. Does the repeated launching and dropping of lawsuits constitute conduct unbecoming a lawyer? In a 2015 interview with me, Sask Law Society Executive Director Tom Schonhoffer said the law society has never had a prosecution of a lawyer with a high launch-and-drop rate, but hypothetically could, if a complaint were lodged.

At the coroner's inquest into the death of Rodney Naistus, October 30 to

November 3, 2001, Munson and Hatchen originally had not been asked to testify because there was no evidence they were involved. However, on the second-last day, with only a few hours' notice, inquest lawyer Hugh Harradence changed his mind and asked them to appear. Both immediately attended. Munson told the jury, "I want to be questioned because I know we're innocent. ...In respect for the family, I had to be here. I feel sorry for the Naistus family. I will help in any way I can; whatever it takes."

Lawyer Winegarden suggested that the officers' one hour and six-minute meal break between 1:18 and 2:24 a.m. was adequate time for them to pick up Naistus and drive him across town to the location his body was found, five blocks from a residential area. Their cruiser computer indicated, however, they were at the police gym, as the officers had maintained.

From questions asked, Hatchen believes that Winegarden "was trying to 'do a Stonechild' on us. That is, manufacture a causation outside of our usual protections under the criminal code and therefore convict us [at the inquest] without trial, as was later done to Hartwig and Senger at the Stonechild Inquiry."

National Post columnist Christy Blatchford covering the Naistus inquest had shown little sympathy for Saskatoon police until she watched Ken Munson's testimony:

"A little later, holding up a single finger, Munson said, 'Apart from Darrell Night, I certainly have never dropped off an aboriginal person before and I never will. I have many aboriginal friends ... Darrell Night was a mistake.' In his evidence, so eagerly given, Munson occasionally referred to himself as a police officer in the present tense; he talked at length about the sorts of calls he would get and how he would handle them; at one point, he even described the two doughnut stores he and Hatchen most often favoured. It was a portrait of a trying job, often grim – stories of breaking up drunken fights; returning drunks home to their families; answering calls for doors that had been kicked in – yet one that he transparently misses badly.[90]

No one at the Naistus inquest made the recommendation that an RCMP officer in Fort St. John, B.C. had made in a different case three years before: First Nations must do a better job of taking care of their members. "We have, as a police force, done a lot of initiatives to help our street people," RCMP

Const. Bob Charron told a coroner's inquest into the death of a woman who died of pneumonia while in custody. Mounties had been called to a drinking establishment to "deal with a drunk," but later learned she was ill rather than drunk. She had been detained by their detachment about 65 times in the previous five years. *"The constable said 99 percent of the street people are 'alcohol dependent. While not all are native, Treaty 8 is not helping those who are.'"[91]*

Outside the Naistus inquest, Morris Bodnar had harsh words for reporters: "All too often … the media has very unfairly portrayed Mr. Munson and Mr. Hatchen and linked them to the deaths of individuals in the city, which is absolutely false, false, false!"

At that same media scrum, Hatchen spoke of the coincidence between the Night drop-off and two freezing deaths: "This, today, is actually the very reason why I came forward. I knew there would be lots of questions about the coincidence of all this, and that's why I made myself available for that, as well as the investigation. I'm glad it finally took place and I hope maybe there's some resolution for the family. I'm not a murderer; I don't want to hurt anybody. I don't know if some people, because of their pain, might want to believe what I've been saying, but I'm glad I was able to come forward and speak, finally."

Remarkably, the Naistus inquest concluded with the jury aiming seven of its eight recommendations at police, including that they keep notes about any civilians who enter their cruisers, notify their dispatcher about it, and employ more Aboriginal officers. According to Scott, "There is not a police department or any company that would not like a greater Aboriginal presence in their workforce. Competition is strong in trying to recruit Aboriginal workers. Some choose not to go into policing because of the resistance they receive from their own people once they are on the street. There are simply no easy answers."

Other recommendations: that police patrol non-residential areas when not responding to a call; increase the number of police patrols in high-incident districts, particularly in winter; require all SPS employees to take an Aboriginal cross-cultural workshop (which they had been doing for years); and have an Aboriginal elder on call for an unruly situation with an Aboriginal person (also in place under Scott's watch). The eighth recommendation was that a government-funded agency other than police patrol the streets to assist people in questionable circumstances.

The new president of the Police Association, Stan Goertzen, released a statement that police were confused that most of the inquest's recommendations were aimed at police, even though there was no evidence police had any contact with the man leading up to his death. Police had been looking for closure as a result of the inquest, Goertzen said, but the recommendations had prevented that occurring.

Interim Police Chief Jim Matthews announced: "[It's] my understanding that nowhere within the testimony provided was there any information or evidence to suggest that the Saskatoon Police Service or anyone else had any dealings with Mr. Naistus on the day in question. There was nothing to tie the cops to this. There was nothing to tie anybody to this."

Matthews even dared voice a terrible fact about freezing deaths: there would be more. "Invariably when the weather gets really cold for a period of time, we have people succumbing to these types of circumstances. And this, as far as I know, is the only jurisdiction where the automatic assumption is: it was the police. So it's going to be interesting, because this is going to happen again. *As long as there's homeless people and winter it's going to happen.*"

His words would be echoed in 2005 when FBI serial homicide experts investigated the large number of missing persons in Nome, Alaska. Associated Press reported ominously:

"Whispers that danger awaits travelers on the streets of Nome have circulated in the region's Inupiat and Siberian Yupik villages for years. The accounts of missing cousins and in-laws have been colored by allegations of police indifference and even hostility toward visiting Natives, especially those who pass through the bars on Front Street.

"But no official investigation ever was launched until earlier this year, when the region's Native community was galvanized by the sensational murder trial of a Nome police officer who stood accused of killing a young village woman.

"The trial added to community concerns over yet another disappearance. Eric Apatiki, 21, had come from St. Lawrence Island in October 2004 to meet his pregnant girlfriend and spend his Permanent Fund dividend check. After he vanished, his mother wrote a heart-rending letter to the Nome Nugget.

"By February, villagers trembling with emotion were stepping forward in meetings to tell stories of missing family members. The U.S. attorney for Alaska and the commissioner of the state Department of Public Safety flew to Nome with FBI officials in June. ...

COMPLAINTS OF POLICE MISCONDUCT

"The fog of intrigue and suspicion is thickened by a history of mistrust and bad feelings between the region's Native villagers and the Nome police. The investigations of the past few months have included Native complaints of a too-ready willingness by officials to shrug off each succeeding case as another accident or suicide.

The cases never would have lingered had the victims been Nome residents instead of villagers, [tribal council member Delbert] Pungowiyi said.

'Can you imagine the outcry they would be having, demanding that these be solved?' he said. 'It should have been given attention years ago. I'm just really glad it's finally happening. ... The region is just overwhelmed with this. They're tired of this. They're tired of living with these big gaping holes and no closure.'"[92]

Months of investigation exposed Nome's "whispered danger" – and it was not police. Unlike other villages with strict regulations, Nome was found to be unique in its *lax regulations for alcohol consumption*. The FBI reported the deaths were not murder. The common denominator in many of the suspicious deaths were unforgiving winter weather and excessive consumption of alcohol.

In 2008, the U.S. Centers for Disease Control and Prevention found that almost 12 percent of deaths among Native Americans and Alaska Natives between 2001 and 2005 were alcohol-related – more than three times the percentage in the general population. To their great credit, "advocates for Native American tribal health took the numbers as a 'call to action' for an issue that has long been ignored and swept under the rug on reservations around the U.S."[93] The greatest number of tribal alcohol-related deaths – about one-third of the total – occurred in the Northern Plains. Author Dwayne Jarman said the study did not look at why there may be more alcohol-related deaths in the Plains but found it consistent with previous studies.

~ ~ ~

Is it possible police were involved in the freezing death of Lawrence Wegner? Neither Munson nor Hatchen were working the night of Wegner's death, and the RCMP investigation showed no evidence of police involvement.

Wegner, 30, the son of a Saulteaux mother and German father, was described as soft-spoken with a warm and gentle nature. He had lived three years in a mental-health care home, struggling with both schizophrenia and drug addiction, while taking classes in social work. Evicted from the group home on January 23, 2000 for stealing prescription drugs, he moved into an apartment with friends.

As outlined earlier, on the -20 evening of January 30, he ingested a disorienting mixture of prescription drugs and then smoked marijuana. Between 11 p.m. and midnight he was seen by a woman who said he was wearing neither jacket nor boots, pounding on her door. A man matching Wegner's description – dressed in only a white T-shirt, jeans and socks – was seen by three workmen and a truck driver, stumbling along the railway tracks as though his feet were bothering him, walking toward the power plant. He did not respond when called to. Several days later, he was found nearby, frozen to death, a single footpath to his body, and three impressions in the snow indicating where he had fallen earlier. (One of the men giving evidence at the inquest broke down and sobbed, regretting he had not called police.)

RCMP conducted an extensive door-to-door investigation, surveyed hundreds of police records and interviewed dozens of police officers. They discovered no police involvement in Wegner's death, and no charges were laid. (Lawrence Joseph then told reporters that the RCMP and city police "bungled" the Wegner investigation: "The RCMP cannot and should not be trusted by First Nations people and marginalized people."[94] The RCMP then sent a "strongly-worded" letter to FSIN.)

But at the month-long coroner's inquest two years later in January 2002, three surprise witnesses who all admitted they had never spoken to any living person about any of their evidence (only to someone who had died), suddenly came forward to say that they had seen police throwing Wegner head-first into their cruiser in front of St. Paul's hospital. This gave them the chance to see that he was wearing only socks.

First Chatsis was discredited regarding his frigid midnight walk, during which he claimed to first see police throw someone into their vehicle, and then, when he walked in a park several miles away and out onto a train bridge, claimed to see, almost a mile across the river and through the trees, police dropping someone off near the power plant. Next, two women, Benita Moccasin and Darlene Katcheech, were discredited as witnesses when descriptions in their testimonies varied significantly from one another's and from Chatsis'. A fourth potential witness, Dwaine Sutherland, went to police claiming to have seen Wegner being thrown in a patrol car, but when the investigating RCMP asked him to take a polygraph, warning that if he failed, he would face a five-year jail term, he backed down.

A letter to *The StarPhoenix* described the inquest as a "three-ring circus":

"At first [the inquest] heard from a witness [Chatsis] who suddenly remembered events that took place two years ago. Now two people have suddenly come out of the woodwork with information that was widely reported in the media as having been presented by a witness [Chatsis] that the inquiry has already heard from and deemed less than credible. Their reason for not coming forward sooner: fear of retaliation, although several [anonymous] 1-800 hotlines have been open since the events of January 2000. As the Wegner family lawyer speaks in a cryptic code-like language of other information still to come, FSIN's Lawrence Joseph urges us not to doubt the credibility of his newest star witnesses but instead to applaud their bravery. Isn't doubting witness credibility the basis of our system of law? Isn't determining whether reasonable doubt exists, the way we reach verdicts?
– Patrick Barbar"[95]

"The witnesses were so debunked that it all meant nothing," states Stan Goertzen. "Those discredited witnesses also point to a conspiracy." Who might have worked together to cast cops into disrepute? Who might have been capable of such a snow-job?

At the time, Goertzen had been quoted:

"Saskatoon Police Association president Stan Goertzen expressed his sympathy to the Wegners, and said he hopes their questions are answered. … Goertzen also questioned the agenda of anyone who may be bringing forward new information at such a late date.
'Is it damage control? Everything is being laid at the feet of the police. This feels like a witch-hunt,' he said.
'Everyone around here has been beat up for so long. We have a good organization here.'" [96]

At the inquest, a city worker caused consternation when he reported seeing a boot print on the back of Wegner's shirt, a fact some viewed as suspicious or disrespectful. An officer later sought me out, saying he wanted the public to know: "It was not something we wanted to do, but it was really difficult to move Wegner's body. He was found lying on his stomach and frozen solidly to the relatively snow-free stubble and soil. After trying everything we could to move him [including portable heaters in an improvised tent], an officer finally had to use his foot to rock the body and free it. We *had* to bring the body inside and, after trying other methods, it was the only way we *could* do it!"

A mystery emerged at the inquest which some still point to as suggesting Wegner was driven out to the power plant. When his body was found, Wegner's socks were clean, the outer, grey socks had worked their way down to the toes of the inner white ones, and the soles of all four socks were intact. During the RCMP investigation, a Mountie walked shoeless from St. Paul's hospital to the power plant, concluding that the 6 km (3.7 mile) *walk could be done in that weather but* at the end, his socks were filthy and shredded.

Previously unrevealed, it was the Mountie who did that walk who found the witnesses who removed suspicion some were casting on police. A police source reveals that, as RCMP Const. Wendell Reimer surveyed the area, he wondered, "Who might have been out here at that time of night who could have seen Lawrence Wegner?" Noticing the huge, round flat-topped oil storage tanks in the area, he wondered if they were filled late at night. His resourceful investigation located the men who testified. Had it not been for his work, which SPS officers might have been targeted for Wegner's death?

Reimer also believed the socks would not have been as shredded if they had remained frozen, had he stayed outside the whole time rather than warming up periodically in the accompanying car.

Wegner's roommate testified to Wegner's attire when he left the apartment between eight and 10 p.m.: "Plaid shirt, pair of jeans, a jacket and a pair of boots," while the Whitecap witness claimed that, as he ran away from her house, he was not wearing boots. Is it possible Whitecap was wrong? Wegner's socks were likely intact for the simple reason that *he did not walk the entire six kilometres in his socks.* Like other freezing victims, he probably did not lose his footwear until shortly before succumbing to the cold – when the four witnesses saw him walking along the tracks as *though his feet were bothering him,* unresponsive to their calls. Nobody knows whether he had been driven to that point (in a vehicle which the witnesses missed), or whether he had lost his boots after walking some distance, but he had to have walked bootless only far enough for the outer socks to work their way down to his toes, but not fall off.

Inquest coroner Hugh Harradence told the jury that the inquest had not heard "evidence of a dumping practice" by Saskatoon police. The six-person (half Aboriginal, half Caucasian) jury determined that Wegner had died of hypothermia. No determination was made regarding the circumstances leading to his death, and no police involvement was found. An SPS officer did tell me, however: "The guy who took the call in communications had been a police officer who developed multiple sclerosis, so he was put on light duty and was answering phones. Saskatoon is one of the busiest police departments in Canada, they just go all the time, so calls get stacked. In addition, this was one of the busiest night shifts he had ever worked. The officer never did send anyone out to look. Maybe that would have prevented Wegner's death, but we don't know that. *So there was police involvement – not with any intent to harm anyone, but a bad bureaucratic screw-up, nevertheless."*

Meanwhile, some SPS members were left frustrated. "Things we found in our own investigation never came out as evidence," says retired Staff Sgt. Murray Zoorkan. "For example, we located and spoke to a trucker who had been driving on 11th Street and turned South onto Dundonald that morning. As he did so, another truck's headlights revealed someone he later realized matched the description of Wegner, walking on the road alone. If the driver hadn't slammed on his brakes and swerved, he would have hit him. That was only a few hundred yards from where Wegner was found deceased. That was a key piece of evidence we found, but it never came out as evidence. And he was not the only person who wrote a witness statement for us who was not called and should have been! **That's been jumping out at me for years – the crucial evidence that was not presented by the RCMP. Is that intentional or is that stupidity?"**

During this time, Zoorkan saw something troubling. As part of his police duties, he had been assigned to monitor several inquests into the deaths of Aboriginal males. "The focus in peoples' minds [at the Wegner inquest] was the credibility of the two surprise witnesses," he says. "There were a lot of closed-door discussions and a lot of waiting for testimony. My focus was: were they going to polygraph the two prior to testimony?" (They did not.) He continues:

"At one of the inquests – I believe it was at the Wegner inquest because Prosecutor Lane Wiegers was present, but I am not one hundred percent

sure, as I was at several of the inquests. I am, however, one hundred percent sure of the comment I heard.

I observed Donald Worme come into the courtroom on the main floor of the Queen's Bench courthouse. It was just prior to starting again at two o'clock in the afternoon when everyone was waiting to resume the hearing. Donald Worme was not sitting as counsel at the inquest. He was in a jovial mood, and he walked into the room motioning and moving all his fingers. He made a comment, almost as a greeting: 'Don't you see my fingerprints all over this?' I took that to mean that he had engineered something to do with the inquest, that he had some sort of input or influence over the present proceedings. It stuck in my mind, as it seemed nefarious, due to the wording.

Q: Why would Donald Worme say that, when there were all these police officers and lawyers as witnesses?

A: There weren't a lot of police officers there. I was off to the side, there were a few civilians and it was a very small courtroom with only two or three rows of seating. There was a pillar there and he walked straight into the room, I was on the far side of the pillar and the prosecutor was behind the bar by his desk, and again, all in this very close area and he said it almost as a greeting: 'Don't you see my fingerprints all over this?'

Q: Do you know who he was speaking to, directly?

A: There were some civilians as he walked in towards them, and I can't remember today who it was."

Donald Worme denies making such a comment. He would later ignore the RCMP's findings and the workers who saw Wegner walking, and tell a 2002 talking circle filmed by the NFB that Wegner had been "left to die," saying "Mary Wegner chose not to fall into … characterizing the death of her son as a matter simply of racism. …Instead to ask the question as to why her son could be *left in such a calculating way* to die in such an undignified way." When asked about changes made in the police service, he again appeared to implicate police in murder: "Well, tangible change, I think, can be brought about really by one thing and that is goodwill. And the fact is that there has not been a lot of goodwill displayed, at least towards Lawrence Wegner, towards Rodney Naistis, towards Darrell Night or Lloyd Dustyhorn or Neil Stonechild. I mean, these are people that, that have met a very tragic end to their lives. [Last time this writer talked to him, Darrell Night was very much alive!] …And until there are real concrete answers brought forward by those who have those answers, I don't think that we have real, tangible change."

Asked about Const. Bruce Ehalt, the officer dubbed by the *StarPhoenix* as "The One Good Cop" for convincing Darrell Night to come in and make a statement about having been dropped off by two officers, Worme replied that Ehalt had merely done his duty and "has been criticized by some other police officers who suggest that he has broken rank with them and that he ought not to have done that." Bruce Ehalt specifically denies that allegation. "No one at the station ostracized me, or even treated me differently," he says. In fact, within months, he was promoted to sergeant. **"Nothing negative happened to me because I was a whistleblower,"** Ehalt says. **"There was none of this 'blue wall' stuff going on."**

As in the Naistus inquest, many of the Wegner jury's recommendations were aimed at police – in this case, eight out of 22. Wegner's father, Gerry, probably was not alone in interpreting this as: "[The jury] ruled in our favour, that the police need to learn more how to deal with people one on one," as he later told the NFB.

The less-publicized recommendations addressed gaps in caring for the mentally ill, such as "Mandatory 48-hour advanced notification of a pending eviction to the resident's mental health case worker before an eviction is carried out." Gaps which accounted for Wegner being outside on a winter night under the influence of drugs without a caregiver. Gaps for which police ended as scapegoats.

"There just was no news in these recommendations for police," says Dave Scott. "They had already started to slaughter the lamb and simply could not stop. The smell and taste of blood were too delicious!"

CHAPTER 10 - Body Exhumed;
Information Buried

'They obviously didn't want the truth to be found. They wanted it buried deep!'
– Saskatoon ambulance attendant

Saskatoon's Woodlawn Cemetery, 6 a.m., Tuesday, April 24, 2001:

"Careful! Bring it up slo-o-o-w." The men spoke in low voices in case anyone was lurking around the cemetery, although at this hour, they shouldn't be. The first weak rays of sun threw the men's shadows wavering 15 feet across the frosted grass. Chains creaked under the strain of hauling the wooden coffin and concrete burial vault up from the frozen grave. Sgt. Warner and Insp. McFadyen of Operation Ferric observed, along with the province's chief coroner, John Nyssen.

Nyssen had made the order to exhume Stonechild's remains at the request of the Mounties, the first such request in the province in over 20 years. The task force had spoken to family members and friends who said that, at the funeral, Neil looked beaten up. They therefore wanted to determine whether SPS Sgt. Jarvis' conclusion, that the cause of death was accidental due to hypothermia, should now be upgraded to murder.

They had many questions. Did the skeletal remains indicate any injury other than superficial scratches noted in the original autopsy? What could account for the bumps on Stonechild's head, or the broken nose suggested by someone at the funeral? Was there foreign DNA on the hands or elsewhere indicating a struggle? Had someone done a cover-up about this death?

"Almost there. Slow ... slow ... *good!*" The casket descended gently onto a trailer. In the move, the concrete lid on the vault had broken. Beneath it, a plastic spray of three dozen red carnations, placed atop the inner coffin 11 years ago, still seemed to bloom, crimson and lifelike.

"Oh no! The media! How could they have found out about this?" One of the men walked over to consult with the cameraman behind a bulbous telephoto lens, returning with the news: "They say the family told the media about the exhumation. Why would the family want this publicized?" And why would RCMP order the disinterment when, a month earlier, they had been handed a copy of Jason Roy's original hand-written statement in which he had not mentioned police involvement at all? Why were the RCMP pursuing police regardless of whatever clearly exculpatory evidence they were handed?

In all of Canada, where forensic pathology was not yet a recognized sub-specialty of medicine, no one was more qualified to do the job of re-examination than Dr. Graeme Dowling. Chief medical examiner for Alberta, he had trained in the investigation of unexplained deaths, and was also certified in forensic pathology after a year-long fellowship in Dallas, Texas.

A year earlier, in March 2000, Lyons had sent Dowling the SPS documentation on the death. Dowling's reply, not released to the public, suggested exhumation was not required:

"Your primary reason for asking me to review this case is to provide any further interpretive information regarding the skin injuries described in the autopsy report and depicted in the photographs. All of the injuries depicted and described are minor "blunt" injuries called abrasions (otherwise known as scrapes). They are caused by the skin coming in contact with a blunt, as opposed to a sharp, object, such that some of the skin is scraped away. Although the injuries on the nose aren't completely clear in the photographs, I do believe that these are also abrasions. The skin within the depths of these two abrasions may be broken (i.e. which would then make them superficial lacerations), however these would still be blunt injuries. I do not believe they have been produced by a sharp object such as a knife. The same applies to the minor injuries on the right hand which are simply small scrapes or abrasions.

With respect to whether these injuries were caused by an assault or by a fall, this is not a question that can be answered by looking at the injuries in isolation. There is no visible difference between the injuries caused during the course of an assault as opposed to those which result from a fall. In this case, however, if you look at the injuries in the context of the position Mr. Stonechild's body was found in (i.e. face-down in frozen crusted snow), it appears to me that his injuries would be entirely consistent with his falling onto the snow at this site prior to his death. Just to be clear, I cannot definitively say whether any of these injuries are a result of an assault as opposed to a fall. I can only say that the injuries are consistent with his collapse into the hard snow just prior to his death. Your only other question was whether the dark discolouration of Mr. Stonechild's lips was actually an injury or was caused by freezing. The dark discoloration is a post mortem change caused by a combination of drying and freezing of the lips (at the scene of his death) followed by thawing of the lips prior to autopsy. This is not an injury."

The task force was not satisfied. Why? A photogrammetrist (who takes measurements from photos) with questionable credentials who would be labelled in the inquiry judge's final report as "the most controversial witness," had suggested the marks on the face were not caused by crusted snow, as reported in the original pathologist's report and the forensic pathologist's report.

Even though, as Dowling would write of his re-examination, "*Post mortem darkening and desiccation* [extreme drying] *of the skin does not allow for proper examination for the presence or absence of injuries,*" nevertheless, today the RCMP had exhumed the body and, rather than fly Dowling to Saskatoon to re-examine in a local hospital, would fly the body to him in Edmonton by RCMP aircraft.

The RCMP had willingly been pre-judging. Dowling wrote: "Prior to my examination of the body, I am informed that this was a 17-year-old Native Indian male who was found dead in an industrial area in the north end of Saskatoon on the afternoon of November 29, 1990. The decedent *was last seen alive in a police vehicle.*" Not true, actually. Only *one* witness (with a long record of breaking the law who admitted he was very drunk at the time) ever *claimed* to see Stonechild in a police vehicle – and a student counsellor said Roy "remembered" that sighting a year after the event when she did a visualization exercise with him. Another witness, Stonechild's cousin, testified that Stonechild was definitely *not* in the police car when checked by police at 12:04, eight minutes after Jason Roy claimed he was in the police car at 11:56. Yet, remarkably, the RCMP informed Dr. Dowling of the "fact" that Stonechild had been in a police car.

During the two and one-half hour re-examination, overseen by five high-ranking authorities, Dr. Dowling did a complete series of body X-rays, re-examined old tissue slides, probed, analyzed, and finally, for the second time, agreed with everything that the Saskatoon pathologist and coroner had determined a decade earlier. Dowling's July 3, 2001 written summary: "… there is no evidence of any injury or other natural disease process to refute the original autopsy findings and conclusions."

Specifically, Dowling noted:

- *Unable to identify minor external injuries, documented at the initial autopsy, due to degree of post mortem desiccation.*
- *No evidence of injuries not identified at initial autopsy*
- *No evidence of fractures of nasal cartilage or nasal bone.*
- *No evidence of bony injuries of wrists, where handcuffs may have been in place.*

The hair and scalp had been altered by those who prepared the body. Nor was any foreign DNA found under fingernails or elsewhere.

Following re-examination, the RCMP purchased new caskets and flew the body to Manitoba for reburial near where Stella Bignell now lived.

The results – no signs of injury on the body, or DNA of any sort on Stonechild's fingernails, and much more– were exactly what "Fred Smyth," the ambulance attendant had told the RCMP. His information, however, seems to have been repressed – by either RCMP or Sask Justice which handled the Stonechild Inquiry.

RCMP SUPPRESSION OF EVIDENCE IN STONECHILD CASE
Ambulance attendant speaks out **(from "The Reality Test" by retired Const.**
Larry Lockwood and Candis McLean, published on
The Western Standard **Newsmagazine website)**

"I was one of the ambulance attendants who picked up Neil Stonechild's frozen body. Because the body had not been changed by the thawing and drying process seen in many of the photos later publicized, I could clearly see that Stonechild had only very superficial scratches on his nose, and that the marks in the wrist area were clearly made by the tight, 1-1/2 inch-wide elasticized storm cuffs on his bomber jacket. When we moved him, the cuffs pulled back from his wrist and revealed marks which exactly matched the jacket cuffs. Those were not handcuff marks; the skin was puckered just like mine when I wear my bomber jacket, and there were ridge marks at right angles to where any handcuff would have been.

"I told all this to the RCMP when they came to question me. What I want to know is: Why were we not called to testify at the inquiry? I've had people at work say to me, 'You know all this stuff. Why weren't you called to testify?' I answer, 'They obviously didn't want the truth to be found. If I had been asked to testify, my testimony would have collaborated Dr. Emma Lew's testimony and contradicted the photogrammetrist, the only person who ever claimed those were handcuff marks, and there would have been justice. Because facts were excluded, justice did not have a chance to be done.'" -- Saskatoon Ambulance Attendant, 2008

"Smyth" says he gave the same information to an RCMP officer who, I suspected, wrote a summary which I obtained under access to information legislation. That summary stated that on Apr. 10, 2000, an ambulance attendant with birthdate 1956.09.02 advised the following, and then mentioned only that he remembered the body lying face down, wearing a bomber jacket with "Mount Royal Collegiate" written on the front, "not wearing shoes," about 19, with frostbite patches on the cheeks, and "could not make any comments on injuries that may have been on the deceased." "He remembered bagging the feet of the deceased with the police." "He did not retain any notes."

After reading this RCMP summary, I interviewed "Smyth" a second time:

"Q: [Fred], is your birthday Sept. 2, 1956?
A: Yep!
Q: Good! That's the DOB of the ambulance attendant referred to in this RCMP summary. Now, when you were interviewed by the RCMP in 2000, are you sure you told them about the marks you saw on Neil Stonechild's hands?
"Smyth": Yep! Absolutely. He asked if there were any markings and if they looked like handcuffs. I said, 'Those were not handcuff marks. The marks in the wrist area exactly matched the storm cuffs on his bomber jacket.' Most of his questions were not open-ended questions. It was more like being in court where you answer questions with a yes or no. I told them about helping the police bag his hands to preserve evidence, that there was no trauma to the hands, knuckles weren't bleeding, none of the fingernails were broken as I have seen on other people that have been in a fight, I told them that when we pulled the sleeves back to bag the hands, the marks in the area of the wrist exactly matched the storm cuffs of his jacket. They asked, 'How do you know they specifically matched?' I said, 'The marks were exactly like the ones left by the storm cuffs on my jacket. The marks were at right angles to what handcuff marks would have been.'"

"Smyth" continued:

"The RCMP had seemed very interested in coming to talk to me. One officer asked me on the phone: 'Does the name, Neil Stonechild, mean anything to you?' I told them I was one of the ambulance attendants who picked up his body. It was between 56th and 57th in the north end behind

the Hitachi building.

I caught their interest. They said, 'We'll be right over!' When they got here in their black Suburban, we sat down at the kitchen table and they started asking questions. I kept wanting to give more information but they'd interrupt with another question: 'So how come you can't remember your partner?' Well that changed every day. 'Why were the files destroyed?' Files are only kept so long. They seemed to dismiss things they didn't want to know about.

I drew out on paper the location of the body. I said: 'He was lying prone in this direction. And I drew the place to the north-east where it appeared that he had fallen down earlier.' [Why was that not disclosed in RCMP information?]

They asked if there were any other footprints? 'Nothing else but ours. It was a very unkempt area with lots of sage brush, so it would have been easy to trip.' They asked about a search dog. I said, 'Yes, because they were looking for his missing shoe,' but when I tried to describe things, they would change the question.

I said, 'The snow had drifted around him. There was no trauma to the face, only a scratch on the nose – a scratch, not a gash – one little mark on the nose that could have been caused by sagebrush or any of the vegetation there. It wasn't significant of anything. It didn't look like a trauma mark, or like a ring mark, or anything like that, that I'd ever seen before.'

I said, 'There was no blood on his chest, no matting of the hair.' I also stated, 'There was no damage to the clothes, no tears in the jacket, no mouth trauma, and the clothes were not in disarray as if he had been in a struggle.' I told them, 'He had white marks on both cheeks the size of quarters which I took to mean that he had been out in the cold for some time before he died; you don't get frost bite after you die.' I told them he'd been seen in the north end. I had heard that on the street.

When I asked, 'How come you guys don't want to know more stuff in detail?' he said, 'We'll just move on; we have lots of questions we want to ask.' I said, 'I didn't know there was a time limit.'

Q: Was the interview was taped?

A: No, and I wondered why not. When they left, I was very frustrated because of their specific questions. I did not feel I had been heard. I did not feel I had had my say. I did not feel good about it. It was poor police work. When you are asking specific questions, you only get what you *ask, and then cut the person off. I wished they hadn't come, because they hadn't really listened to what I said. **It ticked me off. I thought, 'What the hell? You guys don't want to know about this!'** I felt the RCMP believed I was not important. They discredited what I said and didn't let me continue with what I had to say. It was like the interview was just a formality. I thought, 'What the heck kind of interview was that? Thanks for wasting my time, guys!'*

*I kept waiting for someone to be charged, and when I heard that Hartwig and Senger had not been charged, I thought, 'Well I must have said enough that they were not charged.' **But why wasn't I asked to testify at the inquiry? I think I knew too much!***

The RCMP kept asking me how I remembered things so clearly. I said, 'That's my job. Just the other day I ran into a patient from 1999. I said, 'How's the leg?' They said, 'How do you remember that?' I said, 'How's your son who's going to take over the farm?' Well, sadly, he had died. I just remember things."

This Journalist's Thoughts on the RCMP Summary:

The Mountie did not mention "Smyth's eidetic powers of recall, and omitted his important "one little mark on the nose that could have been caused by sagebrush or any of the vegetation there. It didn't look like a trauma mark, like a ring mark, or anything like that, that I'd ever seen before." The Mountie wrote, "The subject was not wearing shoes [plural]" when "Smyth" had always told me "one shoe." The Mountie omitted: no blood on clothing, no defensive wounds, no damage to the jacket, clothes not in disarray. Nothing about the "pucker marks" near the wrist area, nothing about the important observation: *"Those were not handcuff marks. The marks in the wrist area exactly matched the storm cuffs on his bomber jacket."*

Was the RCMP summary written deliberately vaguely so that no one could possibly say: "This guy has a detailed and provably accurate memory. He would make an excellent witness for the inquiry"? Curiously, nowhere does the Mountie mention interviewing "Smyth" in the presence of another officer. Who was he protecting? Why is there no mention of the diagram "Smyth" drew illustrating how the body lay? Instead the Mountie reported: ""Smyth" did not retain any notes…." He also summarized: "…did not remember the date." This is, I believe, one of the few things "Smyth" does not recall about that day.

Observations:

1. On March 27, 2000, ten days before "Smyth"'s interview, RCMP officers Warner and McFadyen had discussed evidence. They agreed injuries to Stonechild

were not inconsistent with an assault. Also marks were not inconsistent with a handcuff mark. It appears their hypothesis had been established a mere six weeks into the complex investigation.

2. *Why not document "Smyth"'s information on bagging the hands, finding no defensive wounds? Why note only bagging the feet?* This makes no sense, suggesting a deliberate cover-up of crucial information. Did the Mountie wish to repress the observation that marks near Stonechild's wrists exactly matched storm cuffs on his jacket and were not handcuff marks?

The Mounties had obtained audiotaped and even videotaped statements from many other witnesses. Why not tape "Smyth" who had so many provably accurate memories from the scene?

What was going on?

CHAPTER 11 - 'Reality Test' by
Const. Larry Lockwood

'This chapter is my final contribution to the book....'
– Const. Lockwood, five weeks before his death

The term "Post Mortem" means "After Death." To forensic pathologists, specialists who determine the cause of injuries on corpses, this means that whatever made the marks found on Neil Stonechild's hand had to be present both before and after he died. Since he had no handcuffs on when found, *any such handcuffs had to have been removed after his death.*

There is a very simple experiment you can perform yourself to examine what *post mortem* means. Press a finger against the back of your hand for five seconds, and then remove it. The white mark you see is caused by the pressure of your finger pushing the blood away from that portion of your skin. Because you are alive and your heart is pumping blood, the white mark soon returns to its normal skin colour. If you had died with your finger pressed against your skin, the white mark would have remained visible after your death. It would remain indefinitely, *even after* the instrument that caused the mark (your finger) was removed. In order to leave that mark, your finger must be present both before death, and *after you have died.*

All police officers investigate files differently, but at the end of their investigation, before their evidence is presented to a judicial body, their findings and theories must pass the "Reality Test." A crucial reality test question: *"In the real world, is my theory even possible?"*

All the experts at the Stonechild Inquiry, except the RCMP witness, testified that whatever caused the marks on his hand was *post mortem.* In other words, it was on the hand after death and *had to have been removed after death.* What would this mean then, if we were to apply post mortem to a "reality test" to evaluate whether or not handcuffs could have caused the marks found on Stonechild's body? If we are to believe that the marks were most likely the result of Stonechild having been in police custody, this is what would have had to occur – not what *might* have occurred, or *could possibly* have occurred but what *absolutely would have had to occur* – in order to leave the marks found on Stonechild's hand.

Stonechild's friend Jason Roy stated that Stonechild was seated in the rear of a police car, bleeding heavily from the face, handcuffed behind his back, and screaming, "These guys are going to kill me!" This is what the inquiry would have you believe: that Stonechild was taken into custody by the police, beaten across the face in some manner to cause a bleeding injury, transported to a remote location wearing police handcuffs on only one hand, dropped off and left to freeze to death.

This is not what actually happened. This is what would have had to happen for there to be any truth in what was claimed. If what the inquiry judge said was true, the police *had* to have taken Neil Stonechild into custody and beaten him up, causing the facial injury that Roy described (and which four specialists described as scratches, likely from the vegetation into which he took his final fall). The police *had* to have locked Stonechild in handcuffs that can be traced back to the police. In fact, their serial number can be used to trace them back to the very officer to whom they were issued! And only put the handcuff on one hand!

Then, a short time later, the officers *had* to have stopped and talked with Jason Roy while his friend Stonechild was seated in the rear of the police car, screaming, "These guys are going to kill me!" Thus creating a witness to potential misconduct. After speaking with witness Jason Roy, the police then *had* to have transported Stonechild to a remote location in Saskatoon's north industrial area and removed Stonechild from their car, leaving him in traceable police handcuffs to wander around in any direction he chose, while the police officers would have *had* to leave and return to duty, where they took many other calls for service that night.

(And if the officers were going to drive anyone anywhere from Snowberry Downs to let him roam around and freeze to death, why would they drop him within the city for other police to investigate? Why not drive him outside the city and then it becomes an RCMP problem. They would have wanted to get out of town and back as fast as possible, so they would have driven him, not to the north side of the city, out 33rd to the west, outside the city, where it was desolate and the next city miles away, so there would be less chance of Stonechild – or the cops – being seen.) You can see how absurd the whole idea is!

The pathologists all agreed that it would take a person anywhere from two to three hours to be overcome by hypothermia. So now, with Stonechild having been released from custody, this person who was in fear of dying at the hands of the police, according to his friend Jason Roy, *had to have not run like hell*, far away from the area, as soon as he was no longer under the control of the police, while the officers left and took other calls for service. He had to not flag down a car for help, or walk to one of the plants operating around-the-clock in the area. Instead, he *had* to get extremely cold and walk out into a snow-covered field, lie down and die.

The police, anywhere from two to three hours later, then *had* to have returned to the area where they dropped Stonechild off, wearing traceable police handcuffs. They *had* to have searched and located Stonechild frozen to death in this dark, wide-open, snow-covered field, and removed the handcuffs. (Remember, the marks were *post mortem*; he had to be wearing the handcuffs *after death*.)

There are only three problems here. One: there was only one set of footprints left in the snow where Stonechild's body was found, and those were Stonechild's. Two: there was no blood found on Stonechild's face, clothing or the snow beneath his face. Remember, Roy told RCMP that Stonechild was "gushing" blood from the face and said on CBC news, "his face was cut open pretty good." Three: the "handcuff" marks were down below the bone in the wrist which holds handcuffs in place. Dr. Emma Lew, at the Police Act hearing, testified that enlarged photos clearly showed the detail of a cloth weave on his skin along with microscopic fibres – probably the result of Stonechild having pulled his hands inside his jacket cuff for warmth.

Now, what would the officers, who had never worked together before, have to be thinking as they abandon Stonechild wearing handcuffs that could be traced back to one of them? These officers would have to believe that, one: they would be able to locate Stonechild in the dark, anywhere from two to three hours later, so that they could retrieve their handcuffs; two: that Stonechild would not be found by a passer-by before they could return; three: that they could clean the blood impeccably off Stonechild's clothing (and the snow under his face); and four: that, as they went about their duties, they would not be involved in some other situation that would tie them up for the rest of the night and prevent their returning to find the body so they could retrieve their traceable handcuffs. Does any of this pass the Reality Test?"

Constables Hartwig and Senger were both fired from their jobs as a direct result of the Stonechild Inquiry, which left both officers branded in the public eye as murderers. No charges have ever been brought against these officers in a court of law, and these officers have no way of clearing their names, yet here we are, many years later, with the lives of these officers and their families destroyed by a process that was neither fair nor impartial, based on the false assumption that Stonechild was in police custody the night he went missing!

There have been countless articles and books written about this affair. But all the writings of the politically-correct, all the media hype, all the words of all the lawyers and witnesses that lined up in support of the "starlight tour" myth, will never change *the one cold, hard fact that remains constant: the marks found on Neil Stonechild's hand were left there post mortem.* In addition to all the events that must follow from that fact, in terms of getting those marks there.

Neil Stonechild was never in police custody [Lockwood concluded]. The Saskatchewan Department of Justice knows this; that's why no charges have ever been brought against these officers. I believe that the Stonechild Inquiry had one purpose only, and that was to find scapegoats to satisfy special interest groups which are now the tail wagging the Justice dog. In the 'starlight tour' cases, hillbilly justice was alive and well in the Province of Saskatchewan!

CHAPTER 12 - 'Total chaos and mayhem!'
Events Leading to Neil Stonechild's Death

'Randy Lafond had grabbed the axe and as we went in the back door, Eddie – deceased Eddie Rushton and Pat Caisse were coming up from the root cellar where the guns were and Randy chopped – well, hit Eddie in the head with the axe and knocked him into the basement again and they went down there and, I don't know, it was just total chaos and mayhem and ....'
– Gary Pratt testifying at the Stonechild Inquiry

In August, 1990, three months before his death, Neil Stonechild, 17, and another youth broke into a Saskatoon home where they stole some guns. They took the firearms to the home of another associate, Eddie Rushton, where the guns were stored. Two older males, Gary Pratt and Randy Lafond, then went to that house and tried to take the guns, but Rushton leveled a gun at Pratt and threatened to shoot him. A few hours later, Gary Pratt, Errol Pratt, Spencer Bear and Randy Lafond returned and stole the guns in a "home invasion" robbery. Neil Stonechild and others were hit with the butt of an axe, and punched and kicked by Lafond and the Pratts. They were threatened with death if they ratted out the people who robbed them. Stonechild and friends were supposed to testify against the four, and were terrified.

Thirteen years later, Gary Pratt would tell the Stonechild Inquiry:

"I was invited to a party [sic] at Mr. Rushton's place and upon arrival I had sat down, and there was quite a few people there, including the deceased Neil, deceased Shane Bird, deceased Petrina Starblanket, Eddie Rushton. And we were having a party, and Eddie had come out of the kitchen with a gun and pointed it at me and told me if I made it to the door I'd live. And so I attempted to make it to the door; I did and I lived. And I told him I'd be back, and I came back.

Q: When you came back was there other people with you?

A: Yes, there was. There was my deceased brother Harold, Randy Lafond, Spencer Bear and myself.

Q: And can you tell us what took place, then, when you returned?

A: When we returned we had went through the back door and at the back door there was an axe and Randy Lafond had grabbed the axe and as we went in the back door Eddie – deceased Eddie Rushton and Pat Caisse were coming up from the root cellar where the guns were and Randy chopped – well, hit Eddie in the head with the axe and knocked him into the basement again and they went down there and, I don't know, it was just total chaos and mayhem and –

Q: Was Neil still at the house at that time?

A: Yes, he was."

Pratt testified that Stonechild, who had been in a bedroom with Petrina Starblanket, came out to find Eddie Rushton rolled in a carpet, unconscious after being hit in the head with the axe, and that Pratt's brother, Errol, later announced within Stonechild's hearing range, words to the effect: "You don't see anything here, or you don't know anything, or you don't tell anything to anyone, or you're dead!"

Police were called to the assault in progress; several officers, including Const. Larry Hartwig, responded. At the Stonechild Inquiry, District Const. Neil Wylie would refer to his notes and state that Hartwig spoke to Neil Stonechild and other victims briefly and then departed, as his presence was not required: the assault and disturbance were over, the scene secure, and the district constable was there to take the report. Justice David Wright would then claim that since Hartwig took a "statement" from Neil Stonechild, he should have remembered the call and was hiding something, since he couldn't remember the event. The disturbing problem with the judge's claim was this: Hartwig had not taken a statement, and no one at the inquiry said he had taken a statement. Is it possible the judge had the same blinkered determination as the RCMP?

Asked today whether he would have remembered taking a statement, Hartwig replies, "Absolutely. Getting hit with an axe would have been significant."

Father André Poiliévre who has worked with many troubled youths says that Stonechild did not stick around long, either. "The night that the Pratts went into this house, Neil was there and he was in bed with his girlfriend [who some claimed was also Pratt's girlfriend]. And he ended up running out of the house with no clothes on, just a blanket, and ran to his mother's house. Many people don't know that."

The four assailants, the Pratts, Bear and Lafond, were charged with robbery with violence. At the time of his arrest, Gary Pratt was also unlawfully at large on a recognizance in relation to another charge—an assault on his own mother. Pat Caisse and Stonechild were called as witnesses against Pratt for the assault. In October, 1990, Neil was taken to the courthouse to testify, but the hearing did not proceed, as other witnesses did not show up. Stonechild and his family were aware of the danger to him regarding his testimony, and feared for his life. The operator of the group home where Stonechild was in custody at the time would state that Stonechild would have rather "cut his legs off" than testify against the group, but, because of his subpoena, she delivered him to court.

Pratt had spent three months in remand, from August 10 until October 24, 1990, and was released about a month before Stonechild went missing. Pratt claimed at the inquiry, however, he hadn't realized Stonechild was in court to testify and held no animosity toward him; their last contact after his release, Pratt said, "was just basically, hello, hi, how you doing, and no hard feelings." He denied any involvement in Stonechild's death.

The "robbery with violence charges" against the others were still in effect after the time Stonechild died. The following year, on May 19, 1991, the charge against Lafond was stayed. Rushton, whom Lafond had axed in the head, died of a suspicious gunshot wound to the head sometime in 1991. The rumour going around was that he had been playing Russian roulette with a 9 mm. automatic pistol. The problem with that story is that a pistol does not have a cylinder to spin like a revolver does. Which means, as a street kid said to me, "If there is a bullet in a pistol, *whenever* you pull that trigger, it's gonna go, 'Bang!'"

I learned from one of Stonechild's friends that the "street word" at the time was that the Pratts had taken Stonechild out to the industrial area and left him to die. "The people on the street, they know. They see everything," said the Native man, then 34, who requested anonymity. "Even today, if you go on the street, you'll find half the guys say Gary Pratt did it, but nobody wants to rat to the police. It's like an oath." On the other hand, he said, "The police are an easier target to blame; they can't fight back."

After Stonechild's body was found, he continued, "the whole Pratt family, who used to be big mall rats, disappeared!" The Stonechilds, MacDonalds and Carons, three large Native families, were making plans to go after the Pratts, the source claimed, but Stella Bignell stopped them, fearing "a big family war." Whether or not that source is correct, at some point Bignell apparently "made plans to go after" the police. The interesting question is: was it her own idea, or someone else's? If so, whose suggestion might it have been? (In September 2008, Mrs. Bignell had agreed to an interview with this writer at her Manitoba home. Before the appointed date, however, she informed me that her lawyer had told her not to talk to me.)

Pratt testified that Jason Roy, like Stonechild, was part of neither the Rushton nor Pratt factions, which had numerous "violent interactions." Jason Roy, Pratt said, "just liked to drink with the guys."

Stella Bignell would tell Const. Warner that Gary Pratt, then 20, talked to her about Neil's death. She gave a remarkable reason for believing him:

> "I talked to him later. Musta been... ohhh...it was further on in the summer time, after his death...in '91 anyway...in the summer time, sometime. And he came an' talked to me, he said, 'Stella,' he said, 'you know,' he says ahh... 'I would never do that to Neil,' he said, 'I respected Neil... for the...type of ahh...person he was. I had a lotta respect for him. And,' he said, 'I grew up with him. I would never do that,' he said. And I...and I believed him, you know. And then after where we had a talk... I talked to the boys and Erica, my daughter... we were talking about [name redacted] ...and Erica said ahhh... 'You know,' she said, 'if those guys had beat him up, you wouldn't a been able to recognize him,' she said. So that's where I knew, I knew that they didn't. They had nothing to do with it. And I believed [him].
> Const. Warner: Okay, those are pretty much all the questions I have, Stella."

Having believed Pratt's denial, despite knowing he had earlier beaten Neil with the butt-end of a shotgun, and that he had even been charged for beating up his own mother, Mrs. Bignell then went on to suggest to the RCMP that police might have been involved in her son's death:

> "I phoned my sister up in Caronport, Marcie, and they came down right away. She was making some inquiries as to what might have happened to him...and I said, 'I think he was doing a B & E.' I told her, 'Maybe the police would know something about it,' I said. 'I heard that they were in a B & E and the police were called,' I said. So she phoned the police station and asked about it. And he said there was no police ever sent out for Neil. But I know that there was."

(Justice David Wright, in his report on the Stonechild Inquiry, would also reject the probability that Pratt might have been involved in Stonechild's death. Despite the fact that a number of tips to police had linked the two, and although Bignell "had heard rumours that Neil might have been beaten up by a member of the Pratt family as a result of her son's involvement with the Pratts in September 1990 in a gun transaction [two months before his death]," Wright concluded: "Gary Pratt visited her and told her that report was untrue, and she accepted his explanation." Apparently the judge did, too.)

Const. Ernie Louttit and Hartwig had been in the same recruit class, and by November 1990, were both three-year members of the SPS. Louttit had a reputation as a keen police officer; he was a friend of the Stonechild family, trusted in the Aboriginal community. ("He's like a guidance counsellor with a badge," Marcel Stonechild would tell the inquiry.) According to his notes, Louttit was consulted by the Stonechild family and asked to make inquiries on behalf of the family, as they wanted to ensure that Gary Pratt was properly investigated as a suspect in Neil's death.

At the inquiry, Louttit testified that a few days after Stonechild's body was found, Stonechild's brother, Jake (Jason), told Louttit that Stonechild had been killed by Gary and Danny Pratt. Reading from his notes made at the time, "that he'd been picked up at a party when he was very drunk in the north end, somewhere up by the 7-Eleven, and that he'd been beaten up and then – and dumped off." Louttit continued:

"Neil was with an unknown female, or unidentified female, first name starts with F, she witnessed Neil get in the car, very loaded.

Q: During this time period, 1990, 1991, did you receive any information during that time, Constable Louttit, that Neil Stonechild was in the back of a city police car on the night that he disappeared?

A: No, not at all. And if I had received that information, I wouldn't have stopped on this after I was speaking with Sergeant Jarvis; I would have went to somebody else. I have no problem arresting a police officer that's taken part in a crime. ...

THE COMMISSIONER: Other questions?

MR. [JAY] WATSON, examining:

Q: Good afternoon. Just picking up on that last point. You, if you had had any information that police officers were involved in this, you, if you didn't get satisfaction from the Saskatoon City Police, you would have gone to the RCMP, or you would have gone somewhere until you got attention, is that correct?

A: Absolutely.

Q: Now, you mentioned all of the names that were that you heard that may be people involved in this, the Ts, Ps, Rushton, K. All of those names were names that you recognized?

A: Yes, that's correct, sir.

Q: Because you've been on Patrol basically your whole police career, correct?

A: Yes, in pretty much the same area. …

Q: Now were these names that you heard, were those names that you knew from your experience had been involved in criminal activity?

A: Yes.

Q: Did you feel that those were names that should be investigated to see if they did have something to do with Neil?

A: Yes.

Q: Now, one name that was mentioned here at this inquiry that I don't believe necessarily was in the documents we have received, but M brothers, do you have any knowledge of any M brothers being around in 1990?

A: Yeah, to put it in the right perspective, at the time, in 1990, there was several families vying for a large portion of the drug trade and control the prostitutes in Riversdale and Pleasant Hill. Among those families were the Ps, the McDs. The Ms were peripheral; they were usually associated to one group or the other at the time. There was the Cs. The Ts were at the, I think at the tail end of that power struggle; they were done. The Ms, I dealt with several of the M boys, if you want to call them that; M men are the menfolk for different offences. In 1990 there was a considerable amount of violence on the street that was going unreported, that I was hearing about but never receiving an actual complaint that you could act upon, in that perfect world sense.

Q: So some of the violence that was taking place between some of the factions, neither side would phone the police?

A: No. No, and what was happening is, it was almost peripheral. You were picking them off on drugs, on weapons charges, on bail violations, but you weren't getting them for the main substance of what they were up to. And nobody was willing to come forward.

Q: And in these disputes, wars, and I -- the term "gang" wasn't used at that time, is that fair to say?

A: No, it wasn't.

Q: More families and factions?

A: Yeah, I would describe it as factional fighting.

Q: But certainly violence did take place between those two, between the various factions, and people would be seriously injured at times?

A: Yes, and -- yes. Stabbings, et cetera.

Q: And that's, in particular, why you thought at the time those people should have been spoken to about Neil's death?

A: Yes.

Q: Thank you, sir. ...

THE COMMISSIONER: I have a question for you, if you don't mind. Given your obvious experience and thorough knowledge of the activities that were going on between the various family groups who were in conflict, were there many homicides that you know of that occurred as a result of that inter-family conflict? Or were there any?

A: Yeah, there was -- there was several, sir. In fact I think in 1990 and '91, '92, in those years, we had the dubious distinction of having the highest murder rate per capita in Canada.

THE COMMISSIONER: And were these, some of these at least, murders or homicides that occurred because of conflicts between ... families in 1990?

A: Yes, it was not uncommon."

Retired SPS officer Lockwood told me that after the Stonechild death, Errol Pratt was murdered with a baseball bat by a member of the Gamble family, closely associated with the Caron clan. "All of these people – the Carons, MacDonalds, Pratts, Caisses – were involved in the 'Hooker Wars' of 1985," Lockwood said. "Two factions got into a turf war over prostitution territories. There was a big shoot-out at Baldwin Hotel, windows shot out of houses, and we had to dispose of two bombs in the city planted next to houses associated with members of different prostitution rings." The bottom line, Lockwood says, "In my opinion as a street officer of 27 years, if Stonechild's death was a murder – and I'm not convinced it was – I would look for connections going back to the family feuding of the Hooker Wars."

Indeed, Gary Pratt said something similar to an Operation Ferric investigator in an inexplicably unrecorded 45-minute interview. Const. Mayrs summarized Pratt's words: "Pratt stated that the police did not like him, his brother Errol Pratt (now deceased) and Errol's wife/common law Margaret McDonald due to the 'pimp wars and hookers' which went on during the 1980s."

In a 2008 interview with me, Jason Roy, then 33, recalled the last day he saw Neil Stonechild:

"Back in those days, the bus terminal that's downtown where all the buses meet, it was a newer thing to Saskatoon, and there was arcades down there, so a lot of us used to hang around the bus terminal. It was just somewhere where we'd all meet up after school or on the weekends, at nights, you know, 'til whenever. And so I mean, I got down there and I happened to meet up with Neil there. And, uh, we just started talking, and back then I was, I was, I was into a lot of crime, I, I liked to do a lot of crime, and I was good at it, you know, good but bad, I guess. As soon as we met up we kind of, you know, it's, it's uh kind of an unwritten thing, I should say more of an unsaid thing that, like: 'Okay, well hey! We met up with each other, let's go do some crime and make some money, make some money to go drink.'
So we just started saying, 'Okay, well, let's go do something; let's go find some booze or let's go find some cash.' And so, yeah, that's what we did; we took off and we headed up to 8th Street on the east side to go cruise around there and see we can get. And, like, you know, being up there was pretty much uneventful, you know, like, we didn't really find too much shit to get into, eh? And, so, I had a pair of gloves – we were gonna go sell them to Neil's older brother Marcel, so we made our way back up to this side of the river."

In material obtained under Freedom of Information (FOI) legislation, a person whose identity was concealed told Operation Ferric that he had done B & Es with Neil for five or six years. Shortly before his death, Neil had attempted a B & E, police tracked him back to a house where they managed to find him in the basement, hiding in a freezer. This person added: "Neil could be abusive if drinking."

Boarding a city bus, they met Neil's ex-girlfriend, Lucille Neetz and her new boyfriend, Gary Horse. Stonechild had dated Neetz until the day they learned they were close relatives. Jason Roy continued his account, revealing something I had not heard before:

"Neil just hated that so much, because he really loved her and he really cared for her and he was just torn apart that he couldn't be with her.

Q: Were they first cousins?

A: No, more than that, more than that. [If Roy is correct, that means Neil and Lucille were either half-siblings with one shared parent, or they were brother and sister. Why didn't the RCMP learn that?] They were related and so she didn't want to be with him. But it really tore him up. And, uh, he kind of had a hate on for Gary [Horse] 'cause Gary could be with her and he couldn't. And so we started talking, and Gary was always my friend. He's more like a brother to me, Gary Horse.

You know, like, no conflict or confrontation arose while we were on the bus, but you could just kind of tell from Neil's demeanor that he was, uh, pissed off; he didn't like the fact of seeing them together. And we were talking and then they told us that they were gonna go babysit at her sister's place in Snowberry Downs...."

They went to Stonechild's house, by some reports arriving at the residence in a car, even though neither owned a car. Marcel bought the vodka for the teens (not of legal drinking age) so they could go out partying. Neil had a phone conversation with Pat Pickard, the operator of his group home for young offenders. She wanted Neil to turn himself in, but he said he had already been drinking and wanted to go out for one more night partying and would turn himself in the following day by 1 p.m.

Pickard was a designated "peace officer in and for the Province of Saskatchewan." When she confirmed that he was at the Bignell residence, she had a duty of care to Stonechild – either to take custody of him or notify police of his whereabouts. Either move might have prevented the tragedy; she did neither. Nor did she report any suspicion of police involvement in Neil's death, although 10 years later she would claim she had. Yet no one would take her to task.

Although it was too small for him, Neil borrowed his brother's jacket to wear. Stella Bignell told the inquiry that, calling him by his nickname, she had said, "Harry, you have to be careful. It's stormy. Please stay inside." Several years earlier, she had told an RCMP investigator, "I think he went out to do a B & E." She did not mention that possibility at the inquiry.

According to Mrs. Bignell, he left about 9 p.m. for the Binning residence three blocks away. Julie Binning would tell RCMP that Neil and her boyfriend, Jason, arrived about 9 or 10, already "pretty drunk." Neil's aunt and uncle would testify at the inquiry that a late-1970s model General Motors vehicle, possibly a Nova, was at the Stonechild residence and they may have caught a ride to the Binnings in that. (A call was made to police about midnight that same night: three males were trying to push someone into a car matching the Nova description at the Husky House on the corner of Circle Drive and Idylwyld Drive. That was a 40-minute walk from O'Regan Crescent, and 20 to 25 blocks from where Stonechild's body was found. When police attended, however, the males were GOA. There is no evidence that the RCMP later verified whether or not that Nova information was relevant to the Stonechild case. This despite Julie Binning telling Warner that when Jason Roy returned to her home without Stonechild, "I think he said he… he… he saw them putting him in the…in the back of the police car and then… but ah… we're ah… we're trying to find out if he remembered any number or anything like on the police car but he … he said he was really drunk and he couldn't remember anything and he wasn't sure if it was the police or not….")

At the Binning's, according to Roy's written statement, they drank most of the 40-ounce bottle of vodka between the two of them.

Jason Roy explained to me:

"And there was a house that my girlfriend [16-year-old Cheryl Antoine] was living at, up in Confederation on Milton Street, and I stayed there with her off and on. My girlfriend was pregnant with my oldest daughter at the time, and, uh, we went there and started just sitting around playing cards with Sharon Night and my ex, Cheryl, and me and Neil. And we're drinking for a few hours; there's just me and Neil drinking – Cheryl was pregnant and Sharon didn't want to drink.

I didn't realize it at the time, but Neil was fuming about meeting up with them. And he had it going on in his head about Lucille. And as we started getting a little more inebriated, now it just started hitting him more and he wanted to do something about it; he wanted to go and see her, I guess was his plan; just go see her and talk to her.

Q: How long before that had they broken up?

A: I'm not sure. But he was still raw about it. And then all of a sudden Neil says: Well, let's, I'm gonna, he says, he asked me, let's go see Lucille and Gary. And I says, you know, I didn't want to do it – it was freezing out. It was, like, it was colder than minus 25, [at midnight, with wind-chill, the temperature was –29.8 C[97]] and, you know, like, it was night time and I said – I tried to talk him out of it, that I didn't want – I said, you know, 'What for, man? Like, they're babysitting!' He says, well, he was saying that he wanted to just go see her and talk to her. And I told him, and he knew that Gary was there and who knows whatever woulda happened like, if they woulda found each other, if they woulda fought or whatever. But I couldn't talk him outta wanting to go. And so, finally I just resigned myself to the fact that he was gonna go whether I liked it or not. And I didn't want him to go, go alone. And so we got suited up and dressed up as warm as we could with what we had, and we headed out into the night."

At the inquiry, Roy discussed another reason they went out that night:

Fox: "And one of the possibilities to obtain more -- more liquor would be to -- to do a Break and Enter and either find some liquor in the place you broke into or get some money that will let you buy some more liquor?

A: Yes.

Q: And when you left there, that wouldn't have been your prime objective, to use your words, but it was one of your objectives that, we're going to get some more liquor, and a B and E would be a way of doing it?

A: Well, if I can explain that, that wasn't our primary objective. It was just one of those things where, if it happened to came along, great; if it didn't, oh, well."

Roy also described the weather leading to their dropping into the 7-Eleven: "The snow was blowing pretty hard and the snow was relatively – it was like, up to the ankles anyway, so it probably took within – took about ten minutes."

Meanwhile, Const. Brad Senger had started his shift at 7 p.m., assigned the downtown beat (foot) patrol. (A group of retired police officers working with Police Association President Stan Goertzen developed a PowerPoint presentation, complete with maps and photos, which outlines the documented timeline from that night: www.whenpolicebecomeprey.com/PowerPoint.) Hartwig started his shift at 8, working alone in his regular patrol area in Saskatoon's west end. He was dispatched at 9:47 p.m. to the 300 block of Tache Crescent to attend a call regarding a missing girl who had threatened to kill herself. He attended the scene, took information for a report, checked another address and looked around in an effort to locate the missing girl. He cleared the call at 10:28.

Hartwig's regular partner had been seconded to other duties, which left Hartwig working alone in his district. SPS officers work alone during the day but partner up at 11:00 p.m. for night shifts (the result of RCMP Const. King's murder). In the late evening of November 24, 1990, Senger was assigned to work with Hartwig for the rest of the night. The two officers did not know each other well, and this would be the first time they would work together.

Hartwig drove to the downtown police station where he arrived at approximately 10:43 p.m. He picked up Senger in Car #38, and started heading to the West side when they were dispatched to a suspicious vehicle in the 200 block of Tache Crescent at 10:52 p.m. The caller stated that there was an intoxicated male passed out behind the wheel of a running vehicle and he had been there for approximately three hours.

Hartwig and Senger arrived at the scene at 10:59 p.m. They spoke to the young Aboriginal male and instead of arresting him and charging him with a criminal offense; they decided to drive him home to the 1000 block McCormack Road. They cleared the call at 11:18 p.m. and drove to the 300 block Havilland Crescent (bottom left of map), arriving at 11:34 to conduct a property check. Hartwig had been there frequently and knew that address was subject to chronic nuisance (unfounded) complaints; they spent approximately five minutes checking the area.

In the meantime, Neil Stonechild and Jason Roy left the Binning residence at 3269 Milton Street, just off Confederation Dive. Some witnesses, including Neil's own mother, told RCMP that when he left the house, Neil said he and Roy were going out to do a B & E to get more liquor. This Break-and-Enter allegation was completely omitted from the RCMP investigative summary submitted to Sask Justice. Instead, remarkably, the RCMP chose to write about only the other two reports: "Neil wanted to go look for Lucille Neetz, his old girlfriend and cousin, and perhaps to get snacks from 7-Eleven."

By Roy's account, they went to find Neil's ex-girlfriend. Cheryl Antoine testified that Neil told her and Julie Binning (whom Neil had recently begun dating) that they were going out for "munchies."

They went to the area of the Snowberry Downs apartment complex in the 3300 block of 33rd Street West (on the map, just north of 33rd St., above Cartier Cres.). Snowberry Downs consists of three large apartment buildings, each containing 60 suites.

Jason Roy continued with his account to me:

"We went walking towards Snowberry Downs, and we both didn't know where we were going, we just knew we were going to Snowberry Downs. It

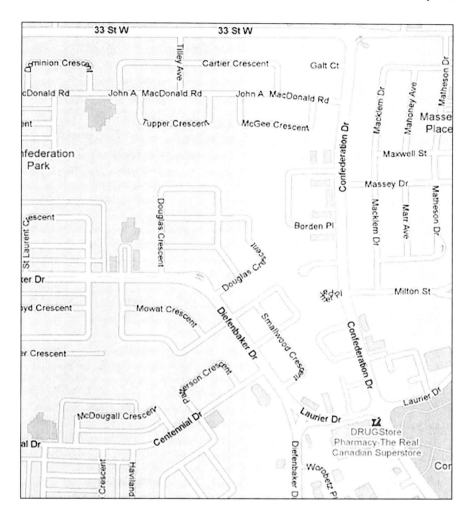

was cold, so we stopped at the 7-Eleven across the street from Snowberry Downs and warmed up for a while. The kinda deal that I struck up with him was that, 'OK, if we didn't find Lucille's sister's [Claudine Neetz, later Claudine Wright] boyfriend's name, Trent Ewart, in the directories, then we would go back.'

So we went to the buzzers, looking for the name, Trent Ewart. We got around to the first one, looked, buzzed a few buzzers, I guess, you know, I'm pretty sure we did, probably did. And, uh, when we got to the next building, where we did the same. We talked to a few people but, ya know, we got denied and rejected, whatever, 'cause nobody knew us and obviously we were drinking. And, uh, so we went around the whole complex to each buzzer, and we didn't find them, and so I tried to talk him into going back to Jule's – that's the girl's name where we were at, Julie Binning.

I was, you know, trying to persuade him into coming back to the house there. And he was very, very adamant and wanted to keep looking for Lucille. He still wanted to look for her. And, you know, I thought, 'OK, well, if I just kind of, uh, just say, "Well, OK I'm gonna go, and you go and keep looking," maybe he'll come along with me.' So I tried that with him and I says, 'OK well, I'm gonna go, I'm going back to Jule's,' and he says, 'Well, go ahead, go then!'

"So I made like I was gonna walk away. And he obviously was still gonna go look for her, no matter if I went with him or not. Um, so we walked a few steps apart from each other, and I kinda thought, 'OK, well, he's not gonna come, so I better turn around here.' So I started calling after him, and I was saying, 'OK, well just wait then, c'mon, like, I'll come with you.' And he's saying, like, 'F--- that!' and 'Never mind , that's OK, just go your own way, just go back to Jule's,' he's telling me, 'Just go ahead and go back, I'll do it myself!'

And so I started, I turned around to go chase after him, and I was calling after him, and then he seen that I was gonna come – I dunno if he seen me or whatever but, I was starting to go towards him – and I, I started running, going towards him and I tripped and I fell. And I seen him. He turned the corner, and I got up and I was yelling at him for him to come and, uh, to come and to wait for me and I was gonna come with him. And (tsk) he wouldn't wait for me. He just wanted to keep on going. And, he's telling me just to go back to Jule's, like, "Just go!" And he kept trying to run away from me. He kept just trying to go his own way. And I was running to get him to wait for me, but he kept—yeah, I dunno if he found it to be a game or what; whatever he was trying to do or whatever he was trying to pull, you know, and I was trying to stick with him. But he just kept taking off on me and, uh, I was yelling for him and I could hear him off in the distance, saying just to go and to f--- off or whatever, and I could hear him in the distance 'cause it was an apartment complex and it was winter so things were echoing pretty good, and I could hear him but I really couldn't tell which way he was coming from. (Sigh) And, uh, I tell you, I circled the buildings looking for him again; I went circling around again. And, uh, yelling for him.

Q: Was he terribly drunk?"
A: Well, no, we weren't that drunk! We weren't that drunk, you know, like,
obviously I'm remembering, I can remember everything that happened.
I went around the building again. I went around the building and then I
went to the 7-Eleven across the street, and I stayed there and I warmed
up and I waited for a while. I waited as long as I could."
[In his first statement to police five days after this incident, Roy had
said that he was so drunk that he blacked out and couldn't remember
anything that happened after leaving Neil. He later told the inquiry
"Well, he [Stonechild] was pretty well out of it."]

After Roy left, Stonechild gained entry to one of the buildings at Snowberry Downs. After banging on a number of doors, either guided by tenants or strictly accidentally, he walked into the correct apartment, unannounced. That tenant, Trent Ewart had just arrived home after a night of drinking, and according to his statement, grabbed Stonechild and pushed him out the door. Stonechild was seen in the hallway a few minutes later by the occupants of the Ewart apartment, Lucille Neetz and Gary Horse.

11:49 p.m., Trent Ewart called the SPS to report that Neil Stonechild was drunk and causing problems at his residence. Other tenants also called to complain.

11:51 p.m., Hartwig and Senger were dispatched to a disturbance call at 3308 - 33rd Street West where Neil Stonechild was drunk and causing problems. They arrived in the area at 11:56 p.m. and immediately checked Jason Roy who was leaving the area on foot. Jason Roy lied about who he was and stated his name was Tracy Lee Horse of 418 Avenue I South, Date Of Birth (DOB) April 19, 1973. The name Tracy Lee Horse was queried by DOB on CPIC at **11:56 p.m.** by Senger. Since Hartwig and Senger were looking for Neil Stonechild, his name was also queried by approximate age (18 years). Querying the subject of a call is routine, as an officer would testify at the inquiry, in order to determine if the subject is wanted on outstanding warrants, if there are any court-ordered conditions the person was to abide by, or to obtain a physical description of the person being queried.[98] Hartwig and Senger confirmed that Stonechild had a warrant for his arrest for being Unlawfully at Large. Jason Roy was sent on his way.

At the time of Stonechild's death, Roy was only 16, but already had accumulated a lengthy criminal record and numerous criminal associates, was actively abusing alcohol and marijuana, and been in and out of custody for years. Roy continued with his account to me:

"I waited for him [Neil, at the 7-Eleven], and he didn't come. I started walking back to Jule's, walking down Confederation Drive (sigh). All of a sudden there, you could kind of see the shadows of a car coming down the alley, just as I was hitting the one alley. And as I got closer to the alley, that car got closer to the alley, and that car was a police car. As it pulled up to where we, we all met, we met at the corner, and, uh, the car pulled up, I got there and obviously what I do and, like, what we all do, is, like, we see if there's anybody in the car. And that's what I did; I saw him. That's where Neil was. He was in the back of the cop car. And he was pissed off; he was really pissed off, right away you could tell. He was agitated about being there, and, you know, I just kinda—and I, I was wanted at the time, I know I was wanted, for whatever, whatever reason. There wasn't a time in my youth where I wasn't probably either wanted or in jail. And so, uh, I pull up to the cop car, and the cop asked me who I was, and I just, uh, I told him my name was Tracy, Tracy Horse – this is Gary's brother. And I gave him Tracy's birthday, 'cause I knew that Tracy was, you know, he's a straight-Joe kinda guy where he didn't get into trouble and, ya know, he wasn't any kind of, he wasn't another criminal element, I guess. And, uh, I used his name and then they checked the name, and as this is all going on, Neil's in the back of the cop car, and as soon as he heard that I was using a different name, he was just saying something about, you know, like—the order in the way in which it went down, you know, like, getting in the car, and (long pause) Neil was, like I said, Neil was obviously pissed off about being in the back of that cop car. And, uh, he just started freaking out. And then, once he realized and, uh, he heard that I was using a different name, he was saying, "Oh Jason, don't lie about your name! Just tell em who you are!" And I was just trying to, ya know, tell him, ya know, "Keep it down, ya know, relax man, I'm gonna go to jail, too, here if you keep bugging me, keep acting up here," ya know.
Q: But when he said, "Don't lie about your name," didn't the police get upset?
A: Yeah yeah yeah, no no, they, they, they just said, 'Well, what's your name?' And I said, 'Well, my name's Tracy Horse,' and they checked it out or whatever. Back then they just had little, really simple computers in their

cars, not anything near what they have today. So they only had limited information about what Tracy Horse looked like, eh, if they even knew what Tracy Horse looked like because Tracy doesn't have a criminal record. And, uh, so they had no other choice but, you know, I was telling them my name and half the time, like I just, I didn't carry a wallet or anything so I didn't have no ID, and, so, you know, they had to take what I was saying as, as what I was saying. And this whole time, you know, Neil's freaking out, and he's pissed off and he's bleeding. And then they checked my name—they checked that name—and they, uh. And then, uh, I asked them what they were doing with that guy—they asked me if I knew him and I said no. I'm ignoring him, because, if I did, then they would put two and two together, you know, that he's obviously using a different name. So, uh, they had to just, they just, they let me go."

In this interview with me, Jason Roy did not mention anything about Stonechild being handcuffed, or yelling, "They're going to kill me!"

Here is how Roy was quoted anonymously in the February 22, 2000 *StarPhoenix* story in which his allegation first became public:

"A few minutes later while the friend was walking south along Diefenbaker Drive, he says two police officers drove up to him from an alley. The officers asked for his name and they asked if he knew the young man sitting in the back of the car. The young man in custody was Neil Stonechild.

The friend says he gave a false name to police and denied he knew Stonechild, who was swearing and bleeding in the back seat. The friend says he lied because he was wanted by police at the time and he already had a lengthy criminal record.

'Neil was screaming my name, telling me to help him. Seeing him sitting in the car like that, I was in no position to want to get in that car with him. So I lied,' he said.

'I know it was him. I couldn't be more positive. He was screaming my name. It couldn't have been anyone else.'

As the car drove away, the friend says Stonechild swore and screamed: 'They're gonna kill me, they're gonna kill me.'"

This is how RCMP investigators reported what Roy told them in 2000:

ROY's recollection was that there were two officers in the vehicle and one of them asked if he knew who the person was in the back of the police car.

ROY told the officers he did not know the name of the person, fearing that to identify him would possibly identify himself and that he would be arrested on the outstanding warrant.

STONECHILD began pleading with ROY to tell them who he was but ROY maintained his denial that he did not know who STONECHILD was.

ROY was then asked by the police officers what his name was and he provided the name of Tracy Horse and a date of birth of 1973.04.19.

ROY advised that the police officers did a CPIC check of that name and he was allowed to go.

Other observations which ROY made at the time were that STONECHILD was handcuffed and had an injury to his face which was bleeding. [Roy's actual words: "gushing blood." Did the RCMP repress those words because none of the medical or police officials who dealt with Stonechild's body saw any evidence of blood on his clothes?]

Roy described the injury as being a diagonal cut starting below one eye and running across the bridge of his nose. He was uncertain as to whether it was left to right or right to left.

The police vehicle drove away and ROY's last recollection of him was STONECHILD screaming at him, "They're going to kill me."[99]

Hartwig and Senger then left the back alley, drove to their right (south) down Confederation Drive, made a U-turn around the median, and drove back to within a block of where they had spoken to Roy, where they stopped a second young man. Eight minutes after CPIC-ing "Tracy Horse" (actually Jason Roy), they checked a second male leaving the area on foot. He identified himself as Bruce Genaille, 23. Senger did not believe Genaille was telling the truth and challenged him further about being Neil Stonechild; he was able to produce ID (without a photo), was queried by Hartwig on CPIC with a DOB, and when results were returned with no warrants out for his arrest, he, too, was sent on his way. Genaille later told the task force:

"I was stopped by two city officers and they motioned me to come over to their car and they asked me who I was and I told them who I was and they asked me again, "Are you Stonechild?" Well, they asked me for my IDs and I showed them my IDs. They were askin' me, "Are you sure you're not Neil Stonechild?" "Yeah, I'm sure. That's my cousin," I told them. And they asked me again... like... it's like they didn't believe me."

If Stonechild had been in the back of their car, would the police have been so insistent with Genaille that he was actually Stonechild? Genaille later testified that while he spoke to the police for five to 10 minutes, he saw no one in the back seat. Stan Goertzen says, "Genaille was checked about a block from where Jason Roy was checked. He saw no one in the rear seat. Jason Roy is a liar, in my opinion."

Warner also asked Genaille:

"When you were travelling around at that time, just before and just after the police spoke with you, Bruce, do you have any recollection of seeing any other people around that you knew, walking on the street or driving? Genaille: Uhm-mmm [negative]. I just went to Guy's place and I didn't see anybody else. After there I just came home about...probably two in the morning or something like that. I didn't see anybody else."

Hartwig and Senger then attended to Ewart's apartment, where he confirmed that Neil Stonechild had left several minutes earlier, after being told that the police had been called. According to SIMS records [Saskatoon Information Management System], Hartwig and Senger cleared the call at 12:17 a.m. and noted that Neil Stonechild was GOA, Gone on Arrival.

At 12:18 a.m. they were dispatched to a suspicious person hiding in a yard several blocks away, at 118 O'Regan Crescent. The caller had arrived home shortly before 11:56 p.m., when she noticed a suspicious person hiding beside the driveway, and actually chased the person away. She phoned 911 at 11:56 p.m. – the very same minute Jason Roy was being checked by police, and when, he later claimed, he had seen Stonechild in the cruiser.

The description of the person hiding in the yard on O'Regan Crescent matched that of Neil Stonechild, as a witness later revealed to me. He could easily have made it to that area within the seven-minute time period between when he was last seen at Snowberry Downs (23:49) and when a woman called 911 about a male crouched beside her driveway (23:56). Having driven from Snowberry the five blocks to O'Regan in about eight minutes (which included first having to turn the wrong direction to go around a centre median), I tried running from outside Snowberry Downs, and found that a series of interconnecting walkways provided shortcuts between streets and actually "funnelled" me into O'Regan Crescent, two blocks away. I did it in 3 minutes, 12 seconds.

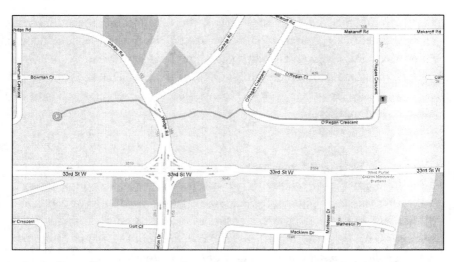

Route for walking or running from Snowberry Downs on left to 118 O'Regan:

Driving route (Maps courtesy Saskatoon City Police Association)

Stonechild would have known about the pedestrian shortcuts, because as witness told RCMP Const. Warner, he knew the area well:

"Const. Warner: Can you comment whether or not... or whether you believe... Neil was known to the police that... that worked that area? Witness: Yes. He was... 'cause ahh... all we... when we got into trouble, we usually picked the Confederation area 'cause ahh... we knew the area, like the back of our hands. We knew all the ins and outs, we knew all the walkways, all the catwalks [paved walkways between houses leading from one street to another, wide enough for pedestrians and bikes only,

so they are not forced to travel the long, car-route around] ... *we knew the back alleys, we knew different routes through yards and stuff like that... ways of getting away from cops. So Confederation Park was our choice of... trouble making. And ahh... we knew like, as long as we ahh... if we were to go to another area, we would get lost. We would get caught right away if we went and did... something in another area of town.*"

In a more formal time-trial than mine, Sgt. Goertzen had two men, each about Stonechild's height of 5'8", walk the further distance from the door of apartment 306 at Snowberry Downs, down the stairs and through the walkways to 118 O'Regan Crescent. It took them 4 minutes, 14 seconds. Tacking on 40 seconds as the approximate time for the woman at O'Regan to chase after the prowler and then return home to phone 911, it adds up to 5 minutes. If Stonechild had run the same direction I did, he would have had seven to eight minutes to make that run, according to the documented timeline.

Hartwig and Senger arrived at O'Regan Crescent at 12:24 a.m. Knowing the suspicious male had run away almost half an hour earlier, they searched three minutes and cleared the call at 12:27 a.m., listing the suspicious person as GOA.

Jason Roy, meanwhile, returned to the Binning home where he and Stonechild previously had been drinking. When asked, "Where's Neil?" some witnesses claimed, 10 years later, that Roy replied he didn't know; other witnesses that he said they had become separated and he didn't know what had happened to him; still others, that Stonechild got "picked up." This would have been a logical conclusion considering the disturbance that Neil Stonechild caused at Snowberry Downs, combined with the fact that Roy himself was subsequently checked by Hartwig and Senger.

Hartwig and Senger went on working throughout the early morning hours, taking six more calls together in five hours before their seventh call, at 5:28 a.m. At that time they were dispatched to advise a woman that her two young sons had been shot by her estranged husband. That call, neither officer would ever forget.

CHAPTER 13 - Was Stonechild Really in that Police Car? Or was he this 'Suspicious Person' Hiding Nearby?

'Was Neil Stonechild actually a couple of blocks away from where Jason Roy claimed to have seen him at 11:56 p.m.? Probably.'
– Sgt. Stan Goertzen

In 1990, Saskatoon insurance claims officer Darlene Nadeau and her husband owned a home in Dundonald subdivision near Snowberry Downs.[100] In 2009, as she and I stood viewing her former home, she recalled the night of November 24, 1990, when, around midnight, she was alarmed to discover someone hiding in the yard:

"This is our old residence, 118 O'Regan Crescent. That evening we – my husband Wayne and the Grigoroviches, Ken and Shelly – came home from a concert. There was a truck in the driveway just like the one that's there now, but it was parked a little bit back from this one. We drove into the driveway and in between the back of my husband's truck and the bushes, that's where the gentleman was crouched. As we came into the driveway, it was night and our lights hit him, and I think it kind of spooked him. He was crouched down but we could see his legs in between the tires and the bush. From my memory, Shelly got out of the car and yelled at him, "Hey! What are you doing?" He popped up when Shelly opened the door and screamed something out to him. There was no fence there [beside him] at that time, and he dashed off to our right, down the street toward the south and then took off west toward that church over there. Shelly ran after him and my recollection of what she later said was: she passed the church and went a couple of houses down. I don't know that from sight, just from her telling me that. I just know they ran off into that direction and the last I saw, she was passing the next-door neighbour's house and going on toward the next one.

Shelly said that he dove into someone's yard on the same side of the street as the church, and she got kind of spooked; she didn't want to follow him in there. My thought was that he was trying to get out of a residential street that he thought he was going to get locked into.

After Shelly took off, my memory is that her husband, Ken stayed outside, because I think he was concerned that his wife took off after a strange guy. My husband, Wayne, and I immediately went into the house because we thought he had been either attempting to break into our house or he was exiting our house and that we caught him on the way out, so we thought there was a possible Break-and-Enter there.

We were kind of laughing at her because we thought she was being kind of crazy and she just said: Well, I wasn't going to chase him into the back yard because that was getting kind of crazy because it wasn't in an open place then.

Q: Can you describe the guy in the driveway?

A: He had long, dark hair, probably shoulder-length or just past shoulder-length because I could see a few strands just on the front part of his shoulder as he crouched. Definitely not dressed for winter, because it was cold out. I remember what I thought looked like a very small blue jean jacket – just one of those little short jackets that just come down to the top of your blue jeans. It was a dark jacket and it was open. He was thin, of average height, not what you would consider tall or short, so shorter than five foot-ten or -eleven [Stonechild was 5'8"]. And he was Aboriginal; that was definite.

I just got a quick glimpse of him, but if I close my eyes and think back about what he looked like, I wouldn't have thought he was 17. He looked young, but he looked like he had had a little bit of a hard life. It's hard to tell peoples' ages sometimes.[101]

The only pictures I had seen of Neil Stonechild, up until the point of meeting you, were pictures in the newspaper. They had the same picture run over and over and over; Stonechild at a lot younger age than 17. He looked fairly young, like it was a school picture. And the person that I saw didn't look like a little kid, or as though he had short hair, and I think that's one of the reasons I never really thought of it. The picture in the paper looked like an innocent child that might be a little mischievous, but not into crime. The guy I saw looked 20, 21. He was definitely a young person, he just looked like he had not treated himself well in his life. You can tell if people are hard on themselves – drink hard or drug hard or live on the street. Looked like he had been hard on his body. You could tell he was a young man but he looked like his body had aged beyond his actual years. You can't make a judgment call, but the person I saw pop up, if I had seen him walk down the street, I would have thought he was capable of robbery, and that he drank too much because you could tell that physically, he just wasn't in good shape. It was a totally different thing than I was seeing in the paper.

Q: *Did he appear to be intoxicated?*

A: *Well, he wasn't falling-down drunk because he ran faster than Shelly!*

Q: *When you heard a few days later that Neil Stonechild had frozen to death, did it occur to you that that person you saw might have been?*

A: *Not at all. Actually I didn't even refer back to that night at all. The first indication that I had that the two events were on the same night was [10 years later] in 2000, when the RCMP officer who was investigating for the inquiry came to my door where I currently live and asked to speak to me regarding that evening when we reported this to the police department.*

Q: *What did the RCMP officer say?*

A: *He, to my memory, just announced himself, and gave me his card, but I don't remember who he was and I don't have the card any longer. He didn't start with anything about Stonechild. He referred back to the evening in question and I think he started with: Are you Darlene Nadeau; is your husband Wayne Nadeau? Then he asked if I had resided at 118 O'Regan Crescent on such and such a date, which I had. Then he asked if I remembered phoning the police for having someone at my residence. At first I absolutely looked at him and said, "No," because I didn't remember anything happening. Then he said: I believe it was Shelly Grigorovich who phoned the police that night reporting that you had seen someone outside your residence. And all of a sudden it kind of clicked. He asked me if I remembered the particulars and I really didn't, so he asked me if I knew Ken and Shelly Grigorovich. He had been phoning the right Shelly Grigorovich but she thought he was phoning the wrong one.*

So I phoned Shelly while he was there and asked her if she had remembered calling the police from my home and she started to laugh and said, 'Yeah, don't you remember? That was the night I chased that guy down the street!' And that went BOOM because that I remembered! We had teased her about that for a while. Other than that I would never have connected the two. I never really followed the case. My comments and my husband's and Ken Grigorovich's comments to the RCMP were obviously not significant enough to have us testify at the inquiry. Shelly must have had more information because she had run after him and had her eyes on him longer and probably had a better description of him. But I never have spent a whole long time thinking about it until you contacted me.

Q: Did you see the police come looking for him after you called 911?

A: No. We just went on with our evening and played some cards, is what I think we did. We didn't watch for the police. We just assumed that if they wanted to talk to us, they would ring the doorbell. It didn't surprise me that they didn't because really, we were just saying that we saw someone in our driveway but we didn't find anything broken into or anything missing, we were just reporting it because we know there was a suspicious guy in the neighbourhood. It would make more sense if they just drove around the neighbourhood to see if they could find him. There's no burglary for them to talk to someone about or put in an occurrence report. [In addition (see Stonechild Timeline), the officers did not receive their dispatch to this address until 14 minutes after Grigorovich's 911 call; they continued searching for Neil Stonechild at Snowberry Downs for another 8 minutes, and did not arrive on scene until 6 minutes after that. They would have known that the likelihood of success in finding him, 28 minutes after he was spotted, was slim. Indeed, three minutes after arriving at 118 O'Regan, they cleared that call, signalling they were ready for the next.]

Q: Did you often see Aboriginal youths in your neighbourhood?

A: Not often. Previous to that, but I'm not sure how many years earlier, we had had someone attempt to break in and the neighbour on the right-hand side had actually caught him. There was an Aboriginal person crouched between my husband's motorcycle and the window, trying to pry the window open. Instead of calling the police, she actually walked into our back yard and tapped him on the back and confronted him. She was 50-some years old; he pushed her aside and ran. She ran out into the street after him, our other neighbour was pulling up across the street and she yelled at him and they chased the guy with a car, but no one was caught.

Other than that, we never had any problems; I've never seen anyone of any kind or sort in the neighbourhood. However, our neighbours had had some break-ins a few weeks prior to us seeing this gentleman on our property, so that was another reason why we called. Nothing significant was stolen, just cigarettes, pocket change and alcohol, which made it look like it was probably kids. But their dog had been kicked and brutally beaten. And that was why Wayne and I were so panicked, not so much for our property, but because we had a little tiny dog in the house and we thought if it was the same characters, they might have hurt our dog.

Q: Did anyone in the neighbourhood get broken into that night – either before or after you saw this person? A: No. [If he had not committed a crime, what other reason could this person have had for hiding, unless hiding from the police he knew were looking for him?]

Q: Do you think that might have been Neil Stonechild you saw?

A: It wouldn't have been hard to go from Snowberry Downs to our yard. He could have been just hopping fences, not wanting to break in, but just exiting Snowberry Downs. If you're inebriated, you just do what you do. And it's a quicker way to cut cross-country than going all the way around on the sidewalks. I did think of that – I just thought, "It's not so impossible that somebody would have left Snowberry Downs and entered our yard. It's very easily done." But who that person was, I guess I'll never know.

Q: It's tough to estimate times. I ran through the walkways from Snowberry Downs to your house and I thought it would take a long time but it only took a few minutes. So maybe what we could do is, I could just run as far as you think it would have been and we could time it?

A: That would give us an idea. Shelly would have been quick because she was in her twenties at the time and athletic. She golfed and roller-bladed and played ball. Her dad was inducted into the Sports Hall of Fame for being a baseball player. Her whole family was athletic and physically fit. Alright, the distance would have been to where that car is, and back. I'll time you with the second hand on my watch. When I put my finger down, go!

~ ~ ~

Q: (Gasp... gasp...) How long did that take?

A: That took you, for approximately the same amount of distance, 40 seconds. To go there and back.

Q: When you think about it, could it have taken Shelly that long?

A: You know, if it only took 40 seconds for you to do this, it could have been very plausible because she got out of the car, she yelled at him, he bolted, she ran after him, turned around, ran back. I don't know if she stood there for a while or not, but I don't think so because I remember her saying to me that when he ducked into the back yard, it kind of spooked her because she thought, "Well now I'm going to be in the dark because there are no street lights in the back yard. He could have ducked around a corner and be waiting to attack me." So all of a sudden, I think it clicked in. So I can't see her standing there for long if she was worried about him doing something to her. So if she jumped out of the car, said, "Hey! What are you doing?" And then he bolted, she ran after him, then ran back, came into the house, I think she probably asked, "Did anyone break in?" or whatever, and then I can see something being said to the effect of, "We better phone the cops in case he breaks into someone else's house." And then she would have probably dialled the phone and that would have been it.

Q: So let's look at the documented timeline ....

A: Trent Ewart's call came into the police at 11:49, and our call came in at 11:56, so that's seven minutes later. And Stonechild could have left before Ewart called. I was thinking that the timing was right: it would have taken him a few minutes to run here, Shelly would have chased him down the street and run back in 40 seconds, I think she phoned the police pretty much when she walked in the door, so it makes sense. That could have all been done easily under seven minutes. Whether that's what happened or not, I don't know. But it's a possibility.

To what does Nadeau attribute her remarkably detailed memory of the 1990 event? "Both personality and training. I have worked with the city in legal matters, and now in the insurance industry I have an investigative role to determine fraud and investigate the causes of loss. I've learned to pay attention to detail as well as the larger picture, looking for things around the situation to see whether they support what the person is saying in their statement, or not. That becomes part of who you are."

A note in the RCMP file states: "Const. WARNER drove by the O'Regan address and it was observed that the location was within a couple blocks of Snowberry Downs." From that information, it appears that Warner recognized the importance of the complainants' testimonies. Quite simply, they might have proven the accused police innocent.

Next is the manner in which Mountie Ken Lyons, by now promoted to Staff Sergeant, handled one of the most crucial interviews in the entire investigation. Here was an independent, unbiased witness who did not know the RCMP officer was inquiring about Stonechild, or even an Aboriginal person, yet her description matched Stonechild's to a significant degree. If someone with Stonechild's descriptors had been hiding in Nadeau's yard at 11:56 p.m., then it was far less likely Stonechild could have been bleeding in a police car four blocks away at the same time, 11:56 p.m., as Jason Roy later claimed.

RCMP statement of [Darlene Nadeau]   2001/07/19

"Lyons: [Redacted], the call to service at your old residence on O'Regan, what can you remember about that? And, uh... before you begin, I'll just get you to go back and explain, as best as you can recall, who you may have been with and what was going on at the time.

Nadeau: Okay. Uh... yeah, like when you and I first talked, I didn't actually recall anything that night but I did contact the lady who made the call, [Redacted, Shelly Grigorovich], and this is kind of based off of what she said. Now, I don't really know if this is the night that this event happened. I just know that this event did happen and we're assuming that it may be the night in question of November 25 [sic], 1990. Okay? I think that's important for you to know, that we're not sure of dates, or...

Q: Exactly

A: ...years or whatever. We're just takin' a wild stab...

Q: And that's understandable

A: ...at it. She had some recollection and it took me a little while to recall some of it but from what I remember, we believe we were coming back from a concert and, uh...that's kind of where it all begins, but uh...there was an event that happened with [Shelly, Wayne, Ken] and I and we're thinking this may be the event because we can't recall anything else where we were coming back from some place with them. Uh... my husband and I had a really long, narrow driveway beside our house on O'Regan, uh...and a garage at the end and he had his truck parked on the driveway beside our house. We pulled up on the driveway, it was late in the evening or early morning, and when the headlights of the vehicle we were in shone on the back of my husband's truck, we noticed that there was a person crouching on the passenger rear side of the truck near the box, kind of jammed... we had a row of Potentillas that were all the way down the driveway, and in the winter the snow would pile up against them and the person was kind of jammed in between the truck and this mound of snow.

Q: Okay.

A: And what I remember is pulling up and [Shelly] who, I believe, was in the front passenger side of the car, was the nearest to him and saw him first and I remember her saying, "Oh, what is that? There's somebody crouched beside your truck." And as we started opening up the doors, we startled the person and he stood up and why I remember that is because he turned and he kind of fumbled over the mound of snow over these Potentillas and kind of got a little…

Q: Okay.

A: …tangled up. I was in the back seat but that's kind of why I got a glimpse of the person at all because he kind of got tangled up in that clump of snow.

Q: Okay. … What do you remember of, uh…

A: Well, it's kind of funny…

Q: …of that?

A: …cause if I close my eyes I can have a little image of him and…and stuff, but it's really brief. Uh… from what I can remember, he may or may not have been native. If the police had interviewed me that night, my impression probably would have been that he was native.

Q: Okay.

A: Uh… but he may not have been. The reason why I'm saying that is cause I…he… wasn't blond-haired and he was definitely dark-haired, either dark brown or black. It was straight. It was past shoulder-length. Uh…from what I remember seeing he either had a really light jacket on…I believe it was a blue jean jacket or something like that, you may not have been able to easily distinguish. He wasn't dressed for the winter.

Q: It wasn't a heavy coat at any rate?

A: No. The feeling I have strong is that it was not appropriate wear for the winter, but it was a jacket of some type.

Q: Hm-mmm.

A: Open because I…closing my eyes I see a difference between the colour of his shirt and his jacket, you know… like there was a distinction there…

Q: Right.

A: Uh…either khaki canvas or blue jeans and running shoes.

Q: All right. Uh…any headwear? Cap or hat of any sort that you can remember?

A: I don't think so. I just remember the hair…

Q: Yeah.

A: …being longer.

Q: You mentioned a male.

A: It was definitely a male.

Q: Are you able to offer any opinion as to how old he may have been?

A: (pause)

Q: Or...?

A: I would say...I would say definitely, definitely not over forty... could have been anywhere from his dark...he could have been anywhere from twenty-five to thirty-five, thirty-eight.

Q: Hm-mmm.

A: Like it was really hard. Like he was... he was youth...youthful but not necessarily...

Q: A kid...

A: A kid, you know?

Q: I see. Okay, [Shelly] is your friend. Uh... you socialized with her from time to time? ...."

This is how someone within Operation Ferric summarized that interview in seven bullet points (more, below):

"[Darlene Nadeau]

-she believes the group, her husband, [and the Grigoroviches] came to their place from a concert

-they had a long narrow driveway where 3 or 4 vehicles could park"

This was untrue! There was absolutely nothing in Nadeau's statement regarding "where 3 or 4 vehicles could park." This is fabrication of witness information by the RCMP. What could have been their motive? Were they trying to invalidate her information by suggesting she was too far away to see the suspicious person clearly? Asked about this point, Nadeau says today, "The front of our car was almost touching the bumper of the truck, so we were just half the length of a short-box truck away from him."

Intriguingly, the only mention of the numbers "3 or 4" was in the RCMP summary of Grigorovich's– not Nadeau's – statement. That summary claimed *Grigorovich* said the male ran "3 or 4 houses away and cut between some houses." How could the Mounties have transposed those numbers about houses from one person's summary, to another person's summary regarding vehicles? Moreover, here are Shelly Grigorovich's actual words in her taped interview with RCMP Staff Sgt. Lyons:

Lyons: You mentioned, uh...also, that if you drove by that house you'd be able to tell the number [of the house which the male ran behind]. How many houses away from, uh... would it have been...uh...just roughly and really, uh...

[Grigorovich]: Three.

Q: Okay. Would, uh...would you be prepared to do something for me?

A: Sure.

Q: At your leisure, would you drive by and just see if you can pick out the house and the number and let me know what it was?

A: Sure.

Q: Yeah. It doesn't need to be done immediately.

A: I remember it was... it's got, uh, kind of goldy colour siding on it.

Q: Is it on the same side of the street as...?

A: Yes. As [Darlene Nadeau's], yes.

Q: Is there, uh...is there a garage there?

A: (pause)

Q: Well, you'll be able to...

A: I don't believe there is.

Q: ...you'll be able to...

A: ... but uh...

Q: You'll be able to tell me the number anyway and I... I won't bother driving by.

Why would the RCMP officer not take Grigorovich right to the scene of the suspicious person, a mere 20-minute drive away? Why would he ask the witness to do his work – at her leisure? Why, on this crucial matter, which could have helped determine which direction in which the suspicious person – possibly Stonechild – had run, and may have helped the witness to remember more, instead actually say to a witness: "I won't bother driving by"?

The RCMP seven-point summary of Nadeau's statement concludes:

"person was crouched behind her husband's truck [Information repressed. There was nothing in this RCMP summary about the person jumping up and getting tangled in the bushes and snow which, as Nadeau pointed out to the RCMP, gave her the opportunity to observe him.]

person believed to be native (unsure) wearing a jean jacket or light coat and looking cold

[Grigorovich] followed the person for a while before returning to the house

[Darlene Nadeau's] attention was on the house wondering if someone was or had been inside [Suggesting that she did not focus on the person?]

[Nadeau] does not remember police attending or any contact with police, if there was any."

-

Many details in this RCMP summary seem designed to detract from Nadeau's credibility as a witness. In addition to fabrication and repression of information, there is only one line regarding the purpose of the entire five-page interview, which was *to determine whether that suspicious person might have been Neil Stonechild.* That single line reads:*"Person believed to be native (unsure) wearing a jean jacket or light coat and looking cold."* Remarkably, in that one line, there are three important errors or omissions:

1. Nadeau did not ever use the word "coat"; she described a "jacket" (a match with Stonechild). Lyons then introduced the word "coat" and Nadeau corrected him:

Q: It wasn't a heavy coat at any rate?
A: No. The feeling I have strong is that it was not appropriate wear for the winter, ***but it was a jacket of some type.***

How could the RCMP summarizer misconstrue who said what in that interview? Was the summary deliberately written this way (Nadeau said he was "wearing a jean jacket or light coat") to make her memory appear less precise than it was?

2. Nadeau's exact words were: "he wasn't dressed for the winter" (a match with Stonechild); she said nothing about his looking cold, which is useless in identifying Stonechild, since it could apply to anyone. How difficult can it be to summarize accurately from one page to another? However, if the aim were to sabotage Nadeau's information, the summary is a masterpiece.

3. The RCMP summary mentioned nothing about Nadeau's many details which match Stonechild's description: "he was definitely dark-haired, either dark brown or black. It was straight. It was past shoulder-length"; "closing my eyes I see a difference between the colour of his shirt and his jacket, you know... like there was a distinction there" (when found, Stonechild was wearing a blue jacket over a red lumberjack shirt); or the fact that he was

wearing "either khaki canvas or blue jeans and running shoes," or "he either had a really light jacket on…I believe it was a blue jean jacket or something like that." Nothing about: "He was youthful but not necessarily a kid."

In addition, the RCMP could have learned from police records whether Nadeau was correct that there had been no other disturbances in the neighbourhood that night. If the person had not committed a crime, he had to have some other reason for hiding – such as evading a police search.

Would anyone reading this summary believe there was anything useful to be gained by reading Nadeau's interview? In his interview, Lyons did not ask Nadeau which direction the person had run, nor about the person's height, whether he was slim or heavy, or other questions to elicit information she gave me, such as he was shorter than 5'10", thin, the jacket was short, just to the top of his jeans,all of which matched Stonechild's description.

Stan Goertzen comments:

"RCMP investigators would have been trained to dig out the details, but by this time, I believe some of them, Jack Warner in particular and possibly Ken Lyons, seem to have already formed their own opinions that the city police must have done something wrong based on the words of their only so-called witness, Jason Roy (even though Warner and Lyons were aware of a number of lies and inconsistencies in Roy's story by that time). I believe that media pressure, combined with RCMP disinterest due to what they believed they 'already knew' to be facts, resulted in the RCMP not doing a complete and thorough job."

Given the significance of the evidence from 118 O'Regan Crescent, Goertzen questions why the witness interviews were not conducted by lead investigator Warner. "Even when the lead investigator is acting as a file manager and tasking others to investigate, he should be more in touch with things where there is a real possibility of exculpatory evidence that potentially could have exonerated Hartwig and Senger. Lyons probably didn't know the rest of the file and he wasn't the lead investigator. Given Warner's overall knowledge of the case, Warner should have done it."

In addition, the facts that RCMP rarely took "pure version" statements, and often editorialized, leads Goertzen to believe there was potential that the Mounties were directing the investigation rather than "going where the evidence takes you." The facts that Lyons devoted 10 minutes to Grigorovich's interview and 13 to Nadeau's, and did not conduct them either at the scene or with photos to assist their memories, Goertzen says, is "shoddy, lazy, poor police work. What else did the Mounties miss?"

After reading the RCMP summary of her interview, Nadeau said to me: "None of the pertinent material from my interview was mentioned, so other investigators probably never read my interview. I always thought it strange that Shelly got called to testify at the Stonechild Inquiry, but not my husband or I, since it was our home and our event. Why would they not involve everyone?"

Particularly since excerpts from Lyons' interview with Shelly Grigorovich indicate she clearly remembered where she chased the person, but nothing about his appearance:

"A: I don't know what he had on.
Q: Yeah.
A: Uh...like, having said that, I know that he wasn't dressed for the weather. If you'd ask me what he was wearing, I don't know.
Q: Okay.
A: It was just a mental note that I had made at the time. Uh...it was a male and, you know, again I couldn't tell you if he was Caucasian or Native or Black. I have no idea at all and I've thought about it and thought about it and I ... I don't recall.
Q: Would you be able to give any opinion as to a rough age?
A: No, I really wouldn't.
Q: Or whether we're talking uh... an elderly person, middle-aged, youth, or even a young, uh?
A: Oh, he definitely wasn't elderly 'cause he moved quite well. (laugh)
Q: Yeah. (laugh)."

As Nadeau said to me: "My comments and my husband's and Ken Grigorovich's comments to the RCMP were obviously not significant enough to have us testify at the inquiry. Shelly must have had more information...." Logically, the criteria RCMP used to determine who testified should, indeed, have been: whoever "had more information." Yet, remarkably, Grigorovich rather than Nadeau was the witness called by the RCMP to testify at the Stonechild Inquiry. There Grigorovich repeated herself:

"Q: Are you able to describe the person that you saw that night at all?
A: I'm not.
Q: Any recollection as to clothing or dress of the individual?
A: I don't recall if I had given a description at the time when the call was made. That would be the accurate description. I'm unable to recall any specifics of it today."[102]

Those attending must have wondered who had wasted their time with a witness who recalled nothing. Is it possible that Warner – as well as Commission Counsel Hesje – recognized the significance of Nadeau's evidence, but minimized, even repressed it, since it provides evidence to refute Jason Roy's allegation that he saw Stonechild in a police car at the identical time? Goertzen says, "I wasn't aware of Nadeau's evidence until after the inquiry, and it just made me feel more frustrated and angry with Hesje. It was his job to determine who needed to be called, and he would have been meeting with Warner et al weekly, leading up to the inquiry."

Importantly, the RCMP easily could have determined whether the person hiding in the yard was Stonechild by utilizing a simple, common-sense method that any other officer or organization would use in a legitimate investigation: show the witnesses a photo of Stonechild and ask if that was the person they saw. The RCMP did not do this. Were they concerned it would further undermine the credibility of Roy's allegation?

Goertzen believes the summaries for the RCMP report were prepared by Operation Ferric lead investigator, Sgt. Jack Warner. Regarding Warner, Goertzen recalls:

"A number of months after the inquiry had concluded in 2004, an RCMP investigator attended at Bowden Prison in Alberta to speak with a serving inmate about possibly being the victim of child abuse at a Regina youth facility 10 years earlier. After the interview, the inmate asked about Stonechild and said he had info. The RCMP investigator taped an interview with the inmate about his information regarding the Stonechild freezing death.
The RCMP member had that taped interview transcribed and turned the transcription over to Regina RCMP major crimes so that it could be looked at and added to the open file on the freezing death of Neil Stonechild.
I was told that a number of weeks later, the RCMP investigator who had taken the Bowden Stonechild statement checked to see if his efforts had helped further the Major Crime file on Neil Stonechild. My understanding

is that he wasn't able to locate any indication that his statement had been attached to the file and nowhere in the file was there any mention of the Major Crime investigator speaking with him or receiving the transcribed statement.

Apparently he voiced his concerns and those concerns were made known to one of our lawyers who advised me of this. I instructed our lawyer to contact RCMP legal counsel to informally inquire if there was any validity to this story that an RCMP major crimes investigator had failed to include evidence in a death file.

[Goertzen continues:]

I was troubled with the thought that any evidence that was contrary to the findings of the Stonechild Inquiry report might have been excluded from an open police file. This concerned me because, if it was the result of neglect or laziness, that was troubling, and if it was withheld from the file intentionally, then it was potentially a much more serious matter.

It is my understanding that the Bowden Stonechild statement had been turned over to RCMP Major Crimes investigator Jack Warner by the Bowden investigator. Several months after having our lawyer make informal inquiries into concerns that evidence had been mishandled or repressed, I was advised that Jack Warner had retired from the RCMP.

I spoke to a colleague who'd worked with Jack Warner and he said that Jack's retirement had caught him off-guard. What was more surprising to him was that Jack Warner retired from the RCMP and almost immediately got hired by the FSIN as a special investigator looking into allegations against police, including complaints against Mounted Police. I was troubled by this and would have pursued it, but, under RCMP rules and regulations, a person cannot make a formal complaint against a retired RCMP officer.

My thoughts at this point were: if this statement was mishandled or withheld, were there similar occurrences during Operation Ferric when Warner was lead RCMP investigator? I don't know that I will ever have an adequate answer to that question."

This information also suggests Warner might have been pandering to FSIN and raises the question: What did Warner say to other Ferric investigators before they did interviews? "Looking at the whole thing in retrospect, with Warner going to work for the FSIN," says retired Staff Sgt. Zoorkan, "I think at some point he got tunnel vision, and he made the decision that he needed a bad guy, and if it was truthful, that was fine."

Having served 15 years as a Member of Parliament and, prior to that, 22 years as a Calgary police officer (including five years as a major crimes investigator), Art Hanger observes:

> "What's interesting on the RCMP summary is that the officer appeared to use his own words regarding the clothing description, driveway length, and proximity of intruder to the witness, rather than the descriptive words of the witness, which is odd. Having received Nadeau's statement, my next move as an investigator would have been to compare it to the Grigorovich account and then include my personal account by visiting the site where the intruder was seen, along with the witnesses. Given what was at stake, why wasn't this effort made? In such a politically-charged event, it would not be surprising if investigators who were willing to compromise were selected in order to reach a certain conclusion.
> **This was a circus extraordinaire! Was it the agenda of a few politically-correct department heads who wanted to make a name for themselves? Or could government bureaucrats in the justice department have wanted this to happen? The whole thing smacks of politics right from the get-go, filtering from the federal to the provincial level."**

Dave Scott's analysis:

> "This is evidence that further verifies the lack of credible attention to detail by RCMP investigators regarding a serious criminal allegation that could and would ruin a fine police service and some of its police officers' and their families' lives forever. It is this kind of unsupervised investigative incompetence that makes one suspect of the RCMP's intent from the beginning. Saskatchewan Justice, I believe, wanted to find a police service or police officers to cast a shadow of doubt over, as they were embarrassed by the international attention focused on Saskatchewan by Amnesty International. For their part, the RCMP wanted to move any

attention away from themselves, based on the FSIN's [1-800 line] reports, while also maintaining favour with the FSIN.
I cannot believe I am writing this about my own career as a police officer. Those were evil times influenced by wicked people. None of us believed people would do this. I regret telling Larry Hartwig, when I was his chief, to trust them and take the high road. What a terrible mistake!"

In an interview with me, retired Saskatoon RCMP Sgt. Colin Crocker said he believes his colleagues, Regina Operation Ferric investigators, were wearing blinders:

"Stan Goertzen thought the RCMP were wearing blinders rather than following the way the investigation would lead. I think that's true. If you're doing an investigation, you start from the body and work back to what happened. If someone says they saw someone squatting behind a truck, you go to the neighbours and say, 'Can you add anything?' The investigation could take off on a different path. But it seems the RCMP had someone in mind and thought, 'I won't worry about anything else.' You have to go where the investigation leads: 'Well gee, these guys said this and that's contrary to what was passed on to us in the original complaint....'

[Crocker continues.]

The FSIN's investigator had too much influence. RCMP investigators used his evidence as gospel and wouldn't look in any other direction. One witness said somebody might have dropped Stonechild off from a party. Why was that not followed up on? The big thing is: where would the party have been? I don't know if they followed-up who else was at the party. [It appears they did not.] It could have taken a long time, but you have to cover all the bases. We had a major crime once with 2,800 tips, and we had to follow up on them all. If our investigation didn't go the way I believed it should have gone, I would have said, 'Well we should be going in the new direction the evidence is leading,' because that sometimes happens.
I also wonder why the summaries differed from the content of the interviews. The summaries should have been reviewed.

If investigators were the least bit suspicious that either Hartwig or Senger was guilty, then charges should have been laid under the criminal code. Why weren't they? Whose decision was that?

*I had a horrible feeling, hearing you come out with evidence I hadn't heard. The more I hear about it, the more I realize that a lot of things should have been brought forward that weren't. But the final decision was not in the hands of Warner or Lyons. **They put their report in to Sask Justice and Sask Justice decided who was called.***

*I don't know why they didn't call everyone to testify [at the inquiry]. If it takes three weeks or twelve, so be it; at least everything is put on the table. In an inquiry, you want to find out what happened. **Maybe they were told just to rely on the evidence toward Hartwig and Senger.***

*The guys I worked with wouldn't repress evidence. I know Jack [Warner] quite well and Lyons and Mayrs – I wouldn't think they'd intentionally do anything against the law. **Whether or not stuff was vetted when it went to [Sask] Justice, I have no idea. But I don't feel good about it if something like that was done.***

This doesn't look good for the Mounted Police. I still consider myself a member because I spent thirty-six years of my life there; ten years in major crimes. I know that if the guys I had working for me on major crimes had investigated, they would have covered all the bases so that no one could out and say, 'This is wrong!'"

Concludes Dave Scott: "Something very, very bad happened, and that happening was purposely coordinated and directed by people of influence and power."

CHAPTER 14 - 'Inadequate!'
SPS Investigation into Death of Neil Stonechild

'As for the marks on the hand – that jacket had elastic ribbed cuffs and he had his hands pulled into the cuffs for warmth. His hand was underneath him as he lay slightly on his right side. I believe that a close check of the photos today would show that the marks on the hand came from the jacket cuff.'
— **Staff Sgt. Robert Morton, retired**

The alarm was raised about one p.m. on Thursday, November 29, 1990. Earlier that morning, two men installing a fence for a new business had noticed something in a field south of the Hitachi plant at 826 – 58th Street East. Deciding several hours later to investigate, they discovered a human body lying in the snow. Inside four minutes of their call, officers arrived. Approaching the body from the direction opposite the existing footprints, Const. René Lagimodiere checked for signs of life. "I touched the body, but it was frozen quite solid," the Métis officer wrote in his notebook.

The area was immediately cordoned off and treated as a crime scene. A supervisory sergeant, a crime scene investigative sergeant, and at least four other police officers attended. The coroner and a K9 unit were called. Speaking in low voices, staying well clear of the body and tracks, the officers struggled to make sense of the still, silent clues laid out before them on the shimmering snow. Suspended in time.

All was a mystery since, unique in the world of forensic science, glacial temperatures arrest bodily decomposition. Death might have occurred within hours or within weeks. And next, they knew, bodily thawing and drying would radically distort evidence. Not a job for amateurs, freezing deaths make a mockery of common sense, creating curious, specialized issues for every aspect of inquiry.

The officers squinted into the blazing, snow-stoked sunlight, working to bring the deadly event to life. "We look at the scene, what is the scene telling us about how this individual died?" Dr. Dowling would explain at the inquiry. "And we look at the body of the individual, what is the body telling me about how this individual died?"

They started with the snow. Rather than feathery, it was crystallized, and so hard and crusty that, when stepped on, it broke into large plates. The person who first noticed the body had preserved the scene by not approaching too closely, and by taking the same path in and out. Several other workers had come to take a look, but also stayed well back. Only one set of footprints led to the body; these had been left by the deceased. The footprints were blown over, indicating they were not fresh, possibly several days old. They revealed the person had come from 57th Street, and that he had walked through the knee-deep snow in a northerly direction. After a while, however, he began walking in a meandering fashion, as though staggering. Reaching a shallow ditch, he stumbled and fell face-first into it, before crawling back out in the same direction he had entered.

Police photo 15:
Weaving, shuffling footsteps heading in S-shape toward the ditch

(35) Steps stumbling into ditch[103]

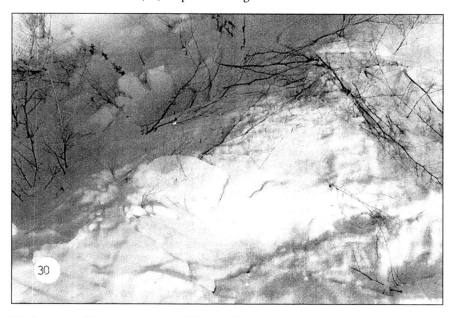

(30) Imprint of the body in ditch full of willow bushes. Sgt. Keith Jarvis wrote: "The deceased had walked North in this empty lot and then fell into a depression in the center portion of the lot causing himself to fall over to the right and land spread-eagle down in the snow."

(33) Impressions exiting ditch

On hands and knees, the unknown deceased had struggled on a further 10 feet before falling a second time face-down into the snow, rolling slightly onto his right side and moving no more.

Why had he left the road and walked into that snowy field, they wondered aloud? The nearby Hitachi plant was operating 24 hours-a-day these days, building generators. Had he realized he was in trouble, seen the lights at the plant and attempted to walk to it? If so, he might have made it to help at the plant, 150 yards further north, had it not been for the ditch!

The disorientation of freezing to death, as in a final attempt at survival the body hoards oxygenated blood for the central organs, depriving the brain and extremities, is described by the editor of *Ottawa Outdoors* magazine:

"You're in disbelief and borderline desperate as to your predicament. You're lost, in pain, and trying to find your way to a destination of warmth and security, willing to risk shortcuts to get there.
You hunker down with renewed energy and tromp your way through the knee-deep snow when you begin to sweat more profusely. When you stop to gather your bearings, the sweat cools and lines your body with a coat of

Aerial Photograph of Area Where Body Located
Exhibit P-42

A) Location of Neil
Stonechild's body

1990 map courtesy of Saskatchewan Department of Justice

water. Cold water robs the body of heat 32 times more quickly than cold air, and right now you're drenched.

Your extremities begin to ache from the cold, and as mild hypothermia sets in, you begin to shiver violently. It's natural, of course, just your body trying to generate warmth. But you hear your teeth chattering and feel your body convulsing and your anxiety rises. You may even start laughing or cursing that you were so stupid to be in this state. It's situation critical. So critical, in fact, you continue to take further risks with a body that is no longer working as it should. Your muscles ache and each step or glide becomes more awkward. ... All around you it's getting colder, you're less mobile and your body temperature continues to drop at an alarming rate. To rest, to rest, you think, just for a minute. You remember how comfortable a bed of snow felt when you were a child. If I can just lie down and get my energy (you think), up I'll jump and keep going.

You do jump up, but not with renewed vigor, but instead rip off your clothing. Why? Because now you're in a state called paradoxical undressing, defined as a sensation of extreme heat against the skin. Your temporary insanity and very real pain is brought on by constricted blood vessels dilating near the surface of your epidermis.

You're doomed."[104]

After taking a video, dozens of photographs and measurements of the scene, having directed the K9 unit to search for outlying clues, and talked to those who discovered the body, only then did three officers make their own tracks into the scene, taking photos every step of the way. Finally, they rolled the body over.

So thoroughly was the body frozen that it retained its original position even when turned over, feet suspended in mid-air. The eyes were closed. Hugely swollen, the face was flattened on the right side where it had been lying. Typical of all such deaths, as water in the cells had expanded with freezing, the face had puffed up and become grossly distended. Near the nose, some small vegetation was stuck to the cheek.

The deceased was dressed in a short, dark-blue cloth "baseball-style" jacket with a "Boy's Town Cowboys" crest on the back. The jacket was open, revealing a red and black lumberjack shirt beneath. He was also wearing a white T-shirt, striped blue jeans, underwear shorts as well as thigh-length spandex shorts. He wore one "Asics Tiger" running shoe on his left foot, laces undone. In it was a flat stone. Sgt. Robert Morton observed, "It looked like he'd been [walking] on it for some while, as there was a noticeable depression into the foot."[105] On his other foot, the white sports sock was worn through at the heel, suggesting he had walked for some time without the shoe. The K9 unit searched the deep snow, but they were unable to locate the running shoe.

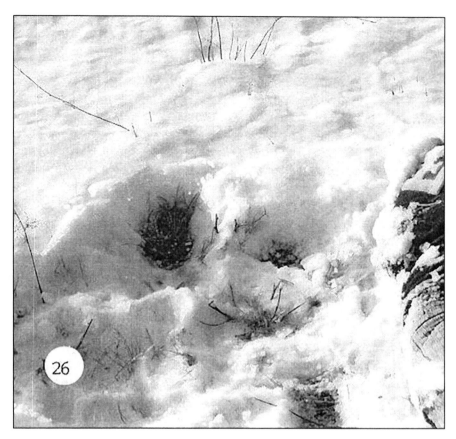

(26) Location where the face lay, melting through the snow before death

Coroner Dr. Brian Fern examined the body for physical evidence such as signs of obvious injury to the chest or stomach, and found none. Nor did anyone find evidence of blood on the clothes or snow. Finding no ID on the body, they estimated the age at 30. Lagimodiere observed poignantly: "Victim's hands were tucked in his sleeves and cuddled close to his chest like he was trying to keep warm."

Now-retired Staff Sgt. Morton, who worked Ident for 12 years, recalls how he captured video footage of the scene, and more than 40 photographs. In some, his own shadow loomed large:

"I dealt with the Stonechild death the same way I handled any other death. My philosophy in any death was always to investigate the death as

completely as if it were a murder. In the past, I had found people would investigate a death as a suicide and then, three years later, discover it was a murder. I didn't want that ever to happen to me. I did the work as thoroughly as for any murder case – you try to cover every base.

It was standard procedure to take photos long-range, then continue taking photos as I moved toward the centre. You don't want to contaminate the scene. The first officers on-scene followed normal procedure of going to the body to see if the person needed medical attention, and then, upon discovering the person was dead, backing off and calling the identification officer. I took a number of photos, and then did a video, which was a replication of the still photos.

As for the marks on the hand – that jacket had elastic ribbed cuffs and he had his hands pulled into the cuffs for warmth. His hand was underneath him as he lay slightly on his right side. **I believe that a close check of the photos today would show that the marks on the hand came from the jacket cuff.**

I was never asked my opinion on the marks on the hand or the two scratches on the bridge of his nose."

After police investigated two and a half hours, an ambulance attendant helped them bag the hands and feet for evidence, and they drove the body to St. Paul's morgue for autopsy. They were accompanied by an officer to maintain continuity of the body and preserve evidence. Saskatoon police personnel, including the crime scene investigative sergeant Neil Wylie, attended to the morgue where experts examined the body for any evidence of foul play as well as cause of death. Photos of marks on the deceased were taken, including scratches to the face, chest, and knees. Just as pyjamas, under the weight of a sleeping body, leave marks on the skin, so the clothing had left indentations on the front side of the body, particularly the torso. The difference between marks left while sleeping and while dying, is that the latter, like the stone's mark on the foot, are permanent. The body was locked in the morgue until thawed, when the autopsy could be performed.

Strangely, no missing person complaint had been filed by either the Stonechilds or the group home operator, and with identification complicated by difficulty estimating age, Const. John Middleton acted on the few clues he had: a photo in the pocket of the deceased addressed to "Neil," and the initials "N.S." tattooed at the base of his right thumb. Sgt. Morton wrote in his notebook:

"Returning to the police station, Const. John MIDDLETON #285, using the information of the tattoos on this deceased "NS" searched [manually through the vast] identification card system for anybody with the last name starting with S and a first name of Neil. Const. MIDDLETON came up with the name Neil Christopher STONECHILD, pulled the record and photographs, and from the description of the tattooing, it was determined that this would be a good possible identity for this deceased. Cst MIDDLETON should be congratulated on his initiative and ingenuity."

Heading back to the morgue, Morton obtained a thumbprint. This was compared to the one on Stonechild's criminal record. By 8 p.m., 7 hours after the discovery of an unknown body in a remote location, police had the identity confirmed. Morton noted: "All information pertaining to this case has been turned over to Sgt. JARVIS for purposes of notifying next of kin and trying to determine why this individual would have been out into that basically remote business area of town."

No one criticizes the thorough and efficient information-gathering and detective work by SPS up to this point. The same cannot be said, however, for the subsequent investigation.

On the basis of all evidence available, it had been assigned to the Morality Section rather than Major Crimes. At the Stonechild Inquiry, retired Staff Sgt. Raymond Pfiel would be asked about that decision:

"A: Morality came to suicides, sudden deaths, that sort of thing.
Q: Sudden deaths where there was no suspicion of foul play?
A: No suspicion of foul play, yes.
Q: And someone being in a remote area, wandering in an intoxicated condition can occur without foul play, I take it?
A: It could."

Sgt. Jarvis met that same evening with Stella Bignell and Marcel Stonechild, with the terrible task of notifying them that the publicized deceased was their son and brother. Stella stated she had last seen Neil on Saturday, November 24th in the company of Jason Roy, planning to go to Eddie Rushton's residence. The media was notified. Jarvis interviewed Stonechild's group home operator, Pat Pickard, who stated she also had spoken to Stonechild on November 24th about 10 p.m., when he stated he wanted to turn himself in the following day on an outstanding warrant.

The following day, pathologist Dr. Jack Adolph wrote in his autopsy report these important facts: "there were two parallel superficial abrasions across the mid-point of the nose directed obliquely downward to the right. The upper was 2.0 cm and the lower 2.5 cm in length and they were separated by a bridge of skin 2.6 cm in width. There was a curved recent similar abrasion on the cheek on the left side of the face, 5.5 cm in length, and this was convexed forward; there was also a recent abrasion just above this 1.0 x 0.6 cm. There were small abrasions over the lower border of each kneecap each approximately 1.5 and 1.0 cm." Post mortem blood ethanol concentration was 150 mg/100 ml, almost double Canada's legally-defined intoxication level of 80 mg/100 ml.

Dr. Adolph concluded that Stonechild had died as a result of hypothermia and freezing. Required to assign a date of death, he designated it two days earlier, November 27th, since it would have taken 48 hours for the body to freeze so solidly. Detecting no traces of blood on the deceased's clothes, he turned them over to Sgt. Morton. Morton later hand-delivered tissue samples to the Regina RCMP forensic lab for drug analysis. No drugs were detected.

Jarvis discovered five people who may have had contact with Stonechild in the days before his death and started interviewing. Several members of the Stonechild family and their friends reported to SPS that Gary Pratt and the others were responsible for Neil Stonechild's death because Neil had been willing to testify against the group. Youth worker Diana Fraser was aware of the problems brewing between the Pratt and Stonechild family. She anticipated problems at the fast-approaching wake for Neil, and on December 2nd, called the SPS to warn them. She spoke to Sgt. Pfeil on the Crime Stoppers line, claiming that Gary Pratt and Kelly McDonald had assaulted Stonechild about a month before his death and almost killed him. She also stated that Neil Stonechild had been at a party the night before his death; Gary Pratt had been at the same party. She stated that there may be trouble at the wake for Neil Stonechild; as the family gets together they might get themselves worked up.[106] Fraser also told police that a girlfriend of one of the Pratt boys claimed that Gary and Danny Pratt were responsible for assaulting Neil Stonechild at the location where he was found frozen; that he had been left to die as pay-back for Stonechild and Eddie Rushton having been willing to testify against the Pratts. Still others claimed that Stonechild had "fooled around" with Gary Pratt's girlfriend, and Gary paid him back.

On the evening of November 30th, Const. Geoff Brand obtained information from an informant in the SPS detention area, which he passed along. Reading from his notes at the 2004 Public Inquiry, Brand revealed that the informant stated that Neil Stonechild and Eddie Rushton had broken into either one home or several places, where they had a good score on handguns and a rifle. They tried to sell the guns to the Pratts, but the price the Pratts offered was too low and a "big fight" ensued. Stonechild was beaten up by the Pratts and about two weeks later, Stonechild was dead. Approximately one week prior to his death, Stonechild expressed concern to that informant about his safety regarding a threat made against him. At the inquiry, Const. Brand stated he could not remember who gave him this information.

Meanwhile, Jarvis learned that Stonechild had been at an apartment at Snowberry Downs. Jarvis spoke to Claudine Neetz who stated that she had been out the evening on November 24, and that her sister, Lucille Neetz, along with Gary Horse were babysitting for her at the residence of Trent Ewart. Jarvis checked with Communications and noted that Const. Hartwig had attended the Ewart apartment approximately 11:56 p.m. and cleared the call at 12:17 a.m., but had been unable to find Stonechild.

Jason Roy contacted Jarvis, telling him that he had last seen Neil Stonechild on the night of November 24-25th and was possibly the last person to see Neil Stonechild alive. Arrangements were made to meet with Roy at the home of Dina Sunshine to obtain a statement. In addition to Sunshine, Roy's girlfriend, Cheryl Antoine was also present. Jason Roy provided Jarvis with this two-page statement (actual document below):

"Roy, Jason Edward DOB 73/12/22 Date of Statement: 90/11/30 Time: 20:45 – 21:40
Me & Neil were [at] juli Binnings of 3269 Milton street we were sitting around having coffee & neil said lets go see trevor and I said ok we left at about 2:00 p.m. and caught the Bus at the confed terminal. And we were talking to this one white guy about old time fights then we kept on going to trevor we got there at about 2:45 sat around and just talked about custody time & girls. We bus in around & I saw an old friend and he lent me $20.00. we didnt have nothing to do. We went and hung around circle park mall till around 6:30 & neil said lets go to my moms and get some money from his mom so went over there and neils mom wasnt home and sold my gloves to Marcelle and he went & bought us a 40 ounce of Silent

Sam [vodka]. We over to juli's and drank the hole bottle straight just me & Neil. We were sitting around talking about whatever and he said lets go find Lucille. So we started on our way to Snowberry Downs. I dont know how we got to seven-11. We stopped there and tryed buying something but a cant remember if they sold me anything. We started walking over there and stopped on the boulevard and we were arguing but I dont know what about. And we got to one apartment looked for Lucilles sister but it wasnt there so we checked other apartments for the last name Neetz but we couldnt find it any where so we got to the last apartment and we were about to check it then I must have stopped him and we stood there and argued for what I dont know and he turned around and said fuckin Jay and I looked around and blacked out and woke up at juli binnings.

Q: What time approximately did you last see Neil Stonechild alive on Nov. 24, 1990?

A: Could be about 1130 p.m..

Q: When you say the name Trevor, is that Nowaselski?

A: Yes.

Q: What condition was Neil in when you last saw him?

A: Pretty drunk. Well, totally out of it.

Q: Is there anything else you wish to tell me?

A: No that's all I can think of.

Q: Is this a true statement?

A: Yes.

(Signed by) Sgt. K. D. Jarvis, Badge #125, and Jason Roy"

This statement was a "pure version," free-narrative statement (a witness's unprompted recall of events, uninterrupted by directing or "contaminating" questions), written in his own hand. This is the most accurate method in which a statement can be obtained. Jarvis noted the details of the statement in both his report and his police notes. Nowhere in the statement was there any mention of encountering police or seeing Stonechild bleeding and screaming in the back of a police vehicle.

Sgt. Stan Goertzen says of Roy's statement"

"In his Nov. 30, 2000 statement, Roy concluded by saying he blacked out and found himself back at the Binnings. (Probably because he did

SASKATOON POLICE DEPARTMENT

WITNESS STATEMENT

FORM PR23
CASE NUMBER 97411-90
DATE OF STATEMENT 30 11 30
TIME STARTED 2045
TIME FINISHED 2140

NAME: Roy Jason Edward SEX: M DATE OF BIRTH: 73 12 22
ADDRESS: 516 Ave I So

RE: DEATH of NEIL STONECHILD.

Me & Neil were at juli Binning's of 33 milto. street We were sitting around having coffee & neil said lets go see trevor and I said ok we left at about 2:00 p.m. and caught the Bus at the confed terminal, and we were talking to this one white guy about old time fights then we Kept on going to trevor we got there at about 2:45 sat around with trevor and just talked about custody time & girls. We busin around & I saw an old friend & he lent me $20.00. I dnt have nothing to do. wen went and hung aroun circle park mall till around 6:30 & niel said lets go to my moms and gets some money from his mom, so went over there and niel's mom wasn't home sad sold my gloves to Marcelle and went & baught us a 40 ounce of Silent Sam. we over to juli's and drank the hole battle straight just me & Neil. We were just sitting around talking about whatever and he said lets go find lucille, so we started an our way to Strawberry Downs I drnt rember how & we got to seven 11. we stopped there and tryed buying something but a cant remember if they sold me anything, e started walking over there and stopped on the boolevard and we were arguing but I dont what about.

not want to mention being stopped by police and giving them a false name – which is the basis for charges of lying and obstructing justice.) Then the RCMP told him the file had been shredded and they were rebuilding it. Roy then supplies details that were not in the Nov. 30 statement.

Then Ernie Louttit found the Nov. 30 Statement. Roy then says: No I *didn't leave that statement at that time, I left it later.*

So that is not a blackout – supplying details that were not confirmable. What Jason Roy is, is a liar. He picked out specific details and recalled them – that is not a blackout."

That same evening, Jarvis met with Trent Ewart at the police station, where he obtained this statement:

"Ewart, Trent DOB 72/11/08 Date of Statement 90/11/30 Time: 21:45 – 21:55

I was drinking with Lucille neetz 870 confederation Drive and Gary horse. The buzzer rang and the person apologizes for ringing the wrong buzzer and then their was a knock on the door Lucille neetz said it was neil Stonechild she was scared or paranoid I asked what he wanted he said "he wanted a party" I said there is "no party here" he mumbled some things I said "get out of here before I called the cops" he said "sorry dude" and left he came back and Lucille neetz said that I should call the police because he was wanted then the police came and me and garry lied to the police because Lucille neetz didn't want them to give niel her name. We told them we thought it was niel Stonechild.
Q: Anything else you wish to add.
A: I don't think so, it was between 11 p.m. and 12 p.m. on Saturday November 04 [sic; should have read 30] /90.
Q: Is this a true statement.
A: Yes it is."

Jarvis flagged the file. Knowing that further investigation was required, he made an entry stating that, because he was off-duty for the next four days and foul play could not be ruled out, "this file should be turned over to Major Crime for immediate follow-up." He did not, however, phone in the following day, as he should have, to ensure that had been done.

Earlier, on November 30, the SPS had sent out a media release that an Aboriginal male had been found frozen to death in the north end. The following day, a city bank manager phoned the police station to state that he and his wife had seen a person matching that description the night before, walking east on the 51st Street overpass over Idylwyld Drive (12 blocks from the field in which the body was later found, and walking in that direction.) The banker left a message with police requesting that someone contact him, but no one did. He later told me:

"I saw the individual walking slowly in the direction I was driving, along 51st Street on the overpass over Idylwyld Drive between 1 or 2 a.m. It was definitely after 1 a.m. I'm sure it was him [Stonechild]! There was no one else out walking at that time of night and in that cold. He was Aboriginal, under 30, slim with long, dark hair to his shoulders, wearing a checkered lumber jacket. He had no heavy clothes, he was shivering quite a bit, his shoulders hunched up, his head down, hands in his pockets. We didn't

see any blood on his face; if we had, we would have stopped or called the police. I assumed he'd get to the gas station after the bridge. There was a snowplow two blocks back, I thought he might help.

Jeez, you feel like you should stop, but I had my wife and daughter who was a year or two in the car. You don't think that will happen. It bothered me after, when I heard he had frozen to death, so I phoned the city police general line. A female took my information. No one ever got hold of me.

When the inquiry started [13 years later], I told a police officer in the bank what I had seen, and he contacted the RCMP. Two Mounties came to my office and did a taped interview. I supposed they'd call me to testify at the inquiry. I was surprised when they didn't. I thought, 'There must be other factors.'

But how could it be the police if he's still walking after 1 a.m.?"

Jarvis never did contact the banker about his crucial evidence. How his message was missed, nobody knows. In the days before text messages and email, such a message most likely was taken in the form of a handwritten note by the communications section.

Remarkably, at the time of the Stonechild Inquiry, the banker provided his information again – this time to the RCMP – but was not called to testify.

Transcribed, the banker's interview with RCMP ran to 11 pages, including a drawing. With the description matching Stonechild's height and weight, it should have profoundly affected the outcome of the inquiry:

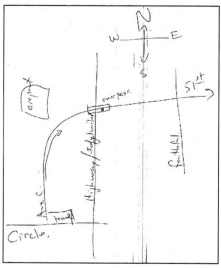

Audio statement:
Date: 2003.10.30

Erica Stonechild
Task #2150

Q = Constable Chris deGALE
A =

Q1. Okay. Today's date is Thursday, October thirtieth, two thousand and three. The time is eleven sixteen hours. Uh... myself, Constable Chris deGALE of the Regina Major Crime Unit, is present here today at the office, uh... in Lawson Heights, Saskatoon, Saskatchewan and I'm here present with, uh...

that, uh... you had some information that you, uh... passed on to, uh... uh... of the Saskatoon Police Service, uh... regarding, uh... regarding a day, uh... quite a while ago in which you, uh... saw the, uh... male walking down the road in... and subsequently heard about, uh... a male dying. And, uh... that male being by the name of Neil STONECHILD. I guess, what could you, uh... what could you tell me about, uh... that day and what you remember?
A1. Okay. Uh... I don't remember the exact, uh... date of the, uh... when it happened. But I do know that, uh... it was on a Saturday night and it was... well, I think it was the first major snow storm of the year.

driving along Avenue 'C', uh... north, which comes from the Travelodge up by J&H Warehouse, uh... by the airport and there's an overpass that connects onto Fifty-first Street, uh... in the north end of Saskatoon. And as we came along the... the corner by the airport and J&H, up over the overpass, uh... there was an... an individual... it was a man, walking on the right-hand side... the same direction I was going, which would have been east, I guess, uh... towards the river. And we passed him... It was still snowing. And he was... you could tell he was very cold.
"Hey, man, he looks frozen." Like... and he was lightly dressed. Uh... my recollection is that it was a male native, younger, uh... under thirty years of age, like... it was my recollection. Uh... dark hair, don't remember the length or anything but I don't recall anything on his head. Uh... I recall a loose-fitting shirt or jacket, uh... over top and it... I don't remember it being buttoned up. I remember him being sort of, uh... hutched up with his hands shivering qui... quite a bit. And, uh... you know, what rings a bell and I... and I'm not a hundred percent sure was that this light covered, uh... jacket or... jacket reminded me of, uh... one of these lumber jacket kind of shirts. Uh... like the plaid checkered ones. And I don't know, because that's, uh... you know, so many years ago but it was something like that that was loose over top, but it... it was not a... definitely not a winter coat. But this gentleman was freezing, you could

tell. Uh... because of the time of night

hoping that, uh... he would get some place there warm.
uh... I think it was either Tuesday morning or Wednesday morning. I'm not sure of the... the date now. But we heard on the radio
they had... somebody had found a... a male frozen to death in the north end of Saskatoon.
                                        "That must have been the person we saw Saturday
night." I don't know who it was but it just made sense to us.

                                        the City Police general line to report that I had
information about seeing an individual walking Saturday night about two o'clock in the morning
and thought that it might be important or connected to the individual they found frozen.
                                        the time and where I saw this individual walking. And they said
that they would take the information and pass it on to the investigator and that is the last I've ever
heard from the City Police or anyone else.

Q2. Okay. Uh... now when you went to... when you, uh... made that call to the Call Centre... or
to the, I guess it was the general line.
A2. Uh-hmm.

Q3. ... of Saskatoon Police Service. Uh... now, how many days would you say that was after,
uh... how long was that after you actually saw that person walking?
A3. Well, Saturday night is when we would have saw the individual,
                                        I'm assuming Tuesday morning or Wednesday.
                                        But why it rings a bell is because
that was the morning it was announced on the local radio station. So whatever day it was
released to the radio station, is when I heard it and an hour and a half or two hours after is when I
phoned the... the general line.

Q4. Okay. And you'd said you'd... talked to, uh... some of the...
A4. Yeah.

now. And probably on the opposite side at that time would have been just open field. Now there's a Petro-Pass or something. It's all commercial built up. And, uh... all light industrial for maybe four or five blocks. And then when you go to Fifty-First and Miller is where a McDonald's restaurant was.

Q47. Okay. And, uh... so would there be any... there wouldn't be any residential, uh... there isn't... there aren't any residential... ?
A47. Within a mile of that location... no residential. Uh... the first residential would be on the other side of Fifty-first and Warman Road. Then you start the Silverwood residential district. Uh... so from where that is, uh... everything, uh... from where I saw him up to the train tracks on... where Warman Road is... it's all commercial.

Q48. Okay. And... I guess if, uh... do you know where... when you heard, I guess, a few days later that, uh... the body of Neil STONECHILD was found. Uh... do you know where it was found?
A48. No. I...

Q49. No?
A49. I... I didn't know a name of the individual at the time. I... I believe the radio said something about a... either a... a male was found or... I don't even know if it said aboriginal male. I don't know. Uh... I remember it said a male. Uh... and it just said in the north area of Saskatoon... north industrial area of Saskatoon is all I recall. So whatever the radio released that day is all I ever heard.

Q50. Okay. And I guess further to that, did you ever, uh... did you ever learn of any, uh... more specific details as... as... as to where his body was located?
A50. No.

Q51. ... found?
A51. And I still don't know, even today, exactly his body was located. Uh... I never saw a picture of his body up until maybe two years ago on the news. Just in the last two years, I've seen whatever's broadcast on the tv where it did show a frozen body. But up until then, I've never seen that. So the first number of years...

Q52. Uh... now... if, uh... I guess you... granted it's been... it's been some years, uh... but the person that you saw walking on the road... if I were able to sh... if I were to show you a few pictures of... of different people, would you able... would you be able to point him out? Do you think you would?
A52. I... don't know. I could tell you his build, uh... that it was, uh... not a big built person. Uh... now, height and weight wise, he was definitely under a hundred and fifty pounds would be my guess. You know, that's just, uh... you know, that's a long time but he was not a heavy set individual and he was younger. So... and aboriginal, definitely. And dark hair. I don't recall the length of the hair. Now that's... about what I recall.

Q53. Okay. And the picture that you saw... I said... I guess a couple years ago, you said you saw

It was "the biggest piece of evidence for the entire inquiry," says Dave Scott, who continues:

Indeed, numerous police officers have stated that in their opinion, there is no doubt this was collusion between the RCMP, Sask Justice and political

officials to appease FSIN, Amnesty International, and other special interest groups. Someone was going to be the fall guy, even though there was no evidence. The RCMP could not walk away from this without finding something amiss.

The police officers who believe this was a conspiracy all said that they are not prone to such theories, but, as one added, "When you consider everything that happened here, how the evidence clearly doesn't add up, what other conclusion can you reach?"

Hartwig states that in a 2008 meeting, he asked one of the lead RCMP investigators about Louttit's March 2001 discovery of Jason Roy's original statement, which had been immediately turned over to them. Since the statement provided clear and tangible evidence that Jason Roy lied about his allegation, why did the investigation not come to an immediate halt? This was their word-for-word exchange:

"Hartwig: When Ernie Louttit found a copy of the original report, with the original statement [from Jason Roy], *what happened with that investigation? That investigation should have come to a screeching halt because now Jason Roy was trapped in several lies.*

RCMP: That had nothing to do with the RCMP, though Larry. By then the process was in place. [This seems to indicate that "process" is more important than evidence – in this case, serious criminal misconduct that threatened the justice system.]

Hartwig: Wasn't it still under investigation then?

RCMP: It was certainly still under investigation, but Justice was the ones that were making all the decisions about what was going to happen next. Were they telling us how to do the investigation? No.

Hartwig: But they were suggesting by...

RCMP: No, there were never any suggestions what to do. Did members of the RCMP consult with Justice on certain things? Yes. That is a part of any investigation. You know that from your own experience.

Hartwig: But I mean, every police officer, every investigator familiar with this case is of the opinion that I am: that it should have ended right there!"

If RCMP investigators weren't making the decisions, who else was there to make them? The Department of Justice? Although this RCMP officer denied any collusion regarding the matter of Jason Roy's statement in which Roy mentioned nothing about police, much less attempted to implicate them in wrongdoing, the RCMP, remarkably, did not bother to conduct a meaningful interview with Roy to address this matter! This move actually may have aided and abetted Roy in keeping his impossible allegation viable.

The former head of Saskatoon RCMP Major Crimes, Colin Crocker, made a similar comment to me: "The more I hear about it, the more I realize that a lot of things should have been brought forward that weren't. But the final decision was not in the hands of Warner or Lyons. **They put their report in to Sask Justice and Sask Justice decided who was called.**"

On December 4, 1990, Const. Ernie Louttit met with Neil Stonechild's brother, Jake, who stated that he heard Neil was at a party somewhere by the 7-Eleven in the north end and that Gary and Danny Pratt picked up Neil. This was apparently witnessed by Petrina Starblanket who was dating both Gary Pratt and Stonechild. Louttit made notes on this and then went to central records at the police station, asked for the Stonechild File, 90-97411, and photocopied everything in it. He passed on the information about the suspects to SPS investigators and met with Mrs. Bignell, who expressed concerns about the way the investigation was handled, but said nothing about possible police involvement.

On December 4th, Sgt. Jarvis returned to work. There was the file still on his desk! Surprised to learn that no one had been available to pick up where he left off, he resumed the investigation. He interviewed Sharon Night who was at the Binning residence the night Neil Stonechild and Jason Roy came over to party. She stated Roy had gone out with Stonechild and returned later that night, telling her that he and Neil had an argument and parted ways. She stated that Roy was intoxicated at the time, passed out, and woke up sick the next morning. (The RCMP never did interview Night about the critical evidence that this was all that happened that night – Roy and Stonechild had an argument! Instead the RCMP spoke to her, but in an attempt to confirm a rumour that Hartwig had been involved in another act of wrongdoing involving Neil. One that occurred while he was not working.)

Jarvis tried to interview Eddie Rushton and Gary Pratt, but made only superficial attempts at contacting them and was unsuccessful. He spoke to pathologist Dr. Jack Adolph who had performed the autopsy; he stated there was no sign of trauma and no evidence of foul play. They discussed the Crime Stoppers tips about Neil having been beaten by the Pratts, concluding that, because there was no sign of trauma, as the tips alleged, the calls must merely have been designed to create disharmony in the community against Pratt.

The following day, December 5, 1990, Jarvis wrote in the file:

"There is nothing to indicate why he was in the area other than possibilities he was going to turn himself in to the correctional centre or was attempting to follow the tracks back to Sutherland group home, or simply wandered around drunk until he passed out from the cold and alcohol and froze. Concluded at this time."

Jarvis did not interview the two suspects or determine what factors led to Stonechild's death. At the inquiry, Deputy Chief Dan Wiks testified that Jarvis should have obtained statements from those who discovered the body, ambulance attendants, and many others named in the reports. "There needed to be a lot more work done," Wiks said.

Jarvis' conclusion may have been based on the fact that the body was found four blocks from the correction centre and heading in that direction. While that seems implausible since a young offender would not turn himself into the correctional centre, Stonechild presumably would have known it was staffed around-the-clock, year-round, so that someone always would be present to assist a person in trouble. Jarvis' other theory was that Stonechild had been attempting to "follow the tracks" and walk back to the group home from which he was UAL, several miles away on the other side of the river, but got lost and froze to death; a plausible conclusion since Neil had promised his mother and Pat Pickard that he would turn himself in the day after the party. (At the inquiry, Gary Pratt would say that Stonechild might have gone to the industrial area because there was a "booze can" – a bootlegger in a house on 46th Street where underage people could buy and consume alcohol.)

The provincial coroner, who had the ability to call an inquest, chose not to. He concluded that the cause of death was exposure, and the manner of death accidental.

At his funeral, many family members were shocked at the condition of Stonechild's head and face. His mother, aunt, and sister all commented his face looked like it had been beaten, that they could see bruising, there was a cut across the bridge of his nose, there were lumps on his head and his hair was cut.

Randy Pshebylo who embalmed Stonechild, told the RCMP, "It is possible that there are bumps or unevenness around the skull during autopsy and the preparation of the body; this is common," and that he "has had people in the past feel the deceased's head and say, 'What did you do to him?' 'Why does he have this?' 'Who did this to him?'"

A Saskatchewan licensed embalmer explains:

"The pathologist likely would have cut the hair before removing the skullcap to examine the brain for trauma or disease. [Dowling would also write: "The difference in lengths [of the hair] appears to correspond roughly with the site of an autopsy incision made over the vertex of the scalp."] *The embalmer who prepared the remains for burial would have replaced the skullcap and spent hours carefully suturing up the top of the head, using a light cord to form a baseball stitch. This leaves a line of small lumps beneath the hair and often a ridge just above the eyes. Post mortem lividity, or pooling of the blood after death, occurs when the blood gravitates to the lower part of the body, so if he died face-down, the face would be discolored, like a massive bruise. Also, when a person freezes to death, their face swells grotesquely. When it thaws, it shrinks back, leaving the face disfigured, which often makes the family question what actually happened to the person. I have handled a number of freezing deaths, and they all looked as though someone had hit them a number of times in the face. One was a man whom I knew fairly well. I did not even recognize him."*

Hence the later front-page headline, prejudicial to the public: "Mom saw bruising: Stonechild inquiry hears tearful testimony during first day."[107] Jason Roy had been present at the funeral and, according to some, including his ex-wife, expressed surprise at the injury to Neil's nose, stating that Neil had not had the injury when he last saw him. Yet he would later claim that he had been saying for years that the last time he saw him, in a police car, Neil had blood on his face. For example, at the inquiry, Roy testified:

"A: He had a cut across his – across his face.
Q: Just to be clear, the last time you saw him alive, did he have a cut across his nose?
A: In the back of a police car."

(In a later interview, I asked Roy why he would be surprised at the funeral if he had already seen Stonechild bleeding in a police car. "Well, you know," he replied, "like, that night that, the night that, the night in question, what happened with him, you know. And then, however many days later, it was probably like a week later, you know, like – everything is a shock to you, everything is a shock to a 16-year-old when it comes to a murder.")

Const. Louttit had previously met with Stella Bignell; they met again on December 30, 1990 (and would meet another eight times over the next few months), as she asked what efforts had been made to establish Neil's activities the night he disappeared, and what, if any, follow-up there had been on her information about the party with Pratt in the north end. Louttit also wanted to know if all leads had been followed, so contacted his staff sergeant, who arranged a meeting with Jarvis's supervisor. He referred Louttit to Jarvis. Jarvis then completely dismissed Louttit's protests. Even though Jarvis knew about Pratt being a suspect in Neil Stonechild's death, only superficial attempts were made to contact him.

Louttit would later testify there were no rumours from the Stonechild family or anyone else about police being involved in Neil Stonechild's death. Louttit kept his copy of the original file with him until he filed it away in a foot locker at his home sometime in March, 1991, and, over time, forgot about it.

The following year, a March 4, 1991 *StarPhoenix* headline read: "Family Suspects Foul Play." Featuring a photo of a much-younger Neil, the article stated, "Aside from some scratches on his nose, there were no signs of physical abuse." Stella claimed that racism might have played a role in the police not investigating the file properly, but did not suggest police involvement in his death. Both Stella and her daughter Erica questioned how he ended up in the north end unless he'd been driven there. Stella stated that Neil would have broken in somewhere if he had been cold, and referred to a run-in with hardened young offenders in which her son suffered a beating: "He got a lickin'. He was beaten with guns and baseball bats. Sure he was drunk, but he had enough sense to run home."

Family suspects foul play

4 Police + murder?

MAR 4 1991

Police say every avenue investigated

By Terry Craig
of The Star-Phoenix

When Neil Stonechild's frozen body was found in a vacant field in north Saskatoon last November, family members immediately suspected foul play.

Three months later, they still subscribe to that theory, even though the police file on the case has been closed.

The official cause of death was listed as hypothermia. Aside from some scratches on his nose, there were no marks of physical abuse. His blood-alcohol level was .15, almost twice the legal limit for impaired driving.

Stonechild's mother, Stella, and sister, Erica, are the first to admit Neil had a problem with alcohol but they say in the months before his death, he was coming to terms with his problem.

They also say that, had Stonechild been white, police would have been more thorough in the investigation of his death.

"It makes me wonder. If Neil was the son of the mayor or commission-

NEIL STONECHILD

er, police would still be investigating," Stella said.

A senior officer within the department guardedly agreed.

But department spokesman Sgt. Dave Scott vehemently denies Stel-

la's assessment of the investigation.

"I don't agree. A tremendous amount of work went into that case," he says.

MORE ON PAGE A2

How Stonechild was depicted at the time.[108]

Family cites altercation with 'gang'

COVER STORY from Page A1

Pointing to a hefty file, Scott says investigators pursued every avenue. The coroner's report said no evidence showed Stonechild, who was 17, was beaten before his death.

"The profile we have at this time was death by hypothermia. It was an unfortunate incident," Scott reports.

Nevertheless, the Stonechild family is convinced Neil was killed.

He was found Nov. 29 lying face down in a field behind 830 57th St. West. According to the pathologist's report, Stonechild could have died Nov. 25.

It is where the body was found that puzzles his relatives.

"Why was he found way up in the north industrial area with only one shoe?" asks his mother. "What kid goes out with only one shoe?"

The temperatures in Saskatoon the week Stonechild disappeared and until the body was found

ranged from a low of minus 28 on Nov. 25 to a high of five on Nov. 29.

He was last seen alive Nov. 24 at a confectionery at 33rd Street and Confederation Drive. He was very drunk.

Stella and her daughter don't believe the police theory Neil was walking to the provincial correctional centre to give himself up.

At the time of his death, Stonechild was a fugitive from a community home, where he was serving time for a break and enter.

"I know my son very well. I know he wouldn't go out there by himself," Stella said. "Even though he was on the run, he always called (home).

"It was a stormy night (Nov. 24). I told him to please be careful. He said he was going to be all right."

"If he was so intoxicated at the 7-Eleven, how did he get to the north end?" Erica asks. "He didn't know anyone. It was too late for the buses to stop. There were no houses."

Both women believe Stonechild was driven to the area and abandoned.

"He was thrown out there," Stella said. "I know him. He would have broken into some place to get shelter."

She feared for her son because of a recent run-in with some hardened young offenders.

In the weeks before his death, he had an altercation with a gang. He suffered a beating — the result of a deal gone sour over the sale of some handguns Stonechild acquired during a break and enter.

"He got a lickin'. He was beaten with the guns and baseball bats," Stella said. "Sure, he was drunk but he had enough sense to run home."

He was assaulted at an inner-city location but managed to stagger his way to his mother's home on Confederation Crescent.

Stonechild was a familiar face to Social Services youth workers, who described him as a likeable, pleasant boy. His major downfall was alcohol.

"He enrolled in an Alcoholics Anonymous program a few weeks before his death and had attended regularly.

"He was learning that a life with alcohol was bad but he was

dealing with the issues in his life," a social worker said. "He was a smart kid with a lot of potential. He had a terrific personality. He could have been anything. His death is a terrible waste."

Stonechild was also a highly regarded wrestler. Wendel Wilkie, coach of the Westside Wolverines wrestling club, described the youth as exceptional "with more potential than 90 per cent of the kids I see."

Stonechild was a bantam provincial champion when he worked with Wilkie.

His high school wrestling coach, Gil Wift at Bedford Road, was shocked when he learned of the death.

Wift said Stonechild was "trying hard" to overcome his problems when he enrolled at the collegiate last fall.

As Stella ponders the tragedy, she declares: "Not a day goes by when I don't shed a tear for my boy.

"It's heartbreaking to know my son is gone.

"I can't let him rest in peace knowing he didn't die naturally. Whoever did it is still out there."

How he actually looked at the time. He had had eight run-ins with the law that year alone, including charges for Break-and-Enter on Saskatoon homes. (Photo from *Report on the Stonechild Inquiry*)

Within that year, Stella Bignell also learned that Gary Pratt had not been charged in the death of her son, and contacted another SPS officer, Const. Eli Tarasoff, whose stepson had been a friend of Neil's. The grieving mother told Tarasoff she was concerned that Neil had been beaten up; she felt the file had not been thoroughly investigated and asked him to review it. He did so, agreed with Mrs. Bignell, and spoke to Jarvis, who dismissed his concerns about the case, as well. Tarasoff advised Stella to consult a lawyer and perhaps the file could be re-opened. In a written statement, Tarasoff would state that there were no rumours from the Stonechild family or anyone else of police involvement in Neil's death. If Jason Roy had done as he claimed and told Mrs. Bignell about his allegation of police involvement in March of 1991, she most certainly would have brought this up with Tarasoff, someone she obviously trusted.

The sad bottom line to the police investigation: "Most parties today agree the SPS investigation was inadequate," states Stan Goertzen. "No one defends it." At the Stonechild Inquiry, deputy chief Wiks testified it was "a very poor investigation," and acknowledged that police had refused Stella Bignell's attempt to have the investigation reopened.

CHAPTER 15 - 'Moonlight Tours' to 'Starlight Cruises': The Cold, Hard Facts

'I said, "You mean, 'starlight tour' is a term taxi drivers use all the time?" He said, "Oh yes, it's been going on for years!"'
– Const. Larry Lockwood

Between 1990 and 2000, 16 people froze to death in the Saskatoon Health Region, which includes a circumference of 100 kilometres around the city. One-third of those people, including Neil Stonechild, died in the very cold winter of 1990-91. Of those five deaths, alcohol was a factor in four.

Victims during that decade ranged widely. A retirement-age Caucasian farmer found by his son beside his back step on a cold November morning, empty beer bottles in his truck and oval imprints in the grass where his dogs had lain close beside him throughout the frigid night. The coroner wrote in his report: "He was on his back, legs crossed, and frozen." A 28-year-old Aboriginal man found one March morning face-down in a snowy intersection in the West end. A middle-aged Caucasian woman in her designer bedroom, empty vodka bottles strewn around the floor, a box over the heating register and both windows open to the -30 C early April weather discovered by her physician husband.

Widely-varying ages, races, situations in life, seasons of death. Some apparent suicides, some who fought valiantly to survive, others who didn't care whether they lived or died. The most prominent features? Superficial scratches on their faces (and elsewhere) sustained during their final falls, and a high level of alcohol and drugs in their bodies. The notation on one autopsy alone read: "No traumatic injury or disease processes; toxicological results showed a drug combination which cause depression of brain function and induce sleep: alcohol, codeine, diazepam, Amitriptyline." (Nortriptyline and opiates were also detected in this body.) Neil Stonechild's body contained no drugs, but the blood alcohol level was .15, almost double the Canadian legal definition of intoxication.

Locations varied. For example, in circumstances startlingly similar to Stonechild's, *the same week* that Stonechild went missing in 1990, an 18-year-old white male, John Webb, walked out of a farmhouse 100 km east of

Saskatoon, "quite drunk," following an argument with his girlfriend. Later that week, Webb's frozen body was discovered in a field near the farm with no shoes on and part of his shirt undone. "The RCMP investigated the area carefully," wrote coroner E.D. Roberts; "there had been a light snowfall and there was no evidence of any tracks except his own to the point where he was found." The death was ruled accidental. Pathologist Dr. T. Moyana described Webb's "multiple superficial lacerations on the forehead, the longest of which measured 1.5 cm in length. There were multiple *small superficial abrasions around the left eye as well as one short recent deeper laceration over the bridge of the nose.*"

Similarly, 19-year-old David Rahm was found frozen in a Saskatoon back alley *three weeks after* Stonechild: "There is a cutaneous [on the skin, as opposed to sub-cutaneous, *through* the skin] abrasion measuring 2.5 x 2.0 cm present on the chin. ...." wrote pathologist Dr. R.K. Waghray.

In November 1999, Timothy Budd, 29, and a friend were inhaling solvent in Saskatoon's Victoria Park when they both passed out. The friend awoke, Budd did not. Coroner Arnold Nickle wrote: "Examination revealed *minor abrasions to the decedent's nose....*" The woman in her bedroom with vodka had "*superficial scrapes*" on her forehead and leg; the man in the intersection had "*superficial abrasions* to the right side of his face."

In his observations at the Stonechild scene, Sgt. Robert Morton wrote: "The deceased had two scrapes or scratches across the bridge of his nose and a small cut on the lower lip." Dr. Jack Adolph, too, made note of two "superficial abrasions across the mid point of the nose," one 2 centimetres. (4/5 of an inch), the other 2.5 cms. (one inch) in length. These two "scrapes or scratches," virtually identical to those on other freezing victims would, a decade later, be overlaid electronically with a photo of a handcuff (its third, centre rail which would have had to cause a third scrape but didn't, had been made to mysteriously "disappear" through the magic of digital photography) – and create the uproar heard around the world.

A third commonality is removal of clothing. While that is widely-known, less well-known is the fact that many freezing victims are found missing one or both of their shoes. The man found in the Saskatoon intersection, Becky Charles near La Ronge, Russell Charles in Saskatoon whose story was soon dropped by the newspaper, John Webb on a farm far from Saskatoon, Rodney Wailing found intoxicated but alive in a Saskatoon alley, and both Wegner and Stonechild were missing one or both shoes. Because feet lose sensation as the body restricts circulation to its core to stay alive, freezing victims possibly don't notice when their shoes slip off in the snow. Alternatively, Russell Charles' uncle, Richard Ross, who has tracked down four frozen bodies in northern Saskatchewan, believes some victims deliberately remove their shoes. "Most people I have found who were frozen to death usually have their clothes off, their shoes off, and their coat like a pillow." As if they had prepared for bed.

In Saskatoon, however, much would be made of missing shoes, some hinting darkly that it meant victims had been driven, rather than walked on their own, to the places found. No one seems to have pointed out that shoelessness is a nearly universal common denominator of freezing deaths.

Many, too, have been led to believe that the only way someone could have arrived at a remote location is if transported, particularly by police. In the words of one officer, "In Saskatoon there have been one to three freezing deaths per year forever, but the constant link between the media and the RCMP is intent on proving that the police are to blame – and they have many citizens convinced."

Observes a female officer, "To think we're killing Native people is just ludicrous. We are highly visible and closely scrutinized. We also get paid a good wage which, throughout our whole career and retirement, amounts to hundreds of thousands of dollars. Why would they think we would kill someone and put that at risk?"

Police Association President Goertzen felt so strongly about it that he asked police detractors to "put their money where their mouth is," challenging them to put up a cash reward for anyone who could prove that the alleged practice of dropping off Natives, or anyone else, was common practice in the city. Not a single person took him up on it. Goertzen said of the alleged police practice: "That's false. That isn't happening. It's easy to lie about someone when they can't defend themselves and you have an axe to grind. As [Nazi propaganda minister] Joseph Goebbels said, 'If you tell a lie big enough and keep repeating it, people will eventually come to believe it.' Hitler coined the expression, 'the Big Lie,' about using a lie so 'colossal' that nobody would believe anyone would dare invent it.[109] That is what we experienced in Saskatoon."

Goertzen knows of three incidents since the sixties when Saskatoon police officers dropped someone off in an improper manner. In the 1960s, a white male was dropped off in the summer, in the seventies, an Aboriginal woman was dropped off in the summer, and in 2000, Darrell Night was dropped off in the winter and had to take a cab home. The only person dropped either near the power plant, or in winter, was Night. In each case, it was the police service that initiated investigations into the drop-offs, and the officers responsible were disciplined. "That was something that was made very clear to us in our training was not to be done," Goertzen says.

Indeed, the only Saskatonian this author found who said he, personally, had been dropped off against his will by police was Caucasian. Now an architect, he said that, as a long-haired youth in the late sixties, he had been taken from half a block from his home and dropped off by police "in the city, some distance away." It was not winter. "I wasn't cold when I got home," he reported, "but I was really annoyed!"

Goertzen continues, "I remember being told about a Calgary officer that dropped a drunk Native off on the other side of some bridge in Calgary where there is a reserve bordering the city. Urban myth has it that the native male rolled down into the water and drowned after he was dropped off. This would have been a few years ago, because I was told that the responsible officer is now a senior executive officer or retired.

"I have never heard of such a practice in Edmonton, Prince Albert, Moose Jaw, Estevan, Weyburn and during my career, the only instance of someone being driven to the outskirts and dropped off was the one with Ken [Munson] and Dan [Hatchen]. Since I started here in 1981, I have heard rumours that cabbies have dropped people off, but I have no specific details to back that up, or even form a reasonable opinion about."

I have spoken to many officers about the issue, and was told by a now-deceased member of the Regina Police Service that in the 1940s and '50s, before social assistance, if police found a vagrant with few options but to survive by theft, that officer would put him on the highway "headed for Moose Jaw. There were very few Native people in the city, so only white people were dropped off. And *only* in the summer!" he added emphatically.

A retired Calgary officer said that in the fifties and sixties, the paddy wagon used to drop drunk people outside of town to walk home and sober up, but only in warm weather. "It was not a malicious thing in the sense of 'We are going to make you suffer,' it was because we had nowhere to take them. It was a way of solving a problem. A lot of them were white; we didn't have many Aboriginal people in Calgary then."

The only other officer who said he had heard of occasional unrequested drop-offs was in B.C. "Senior officers have told stories of the wagon sometimes taking drunks out of town and dropping them off to let them walk it off in the sixties, seventies and probably into the eighties. This was done when weather was not a threat and they were not comatose drunk; in that case they were taken to Emergency before being lodged in cells."

All three older officers said four things: these drop-offs did not target Aboriginal people, they were never done in cold weather, they had not been done in decades, and were never referred to as "starlight tours."

Retired Const. Larry Lockwood:

"I had never heard the term 'starlight tour' until Munson and Hatchen got into trouble in 2000. I was very curious about that. I thought I was a pretty wise street cop and I'd never heard this term. Then one day I was sitting in a coffee shop down on 42nd and Faithful, and there were some fellows in there, some taxi drivers, and I was listening to them. They were complaining about a Native fellow who'd taken them on a 'starlight tour.' And of course my ears perked up right now!

So I went and I said, 'What are you guys talking about – starlight tour?' One of them says, 'Oh, this has been going on for years! That's what we call it when some Natives take us from one address to another address, over to a store and then, a block away from a residence, they bail out without paying. We've gone on a starlight tour.'

I said, 'You mean, "starlight tour" is a term taxi drivers use all the time for what we call "transportation by fraud" – not getting paid for giving someone a taxi ride?'

He said, 'Oh yes, we've been calling that "starlight tours" for years!'

I wanted to start laughing, but it's not a laughing matter. You know, a term that's familiar between cabbies and the Native community when Natives do something wrong to cabbies – nothing to do with police. Suddenly Aboriginal activists claim it means police doing something wrong to Natives!"

A Calgary woman who asked to remain nameless backs up Lockwood's account. "I worked as a civilian secretary for a Manitoba RCMP detachment from 1971 to '74. We used to get taxi drivers coming in often, complaining that they had been taken on a 'starlight tour.' We knew they had been directed all over the place and not paid."

Saskatoon United Blueline taxi driver, Amca Czuli, says this has happened to her. "You drive down to their address, you pick them up, you drive them wherever they have to go, and in the end they don't pay. Just as soon as we say we are going to call the cops, they start saying bad things about racism and they had the land here and the white people did this and that. I don't know why they have to say that all the time because they have the same rights as the whites, the blacks, and so on. They refuse to make better choices and that's the consequences."

Asked if she had ever heard an Aboriginal person say they had been dropped off by police against their will, Czuli replied, "Never. The police here are working very well. I came here from a communist country, Romania, where I know that the police officer has the right to beat you up because nobody was questioning them and so on. So far here, I have seen they are just applying the law. That's all."

Ambulance attendant "Fred Smyth" says that cab drivers are the only people he's heard of making drop-offs in Saskatoon:

"I worked cab in 1985-86 in Saskatoon while going to university. Lots of stuff happened that shouldn't. Someone stiffs you and you drop them off in the middle of nowhere. White or Aboriginal. I didn't have to do that because I'd ask for money up front. You'd hear: 'So-and-so was stiffed. So he booted them out.' I remember asking another driver at the time what 'starlight tour' meant. Apparently it was a term given to people that were known not to have money to pay their cab fare. So if they were slightly intoxicated, then they would be driven away from their destination and kicked out of the car. A kind of punishment for wasting the driver's time. Did I do it? No. Did others? Possibly. I just know that it was explained to me and I didn't ask too many questions."

An Aboriginal woman who knew Neil Stonechild as a youth says:

"I heard something about Neil apparently getting into a cab, that was some of the word on the street. I also heard that, if taxis were robbed or anything, they had stopped reporting it, because the police, you know, there is only so much the police can do, and there is only so much that the justice system does. They slap 'em on the wrist, and away they go, and they get probation, they get community service, and that taxi driver is

still out the money. So apparently, I guess, these taxi drivers were starting to take matters into their own hands, and from my understanding, taking people that weren't going to pay their fare, out of town, and dumping them off, and making them walk back, but it's never happened to me. I don't recall a whole lot of peoples' names that have told me this because it's been a long time. I feel horrible in the fact that I probably can't give anybody any more than the fact that he was an awesome kid and didn't deserve this."

Documents obtained under the Access to Information Act reveal that RCMP received information from an SPS officer, his name in the document redacted (edited out): "He also states he picked up a man near the landfill and brought him into the city after the man had been dropped off by a taxi driver."

Retired Saskatoon Crown prosecutor Terry Hinz says that in the 25 years he had contacts in the criminal community and the defense bar, he never heard of police dropping off people against their wishes. "If it had been widespread or common, you'd think there'd be some undercurrent or rumour about it," he says.

For seven years in the 1970s and '80s, Saskatonian Marie Brown ran a pawn shop in the hood on Ave. H and 18th. She met numerous police officers when they came each week to pick up her reports. As an apartment manager, too, for over 19 years, she called on police for problems:

"Q: Was the term, 'starlight tour,' something you heard often?
Brown: Never. Not 'til I read it in the media.
Q: Do you think you would have heard if police had been dropping people off inappropriately?
A: Yes, I think I would have.
Q: Did you run into any racist cops?
A: (Laughs) I had very little trouble with the police, very little.
Q: Did you ever see them abusing Aboriginal people?
A: No. I've never known any officer in my whole life to ever do physical harm to anyone.
Q: Did you ever see a police officer be rude to a Native person?
A: No. They treated them the same way they treated me, same way they treated everybody."

If "starlight tour" was a term some taxi drivers knew, it seemed unknown to many First Nations Saskatonians. Everyone seemed to use a different name, as in Vice Chief Joseph's interview with CBC television:

"The justice system as it exists today stinks (LAUGHTER). I don't know what else you can say. It doesn't work. The whole system is basically cowboys and Indians: go and find the bad guy and lock him up. End of story. This Moonlight Tours or drop-offs have been happening for many, many, many years."[110]

Joseph was spreading disturbing falsehoods about police around the province as late as 2007, as exposed by journalist Ann Harvey in Yorkton This Week and Enterprise:

"Joseph said [in a speech to Aboriginal students], FSIN is also active and trying to help Aboriginal people who are abused by police. In Saskatoon in 2000, frozen bodies of Aboriginals were found and in some of these cases police had dumped them in isolated places. … The chief referred to two policemen going to jail after a man froze to death."

Harvey corrected Joseph:

"Two policemen were sent to jail for eight months, although many believed they were innocent. But the chief's remarks may have inaccurately led the audience to believe that Night died. No one died, nor was anyone injured from the cold. The chief could not have wanted anyone to get the wrong impression, so I am sure he will appreciate the fact that this press member is listening to First Nations leaders. … I am sure the chief, a man who cares about the First Nations Canadians he represents and who wants the Canadian government to honour treaty promises, is as concerned as I am about maintaining our Canadian tradition of justice for all."[111]

Aboriginal Saskatonian Keith Morvick used the term "Moonlight Rides" when speaking to me. A *Saskatchewan Sage* writer used "Starlight Cruises"[112] (while another *Sage* writer said he had previously heard of police drop-offs only in summer).[113]

Alice Kelsey is one of the few to speak, not of hearsay, but her actual experience with SPS:

"I was trying to hitchhike home from a nightclub on New Year's Eve in the 1970s, and not having any luck. I was 18, wearing high heels and light clothes and it was so cold! All of a sudden a police car stopped beside me. One cop goes, 'You'd better get in; you're going to freeze to death!' I got in the car, he asked me where I lived and I told him, 'The Court.' He goes, 'There's no court at this time of the morning!' and we all laughed. I told him, 'No, the Court apartments!'

They started driving that way and one of them goes, 'Are you hungry? Could you use a hamburger?' I go, 'Yes!' So they went to a drive-through, bought me a burger and pop and drove me home. I go, 'Could you park over there?' (I didn't want anyone to see me getting out of a cop car.) They laughed and drove a little further, said, 'Happy New Year!' and went on their way.

There was no fear on my part because I had never seen any cops roughing up anyone and even when I had apartment parties that went past 11 at night and the police were called, they were always polite and just said, 'People are sleeping; can you turn the music down?' Not like the police here [in Oregon] – they are very different and can be very insulting and make rude comments. The police in Saskatoon were very fair with the Aboriginal people. We were lucky to have those cops."

Craig Nyirfa, SPS Aboriginal Liaison Officer since 1994 says that the only drop-off he's heard of was Darrell Night's. "I've had people who have said they've heard about unwanted drop-offs, as well, but no one who said it happened to himself or herself, and certainly nothing to the extent where they came in and made an official complaint."

Some claim a "blue wall" of police protecting police. People such as Vice Chief Joseph who, in 2001, told media that a "blue veil of police secrecy" is alive and well in Saskatoon.[114] Officers say there are too many checks and balances in the system to permit a blue wall of secrecy, and I had seen it for myself – including SPS bringing Darrell Night in to make a report, and later launching their own internal investigation and phone tap on Hartwig and Senger – but I wanted to talk to someone unrelated to police who could comment on any police drop-offs in the power plant area.

Wayne Erlandson, now of Swift Current, Saskatchewan, reports that from 1987 to 2002, he lived in the Montgomery area near the Saskatoon power plant. For 15 years he walked across acres of open fields to day and night shifts at Corning Cable Systems (since closed). His plant was 300 metres north of the landfill; the power plant is just south of the landfill. In that time, he and 160 colleagues never once saw a police car drop off anyone out there. "If anyone had seen police doing something like that, it would have spread through the plant like wild-fire!" he says. "The only place I've ever heard about it is in the news." (This corresponds with the reaction of the power plant engineer, according to Night's statement: "I told him that the cops had dropped me off out there. He was amazed; he couldn't believe it.")

Renovating his house, Erlandson regularly took garbage to the city dump. "At the landfill there were always four or five street people, often two couples and a couple of kids, picking through the garbage. A lot of them spent a lot of time at the landfill. People walked out there via Dundonald Road or coming along the river or walking on the railway tracks from the west."

The garbage dump is five blocks from the power plant. A field directly beside the fenced south boundary of the dump, next to the power plant, was a well-used area for people to gain access to the dump, while others still use it to turn tricks and inject drugs. On the riverbank are cardboard boxes where people sniff chemicals. The railway track in that area, without much rail traffic, is a highly-used walking path. To this day, many people walk out there on the tracks, or drive there daily, year-round, to party or scavenge. A Caucasian social worker told me that in his youth, his mother and siblings went to the Saskatoon garbage dump every Saturday to obtain everything they used in their house except food and underwear.

Erlandson continues, "The plant went non-smoking, so they put a small tent outside for the smokers. Often we would find street people lying on the bench in the tent, asleep. They frequently seemed intoxicated, but they never said they had been dropped off by police on a supposed 'starlight tour.' They got there under their own steam. Because the plant ran 24 hours a day, we would sometimes find them there at night – we were a light in the dark. My point is that there are more ways, and more reasons, for street people like Wegner to get out to the landfill than being dropped off by cops, and to rule out those other ways is totally wrong."

Nor did reporters stop to ask Aboriginal citizens about "starlight tours" and police racism. Alice Kelsey believes part of the problem is Aboriginal politicians exploiting the fact that Caucasians do not understand Native culture:

"My uncle, for example, lives in the East end of Saskatoon. He wears only a blue jean jacket with a fleece lining over a shirt all winter long – that's what most people wear – and he even walks barefoot to buy beer during the winter when there's snow on the ground. I even told him he was crazy. He's always been like that, and I've seen other Natives – the guys take it as a matter of pride that they have a tolerance for the cold."

Ron Frazer concurs, saying that years after he retired from policing, he picked up an Aboriginal man walking in his hospital gown eight blocks from the hospital in -20° weather. He had been heading for Sutherland, miles away. "They are a tough race of people. I don't know how many people I've picked up walking around in a windbreaker and no hat in -40 temperatures. They'd say something like, 'I'm going to visit my aunt.' I would have been dead in half a block!"

Melvin McGhee, Aboriginal and a veteran Saskatoon social worker, says he's heard rumours of drop-offs made against a person's wishes, but believes most were "a lot of hot air from people with police records as long as your arm and not much credibility. I think they were just jumping on the bandwagon."

McGhee finds it hard to relate to comments about police racism since, in a half-dozen encounters with police over minor offenses, he has always been treated with respect. "They always called me 'Sir,' and sometimes we'd end up talking for a while. Only once I got in a verbal jousting match with an officer but then a senior officer – white – pulled up and said to me, 'Hey man, how ya doing?' and we both calmed down." One time McGhee had accumulated $760 in parking tickets and was pulled over. "I explained to the officer that it was just total disrespect for the law; I'd kept thinking I'd pay later. He could have impounded my car, but when I said I'd be in that evening to pay up, the officer said, 'I believe you.' I went in that night and paid it off."

"It's a two-way street," McGhee continues:

"Often First Nations people are rude to police. The FSIN should be teaching people to treat authorities with respect. You hear so many times that police are just racist. Once we were down at the Sports Bar, a friend was getting rowdy and we'd called him a cab. An officer was called and in a friendly tone simply said, 'You've got to clear this establishment.'
My friend, who looks European, said, 'If I were white, you wouldn't be doing this to me.'

The officer got red in the face and his tone got serious and he said, 'Hang on a minute here! The only reason we were called here was because of your conduct, being drunk and disruptive in a public place.'
After the constable got my friend into a cab, he came over to us and said, 'How's your afternoon going? Sorry about your friend.'
I said, 'I'll bet you're really tired of being called racist.'
He replied, 'Yeah, I don't know why people say that. We're sick and tired of people using the racism card. We're not arresting people for any reason except their conduct. He was breaking the law and we were called here.'"

Saskatonian Phil Braebrook, a retired RCMP officer, concurs. "As police officers, individuals that are in that industry, we become, at times, cynical about certain things, and what it is, it's generally to an individual, not a race, not a religion, not a creed. It's the reputation of an individual that forms our thoughts to them – whether that person is repetitively involved in criminal activity, repetitively displaying their addictions to different substances, whatever, and that's what we may derive a critical opinion from, but we don't gain a bias against a whole community or grouping of people."

"Back in 1973 when I started in the police department, there was no question that Aboriginal people were probably given a bum deal, all right?" says retired Sgt. Ross Campbell:

"The judicial system, police, everything in the judicial system treated Aboriginals differently than they treated everybody else. It was like a two-tiered system, all right? Over the years that changed, and it changed to the better, to the point where I think the justice system tries to treat everybody the same now. I think the police departments have been made a lot more aware of Aboriginal cultures, the differences in the cultures, their beliefs and how they differ from ours, and I think everybody is actually – well, maybe not everybody, there is always gonna be the abstainers – but I think most of the people in the justice system, whether it be police, lawyers, judges, are actually making an attempt now to try and put everything back on an even scale.
The problem is that the Aboriginal people, even though now the balance on the scales of justice has actually levelled out, and things are a lot fairer, and a lot more transparent than they ever were, I think their thinking now is, 'Okay, well it happened to us for all these years, so now we've got

to get even.' And this is where I think this is coming from, and I really, truthfully, don't believe it's all of them; the vast majority, the elders and a lot of people in the Aboriginal community are really, really good people, and they're not vindictive, and they don't want this, but a lot of their leaders are, and because the leaders are the ones that are calling the shots, that's kind of the trail that has been taken. I think this whole deal that has happened from the Munson/Hatchen affair to the Hartwig/Senger affair to whatever affairs are gonna happen in the future, are part of this vindictiveness because the police have been treated totally differently than any other person in the community. The police are being tried and convicted by media, they're being tried and convicted with no evidence whatsoever."

A clergyman who asked to be called "Pastor Mike" explains how he encountered SPS in 2000: "A couple of gentlemen, Murray Zoorkan and Stan Goertzen, came to my door to let me know there was a body buried under my house."

I then, of course, went to talk to Zoorkan and Goertzen. They revealed how they had solved an eight-year-old murder case going back to the same "generalist" era as the botched Stonechild investigation. Despite having no witnesses, no physical evidence, no body, and a very cold trail, they managed to get Lorne Kamm to admit to the killing and subsequent burial of his common-law wife, Dale Beaulieu. Stan Goertzen explains:

"I believe the 1990 investigation into Neil Stonechild's freezing death was inadequate, but it wasn't the only inadequate response to peoples' concern for the welfare of a family member. In 1992, Dale's mother had made repeated attempts to report her daughter missing, yet SPS front desk personnel refused to take a missing person report! In my opinion, we were grossly understaffed, officers were under-trained, and rookies were put at the front desk where, because we didn't respond to all 911 calls, people sometimes had to stand in line 45 minutes to try to get issues dealt with. Finally Dale's frantic mother made a complaint to the head of the local police commission.

Because it was listed as a missing person, the file was not assigned to major crimes, just as Stonechild's wasn't. The investigator did a lot of good work, but never got the break he might have needed to find out where Dale was. She remained missing until Murray was assigned to the newly-created Cold Files. He actively pursued this one, and asked me to assist."

Zoorkan and Goertzen re-interviewed suspects until they "ran into someone who was not straightforward with us" and then began to "focus in on him." Many interviews later, when the officers told Kamm they were hiring an archeologist to help find the body on the site of his former, burned-down rental house in the hood, he confessed and drew a map of where he'd buried the body. Five officers dug for two days, deep beneath Pastor Mike's new home's cemented basement floor, before unearthing the partially-clothed body. The killer was sentenced to six years in prison; eligible for parole in four. Goertzen concludes:

"It was cathartic to recover Dale's body, making up for past SPS mistakes (failure to take a simple report) and provide closure for the family. I believe that cases like Neil Stonechild and Dale Beaulieu proved to be catalysts in improving staffing levels and training with the subsequent benefit of better morale and better public service. I absolutely believe that if a better, more complete investigation had been done into Neil's freezing death in 1990, it would not have allowed room for Jason Roy to fabricate a web of lies about Brad and Larry."

Pastor Mike continues:

"The police were very good to walk me through it, why they suspected this, what they would like to do, and I got to put in my input as to what would keep the dust down in the house and where they could excavate and where they couldn't.
Q: And to get back to my original question, do you deal with many Native people?
A: I live amongst the Native population here in Saskatoon.
Q: Have you ever spoken to a Native person who said they'd been dropped off inappropriately?
A: No. Never."

Pastor James Randall, Minister at Saskatoon City Centre Church, with a congregation of 98 percent First Nations:

"When we're dealing with policing, we're dealing with government authority and the justice system, we need to make sure that we're not acting in defense against the rights of one party or the other. We need to apply the law equally across the colour spectrum. You know, there is not a separate set of rights for First Nations people or white people when it comes to the law.

And I think there's a perception that we have to be careful that we're not prejudicing against the Native population. There is no question that Native people in our community have been prejudiced against in the past, but that doesn't mean that we swing over into the other ditch and start prejudicing against white people so that we can somehow make amends for that. Nobody can undo what's been done in the past. But we have to make sure we move on, treating everybody equal."

Q: So what we need is justice to be not only blind, but colour-blind?

A: You bet! You bet!"

CHAPTER 16 - The Cherub and The Christian:
Intervening Years 1991-2000

'*Q: Do you think that Larry [Hartwig] would have treated Neil
Stonechild worse than he treated you when he arrested you?*
Mark Shule: *No, if anything he should have treated me worse because I
was, uh, I was under investigation for breaking into Larry's own house
at the time. And he knew it!'*

Constables Hartwig and Senger began working together as
regular partners in Saskatoon's West side in 1993. Hartwig recalls one middle-
of-the-night dispatch:

*"Senger and I took a call where a woman's intoxicated ex-boyfriend
had broken into her duplex, grabbed their infant and taken him into an
upstairs bathroom. We arrived and spoke to the hysterical mother. As
we got to the bottom of the stairs, a young Aboriginal man exited the
bathroom and stood at the top of the stairs holding the baby in one arm
and his other arm behind his back. 'I've got a knife and am going to kill
the baby!' he shouted.*
*We drew our weapons and ordered, 'Drop the weapon!' but he refused.
When we tried to talk him into giving us the baby, he shouted, 'Shoot
me!' As we tried to negotiate, he frequently repeated, 'I'm going to kill the
baby!' and 'Shoot me!' It was a standoff and we holstered our guns. After
talking to him a long period of time, we discussed pepper spraying him
but didn't want to risk harming the child, as he could drop him. He kept
shouting, 'Shoot me!' and we finally told him, 'No one is going to be shot
today!' After talking to him a long period of time, he gave up the baby and
revealed he didn't have a weapon. He was arrested and charged. Later he
wrote Senger and me a letter thanking us for not killing him."*

Both officers had excellent service records and were highly regarded in
the Saskatoon Police Service, the justice community, by civic officials and the
community at large. Both had above-average annual performance reviews,
and above-average marks in exams for on-the-job training. By 2000, in their

combined 17 years of service, neither had a legitimate complaint made against them.

Senger had established a reputation as a calming influence on people and situations, possibly related to his years as a psychiatric nurse. Sgt. Lane Cooper gives this account:

Const. Brad Senger, in the photo on his 2004 police ID

"I remember one night – [Constables] Brent Kuemper and Brad were off Avenue I North; they had gone to deal with something, a brawl broke out and they became the targets. My partner and I were in the paddy wagon just a few blocks away. We were en route when another car came on the radio and said, 'We'll get it! We are close.' I knew these guys; I kept going. By the time they got there, we had made sure Brent and Brad were safe and helped their arrests get into the back of the car. I turned around and tore a strip off one of the officers: 'Don't you ever come on the radio and tell somebody you're close, when you're farther away than we are and you drive like a maniac to get there!' I was mad because they would have left Brad and Brent with a wait for back-up of from 30-seconds to a minute longer!

This guy was twice my size. Brad got in between the two of us and said, 'Lane, we're okay.' And I said, 'I know you're okay, but what happens the next time?' He said, 'You'll come, you'll ignore them, and we'll be okay again!' This guy that I was confronting does not back down from anybody. And Brad just kind of looked at him – well, my partner and I called Brad 'The Cherub' – he gets this cherubic look on his face and the other guy backed off, went and got in his car, and drove away. Brad defused the whole situation. He's got that little round face, and when he smiles, you can't be mad!"

This writer had an illuminating experience with Brad Senger. In a taped interview with me, a former street kid who had known Neil Stonechild made a very derogatory allegation about him. When I mentioned it to Brad, he said (and I quote): "You can't use that. Neil isn't here to defend himself!"

In response to a question of mine, Senger also said: "We didn't see Stonechild, we never spoke to Stonechild, and we certainly did not have him in our custody. I had been out of police college for six months, and it was my first night partnered with Larry, our second call. We didn't even know each other! It is a no-brainer – something like that would not happen; it just would not be done."

Larry Hartwig is described by a fellow officer as "an eager beaver, hard worker, a little effusive, quite religious." In 1993, with support of other officers, Hartwig started a Christian Police Officers group, and was involved in a number of chaplaincy initiatives serving poor families of all races:

Const. Larry Hartwig, in his 2004 police ID photo

"I took my inspiration from the apostle James, who said we are to prove our faith by our actions. I firmly believed that we demonstrate our love for God by how we treat others. This respect I applied to all created things. My personal goal was to strive daily to be the best police officer, person, husband, and father I could be, and never miss an opportunity to help others. This was a goal I took very seriously.

"The role of police officer is not only immensely fulfilling, it is both heart-warming and heart-breaking, especially when you witness the harm done to children by their own parents. It is also filled with danger and temptation that only the most steadfast and disciplined people can resist. Police officers put their own physical, mental, and spiritual lives on the line every day for people who view them with suspicion, anger, hatred, or indifference. Police officers save lives every day. They save people from each other, but most often they save people from themselves. This is the nature of service."

Hartwig volunteered his time to several programs initiated by SPS to foster a closer relationship with Aboriginal Saskatonians and break down stereotypes that people, especially in the Aboriginal community, held about police. When people he arrested were receptive, he would ask, "Why did you do what you did?" Despite their various reasons, he found the root of the behaviour was usually some sort of dysfunction. Hartwig felt it was his duty to help out such people any way he could, including providing spiritual care and even food – frequently bringing needy families the deer meat he had hunted.

Hartwig would debate with other Christian police officers his philosophy that if he treated even the "bad guys" well, someday when in a bar fight or other disturbance, if someone were about to attack a distracted officer, one of the people he had treated well would step in.

Mark Shule, for one, says he'd step in: "For sure! Larry is one helluva guy. He looks out for people." In 1988, Shule was one of several teens breaking into Hartwig's home. After they broke a window in the empty house, however, they "heard sirens and all went running!" The SPS K9 unit soon tracked down and arrested the teens. Whenever Hartwig encountered him later, Shule says, even knowing that he had tried to break into his home, Hartwig always treated him fairly:

"Oh, he was good, yeah! He never changed at all; he was just a normal guy. One time that really sticks out is we were at a house party in Dundonald, and the house party got broken up and we were getting kicked out, and I was walking to my jeep, and of course I had had a few drinks. And he was in his cop car, and he got out before I got in my jeep; he's like, 'Mark, you're not gonna be driving that, are you?' I was like, 'Well, no-o-o....'
If he had let me get into that vehicle, he right away could have given me a breathalyzer and arrested me. Instead, he asked for my parents' number, and he called my dad himself, making sure I wasn't tripping him, giving him a false number. He dialed the number and asked for my dad and then I asked him for a ride home. My parents got mad because they thought I was in trouble again with the law, but which this time I wasn't. And he waited there 'til my dad got there. And, yeah, he knew me by name then, even. At the time I didn't care for him because, well, he made me call my dad, and I was kind of mad at it then, but now that I'm older I realize what he was doing.
(Pause.) Uh, one time – that would've been years ago! – I did throw a punch at Larry, once.

Q: Did you hit him?

A: Uh, I was very close. Yeah, for sure. So....

Q: What did he do?

A: Nothin'. Just grabbed my hands and put me under arrest.

Q: Did he hurt you at all, even 'accidentally'?

A: Oh, he could have for sure, yeah, but no. Just took me straight downtown.

Q: And next time he ran into you, how did he treat you?

A: Oh, he was fine, yeah. Didn't treat me bad or any different, no. It was good.

Q: Do you think that Larry would have treated Neil Stonechild worse than you?

A: No, if anything he should have treated me worse because I was, uh, I was under investigation for breaking into Larry's own house at the time. And he knew it!

Q: The RCMP had a theory that Larry Hartwig and Brad Senger did harm to Neil Stonechild because he was a 'troublemaker.' Do you think Larry is the kind of guy that would have taken Stonechild out to that field because Stonechild had done something to him before?

A: No, he wouldn't have never done that. I can't see it happening. We all thought he was a pretty good guy.

Q: Did you ever hear of police dropping anybody off where they didn't ask to be dropped?

A: I never heard of that, no. I knew a lot of police and a lot of kids that knew police and I never heard of that, ever. So I sure can't see Larry ever doing that."

The police department received numerous letters praising Hartwig's work:

"Oct. 31, 1991: *Mrs. [Name Withheld] 18-year-old Métis daughter had to testify at the recent [name withheld] trial. It was a very difficult decision for her to testify, given the circumstances. Constable Hartwig went the extra mile and was extremely helpful and support[ive] for them."*

"June 18, 1992: *We would like to use The StarPhoenix to publicly thank the many people who helped us after our traffic accident on June 12. ... and the many firefighters who attended so promptly and used the Jaws of Life, and finally we are truly grateful to Const. Larry Hartwig for his* *professional and understanding manner."*

"Dec. 1992: *Inspector Fleming has informed me about your excellent teamwork in solving a number of break-and-enters. This is a case in point where the sharing of information, and using good old common sense and police initiative, has paid off. – Chief Owen Maquire"*

"Dec. 6, 1995: *As a result of this information [obtained by Hartwig from a street source], 10 male subjects were arrested with approximately 45 Criminal Code charges laid. This information cleared up approximately 20 B & Es. – Sgt. Al Kopelchuk"*

"On August 24/25, 1996, *while away for the weekend, our home was broken into. When we arrived home on Sunday, we called your service and within 10 minutes two officers arrived. Within 24 hours, the majority of our belongings that had been taken were returned. We certainly appreciate the kindness and service provided by Constables Kuemper and Hartwig and feel they deserve to be commended."*

"[No date]: *In the future, I would highly recommend that Larry be given the opportunity to work in GIS or any of the other specialized investigative divisions. He has tremendous investigative skills and adapts to new challenges with confidence. When Larry gets a little piece of information, he tends to not let go until he has solved the file. He can be very tenacious and stubborn and is never one to quickly write off a file. – Sgt. Jim Bracken"*

Perhaps most relevantly, in the year before Stonechild's death:

"Apr. 20, 1989: *Sir: On April 20, 1989 at approximately 0020 hrs. Csts. Mulder and Hartwig had occasion to attend the initial complaint of a house entry at 526 SHEA Cres. Entry was gained via a ground level sliding window located at the rear of the home, under the deck. The owners came home while the intruders were still in the house, but persons were able to flee. Const. Carlson and I attended at the scene. I was able to develop three finger-prints on one of the windows. As a result of the constables doing street checks some 6 hours after the offense, a Jet Set [paper producing several copies] with the names of four of our more active young offenders was directed to me. Three of these people have fingerprints on file with our department. I compared the scene prints with these persons and identified them to one Neil STONECHILD, SPD #*

*40132. I believe that as a result of the quick work of Mulder and Hartwig, a case was solved, an offender was identified within a matter of hours, thus saving the Identification Section and the Department several man-hours of work in processing the scene prints for submission to Ottawa, and awaiting a possibility of two to three weeks for the results. This type of work shows **the importance our section places on street checks and being advised of suspects found in the areas** of residential house entries. I would, therefore, request that these two constables be given some sort of recognition for their actions and a job well done. Respectfully submitted, Sgt. R. A. Grosy."*

When the SPS, partnering with FSIN, started the "Peacekeepers" program in which police officers take Aboriginal youth in conflict with the law to interact together in a relaxed, non-threatening way, Hartwig was one of the first to volunteer. Their initial canoe trip in 1998 included 12 police officers, 10 Aboriginal youth including three hard-core offenders, three FSIN staff and an Aboriginal Elder. In addition to four days canoeing, they would participate in sweat lodge, prayer, and discussion of a wide range of topics, including the issues that landed them in trouble.

The group included not only young offenders, but hard-core offenders unreachable by any other means. This was viewed as a desperate, last-ditch effort to positively influence their lives. While most of the youth were guarded and apprehensive, some began to relax and see that the cops were not their enemies. Hartwig describes one:

"Ambrose was a kid about 16 years of age who was a serving prisoner in Lloydminster. He was a big kid, over six feet tall and about 300 lbs. He was a shy, quiet, and respectful kid. When I asked what he was serving time for, he responded, "Break-and-Enter and robbery." After a few days of observing him, I asked him why and how he gets into trouble. He told me that his friends bother and bully him to get drunk and do crime. I told Ambrose that he knew that what he was allowing himself to do was wrong and that he was a mountain of a young man and that no one should be able to make him do anything he didn't want to do. He seemed to grow a couple of inches at that point.
Being an outdoorsman, I took extra fishing gear and allowed Ambrose to use my gear, even though fishing gear was supplied by the outfitter. As we

got to know each other, I asked him why he thought I allowed him to use my gear. He replied, "I don't know." I told him, "I know that you respect me, and if you respect me, you will respect my possessions. I trust you." He grew another couple of inches.

When we participated in the sweat lodge, we all said a prayer to the Creator and 'all our relations.' That is to honour and respect all who have passed on to the spirit world before us. I prayed the same prayer I do any time I am lucky enough to participate in cultural experiences: that the 'Creator of All Things' would help all of us to focus on our similarities rather than on the human instinct to focus on our differences. I believed it is only when we do this, that relationships are built and past wounds healed."

The group was returning to Saskatoon at the end of the trip when the officers received word that one of the hard-core youth offenders was planning to escape as soon as they stopped in Prince Albert for supper. Because a youth trusted the police enough to warn them, as soon as the youth bailed out, he was captured.

Two corrections officers met the group when they arrived at the restaurant, saying they were to escort Ambrose back to Lloydminster as soon as they arrived in P.A. Hartwig told them that, of all people on the trip, Ambrose was one of the best-behaved. The correctional officers couldn't believe it. Hartwig personally vouched for Ambrose and asked the correctional officers to wait in the parking lot while the group had its final supper.

"Other police officers had similar stories," Hartwig says. "Several youth would say that this single experience demonstrated to them that police officers were not the 'bad guys' they thought, but people who really cared. Some would even say this changed their outlook on life."

Hartwig says he operated on the belief that "When we open ourselves up to others in such a way, we accomplish several things. First, we learn that our petty little problems aren't so big after all. Second, we demonstrate we genuinely care for them and the way they feel; this builds relationships and understanding. Third, this is scripturally-sound and we meet our responsibilities to others."

Senger returned after his firing to his former job and tried to forget about these years of his life, but Hartwig's firing hit him particularly hard. "That is what people don't get. This isn't about losing a job. It is about losing your mission and purpose in life. It is about losing family history. It is about my children not being able to make a difference as I/they wanted. I am forever stained by this. The things I did as a police officer, my mission to help and protect others will remain unfinished. The guilt and shame laid on me and my family will cause a stain on our history. I will have to carry this burden to my death. This will chase me until then and even after that, because people are so filled with hate."

CHAPTER 17 - Stonechild Timeline

Tuesday, November 13, 1990, 11:12 pm: 17-year-old Neil Stonechild is reported Unlawfully at Large (UAL) from group home for young offenders. He had been in custody since August 29, 1990, following conviction for Break-and-Enter, due to be released December 28, 1990. His day pass for Nov. 13 had been good until 4:30 p.m. He was to have attended court in the morning and then completed that day's community hours at the Friendship Inn. When he didn't show, his supervisor reported him missing.

Eleven days later, Saturday, November 24, 1990: Neil Stonechild, still UAL, was living at his mother's residence, when he met up with his slightly younger, 16-year-old friend, Jason Roy. They spend the day together.

7:00 pm: Const. Bradley Senger starts his shift, walking the beat in downtown Saskatoon. He works with Const. Dave Hudson until nearly 11, when both pair up with district patrol cars.

8:00 pm: Const. Larry Hartwig (in his fourth year as a police officer) starts shift, assigned to his district in the west end of Saskatoon. With different start times and different geographical assignments, it is very unlikely that Hartwig and Senger would have spoken with each other prior to pairing up later.

10:40 to 10:45 pm: Senger pairs up with Hartwig for the first time in their lives. Their first dispatch is to a 17-year-old Aboriginal youth intoxicated and asleep in a car. They drive him home.

11:49 pm: Saskatoon resident Trent Ewart calls SPS 911 line, complaining that Neil Stonechild is drunk and causing a disturbance at Snowberry Downs apartment complex in the city's West end. He informs Stonechild he has called the cops; Stonechild says, "Sorry, Dude," and leaves.

11:51 pm: Junior SPS officers Hartwig and Senger are dispatched to investigate the complaint. They have no description to go on, and know Neil Stonechild is active in property crime. Knowing Neil was likely tipped off that police were on their way, they begin to search from his mom's residence to the south and work their way toward Snowberry Downs.

11:56 pm: 3 blocks south of Snowberry Downs, Hartwig and Senger encounter a male leaving the area and push the "at-scene" button on their in-car computer. They are at Twin Gables apartment. They stop and question the young man who says he is Tracy Horse and provides an address and DOB. This is actually Jason Roy who probably lied as he was just involved in the disturbance at Snowberry Downs. Hartwig writes the information in his notebook.

11:56 pm: (The same time Hartwig and Senger are questioning Jason Roy, who later claims he saw Stonechild in their police car at this time) A woman calls 911 to report having just seen a person hiding in driveway at 118 O'Regan Crescent (three blocks East of Snowberry Downs). Her description later given RCMP matches Stonechild's appearance, height, weight and race, including that he was wearing a lightweight jacket, possibly blue in colour, open to reveal a contrasting shirt beneath. This person was hiding, although no attempt had been made to break into this house or any others in the neighbourhood. What was this person's reason for hiding? Perhaps because he is Neil Stonechild and knows police are looking for him and there is a warrant out for his arrest for being UAL from his detention home?

11:57 pm: Senger and Hartwig check with Canadian Police Information Centre (CPIC) on their computer for the name "Tracy Horse," Senger queries the Canadian Police Information Centre (CPIC) on their computer for the name "Tracy Horse," using the DOB provided. Nothing is found on CPIC. Hartwig asks "Tracy" for his middle name. As if it were his real name, Jason doesn't miss a beat and says "Lee." Senger queries him again with DOB but Horse's record comes back "clean" (no warrant for arrest). Although "Tracy" is intoxicated, they release him, unaware he is actually Jason Roy, 16. Ten years later, Roy publicly accuses them of having had Stonechild – handcuffed, bloodied and screaming for his life – in their police vehicle that night.

11:59 pm: The officers continue on their way to Snowberry Downs and encounter another Aboriginal male (Bruce Genaille) leaving the area. This person later testifies that Hartwig and Senger accused him of being Neil Stonechild. In order to get a physical description of Stonechild, the officers run the name, Neil Stonechild, on CPIC, but do not enter a complete DOB, merely "18" in the age field, while Stonechild was actually 17. (Many police members say this is standard procedure. If Hartwig and Senger had had Stonechild in their custody, officers explain, they would have input his actual date of birth, not an approximate age. The computer-check would also have indicated that there was a Canada-wide warrant for Neil Stonechild's arrest. For two junior officers, bringing Stonechild in would have been a significant arrest.) Hartwig and Senger continue to accuse the young man of being Stonechild for several minutes until he produces identification for Bruce Genaille. Genaille later says Stonechild was not in the police car. **Importantly,**

Hartwig writes Genaille's name in his notebook immediately after the name Tracy Horse. This would indicate that this was the chronological order in which they were encountered. (Ten years later, in his statement to the RCMP, Genaille said this street check occurred between 10:00 p.m. and midnight, about a week before Neil's death. He also stated that the police questioned him about a disturbance at the 7-Eleven, making no mention of Snowberry Downs. There was no record of a disturbance call to the 7-Eleven. The RCMP investigated this alleged disturbance and found it to be "without merit." At the inquiry, there was no mention by counsel that this is when the check occurred. **Nevertheless, the commissioner would "find" that the officers had talked to Genaille earlier, and thus "explain" why Genaille did not see Stonechild in the police car.**)

12:04 am: Hartwig and Senger run his name, Bruce Genaille, and exact date of birth on CPIC. (The way this query was made – by DOB – is consistent with the evidence that Hartwig, Senger and other police witnesses gave at the Stonechild Inquiry about only entering DOB when that person is actually present, as they did, twice with "Tracy Horse.") Genaille (Stonechild's cousin) waits five to 10 minutes beside the police vehicle while his name is run. He later testifies no one was in the back seat. The notes in both police books are consistent with their version of events – that they talked to Genaille (who said Stonechild was not in their vehicle) two minutes after talking to Jason Roy (who claimed he was). Genaille is released and the officers arrive at Snowberry Downs.

Approximately 12:07 am: Once admitted to the building and after climbing three flights of stairs, checking each floor for Neil Stonechild, the officers speak with Trent Ewart, who states he thinks the person causing the disturbance was Neil Stonechild. Gary Horse would also confirm the police arrived. Ewart confirmed in his Nov. 30, 1990 statement that "Neil" had left several minutes before Hartwig and Senger arrived. RCMP ignored this. They would theorize that Ewart witnessed "some interaction" between the SPS and Stonechild that night.

12:17 am: After returning to their patrol car, Hartwig and Senger write down the call in their notebooks as Neil Stonechild being GOA or Gone on Arrival. They clear the call.

12:18 am: Hartwig and Senger dispatched to look for suspicious person who has been chased away from 118 O'Regan Crescent, a five-block drive east from Snowberry Downs, and a three-block walk through short-cuts.

12:24 am: Hartwig and Senger indicate they are "at-scene" at O'Regan Cres. They search the yard at 130 O'Regan, believed to be the one the suspicious person ran through. By now they are at least 28 minutes behind that person, who is believed to be travelling in a northeasterly direction.

12:27 am: They indicate the suspicious person is GOA.

12:30 am: They conduct a CPIC query of Trent Ewart who first phoned about Stonechild. (Many officers say they do this, when they have time, to seek extra information to help solve earlier unsolved investigations and for criminal intelligence purposes. These officers wonder why they weren't called to testify about standard police procedures.)

12:32 am: Perimeter alarm activated at 2213D Hanselman Ave., 5 km walking distance northeast of O'Regan Cres. Checked by K9 member, no sign of entry.

Sometime between 1 and 2 am: Banker and wife see a younger, shivering "Aboriginal" male, "maybe five and a half feet," "under 150 lbs" wearing an open jacket and a "lumberjack shirt." (He said he thought it was blue but his wife thought it was a different colour. She was not interviewed.) The male is walking on 51st Street overpass over Idylwyld Drive in the direction of the field, 12 blocks away, where Stonechild's body was later discovered. "I'm sure it was him!" states the banker. "There was no one else was out walking at that time of night and in that cold."

Sometime, date and time unknown, Stonechild dies of cold exposure in a field in the northwest industrial area, six km (3.7 miles) from Snowberry Downs.

Thursday Nov. 29: Stonechild's frozen body found. Sgt. Keith Jarvis of the SPS Morality (rather than Major Crimes) Unit conducts investigation that most parties today agree was inadequate. Jason Roy, 16, provides handwritten statement for police stating he and Stonechild each consumed 20 ounces of vodka before going out to find Stonechild's girlfriend at Snowberry Downs apartment complex. Roy says he and Stonechild then argued, so Roy left Stonechild at Snowberry Downs, "blacked out" and returned home alone. (What is significant in the statement was that Jason Roy was having trouble remembering such things as how they got to the 7-Eleven, whether or not they purchased anything, what they argued about twice, before he "blacked out" and woke up at the Binnings the next day.)

Dec. 5, 1990: Stonechild file closed. Coroner concludes cause of death was exposure, the manner of death: "accident."

March 1, 1991: *StarPhoenix* story headlined: "Family [of Neil Stonechild] suspects foul play: Family cites altercation with 'gang.'" (No suspicion of police involvement.)

~ ~ ~

Ten years later, Jan. 28, 2000: SPS Constables Munson and Hatchen drop off Darrell Night who gets home with no ill effects. The story is revealed in the media and a firestorm starts when media connect two previous freezing deaths to police.

February 3, 2000: Another Aboriginal man found frozen to death and again widely reported, alleging police involvement.

Feb. 16, 2000: RCMP "Operation Ferric" commences.

Feb. 22, 2000: Jason Roy comes forward with a claim of having seen Neil Stonechild in police custody, bloodied and handcuffed, screaming "they are going to kill me!" On the basis of an alleged 10-year-old memory by one man with a lengthy criminal history who told numerous variations of his story, and despite lack of any physical or supporting evidence, and in the face of extensive evidence indicating Stonechild had had no contact with police, following pressure by FSIN and media, government decides RCMP will investigate Stonechild's death. .

Mar. 7, 2000: RCMP finally take a statement from Roy. He states the first person who he actually recalled disclosing this experience to was a budding holistic therapist who would later claim to be able to retrieve memory lost to alcohol intoxication. Jason Roy states he was having trouble sleeping and "was asking questions about (Neil) being gone" (not dead). He further states that the therapist helped him with relaxation and breathing, "just clearing my head and putting what happened...in my mind and telling her everything that happened."

Mar. 31, 2000: RCMP install month-long "telephone number recorders" on Hartwig's and Senger's home lines to learn if they are calling one another. They then reinstall for 60 days, noting there were no calls between the two officers.

May 18, 2000: Separately, RCMP inform Constables Larry Hartwig and Brad Senger (in the presence of his children) that they are under investigation for the death of Neil Stonechild. Both officers immediately demand polygraphs.

May 25, 2000: RCMP begin 90-day wiretaps on home phones of Hartwig and Senger. Yet there was no reasonable and probable grounds for a judge to grant a wiretap, merely suspicion. (After criminal activity, criminals do most post-crime activity and chatter immediately, so to catch them, RCMP needed to get a wiretap in place immediately. The RCMP didn't do that for a week after informing the officers they were under suspicion for Stonechild's death.)

Oct. 18, 2000: Extension to original RCMP wiretap granted.

Nov. 2000: After Hartwig complains loudly to SPS Staff Sgt. about RCMP investigators who had interrogated him, SPS launch an internal investigation and install three month-long wiretaps on Hartwig and Senger's office phones. Hartwig was so "emotive" in his "venting," and later so suspicious of everybody that Staff Sgt. Murray Zoorkan, who, unbeknownst to most officers, was SPS liaison with Operation Ferric, reported it to Ferric investigators and initiated the investigation. Zoorkan later read the phone tap transcripts and found they contained "nothing of any consequence." The RCMP, however, as with both Hartwig and Senger's interviews, keyed in on one idea: Hartwig and Senger "made no denials."

In a later interview with this writer, Zoorkan explained how things got so far out of control. He is describing the very heart of a moral panic. **"I guess, at the time, I thought these guys must be guilty, or you wouldn't have such a big [RCMP] machine going after them. There's gotta be somebody guilty; there has to be an explanation for this. It couldn't be just that that boy wandered north and died of hypothermia, because why would there be this big task force?"**

"We all became afraid of the big machine that was devouring us," adds police chief of the time, Dave Scott.

Zoorkan adds, "I didn't know Larry well before all this happened, and then when I was assigned to look at the file, reviewing the evidence against them, all I ever saw with Larry and Bradley was just two men that were afraid; that's all I ever saw. There was never a hint of anything that you could even twist that these guys were guilty of anything." Yet the RCMP would claim that Zoorkan thought they were "dirty."

Dec. 12, 2000: After earlier refusing a polygraph, Senger bows under the pressure put on him to clear his name. He wants the RCMP and SK Justice to remove him from suspicion after he passes. They refuse. He tests inconclusive. After initially demanding one, at the advice of his lawyer, Hartwig does not take a polygraph.

Mar. 20, 2001: Const. Ernie Louttit finds Jason Roy's original statement in which he mentions no police involvement. Many expect RCMP would halt, or at least start their investigation over from square one, but RCMP did nothing about it. Did they feel they would lose face, so must continue with their theory? Some believe they completely lost objectivity, or even obstructed justice.

Apr. 24, 2001: RCMP had sent information from original Stonechild investigation and autopsy to Alberta's Chief Medical Examiner. He reports back: "All of the injuries depicted and described are minor 'blunt' injuries called abrasions (otherwise known as scrapes.) … if you look at the injuries in the context of the position where Mr. Stonechild's body was found in (i.e. face-down in frozen, crusted snow), it appears to me that his injuries would be entirely consistent with his falling onto the snow at this site prior to his death." Nevertheless, April 24 Stonechild's body is disinterred for re-examination in Alberta.

July 3, 2001: Second autopsy upholds original autopsy finding: "no evidence of foul play."

Dec. 12, 2001: After Brad Senger had requested polygraph 7 months earlier, he finally submits to it after his memory has been contaminated by countless conversations and news stories. He tests "inconclusive." (At the advice of his lawyer, Hartwig does not take polygraph.)

Hartwig explains, "Brad, like me, after first demanding a polygraph, decided against it because we no longer trusted the RCMP and were advised not to. It was only after many months that Brad chose to polygraph to clear his name, as the investigation wasn't 'going away.' The polygraph was to be conducted by an outside agency, with several polygraphists selected as potential examiners. An examiner was selected but backed out at the last moment. Another was selected and he, too, wasn't available. In the end, and against his own better judgment, Brad agreed to be tested by the same RCMP polygraphist who had concluded that I lied during my interview with Lyons. Brad agreed to be tested only if the 'issue' was determined beforehand. The RCMP refused to reveal the 'issue.' Brad also wanted assurances that when he passed, he would be cleared as a suspect. Both Sask Justice and RCMP refused. He finally relented and took the polygraph which did not test on knowledge or involvement in Neil's death, but only on whether or not he knew he had Stonechild in custody. This was an inappropriate issue to test on because it does not establish 'custody' and did not prove anything – unless you first assume Jason Roy was telling the truth about Stonechild being in the patrol car, beaten up."

Later, again against his lawyer's recommendation, Brad takes a second polygraph and again tests inconclusive. Brad seeks a second opinion from a retired RCMP officer who had been in charge of polygraph training. This former Mountie concludes that the key question was insufficient to determine wrongdoing on Hartwig and Senger's part. The RCMP focused on the issue of custody, which means nothing if Stonechild lied about who he was and was released by them.

FBI consultant Sue Doucette advises, "The polygraph cannot replace good, old-fashioned investigative detective work. You have to really hit the pavement and do the work to make a case. You can't just hook wires up to someone and say that this is going to magically solve a case. The polygraph is not admissible in court and that's because it's not been proven scientifically reliable."[115]

Feb. 8, 2003: Sask Justice finds insufficient evidence to lay charges concerning death of Neil Stonechild.

Feb. 20, 2003: Justice Minister Eric Cline announces public inquiry into Stonechild's death

Sept. 8, 2003 - May 19, 2004: Inquiry into the Death of Neil Stonechild. Jason Roy fails to remember numerous details of previous statements. Saskatoon's deputy police chief, Dan Wiks, testifies that the original investigation into Stonechild's death was incomplete.

Oct. 26, 2004: Constables Hartwig and Senger, with a total 29 years' impeccable service between them, are fingered by the commissioner at the Stonechild Inquiry as "probably" having had Stonechild in their custody. After the commissioner rearranged documented evidence, he also found the officers had time to drop Stonechild off in the north end and implied the officers had contributed to Stonechild's death. "In my opinion, he left no other conclusion for anyone who read that report," states Goertzen.

The officers are suspended, but given a chance to have others plead on their behalf for keeping their jobs. On that day, officers gather in the police station, lining hallways from the main floor, up the stairwell, to the third floor boardroom where Sabo would meet with them. As Hartwig and Senger walk past, the officers offer words of encouragement and support. "Deputy Chief Don MacEwan, afraid of what might happen (a mutiny), ordered all of us to leave," an officer recalls. "Nobody moved. We remained until Larry and Brad entered the boardroom. We were very unhappy with Wright's decision. We considered all going home for 24 hours, but decided that would not hurt our employer; only citizens and the city."

Police officers had stickers made up: "We believe in Brad and Larry." Officers said the stickers were still on their locker doors when they moved to the new police station ten years later.

Oct. 31, 2004: SPS Const. Astrid Pura and partner are working nights when they drive by someone outside Jax nightclub waving his arms at them. They recognize Jason Roy, who appears to be trying to get their attention. As Pura later tells the Police Hearing, they run his name on CPIC, discover an outstanding warrant for his arrest, get out of their car, and tell him they would like to deal with it. Pura says Roy turns around and says to people he's with, "Go get the boys!" Once in the back seat of the police car, when people start coming out of the bar, Roy bangs on the window, yelling, "They're going to kill me!" Mocking himself. And the story that ripped apart lives. Begging the question: in telling that story at the inquiry a year earlier, was Roy really, as the commissioner decided, "sincere"?

Nov. 12, 2004: Police Chief Sabo now has several options, including reassigning the officers or charging them on the basis of inquiry findings, in which case they could defend themselves in court. Instead, Sabo fires them as "unsuitable for police service by reason of their conduct." Why? On grounds they did not write in their notebooks that they had Stonechild in their custody. Why? Because, they say, they did not have Stonechild in their custody.

Police executive and police board immediately make clear to the public there was no allegation of the officers driving Stonechild to the industrial area and abandoning him. More than 200 officers at an emergency meeting unanimously vote to reject Wright's findings and unconditionally support Hartwig and Senger.

Stan Goertzen, on behalf of the association, apologizes to Mrs. Bignell for the 1990 investigation: "My heart goes out to the Stonechild family because I think they've lived with a terrible pain wondering how Neil froze to death, ever since it happened. I don't think enough was done to complete the investigation into Neil's death; it should have been dealt with by major crimes investigators. This investigation will always be a black mark for the Saskatoon Police Service and I apologize for that. This black mark has resulted in a more professional and focused approach to training and overseeing all Saskatoon

Police Service investigations now and in the future. The other tragedy is that two innocent people have been tried in the court of public opinion, without being charged, without a trial, and this has just become a comedy of errors."

Publicly, Chief Sabo accepts findings and apologizes to Stella Bignell for 14 years of "frustration and denial." On Parade soon after, however, Const. Wolfgang Pollman asks Sabo, **"Chief, do you personally believe they had done that?"** (taken Stonechild to the north end). Sabo replies: **"Wolfgang, to be honest with you, no I don't."** Pollman recalls, "Sabo then seemed to realize what he had said in front of 40 officers, and rushed out the door. My next question would have been, 'Why did you fire them, then?' but there was no chance; he was gone. For me, that was the end of believing in justice in Saskatchewan, the end of believing in my job and the dawning realization that I would head for the door at the earliest date my pension would allow. Over all those years, I had two very simple rules for my career as a cop. Honesty and Integrity. And some common sense to boot. But when all that is thrown in your face by the people you trust most in our job – the judges – it was time to fold up."

Hartwig and Senger immediately appeal to the Saskatchewan Police Commission.

May 2 – Nov. 1, 2005: Hartwig and Senger Hearing under the Police Act, in which they appeal their firing. Photogrammetrist Robertson who admitted to lying at the Stonechild Inquiry about his credentials is again judged qualified to testify. Police frustration at repeated suggestions they are lying boils over when a lawyer suggests Const. Louttit deliberately withheld from RCMP the Stonechild file he possessed. Louttit explodes, "If I knew I had it, I'd have turned it over in a heartbeat! We were being accused of heinous crimes!" Decision on firing not handed down until a year later, Nov. 1, 2006, when Police Commission upholds Chief Sabo's decision, based on the inquiry, to fire Hartwig and Senger.

August, 2006: Hartwig, Senger and Saskatoon City Police Association independently apply to Saskatchewan Court of Appeal to throw out result of public inquiry on basis it was outside scope of the investigation for Wright to decide whether or not the officers had Stonechild in their custody, when "he effectively imposed criminal and/or civil responsibility" for Stonechild's death upon the officers. In addition, Hartwig's lawyer maintains that Roy's testimony about seeing Stonechild in the back of a police cruiser on the last night he was seen alive was not only "erroneous, perverse, capricious and made without regard for the material before the inquiry," but "completely contrary to the evidence presented at the inquiry."

June 19, 2008: Saskatchewan Court of Appeal dismisses applications. The three judges who conducted the judicial review could examine only the evidence brought out in the inquiry. They rule that Justice Wright did not have to come to the conclusion he did, but believe they must give deference to his findings.[116]

July, 2008: The former officers seek to have their case heard by the Supreme Court. Although the highest court previously had heard appeals regarding other public inquiries, it denies the officers' application. It is not required to provide reasons for denying a hearing.

May 13, 2011: Hartwig, accompanied by his counsel and representative from the police association, file with SPS a complaint of perjury against Jason Roy and Gary Robertson. Supporting documents concerning the allegation are included, referring to the RCMP evidence disclosed for the Public Inquiry, which the commissioner had ordered at its conclusion to be returned or destroyed. Months later, the SPS responded that the file was not going to be investigated, even though the offences occurred in Saskatoon. The file is "sealed" against anyone ever wanting to access it.

Hartwig says, "Every time we launched appeal after appeal, I became more ill with PTSD and depression. Every time we tried to bring forward evidence and were turned down, I became more ill. Wright's findings were like a stab in the heart; Sabo's betrayal was like a stab in the back; all the other roadblocks were a death by a thousand cuts."

CHAPTER 18 - Stan Goertzen:
The Man who Fights for Justice

'He's the rock that kept everyone going through the hell of the first decade of the twenty-first century.'
– Serving SPS officer

A version of the Stonechild Timeline was prepared by Sgt. Goertzen, who worked countless hours with a team of a dozen retired SPS officers committed to proving Constables Hartwig and Senger innocent. "I was working the night Neil Stonechild went missing," said one of the retired officers. "I was alone in the car that night; I could've been framed with this as simple as anybody else. But I didn't get the call." (The team's PowerPoint presentation on the Hartwig/Senger case: www.whenpolicebecomeprey.com/ PowerPoint.)

After gathering all the permanently documented data and applying several hundred years of experience in various specialties, these officers concluded Neil Stonechild walked to that field, via the route they mapped below.

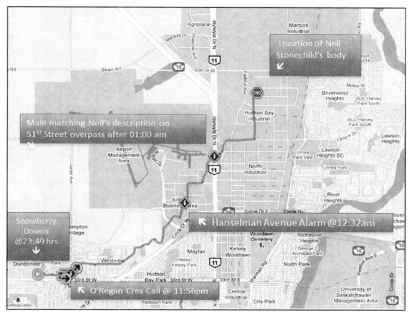

The team of retired officers explained what made them believe Stonechild took this route:

*"**After 12:27 a.m. Where did Stonechild go?***
There are two incidents of interest that occurred after the O'Regan Crescent call.
The first incident of interest is an alarm at 2213D Hanselman Ave at 12:32 hrs.
The alarm location is 5 km walking distance North of O'Regan Crescent via Westview and Cardinal Crescent.
This alarm came in 36 minutes after the suspicious person matching Neil Stonechild's description was chased from O'Regan Crescent.
The Hanselman alarm was checked by a K9 member and there were no signs of entry. This type of call is consistent with someone trying a door and setting the alarm off.
The Hanselman alarm is important to note because it is about 1/2 way in a fairly direct line between the O'Regan Crescent call and where Neil Stonechild was found.
A key witness who was never called to the inquiry by commission counsel is a bank manager who was on his way home to the North end of Saskatoon via the 51st street overpass sometime between 1:00am and 2:00am.
The bank manager told the RCMP task force that he saw a male matching Neil Stonechild's general description walking across the 51st overpass sometime between 1:00am & 2:00am on this particular night. His words were, 'I'm sure it was him.'
Neil would have been suffering significantly from the effects of hypothermia and probably wouldn't know where he was or what he was doing as he was going across the 51st Street overpass. [This also matches the banker's description.]
There are a few things to remember and consider when looking at: how did Neil Stonechild get to the 51st Street overpass.
Neil would know that he couldn't head back [west] to Snowberry Downs, because the police had been called by Trent Ewart [and another two km further west was the city boundary] so his obvious direction of escape was to go North or East to get away from the areas that the police would be coming to look for him.

[Stonechild couldn't go north because one km north was the city boundary.]
We believe that Neil first ran East and then Northeast to get out of the area.
It is possible that Neil may have set off the alarm when he tried a door on
Hanselman Ave in an effort to get out of the cold.
Brad and Larry didn't drive Neil Stonechild up to the North end of Saskatoon.
Neil went there on his own in an effort to avoid getting arrested and eventually
he was overcome by hypothermia and he just kept walking until he couldn't
walk anymore."

Goertzen had an officer of the same height as Stonechild walk that route in
winter; it took him about 90 minutes to get out to the field, which would have put
him right in the middle of the overpass at the time the banker believed he saw
Stonechild there, between one and two a.m., after someone with his descriptors
was seen running away from O'Regan Crescent near midnight.

The man who worked overtime heading up that team of retired officers, and
then several years into his retirement, making Sask Justice aware of the cold, hard
facts, was Stan Goertzen.

On November 1, 2001, soon after the trial for Munson and Hatchen, then-
Const. Goertzen had been elected new head of the Saskatoon City Police
Association. As indicated by his welcome on the Injustice Busters website, "Stan
the man, who'll put us all away if he can," Goertzen had a reputation for taking
no guff. Not only was he a polygraphist who could smell a lie a mile away, but he
had no guilt about growing up with more than anyone else. Because few grow up
with less.

Just before Christmas the year Stan was eight, his father walked out for good,
leaving his mother with four small children. Stan, the eldest, became "man of the
house." In a voice as deep as a tape recording played back at the wrong speed, he
picks up his story:

> *"My mother was at her wit's end. She was sitting there crying and shaking; I*
> *was standing there, patting her on the shoulder, trying to calm her down. It*
> *was obvious there'd be no Christmas that year and even my little sister who*
> *was a toddler knew it. The only Christmas decoration was popcorn Mom*
> *had strung on a thread because it was practical – a decoration we could*
> *eat. Suddenly a man appears! He's from the Salvation Army. He gives me a*
> *present marked in big black letters: 'Boy, 8.'"*

Stan (the middle-aged man) stares at his big, open hands with a look of awe. Slowly he brings them together:

"It was a grey plastic battleship in two halves that snapped together. I will never forget it. Then the man looked around and realized we didn't have a Christmas tree. He went out and a while later came back with a tree. Thinking back, it was a scrawny, needle-bare tree, but I was so thankful for the kindness shown our family by anonymous people that I wanted to do that when I grew up."

His mother worked briefly as a seamstress; but for a period of seven years, they lived on welfare, with little or no food left at the end of each month. Stan and siblings went to an inner city school in the poorest area of Prince Albert, 150 km north-east of Saskatoon. There, a defining moment occurred, for Stan Goertzen and for Saskatchewan. His mother had instructed all her boys not to fight at school, so when kids went after him, he didn't fight back. Until one day that changed. "I decided, 'This is stupid!' and I've never backed away from a fight since then, especially when I knew I was in the right."

Suddenly, life changed for them all:

"Mom married a serving prisoner; a man who was in the Prince Albert penitentiary for attempted murder and armed robbery. She married him while he was in jail, not realizing that, when he went before a parole board, a wife and family would make him appear more stable to them. I got to see first-hand what extreme alcoholism, child abuse and drugs can do to people. We lived in a very violent, dysfunctional home and it was at its worst once he got paroled and came to live with us full-time."

Most of the money Stan earned working late went toward clothing for his sister and two brothers. When something happened that might send his stepfather into a "fury of abuse" directed at the younger ones, Stan stepped in to say that he had done it, so he'd be targeted instead. A very long time later, when Stan was 15, his mother kicked the thug out.

By then, Stan was largely on his own, anyway. A parole officer who knew the family's plight, as well as potential for the lad to take a wrong turn, had offered him a hand up. Gary Brown saw goodness in Stan and, when he turned 14, sponsored him to attend Western Christian College in Weyburn.

There, Stan found sports made him equal to anyone with more money or opportunities in life:

> *"Gary Brown paid the tuition and living expenses to send me to boarding school for grades 9 and 10, a considerable amount of money. When I got there, I was homesick and still accustomed to living in an inner-city world. One day I beat up a kid and was almost expelled. The Dean got us together and said, 'There is only one way you can stay, and that is if this kid says he will forgive you.' Duncan looked at me for a very long time and finally said, 'I forgive you.'"*

Stan went on to become top athlete in his grade both years, as well as provincial gold-medal champion in javelin throwing.

While he was away in grade 10, his mother met a Mennonite man she would later marry. "I was horrible to him," Goertzen says. "I was thinking, 'Here's another guy who's going to come in and screw our family over!' In response, this man just turned the other cheek." A superb carpenter, Henry Goertzen taught his stepson the craft. "We would work silently together all day – two introverts communicating with few words," Goertzen says, adding with tears in his eyes, "He was an angel in our lives. That was the start of my change in attitude toward the world. I learned that being kind and decent was not necessarily a weakness that would be preyed upon."

Today the police association office is elegant with dark wood fixtures – built-in lighting, cabinets and two massive, marble-topped meeting tables. They were all built or refinished by Goertzen while he continued his roles as police polygraphist, association president, and devoted family man. "He's an impressive man: caring and intelligent with impeccable morality," states one officer he helped. "He's the rock that kept everyone going through the hell of the first decade of the twenty-first century."

Goertzen shares a frustration with some other officers: being portrayed in the media as having no clue about lives of marginalized people since they are middle-class, white, male cops (all four classifications currently frowned upon in trendy society). "Our family was marginalized by the fact we were on welfare. We were marginalized by our mother having married several times, once to a serving convict. It had nothing to do with the colour of our skin, but it was very tough. Although marginalization is not an excuse for poor behaviour or doing harm to others, I've always empathized. I understand that if you are angry and trapped enough, you may do something stupid. As a police officer, I've always tried to treat everyone with respect, regardless of their situation, the way I would have liked someone to treat me and my family when we were struggling."

In 2013, Goertzen would learn that DNA samples indicated, with a 99.99% probability, that he is related to the alleged son of former Canadian Prime Minister John Diefenbaker. Goertzen's DNA is also a match with Diefenbaker's closest living relatives, another indicator of family connection. History books recorded that "Dief the Chief," defender of the underdog and leader of the country from 1957 to '63, in whose honour Saskatchewan streets, dams and airports are named, was childless. Goertzen and siblings had suspected the possibility, having heard family rumours and knowing their grandmother worked as his Prince Albert housekeeper. This would mean that Goertzen's father, born in 1939, raised by an adoptive family, and who left his own family in the lurch, was Diefenbaker's illegitimate son.

When the DNA news broke, retired SPS officer Larry Cook said exultantly, "No wonder Stan was our association president for thirteen years. He comes by his leadership qualities honestly!"

Staunch defenders of the underdog with shared DNA: Diefenbaker ca. 1948; Goertzen 2004 following release of the Wright Report on the Stonechild Inquiry

University of Saskatchewan Library, University Archives & Special Collections, Diefenbaker fonds XVII JGD 4908.

CHAPTER 19 - 'Circus extraordinaire!' RCMP Investigation into the Death of Neil Stonechild

'The press are going to want heads to roll over this!'
- 2013 Film, Broken City

As proof of the adage, "In Saskatchewan, everyone knows everyone, or else their spouse does," the original head of Operation Ferric, Insp. Darrell Madill soon revealed that he was related by marriage to one of the key witnesses. He was replaced by Insp. Darrell McFadyen.

As revealed in Chapter 4, since February 2000, the FSIN had been exerting tremendous pressure on the Department of Justice, suggesting that a Native revolt was in the making, and stating that if the government did not move on their demands, it would face a full-scale revolt.

On the basis of the original two freezing deaths, Wegner and Naistus, it was beginning to look as though there was no police involvement in freezing deaths whatsoever. The initial suspects, Constables Munson and Hatchen, had not been on duty the night Naistus died, and, on the basis of witnesses and the polygraphs they demanded, had no involvement in Wegner's death. Indeed, two RCMP investigations would later conclude there was no police involvement in either death.

Responding to an Access to Information request about costs, RCMP advised:

"We are only able to approximately capture the costs of the original team of 8 people for the years 1999/2000, 2000/2001 and 2001/2002. [Another 10 officers had been brought in to assist.] Thus for the year 1999/2000 the costs in salary dollars were approximately $522,083; for the year 2000/2001, $538,550; and for the year 2001/2001, $557,396. Please note that the RCMP does not keep track of hours expanded [sic] on general and/or specific investigations, thus the difficulty in assessing the salary expenses occurred [sic] by the ad hoc members of this Task Force."

Those figures total $1,618,029 for, apparently, half the salaries, and excluding expenses for hotels, meals, transportation, witness protection program and RCMP jet for transporting the body. At the Stonechild Inquiry,

McFadyen testified to an additional "rough estimate of $749,000" for expenses. A source claims "Money was no object; we were given carte blanche for overtime." "The community was very aware of the millions of dollars in costs for both the investigation and public inquiry," says Stan Goertzen. "The pressure was on them to produce some results."

It was indeed "fortunate" that lawyer Donald Worme was suddenly able to bring forth his nephew, Jason Roy, by first approaching the press on February 22, 2000, and keeping Roy anonymous for 11 days while the government and RCMP decided how best to handle Worme's claim that he actually had a witness to police wrongdoing. This information about Stonechild was fresh and new. The government now had a way out of its threatening situation: it could order that the Stonechild matter be fully investigated by the RCMP, and then call for a public inquiry into the death of Neil Stonechild, buying the government time to deal with the approaching crisis.

Const. Jack Warner of the Regina RCMP Major Crimes unit had been placed in charge of the Stonechild investigation. He was a junior RCMP investigator who had just joined the task force, selected to work the file in part because he had a previous working relationship with Donald Worme. What kind of rationale is that? What has an investigator's working relationship with the lawyer for the only person claiming to be a witness got to do with the investigator who is to determine the truth about that self-declared "witness"? Or is that the reverse of reasonable for an unbiased investigation?

According to the book, *Starlight Tour*, upon conclusion of the inquiry and publication of its findings, Warner was Worme's guest of honour at a victory celebration at John's steakhouse. "Worme had seated Stella to his right and Jack Warner on his left. He ordered plenty of red and white wine."[117]

What was Warner thinking? Why would he even consider the impropriety of celebrating with Worme and associates? If this was an ongoing investigation, Warner had completely compromised his objectivity. "I wouldn't do that," states Colin Crocker, retired head of Saskatoon RCMP Major Crimes. "We used to have parties at the conclusion of months of work on a major investigation, but I've never had someone go to a party with defence counsel. That surprises me, and I'm not easily surprised."

Warner later left the RCMP to work for FSIN as their chief investigator. Just what was on Cpl. Warner's mind back when he had attended the second autopsy of Stonechild, or attended as Worme's guest of honour celebrating the Stonechild Inquiry's final report?

Operation Ferric records strongly suggest an investigation loop. A loop is formed when an officer passes on information before a proceeding, which then allows the persons receiving the information to either tailor to, or corroborate, one another's testimony. Or it can be used to plant into a person's thoughts some information not previously there. The investigator, at a later date, asks a question regarding that information he provided. Now the person doesn't know whether the information he or she provides is from memory, or from what they have been told.

One RCMP officers notes, obtained under an FOI request, reveal what looks like choreography between a person unknown and The *StarPhoenix*, with the RCMP puppets in the middle:

Sun. Feb. 20, 2000: "[Name redacted] learned of a Stonechild death by exposure north of city. Will find out more."

Mon. Feb. 21: RCMP meet with person unknown [name redacted] who tells them the newspaper is going to run a story on the Stonechild death. "I advised him I had asked Const. [redacted] for the file."

Tues. Feb. 22: *StarPhoenix* front-page headline: "Decade-old death resurfaces."

Wed. Feb. 23: Front-page headline: "Stonechild case closed: RCMP refuses to add 1990 native death to its investigation of specific deaths." This was news to RCMP. The officer makes a note: "StarPhoenix article says we refuse to do Stonechild investigation." Why should he be concerned what the newspaper says? That story reported that Vice Chief Joseph was angry, since the Stonechild case was one of the "more glaring leads" in allegations of police misconduct related to the deaths of Aboriginal men in Saskatoon. At 8:40 a.m. the Mountie advises someone, identity redacted, "that we wouldn't be doing file immediately but we would be eventually." Much of the FOIPed material is then redacted, until, at 8 p.m. that same evening, he writes: "We will investigate."

Thurs. Feb. 24: Front-page headline: "RCMP accepts Stonechild case." Mountie notes: "Advised [redacted] that we would be doing Stonechild ASAP. … [He] tells me that two well-placed non-aboriginal persons have knowledge of this matter. Will provide names later to investigation." [Why not immediately? Did they require "briefing"?]

This glimpse behind the scene reveals that, between Sunday and Thursday, with the "help" of a person unknown and the newspaper, the RCMP went from first hearing about the Stonechild case to deciding they would not only investigate it, but give it high priority!

In 2000, on top of all the tumult for Saskatoon police, their overcrowded station was undergoing major renovation. A city audit had shown the need for more space, without a budget for larger premises. Everything was disrupted. "It was like one thing after another," says Dave Scott. "We had to get rid of the museum, storage room and commissionaire's office to make room for the renovation. We had no money to go off-site for storage of files. In late 1999 [three months before RCMP demanded the Stonechild file], a staff sergeant had been instructed to destroy *property* files and not destroy any major crime files, either solved or unsolved. I believe Stonechild's file likely was destroyed, when it should have been kept indefinitely. I trusted those responsible to use care in which files would be destroyed. I regret making that decision." [Sec. 6 of the Police Act required retention for only three years, not the 10 years Worme told the media.]

Because the original Stonechild file was missing (although, unknown to anyone, Const. Ernie Louttit had retained a copy), some media and Aboriginal groups alleged the purge was a conspiracy to cover-up police involvement in the death.

The RCMP thus began the Stonechild death investigation with only Jason Roy's allegation to go on, since he was the only person to claim police involvement. Six pages of evidence and limited information on the original file had been retained by SPS, including 49 photos of the original death scene and autopsy. But without the complete file, particularly Roy's initial statement (in which he mentioned no police involvement), there was little evidence to refute whatever Roy wished to allege.

With only one person making allegations against the police, the case was not complex. *Was Jason Roy telling the truth about seeing Stonechild in police custody? Was his evidence supported by any real evidence? Were his supporters telling the truth and providing factual accounts of his allegation?*

Warner makes his first move. Does he track down and do an in-depth recorded interview full of tough questions with the only person to claim seeing Stonechild in a police car the night he went missing? No. First Warner picks up the phone and calls Worme, advising him that he (Warner) will be in charge of the Stonechild investigation.

Worme is already representing Jason Roy – Worme's relative – in allegations against police regarding Stonechild. Worme is already planning to represent Darrell Night in a civil suit against Munson and Hatchen. Worme is representing the Wegner family in allegations against police, while Worme's brother is representing the Naistus family in a similar attempt. And Worme has been a lawyer for the Federation of Saskatchewan Indian Nations. What possible reason could an unbiased investigator give for commencing work by talking to Worme and then taking a trip to his office? To some, it might appear blatant conflict-of-interest. Is it possible Donald Worme is going to steer the investigation?

Feb. 21: Warner meets with Worme, Jason Roy, 26, and his common-law wife, Vanessa Kayseas. Yet, remarkably, no attempt is made to take a statement from Roy about his allegation. Did Roy's counsel, Worme, want Roy's allegation made public first, thereby using media hype to further the cause of alleged police misconduct – an eyewitness to police essentially "murdering" Aboriginal men?

In their report, the RCMP would note very clearly that Jason Roy used the media hype regarding "Starlight Tours" to make his allegation public. They realized, just as others did, that Jason Roy felt guilty for leaving Neil at Snowberry Downs to fend for himself. Surprisingly, however, they did not believe this motive enough for him to make up an elaborate story in order to shift the blame to someone else.

Instead of adding to his investigation a lengthy taped interview with Roy, Warner meets with Roy and his wife who are concerned they are being watched and fear for their safety. Worme had alleged to Warner that Kayseas had been in Ralph's Coffee Shop when she was confronted by SPS. Const. Robin Wintermute with the K9 unit. He told Kayseas that he had information she had recently been the subject of a Crime Stoppers report suggesting she was trafficking in LSD to young people, and she also had a warrant out for her arrest over an unpaid parking ticket. She had never met Const. Wintermute before and had not provided a name to him, therefore questioned how he would know her name and the fact that she had an outstanding parking ticket. The police officer looked in her wallet but did not scrutinize her I.D.

Kayseas had been taken to the police station and searched but later released, as a result of Worme's intervention. Some reports at the time claimed Kayseas was strip-searched on arrest; this was not true. She was arrested on an outstanding warrant and questioned regarding unrelated criminal activity – trafficking in LSD. Worme was concerned that Kayseas was the victim of harassment, or worse, at some risk.

Warner immediately moves to provide VIP security for the man with four aliases and 50 run-ins with the law. Roy and his wife are moved, "no names mentioned," into room 521 of the luxury river-view hotel. Meals are arranged. To their later regret, the Mounties do not inform the couple that their liquor bills would not be covered. In the following days, instead of interviewing Roy, the RCMP conduct an investigation into the SPS arrest of Roy's wife.

March 2, 2000: A week after Roy and wife were installed in the hotel, Worme informs RCMP they have moved out, and no one knows where they have gone. The RCMP go to pay their bill and are appalled at their liquor bill. Nevertheless they (i.e. taxpayers) pay the liquor bill.

A few days later, Worme announces that Roy has resurfaced, but all further communication must go through him because Roy will speak only to him. Warner is finally ready to take a statement but Worme advises he will provide a date *"after he has had an opportunity to speak with Jason."*

The RCMP set up Roy and Kayseas in a residence, in what would become 10 months of paid rent, food, and phone bills. At the Stonechild Inquiry, Roy would inaccurately testify he had been placed in witness protection, not on February 21, but two weeks later, on March 6, after he had made his media allegation of police involvement – *because he was then afraid of what police might do to him.* He would also say that, following the hotel stay, Father Poiliévre hid them in an empty church rectory for a few days, and, finally, they lived under the protection program in Wadena, SK.

None dared call Roy a paid witness, but some did wonder why any witness would want to say anything that might kill the goose that kept laying such golden eggs.

Throughout March, the RCMP make several attempts to interview Roy. Worme, however, claims Roy is afraid they will arrest him on an outstanding warrant for his arrest under the Liquor Act. In the end, Roy does not make a court appearance for the liquor warrant.[118] The RCMP initially were planning to obtain a statement from Roy under oath, along with a warning of repercussions for lying but, for reasons unknown, decide against that. Nor, astonishingly, is Roy ever polygraphed.

In March, Worme requests copies of photos of the scene of the death as well as the autopsy, but RCMP refuse to turn them over. They fax their reasoning: "it may jeopardize our investigation," (since the photos could be used to verify, or even shape, Jason Roy's allegations). In mid-April, however, after Worme threatens to go over their heads, Operation Ferric supervisor Insp. McFadyen overrides concerns about jeopardizing the investigation and shows him all the photos, thus feeding into the "feedback loop."

March 2, 2000: SPS Const. Ernie Louttit meets with RCMP Const. Warner and tells him that when he spoke to Stella Bignell shortly after Neil's death, she told him Neil had been involved in a vehicle theft with Gary Pratt and Randy Lafond. Louttit states there had been animosity developing between Pratt and Lafond against Stonechild which resulted in Stonechild receiving a beating, being dropped off and succumbing to the elements.

Louttit also states there was a rumour in 1990 that Neil might have been dropped off in the north end by Kenny Trotchie. This was the basis for Stella's speculation in the March 1991 *StarPhoenix* story that Neil's death was gang-related. Warner notes that Stella must be interviewed on this specific aspect. There is no evidence that Trotchie was ever interviewed.

Although Const. Louttit is likely the only police officer who could establish whether allegations made by Jason Roy and his supporters were credible or not, *no statement is ever taken from Louttit.* The RCMP will soon want to interview Randy Lafond, but remarkably, not as a suspect in the death of Neil Stonechild. They want to meet him because they received word that Lafond knew of other drop offs and was himself a victim. Although RCMP Const. Dave Yule meets with Lafond on May 4 and again October 16, 2000, he does not interview Lafond as a possible suspect. Lafond is never interviewed by RCMP. Yet, at the RCMP briefing on May 16, 2000, it is stated that Randy Lafond says that police dumpings were common and that it had happened to him as well as 10 others he knows. But how did RCMP receive that information if they did not interview him? Was it hearsay?

March 3, 2000: Warner makes RCMP's first contact by phone with retired Sgt. Keith Jarvis at his Vancouver home. Jarvis, in his mid-60s and long retired, initially says the name Neil Stonechild means nothing to him, but later recalls a boy who froze to death and was missing a shoe. Importantly, Warner notes that Jarvis "doesn't recall any allegations made at the time concerning deceased being in the custody of SPS just prior to his death."

March 4: RCMP has results of the search into calls to CPIC, indicating Neil Stonechild had been queried *the night before his death*. This was untrue, as facts later reveal; it was an assumption made by McFadyen. The fact he made that assumption is one of the first hints that RCMP has serious tunnel vision about SPS involvement.

March 6: CBC's "The National" airs a documentary, *Starlight Tours*. Footage includes the discovery of Stonechild's body, while reporter Mervin Brass speaks of two anonymous persons, one who claimed to have been handcuffed and dropped off at the Borden Bridge, 55 km from Saskatoon, and another claiming to have been dropped outside Saskatoon. Both drop-offs are blamed on SPS. It is in this documentary that Jason Roy's allegation is first made public, although no surname is revealed:

> *"[Mervin] BRASS: There were 2,000 arrests for drunkenness in Saskatoon last year – many on this infamous strip. The action around the Barry and Albany Hotels is testimony to more grim statistics. Natives are charged with half the crimes in the city, and over 70 percent of inmates in the local prison are Indian. That's grist to the mill for the province's native leaders, who say the justice system discriminates against them. Now they've got something else, another case for the RCMP; a death that's resurfaced after 10 years. Another Indian found frozen on the outskirts of town.*
>
> *BRASS: Neil Stonechild's body was found in an empty lot at the north side of the city. It was minus 28 the night before – one of the coldest of the year. Neil was 17-years-old and on the run from a young offender's home with a warrant out for his arrest. Neil's death was a frightening shock for his friend Jay. He says he immediately suspected foul play and he doesn't want his identity revealed. Jay says the two had been out partying when Jay called it quits and headed home alone. Then a police cruiser rolled up.*
>
> *JAY/ NATIVE MAN: The police stopped me and the first question was, is they asked me if I knew this guy. And Neil was in the back of the police car with his face cut open, bleeding. And they asked me if I knew this guy and I said no. Why I said no is because I was on the run from the law and I didn't wanna be back in the police car with him, you know. And Neil was screaming and swearing at me and telling – he was saying, "Okay, help me man, these guys are gonna kill me." He was swearing about a lot of different things, but that's what struck out most in my mind is that he said that. And you know right at that moment it really scared me, because his face was cut open pretty good. …*
>
> *BRASS: That was the last time he saw Neil alive. The frozen body was found five days later. The memory still bothers him. Jay says he made two reports to police, but nothing came of it. Police won't comment on the case now. At the time, police concluded Neil died of exposure – that he was heading to a nearby prison to turn himself in.*
>
> *JAY: That is so far-fetched, I just don't believe it. Neil was wanted by the police. He had more than a few drinks. And he was wanted by the police. And I didn't understand why they had let him go."* [119]

March 7: The day after Roy's incendiary allegations are broadcast across the country, and two weeks after RCMP first met with him, they finally take a statement from him.[120] This is how Const. Warner conducted this crucial interview with the sole witness to allege wrongdoing by SPS officers.

The questions to be answered were quite simple: (1) Was Jason Roy telling the truth about what he claimed to see? (2) Was the key element of his allegation – seeing Neil Stonechild in police custody – credible? (3) Was the information supplied by Jason Roy supported by any 'real' physical or concrete evidence?

Later, at the Stonechild Inquiry, Roy would recall that he had given a statement to the police shortly after Neil's death, but could not remember what he had included in that statement. (While the inquiry was still in progress, that first statement would be found and revealed. In it, Roy mentioned nothing about seeing Stonechild in a police car. Nevertheless, the inquiry does not come to a screeching halt.)

In Jason Roy's initial free-narrative to the RCMP regarding what he claimed to have seen, Roy left out key elements of his later allegation: that Neil Stonechild was (1) in the back of a police car and (2) screaming, "They are going to kill me!" These are huge warning flags that Warner missed or worse, ignored.

Warner asked Roy if there was any doubt whatsoever that Neil Stonechild was in the back of the police car. Roy replied: "None whatsoever. He was wearing the... he was wearing the ja... the jacket that he... no there... there is nobody else... that it could have been... possibly. He... he was... he was screaming my name. He was telling me that they were going to kill him. I didn't believe that, though. I just didn't believe that."

This should have been another warning flag for Warner. Any investigator knows that if a person uses unnecessary language in answering a question, it is a sign of sensitivity, and sensitivity usually means deception. Furthermore, his evidence in this regard would soon change.

Jason Roy provided the following information:

- Considerable detail regarding his conversation with Neil Stonechild.
- Like Neil Stonechild, he was Unlawfully At Large on November 24, 1990, and he lied about who he was so that he would not be arrested on the outstanding warrant. [This was not true; he was not UAL at the time and had no warrant out for his arrest.]

- Neil Stonechild was "making a hell of a ruckus" looking for Lucille, and they had looked for her for approximately 20 minutes.
- When he saw Neil Stonechild in the back of the police car, he was lying across the back seat with his hands handcuffed behind his back and Roy saw the handcuffs. [At another time, Roy stated Neil's face was against the windows and he couldn't see handcuffs. In either case, Neil would have been in the back of a patrol car during very cold weather. When a person is in the back of a patrol car, the lack of air circulation due to the silent patrolman results in the windows almost instantly fogging or freezing up to the point that one can see neither in nor out.]
- He identified Stonechild, in part, because he was wearing the same jacket he had been wearing before.
- Stonechild accused Roy of lying when he provided the name of Tracy Horse, referred to him as "Jay" and told police that he was not Tracy Horse but "Jason."
- Stonechild had a six-inch cut that ran from one cheek, diagonally across his nose, to the opposite cheek, the wound was bleeding and there was "lots" of blood. He also stated that Stonechild did not have the injury when he last saw him less than half an hour earlier. [None of this was discovered by any of the medical people who examined Stonechild's body. Nor did they note any blood on his clothing, or on the snow where his body was found.]
- A few months after the police took his statement, Roy went down to SPS headquarters where he spoke to a homicide investigator who made notes. Again, Warner did not ask Roy what he told him. SPS have no record of any such incident.

According to RCMP records, the RCMP investigators determined the legitimacy and credibility of Jason Roy's allegation solely by comparing what he told them to what he was reported to have said by the media! In other words, they accepted his story as credible because he told the same story twice:

Lyons notes: " [Roy] appears truthful saw Stonechild in PC. Describes wounds to face. [That in itself revealed Roy was not truthful since medical people found neither wounds nor blood.] Provides name and DOB he gave to POs. Describes MDT query on CPIC. ... *All consistent with what was in media.*"

McFadyen notes: "Interviewed [Roy] yesterday seems credible" [no reasons given]. And, "Jack Warner [says]: [Roy] seems very credible" [no reasons given].

With such a serious allegation, one would expect the RCMP to attempt to determine the veracity of what Roy was claiming. For example, Roy expressed fear of the original suspect, Gary Pratt, stating that Pratt suspected Roy of spreading rumours blaming Pratt for Stonechild's death. The RCMP never did question or investigate *why Roy, if he had seen Stonechild in police custody the night of November 24th, would spread rumours blaming Pratt.*

The RCMP seem convinced that Roy was telling the truth, despite the fact that his story would continuously evolve throughout the course of their investigation, and that every time he told it, he would add or change details. It should have been apparent that Roy's allegation could not stand on its own without corroborating evidence. *Which they did not obtain.*

The RCMP also never seem to consider: why would two police officers, who allegedly had Neil Stonechild in custody, drive him around, and stop a random passer-by (Roy) in an attempt to identify him? Why would police, if they had Stonechild in custody, create a witness who may later come forward and implicate them in his death? And why would police engage in such alleged action if they had created such a witness? If the problem had been that Stonechild was so drunk as to be unable or unwilling to identify himself, the police officers would have transported him to detention for being intoxicated in a public place, where he would have been identified. In addition, the RCMP never seemed to ask the very obvious question: "If Stonechild referred to Jason Roy as 'Jay' and told the officers that 'Jay' was lying about who he was, why did the officers not immediately detain Roy on suspicion of obstructing police by lying about who he was, calling himself Tracy Horse?"

On a lighter note, during an Access to Information search, this writer obtained this RCMP interview, names redacted. This was the professional officer's question:

Q. ... here's where I wanna be very careful about how I ask these questions, because I'm not trying to determine what you know. But I'm just simply trying to get an idea of what you may know. Okay? Now I'm not gonna ask you specific questions but I'll... I'll just... I'll... I'll ask a question. You think about it. I'm not gonna ask you who said, who did, who... anything like this at all but... it's... it's a way of evaluating what information you might have to offer, okay? And I'm not gonna ask you... "What do you know and who told you?"... those type of questions. So I'll ask a question, think about it and all I'm trying to do is assess some credibility here for you and that you do know something. Okay? Now, the information that you say you have respecting Neil's death, is that personal information you have? By that, I mean is it something that you've... you've saw yourself? Is it something that someone told you or is it something that somebody told you that they did or they witnessed themself? Is it something of that nature? And just think about the question for a bit before you answer it. And this... I'm not trying to trick you into answering anything. I'm just trying to... do you understand what I'm getting at, I'm just trying to get a vague idea of what your information is, without asking you direct questions about it.

A. And in the event, uh... what you just said there...

While the RCMP's "Circus Extraordinaire" investigation proceeded, SPS Const. Ed Singbeil had a surprising encounter. This was our interview:

"Const. Singbeil: A young Aboriginal man came to the north door of the police station that's adjacent to the alleyway where there were a few of us standing back there on a break. And this young man just, out of the blue, started to say that he had been told the FSIN were paying the witness that was involved in the Stonechild affair, as well as in the Darrell Night affair.

Q: Why do you suppose he would have come and told you that?

A: I think he was frustrated with the lie. He was upset that the police, in his eyes, were being wronged. He was upset that there were these lies being told, and he wanted the truth to be known.

Because this case was being investigated by RCMP, this individual was directed to the front desk of the station where they could assist him in contacting the RCMP. I know that he was advised by the front desk people that he could contact the RCMP at their numbers and whatnot, so whether he did or not, I don't know.

Q: As a police officer, what is your reaction to this, to hearing that the FSIN is paying witnesses in these two major cases against police officers?

A: It makes me angry that any organization would feel that they have the power or - or the right to - to slant the evidence on any individual, or any other organization. In these incidents, I don't think that the truth had anything to do with it. I think it was all a matter of political power, other things that the FSIN wished to gain politically. They seemed to have the political ear of not only the provincial government, but the federal

*government, and as long as they keep the pressure up, then there seems to
be more kowtowing to them."*

The FSIN deny paying witnesses against the police.

CHAPTER 20 - How the RCMP Got their Men

'During the RCMP investigation, I remember sitting and telling Larry to relax. "You did nothing wrong, you have nothing to worry about," I would tell him. I believed in "the system." I work in this system – have dedicated my life to this system – and to find out that the system is capable of this magnitude of corruption is deeply, deeply disturbing.'
– Staff Sgt. Grant Obst

In the spring of 2000, RCMP interviewed a number of people who claimed that, over the previous 10 years, Jason Roy had given them accounts related to the death of Neil Stonechild. In many interviews, these witnesses supplied Roy's details of events verbatim, while others provide minor variations, suggesting these witnesses had been coached. In nearly all cases, prior to their RCMP interview, the witness first had been contacted by either Jason Roy or Donald Worme, or both. Yet in nearly all cases, the RCMP do not ask the witness what Roy or Worme had discussed with them in the weeks and months prior to the interview.

During the same interviews, many witnesses also provided evidence contrary to the allegation. Remarkably, RCMP investigators did not ask these witnesses questions to clarify contradictions. Nor do they ask witnesses why they did not come forward with the information that Roy allegedly provided them years earlier. Several of those interviewed by the RCMP would later change their evidence when testifying at the Public Inquiry and Police Act Hearings – most notably Stonechild's mother.

Stella Bignell, mother

In this initial statement, crucial to reconstructing what happened to her son, Mrs. Bignell says that after her son's body was found in late November 1990, she went to Eddie Rushton to discover who had been with Neil the last night he was seen alive. Told it was Jason Roy, she asked Rushton to ask Roy if he would talk to her. In her recounting to the RCMP, Bignell then skips four months to March 1991 when, she claims, Roy approached her at the Lucky Horseshoe bingo hall and told her about seeing Neil in the back of a police car. (Warner did not ask if she had attempted to contact Roy in the meantime.

Nor, later, point out to her that student counsellor Brenda Valiaho said that when she performed a visualization exercise after Roy allegedly disclosed in the bingo hall, Valiaho thought it was the first time he had remembered it and told anyone.)

Now, a decade after Neil's death, Bignell repeats, almost verbatim, the story Roy has recently told RCMP, including the allegation that Roy had seen Stonechild lying down in the back of a police car. (Bignell also says Roy told her that he and Neil had been chased by police, an aspect of the story never heard of again.) When Const. Warner asks if she had ever spoken to Roy again about the incident, she says no. Nor had she gone to police with this information. Not Const. Loutitt, not Sgt Eli Tarasoff and not even her own children! Remarkably, Warner did not ask Bignell: "Why not?" Surely, if an anxious mother had this information, she would want police to leave no stone unturned! (After the inquiry, she would tell reporters she always believed police had her son in custody the night he died.)

Warner asks if Roy has spoken to her recently about his story. She says Roy had contacted her a month earlier, when he said, "I'm glad this is over with, I'm glad this is all in the open, I'm glad I'm finally getting this off my chest." This seems to indicate Jason Roy was expressing relief at finally telling his story for the first time. Yet, if he had told her back in 1991 about "seeing" Stonechild in police custody, why would he express relief at finally telling his story?

The statement provided by Stonechild's mother is crucial to reconstructing what really happened to her son and what disclosures, if any, Roy made at the time. Yet, once again, Warner fails to make any meaningful inquiries about critical information; in fact, he seems to ignore it altogether. At the inquiry, under rigorous cross-examination, Bignell would recant and say that Roy actually did not tell her about what he allegedly "saw" until after 1991. Yet no one takes her to task. What could be the reason for that? Nor does anyone take her to task for not insisting her son abide by the law and return to the group home from which he was unlawfully-at-large. Everything was heaped on the police. Why might that be?

RCMP investigators state that Roy initially merely told people: "Neil got picked up," but note that as time went on, Roy's allegations changed to having actually seen Stonechild in police custody. Although all those disclosures are hearsay, RCMP nevertheless propose them as confirmation of Roy's allegation that he had seen Stonechild in police custody.

Certainly when another RCMP officer was brought into the task force, his notes indicate he has been informed that in November 2000: "...last time he [Stonechild] was seen which was in back seat of police car."

Jason (Jake) Stonechild, younger brother

Jake Stonechild provides a three-page statement to Const. Warner. Topics include allegations of his own "starlight tour," Neil being roughed up once when he was arrested, and numerous allegations about Gary Pratt being responsible for Neil's death. Jake states that one source of that information was Joanie Pelletier, who, inexplicably, is never interviewed by RCMP.

"Warner: You'd mentioned that as time passed, the stories kind of changed and the flavour then became that the police had something to do with it [Neil's death]. Do you have any recollection of who the people were that told you about the possibility that the police had something to do with it? Jake: Ah....actually it was Gary Horse. Ahm... his brother Tracy...Tracy Horse. Ah...(pause)...I think Jason Roy's brother...ah.... (pause)...ah...just people that we hung out with growing up."

Jake states that the only time he heard Roy mention police involvement was about two weeks before his interview, meaning February 2000 – the same time as the media release making the same claim for the first time. This again seems to confirm that Roy's allegation was a recent confabulation – an invention of imaginary experiences to fill gaps in his faulty memory.

It is inconceivable that Jason Roy would not tell his friend, Jake Stonechild, anything about police being involved in his brother's death until around the time he first made the allegation public, 10 years later. It is also inconceivable that the Stonechild family would keep this information from Jake Stonechild if, indeed, they actually had heard such an allegation from Roy. Remarkably, the fact that all these allegations were completely unbelievable also would be ignored by RCMP.

Corroborating Jake's statement that Roy hadn't spoken to him about alleged police involvement during the entire previous decade, were the cold, hard facts that:

1) Jake had spoken to Const. Louttit back on December 4, 1990, telling

him that Neil had been at a party near the 7-Eleven in the north end, and that Gary Pratt and his brother picked up Neil, witnessed by Petrina Starblanket, and
2) around this same time, Jake had been at Midtown Plaza, very upset. He asked an acquaintance, a security guard, that he knew "who did that to my brother" and was going to settle the score.

Marcel Stonechild, older brother

Const. Warner obtains a taped, five-page statement from Marcel. In the initial free-narrative phase of the statement, Marcel cannot even remember Jason Roy's name, later refers to him as Jason Ross and finally, Jason Roy. *Remember, Roy claimed to have made his allegation widely-known over the years after Neil's death, yet Marcel could not remember the name of the person who claimed to have crucial information about his brother's death. Not a detail one would forget, if the allegation were true.*

Marcel states he got liquor for the boys, they left for the Binning's, and he later went to check on Neil but he and Roy had left. Marcel was told they had gone out to do a Break-and-Enter to get more booze, that while committing a B & E, they were interrupted, fled from the cops and split up. *Significant: if Stonechild or Roy had not yet returned, how could anyone know this information? Is it possible one or both had?*

Marcel says Roy told him he had seen Neil in the back of a police car and "something didn't look right about him," and that was the last time Roy had seen Neil. Marcel looked for information on Neil for next two days. He phoned around and asked Eddie Rushton if Neil ever returned to the Binning's. Eddie confirmed he had not. About four days later, Neil's body was found in the north end. Marcel states that it didn't make sense he would be in the location he was found, given where he was last seen.

Marcel returns to the issue of what Roy had told him: "Jason Roy told me that they were... they were being chased by the cops... and that ahh... all that ahh... he told me on that. That's about what I know." *Once again, the allegation ends with their being chased by police; nothing about Roy's allegation of Neil being in the back of a police car, beaten and bloodied.*

It seems reasonably clear that Marcel is bouncing back and forth between two stories: what Roy told him at the time (the B & E and being chased by the cops), and a second version in which Roy claimed to have seen Neil in the back of a police car. Warner made no attempt to clarify these inconsistencies.

Within a month of Neil's death, Marcel says, he spoke to Jason Roy, who told him "what he saw and stuff like that," that Roy told him what he "thought" had happened and that he "thought" the cops caught him in the act and drove him out of town. *Once again it is clear that, at the time, Jason didn't know what had happened to Neil and that he was speculating that the police had arrested Neil, a logical conclusion, since he and Neil had caused a disturbance late at night. Over time, this speculation would evolve into something Roy claimed actually to have witnessed.*

Warner asks Marcel if anyone had told him that Jason Roy had more information about Neil's death. Marcel replied: "Yah. Like, people have told me that Jason knows more than what he is giving up. But I could never find him after that. He went into hiding and he didn't want nobody to find him." Marcel says that he had spoken to Bruce Genaille and "that's how... I knew that the cops were looking for him [Neil] that night."

Warner then seems to want to cut to the chase. Marcel isn't speaking about Jason Roy's allegation, so he asks him this directed question:

"Warner: That's fine. Thank you. When Jason was telling you about this incident when he saw your brother, Neil, in the back of the police car, did he ever describe seeing any injuries to him at all?
Marcel: Ah, no, not that I know of."

Marcel goes on to state that Jason told him he had seen a body in the back of the police car and he identified the person as being Neil by the jacket he was wearing. Neil was lying across the seat like he "was knocked out or something."

Warner asks what Marcel had done with the information Jason passed onto him. He said he "left it alone" and didn't bring it up with anyone including Ernie Louttit, whom he spoke to later. He then states that he did not share this information with anyone. **It is inconceivable that, if Jason Roy told him anything about seeing his brother Neil in police custody, Marcel wouldn't speak to anyone about it.**

Warner asks how he and his family were "perceived" by the police. Marcel says they were always in trouble and the cops were always harassing him. Warner asks what police thought of Neil. Marcel says the same thing, but to a greater extent. Marcel concludes that the cops have their "own little gang" and it's the "city cops against everyone else."

Marcel will change his evidence considerably at the Public Inquiry.

As for the RCMP investigation of Hartwig and Senger, *even before any evidence* is gathered regarding the officers' potential involvement with Neil Stonechild, the RCMP attempt to gather evidence against them by seeking and obtaining a month-long Telephone Number Recorder Warrant, later extended another 60 days. This would record information on calls between Hartwig's and Senger's home phones. RCMP note there was no contact between them.

April 16, 2000: Const. Brad Senger, in his first interview with Warner, provides a seven-page taped statement. Warner tells Senger that RCMP investigators "are taping all of the interviews." The RCMP had planned to approach Hartwig and Senger under the pretense of interviewing them about what they might know about the Wegner and Naistus deaths, while actually attempting to learn what they would volunteer about Neil Stonechild. Senger does not recall ever encountering either man, and in response to Warner's question, says the only thing he heard about the Stonechild case was recent talk about the K9 officer who, at the time, had attempted to find Stonechild's missing shoe.

Warner advises Senger that the RCMP were being totally objective in investigating the file, that they had no preconceived notions about the evidence, and that although this is his first "kick at something like this," he is working with some experienced investigators.

May 7, 2000: Sgt. Ken Lyons interviews Const. Larry Hartwig for the first time. Hartwig, as many fellow officers have pointed out, is always eager to help in any way he can.

In this case, Lyons decides not to tape the interview because, he would report in his notes, he does not wish to alert Hartwig that he is a suspect in Stonechild's death. Why such a critically important interview is not recorded is not known, but a succession of interviews by the RCMP could suggest why. In Lyons' notes, he paraphrases statements made by Hartwig, often changing the context of how things were said, and omitting information that would speak to Hartwig's beliefs, conduct and character.

May 11, 2000: Warner speaks to Jason Roy again and asks if he had ever told his uncle Donald Worme about his allegation prior to 2000. **Roy states he does not recall ever speaking to Worme about it.** *Although Donald Worme was Jason Roy's uncle, a powerful and influential criminal lawyer, and a person he obviously trusted in this matter, he never spoke to Worme about his* *allegation prior to 2000. Incredibly, the RCMP does not follow up on this very crucial issue by asking, "Why not?"*

The book *Starlight Tour* would later report something else altogether: **Roy told Worme about his allegation shortly after Neil's death.** "*If Donald Worme knew about Roy's allegations against the police in the 1990s, and did not report them to authorities, he should be investigated by the Law Society,*" states William Wuttunee, a retired Calgary lawyer originally from Red Pheasant First Nation near Saskatoon. Likewise, authorities such as Father Poiliévre and the counselling student who did the visualization were required under the law to advise social services if a child was abused. Why didn't they?

May 18, 2000: Constables Larry Hartwig and Brad Senger are separately told they are under investigation for the death of Neil Stonechild. They demand polygraphs.

May 25, 2000: Warner contacts Jason Roy again to clarify some "misunderstandings" in his allegation. The RCMP note in their interview with Doris Binning that she said, "*Jason Roy never said anything to her about seeing Neil in the back of a Saskatoon Police Service vehicle.*"

Roy denies Marcel's claim that he and Stonechild had been going to do a B & E, saying he may have said something about munchies. Warner notes that this was not in Jason's March 7th statement. (And, under cross-examination at the inquiry, Roy would admit they would have done a B & E had the opportunity "*happened to come along.*")

Jason now states that he may have mentioned something about police being called to Snowberry Downs because Neil was causing a disturbance. Cheryl Antoine states that when Jason returned to the Binning's, he told them that he and Neil were chased by the police. This also wasn't in his March 7, 2000 interview.

Roy states that he provided SPS with a statement in which he provided the officer with the alias he used, Tracy Horse.

This attempt to re-interview is very important. In the initial stages of the investigation, the RCMP acknowledge changes in Roy's story and in some ways try to inquire how and why his story changed. *In later stages of the investigation however, the RCMP would fail to clarify some shocking changes to his story.*

May 25, 2000: RCMP begin 90-day wiretaps on Hartwig and Senger's home phones. Yet there was no reasonable and probable grounds for a judge to grant a wiretap. Merely suspicion. Extension to the original wiretap is granted in October. Although required by law to disclose a wiretap once removed, RCMP later disclose only to Senger. Hartwig learns about his wiretap three years later at Stonechild Inquiry. (In the intervening years he assumes they *must* have placed a wiretap on his phone, and is concerned it is still in place.)

July 12, 2000: Jason Roy changes his story once again when interviewed a third time by Warner. This time he states that while he and Neil were on their way to the 7-Eleven, they stopped in to say "Hi" to Jason's mom. He states they were there for about 10 minutes. Warner ignores this change to Roy's statement. This would be the only occasion where Roy included this information.

July 20, 2000: Ken Lyons calls Larry Hartwig. "He asks if I recall speaking to Keith Jarvis regarding this file," Hartwig says. "I tell him that I do not recall speaking to Jarvis regarding the Stonechild file. Lyons states that Jarvis indicates in his notes that he spoke to me and asks me to explain. I tell him that if Jarvis states he spoke to me, then he spoke to me; I do not recall. I say I told him all I know about this file. Lyons asks if I would reconsider taking a polygraph, as it would assist in clearing my name. I tell him that I had already submitted to a three-hour interrogation, that he lied to me, that I told him everything I know and heard about this case, and that I have been truthful throughout. He tells me he lied about only one part of the investigation, and that he spoke to me for one hour instead of three. [Lyons was correct about the length of interview, but he continued to ask Hartwig questions while they drove around for two hours.] He asks again if I would like to take a polygraph. I tell him that I have nothing to fear, nothing to hide, and that there is no evidence to support any charge. He states he isn't so sure that there isn't evidence to support a charge. I tell him to charge me and then I will launch a lawsuit against him, the RCMP and Dept. of Justice."

July 26, 2000: Jason Roy contacts Warner and states that he is thinking about the two officers he claimed had Stonechild in custody. Initially, he told RCMP he could not describe them at all. *He now claims one of them may have been taller and wearing thick glasses* (Hartwig is 5' 7" and 140 pounds, Senger 5' 8" and 180 pounds. Neither has ever worn a moustache, glasses or contact lenses).

August 25, 2000: RCMP officers Warner and Rick Slawson meet with Roy regarding his description. Roy describes the driver of the police car as over six feet tall with a pink face, wearing thick-lensed eyeglasses and sporting a moustache. **Warner decides that the information is too vague, so does**

not take statement from him. Why would the RCMP seek to minimize this crucial change to Jason Roy's story? Because it was exculpatory to the officers?

Roy tells the RCMP that he did not want to meet with Jarvis to give a written statement on November 30, 1990 because he was afraid he would be arrested on an outstanding warrant. He claims that, like Neil Stonechild, he was wanted for being UAL at the time. The RCMP ask him why he was not arrested on the outstanding warrant when interviewed by Sgt. Jarvis. *He claims that Stella Bignell had brokered a deal with Jarvis to assure him that he would not be arrested if he provided a statement.*

The RCMP later confirm that this was not true; Stella did not really know Roy at the time. Had the RCMP simply reviewed SPS documents in their possession (Saskatoon Information Management System or SIMS), they would have realized that Roy must have concocted these details to address the deficiencies in his story regarding the statement provided to police in 1990.

Roy tells RCMP that he met SPS investigator Jarvis and a female detective or counsellor on November 30, 1990 at the Dina Sunshine residence where he and his girlfriend, Cheryl Antoine were living at the time, and that Cheryl was present when he provided the statement. He says that he provided a four- to six-page statement that was written by the investigating officer, and that he told him about seeing Stonechild in the back of a SPS police car, handcuffed, bleeding, screaming, "They are going to kill me!"

The RCMP seek to confirm that a female detective accompanied Jarvis to the interview. They interview all 11 female members of the SPS, asking if they were involved in the Stonechild investigation. None were involved or present when Jarvis met with Roy. The investigator was by himself when Jason was interviewed.

Jason Roy claims that after he provided his statement, he was assured something would be done and someone would get back to him. He claims that when he did not hear anything back, he attended police headquarters to find out why nothing was happening with the file. He states that at that time he spoke to two homicide investigators who took notes and said they would get back to him. No one ever did.

The RCMP attempt to confirm that Roy spoke to homicide detectives, and although records from that time period exist, there is no record that Roy spoke to any of them. All investigators from that time are interviewed and all state they were not involved in the investigation in any way.

The role of the RCMP in this case was simple. They were to investigate the circumstances leading up to Neil Stonechild's death. To investigate means "to carry out a systematic or formal inquiry and examine the facts as to establish the truth." An antonym for "investigate" is "ignore." Did the RCMP investigate circumstances leading up to Neil Stonechild's death and the subsequent disclosures made by Jason Roy and others? Or did they simply record information supplied by Roy and supporters without ever scrutinizing that information and asking questions to clarify details? *After all, Neil Stonechild's own brother and sister did not hear anything about allegations of police involvement in Neil Stonechild's death until 2000. Nor did Jason Roy's friend Gary Horse, who was "like a brother" to him.*

Police/Forensic witnesses

RCMP investigators interview the SPS officers who were at the scene where Neil Stonechild's body was found. Each one has critical information about the scene and the condition of Neil Stonechild's body with which to reconstruct events leading up to his death, *yet none of these police officers or forensic experts is asked to provide written or taped statements.* These included the first police officer on scene, Const. René Lagimodiere, patrol supervisor, Sgt. Mike Petty, Const. John Middleton, and identification officer Sgt. Bob Morton (who later told this writer that, if interviewed, he would have told the RCMP that by examining the photos of the mark on the hand, they could still observe to this day that it was not a handcuff mark). They did not take written statements from K9 officer, Const. Greg Robert, the four ambulance attendants who had attended the scene, the coroner, Dr. Brian Fern, or the forensic pathologist Dr. Jim Arnold.

Yet the RCMP tape recorded the vast majority of their interviews with friends and family of Neil Stonechild. Why would highly trained RCMP officers fail to obtain statements from these very important witnesses? Was it simple neglect or negligence? Or was it something even more sinister?

The Suspects

April 28, 2000: Mayrs interviews Gary Pratt who was considered a suspect in the death of Neil Stonechild in 1990 and since, as indicated by the Stonechild family and others who provided information at the time. Although Pratt was the original suspect with significant evidence in this regard, the RCMP *do* *not record an interview and merely take notes.* They also note in Task 908 that there is "no particular premise" for the suspicion of Pratt being involved in Stonechild's death other than the "altercation" where Neil received a "severe beating." *There is no mention that Neil Stonechild had come to court to testify against him.*

The interview with Gary Pratt did not begin with the subject matter of this investigation but with the way in which Pratt claimed that the SPS had a vendetta against him, and a lengthy narrative of several incidents where Pratt was in conflict and sometimes threatened and assaulted by police.

Pratt confirms the altercation that occurred in August 1990 where Neil Stonechild was assaulted. He states that he and Randy Lafond went to the Rushton residence where Rushton levelled a rifle at them and threatened to kill them. Gary and Randy left and returned with two other friends. Gary states that Lafond "went nuts" and began to assault the people in the house. Lafond picked up an axe and hit Rushton and Neil Stonechild with it. Gary claims to have stopped Randy from hitting Neil *but omits the fact that he had returned to the Rushton residence with a shotgun and that he participated in the assault including on Neil Stonechild.* Pratt states that all four of them were charged with robbery with violence and on remand for three months awaiting trial. He states that none of the witnesses showed to testify against them; the case was adjoined and reconvened two more times. He says the only witness that showed up was one of the victims of the assault and he showed at the last appearance. The charges were eventually withdrawn because witnesses didn't attend court.

He believed he was considered a suspect because of the fact that Neil was to testify against him. He states that he did not bear a grudge against Neil about this incident and denies any involvement in his death.

Although the RCMP are told who the other three suspects were, related to the robbery with violence charges, and that the charges were still before the courts both at and after Neil's death, the RCMP don't bother to contact, much less interview one of those suspects, Spencer Bear. Randy Lafond, who beat Neil Stonechild and Eddie Rushton with an axe, was contacted by the RCMP, but not in order to be interviewed as a possible suspect in the death of Neil Stonechild, but because rumour was that he knew of other incidents of police dumping Aboriginal people out of town. On Oct 13, 2000, RCMP Const. Yule speaks to Randy Lafond who "stated he had no direct knowledge or involvement in the death of Neil Stonechild."

Incredibly, this was one of the original suspects in Neil Stonechild's death, against whom Stonechild was to testify in court. The fact that the RCMP would not conduct any kind of meaningful interview with this person shows *the RCMP had already dismissed the original suspects as possible suspects,* and demonstrates the lengths the RCMP would go in an attempt to prove their case against the SPS. The RCMP did not consider the fact that Neil Stonechild was to testify against the Pratts a suitable motive to want him dead.

Instead the RCMP investigation focuses on Hartwig and Senger. The RCMP make that assumption based on Roy's allegation that those officers found Neil Stonechild, arrested him, beat him up and drove him to the north end of Saskatoon, dropped him off and left him to die.

What the RCMP failed to consider is why the officers would do such a thing? What would be their motive? Most importantly, *how they would benefit* by doing it? According to everyone the RCMP spoke to, Hartwig and Senger were honest, conscientious, hard-working, and well-respected.

Something else the RCMP failed to consider was: Why would the officers drive Neil Stonechild eight km to another area of the city to drop him off, when it would have been easier for them to drive a little over one km to the edge of the city on the West side? This question was proposed to the RCMP and ignored. And why would they drive Neil Stonechild eight km to the north end when they could have driven him to Saskatoon Police detention in six km? Why wouldn't they simply arrest him on the outstanding warrant? After all, the outstanding UAL warrant was a notable arrest at the time. Were they trying to avoid paperwork? In 1990, all that was required of arresting officers was to date and sign the warrant; no report required.

The "Missing" Report: A Critical Juncture in the RCMP Investigation

While going through his foot locker at home in March 2001, Const. Ernie Louttit (the Saskatoon police officer consulted by the Stonechild family in late 1990) found a copy of the original police report on Stonechild, consisting of 20 pages. Louttit had copied the original report on or around December 4, 1990, when he met with the Stonechild family to discuss their concerns about this investigation. He had forgotten he had it and was shocked to discover it. The report was immediately forwarded to the RCMP task force.

This was the report that had been "missing" when the RCMP investigation began, and a critical starting point for the investigation. RCMP now had information from the original investigation vital to determining facts of the case. Instead of having to work backward from Jason Roy's allegation and try to reconstruct events from November 24, 1990, the RCMP could use the report to establish evidence critical to their investigation.

The report contained crucial information about the discovery of Neil Stonechild's frozen body on November 29, 1990 and reconstruction of events surrounding his death. Of particular note: *responding officers had not mentioned any blood found at the scene, and there was one set of footprints leading to Neil's body travelling in a north-easterly direction.* The report also contained information concerning motives to kill Neil Stonechild by the original suspects.

There was the information from Sharon Night in which she told Jarvis that Neil and Jason had left to go to the 7-Eleven, Roy returned home later and said he and Neil "had words" and went their separate ways. She stated that Roy was drunk at the time; he passed out and woke up sick the next morning.

Of particular note, the report contained the statements of Trent Ewart and Jason Roy given within days of Stonechild's death.

In his statement, Ewart had confirmed that he called SPS on November 24, 1990, that Stonechild had entered his apartment, that he had pushed Stonechild out the door, and that the responding officers, Hartwig and Senger, *attended* his suite and spoke to him about it. This statement provided evidence contrary to Jason Roy's 2000 allegation, *as it placed Hartwig and Senger at the Ewart apartment when, according to Jason Roy, they should have had Stonechild in custody.* The RCMP and, later, inquiry commissioner Wright seemed to ignore this crucial information.

The other, and most critical statement, was from Jason Roy himself. *Roy did not mention **anything** about Neil being in the custody of the police. In fact, the police were not mentioned at all in his statement.*

Remember that this statement had been given by Jason Roy five days after he last saw Neil Stonechild. This statement was in Jason Roy's handwriting and provided at Dina Sunshine's residence with Diana and Cheryl Antoine present. These circumstances are *identical* to those at which he had stated he gave Jarvis his statement, except that, in that one, he had claimed he said he **had seen** Stonechild in a police car.

The RCMP investigators noted that the statement provided by Jason Roy was entirely contradictory to his earlier statements made to them and would be evidence of a criminal offense of mischief with intent to mislead the police. The RCMP recognized the serious threat to Jason Roy's credibility and that they had to re-interview Jason Roy regarding the differences between his original statement to Jarvis and his most recent allegations where he claimed Neil Stonechild was in police custody.

The RCMP would meet with *Donald Worme* on a number of occasions over the following days to get to the bottom of Jason Roy's contrary statement.

Instead of re-interviewing Jason Roy concerning his conflicting statement, on March 27, 2001, as revealed at the inquiry, lead RCMP investigator Jack Warner decided against re-interviewing him, and instead gave a copy of Roy's November 30, 1990 statement to Donald Worme so he could review it.[121] This was a grievous breach of any investigative standard and a *grievous breach of investigative integrity*. Although this should have been a fatal blow to Jason Roy's credibility, in this case, it was not.

March 30, 2001, Warner meets with Donald Worme who tells him he will get to the bottom of Jason Roy's contrary statement. *The RCMP essentially ignore this statement.* They do not interview Sharon Night who had information critical to the investigation, nor re-interview parties mentioned in the report including Stella Bignell, Marcel Stonechild, Pat Pickard, and Diana Fraser.

In May 2001, nearly *two months* after the RCMP turned over to Worme Jason Roy's contrary statement, Roy phones lead investigator, Jack Warner, to ask what is happening with the investigation. Warner makes superficial inquiries as to the differences between Roy's statements on November 30, 1990 and March 7, 2000. When Warner mentions that Roy hadn't said anything in the November 30th statement about encountering police, Roy claims there is *"something missing"* in the first statement. He speculates there was a "second" question-and-answer portion with Jarvis and this *"must have"* been where he had made his alleged disclosure. He says he *"may have"* supplied a second statement, but isn't sure.

The RCMP do not conduct any follow-up interview with Jason Roy in this regard, and never do obtain an additional statement to clarify these issues. Instead of considering that Roy's allegation might be a *complete hoax*, they conclude that perhaps Roy hadn't told Jarvis the *"whole story."* They acknowledge the contentious issue of Jason Roy's statement, but do *nothing* to resolve it.

At the Stonechild Inquiry, Jason Roy would come up with another explanation for this deficiency.

Why would the RCMP, faced with contradictory evidence, seek to suppress or ignore this evidence? Was it that, since this was such a high profile case reported worldwide, the RCMP could not admit they had been duped by Jason Roy? Was it that, since none of the other cases they investigated resulted in any evidence of police involvement in those deaths, they couldn't conclude this case as unsubstantiated without arousing significant public criticism?

Hartwig can provide an answer. On December 3, 2008, Hartwig happened to bump into one of the RCMP investigators. Hartwig meets with him over coffee and a number of issues are discussed, with Hartwig secretly videotaping the conversation. The retired officer acknowledges that Jason Roy's allegation required corroborating evidence: "Clearly Jason Roy, without some corroboration, his evidence wouldn't stand. You know that as well as I do!"

As pointed out above, Hartwig asks him why the RCMP investigation did not come to a halt when Roy's statement was found and his credibility destroyed:

> *Hartwig: When Ernie Louttit found a copy of the original report, with the original statement, what happened with that investigation? That investigation should have come to a screeching halt, because now Jason Roy was trapped in several lies.*
> *RCMP officer: That had nothing to do with the RCMP, though, Larry. By then the process was already in place.*
> *Hartwig: Wasn't it still under investigation then?*
> *A: It was certainly still under investigation, but Justice was the ones that were making all the decisions about what was going to happen next."*

By the end of their investigation, the RCMP interview more than 100 SPS officers. All state they had heard nothing about the SPS being involved in any way in the death of Neil Stonechild or any other freezing death. *All officers speak highly of Hartwig and Senger, and state that they can't imagine their being involved in any wrongdoing.* Furthermore, investigators acknowledge that "all indications are that Hartwig is quite religious." In fact, Hartwig was involved in a leadership role both in his church and within the Saskatoon Police Service, and *devoted weeks of his own time to running a police charity helping families in need at Christmas.* RCMP discuss the idea of interviewing the pastor of Hartwig's church and the Saskatoon Police Service Chaplain, but decide against it.

RCMP investigators claim they received the full cooperation of the members of the SPS. Not entirely true! After Hartwig and Senger were interviewed, word got around about their being suspects, and the way in which they were treated. Sgt. Cooper and others took their own tape recorders when they were interviewed so that RCMP couldn't state they had said things they hadn't. Const. Larry Cook and another officer absolutely refused to speak to the RCMP.

Cook told me his suspicions about what happened next:

"We got a brand new district car, and a brand-new car never goes out of service right away. I came to work after it had been in service about a week, and it was out for service. I asked the commissionaire why; he didn't know. So I asked the mechanics; they informed me that the car had not been taken out of service by the mechanics. That put up some red flags!

The next shift when I came back to work, the car was back in service. That's when I really suspected that it had been bugged by the RCMP. So what I did was: I used the car on day-shift, when I was by myself in the car, but I never used that car on night-shift when we were paired up and might be heard talking. This went on for about two weeks and then, when I came back to work, three or four blocks [of shifts] later, the car was out of service again. So I went and asked everybody again why it was out of service. I was informed that none of them had taken it out of service. So I am assuming the car was taken out of service the second time to remove the bug that was in there.

I never had any confirmation that was going on. But, because I had worked with officers over the years who had quit the RCMP and joined SPS, I learned how they investigate. What they do is they will bug cars, they will bug tables at restaurants where the members go to have coffee. They don't have warrants for these bugs, so they are illegal and can't be used in court, but what it does is give them a hint regarding who to go after, what questions to ask, and how to handle their investigation. So if you say anything over coffee to somebody, that might trigger something for them to call you in and ask you questions about. That's how they investigate their own members. It gets to the point where someone who's trying to get ahead in the organization – well, you know who they are and you stay away from them!

Q: Did you inspect your vehicle to see if you could find a recording device?
A: No. I thought about it but I didn't do it. I thought, 'What's the point?'
since I wasn't talking to a partner during day-shift.
Q: What was your concern about talking to RCMP investigators?
A: I didn't agree with what they were doing. I wasn't going to play their
game. I told them point-blank that I wasn't going to talk to them. I'm not
going to be interviewed for stuff I had nothing to do with!
Q: Were you concerned they might do to you what they were doing to
Hartwig and Senger?
A: No, I wasn't concerned at all about that. My motto has always been: 'If
you've got a charge, lay it. We'll see you in court!'
Q: Larry Hartwig brought up the name of Neil Stonechild, and the RCMP
thought that was suspicious. Yet it might have been interpreted as a sign
of innocence, because he was willing to mention that he had dealt with
Stonechild.
A: Yes. Larry wants to help and he thought he was helping out in an
investigation. And that's just who he is. He trusted everybody. He wanted
to help with the investigation, not realizing they were actually trying to
get him. I knew that from Larry, and decided I wouldn't talk to the RCMP.
You start talking to them about something and all of a sudden they're
interested in something else. We had a good relationship with the RCMP
from the time we helped find the killer of murdered RCMP Const. Brian
King [April 1978], but after Operation Ferric, we really didn't have one.
Q: Having a good relationship and good communication and information-
sharing between the RCMP and police presumably aids in combating
crime?
A: It does, and it was too bad it had to happen that way. But they were
out on a witch-hunt, and I wasn't going to be part of it. I think it was
just political – people trying to get ahead, and they were going to go after
absolutely everybody. And they didn't follow up any other leads that were
leading away from the Saskatoon Police Service. They would just go after
the police. Even when it went to the inquiry, the RCMP didn't have to
testify to anything. So what was that all about?
In my opinion, it was a witch-hunt. The Saskatchewan government was
trying to appease the Native population and they thought this would be
a good way of doing it. I believe it came down from the justice minister.
It was not the RCMP, it was the NDP government of the time trying to

appease the Native population, and they, of course, put the RCMP in charge because they go right across Canada. I believe the government told them: This is your mandate – to charge members of our police force for doing something wrong with the Native population. They were afraid of the Natives getting upset and going violent. The government had a lot of political pressure on them, so that's what they decided to do. Even though I didn't talk to the RCMP, I'm certainly not blaming them; they were given a mandate from the government. The Natives weren't happy with a lot of things going on at the time."

When, on July 3, 2001, the man in charge of Operation Ferric, Insp. Darrell McFadyen, wrote to Richard Quinney in charge of public prosecutions about possible criminal charges regarding the death of Neil Stonechild, McFadyen pointed only to Hartwig and Senger:

"...Jason Roy and Neil Stonechild separated at or about the same time as the call to the police. Jason Roy began to make his way back to the house where he and Stonechild had earlier been drinking. En route to that house, he encountered a marked police vehicle with two officers who asked him for his name and also asked him if he knew who the person was who was in custody in their back seat. [In this very important letter, why not state that 'Roy claimed' there was a person in their back seat? Why not point out Jason Roy's background?] Jason Roy observed Neil Stonechild in the back seat in handcuffs and having been beaten. [Why not point out that it was a lie he had been beaten according to the autopsy and lack of any traces of blood on his clothing? And why not point out that, if the police had beaten this guy up, they were then unlikely to stop someone and display him.] Fearing he too would be arrested [Why not point out this was a lie; there was no warrant for Roy's arrest?], Jason Roy gave police a false name and date of birth and was allowed to proceed on his way. That is the last time Neil Stonechild was seen alive. His frozen body was found in the north industrial area of the city some four days later.

According to the witness evidence, Jason Roy disclosed that same night that Stonechild had been arrested and over the years he has told that story to others [and according to other witness evidence – close friends and members of Stonechild's family – Jason Roy did not disclose anything at all until his allegation hit the media, 10 year later. And what about the student counsellor who claimed that the first time Roy 'remembered' it was during her visualization a year after Stonechild's death?] He also maintains that he told the investigating officer responsible for the sudden death investigation of what he had seen. [What about Roy's original hand-written statement, found and turned over to RCMP three months earlier, which revealed that all these claims were lies?]

There is compelling independent evidence through CPIC to show that [names redacted, but obviously Hartwig and Senger] did have Stonechild in their custody. There is compelling evidence to suggest that Neil Stonechild had been struck on the face with a set of handcuffs and that he had handcuffs on his wrist prior to his death. [And much compelling medical evidence to prove that he distinctly had not. And the marks were on the hand, not wrist.] There is compelling evidence to show that the outstanding warrant for Neil Stonechild was on the CPIC system and that the system was working properly at the time he is believed to have been in custody. [Which strongly suggests the rookie cops did not have him in their custody or they would have brought him in, a laudable achievement.]

What we have not been able to determine is what transpired between the time that [again, presumably Hartwig and Senger] encountered Neil Stonechild and the date his body was discovered.

During the course of the investigation, close to 200 interviews were conducted and a number of investigative steps employed. The majority of those interviews and many of the investigative steps did not yield any evidentiary information. For that reason, this investigative brief does not cover all of those steps and interviews. Once you have had the opportunity to review the brief, I would appreciate the opportunity for the investigators and I to meet with you to fully discuss what criminal charges, if any, might be appropriate at this time.

Sincerely,

Darrell McFadyen, Inspector"

Sask Justice did not, however, charge Hartwig and Senger. The subsequent Minister of Justice, Frank Quennell, would tell the *StarPhoenix*: "I look at inquiries, like the Stonechild inquiry – from which I've received a report and which I think was an inquiry that had to take place because *there wasn't evidence that could possibly have led to a trial in that case* ...."[122]

The conduct of RCMP officers during their investigation seems unprofessional, biased, malicious, and even to constitute criminal mischief. Worse, it seems this can also be said for those who followed the lead of the RCMP (those in charge of the inquiry and Police Chief Sabo), as well as those Sask Justice officials who may have directed the RCMP investigation in the first place.

CHAPTER 21 - Physical Evidence:
The Handcuffs (Graphic photos)

'There are two ways to be fooled. One is to believe what isn't true. The other is to refuse to believe what is true.'
– **Soren Kierkegaard**

When the RCMP investigation began, the original SPS investigation report concerning the death of Neil Stonechild had been purged from the SPS database, but the original crime scene and autopsy photos, 49 in total, were available and turned over to the RCMP. These photos should have been a critical investigative aid to help RCMP reconstruct facts of the case, but they were not fully and reasonably understood. Repeatedly, RCMP investigators would state that Jason Roy fairly accurately described injuries to Neil Stonechild. But is this true? Not according to the many photos captured at the time.

Jason Roy described a six-inch diagonal cut across Neil Stonechild's cheek and nose, and "lots of blood." Yet any reasonable examination of the photos shows there was no blood in the snow where Stonechild had fallen face-first and died, and no blood on his clothing or face that would corroborate Roy's allegation.

The same held true for autopsy photos: no evidence of blood, no mention of blood by the coroner, identification officers, or medical examiner, and no blood in his stomach, which forensic experts stated he would have had to swallow if the facial injury described by Roy were accurate. Furthermore, it seems the RCMP did not realize that the injury depicted in the autopsy photos did not accurately depict the nature and condition of abrasions originally sustained, hence the appearance of those abrasions in field photos. This would later be addressed in the Public Inquiry. But why aren't all Canadian investigators trained in results of "Death by Winter," which vary substantially from every other cause of death?

Similarly, photos of marks on the remainder of Stonechild's body were largely ignored by the RCMP, as were other impressions on the right hand. Although facts captured by the original photos were ignored by the RCMP, these same photos would be manipulated in a vain attempt to prove Jason Roy's allegation.

At the end of March 2000, Lyons and Warner discussed the appearance of the injuries to Stonechild's face and hand. Lyons wrote in his notebook: "I agreed the injuries to Stonechild were *'not inconsistent'* with an assault. Also that marks on wrist were not inconsistent with handcuff marks." The investigators did not differentiate which marks were "not inconsistent" with handcuff marks but, since handcuffs are designed to restrain the hands, one could assume they were referring to the mark to Stonechild's right hand.

In evaluating that mark, a reasonable person would ask why there was only a mark on Neil Stonechild's right hand and not his left. Handcuffs are designed to be used in tandem. A handcuff attached only to one hand is not very effective as a restraining device. Secondly, a reasonable person would question if a handcuff could fit around the mid-point of the hand where a handcuff is not designed to fit.

Although the casual observer may draw conclusions that the mark was caused by handcuffs, these highly-trained RCMP homicide detectives were not casual observers. They know that the only way a handcuff is designed to be applied to the wrist is from thumb to pinky finger or pinky finger to thumb, and then rotated to place the chain between the two hands. When applied in this way, the hinge portion is in the centre of the back of the wrist, and therefore could not make the mark shown on Stonechild's hand. The RCMP also made no attempt to determine if handcuffs could fit around the area of the hand in the location where the marks were on Stonechild. Note photo below:

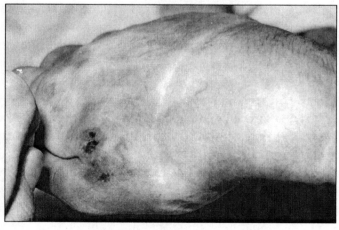

Mark across back of Neil Stonechild's right hand

This is one of the photos of the mark on the back of Neil Stonechild's hand that was available to the RCMP and which they determined was "not unlike" handcuff marks.

First, note the location of the mark from the joint at the base of the thumb to across the back of the hand to the approximate midpoint between the knuckle of the little finger and the wrist. The first question a competent police officer would ask themselves would be: "Could a handcuff fit around that portion of the hand?" The second would be: "Why was there only a mark on the right hand and not the left?" Handcuffs only work if used on both hands.

Finally, the mark is relatively uniform across the back of the hand with the exception of indentations along the mark (see below). The first is at the base of the thumb, the second is in the web between the bone of the thumb and the bone of the index finger, where there is a triangular indentation along the right-centre of the back of the hand and an indentation on either side of the bone of the ring finger.

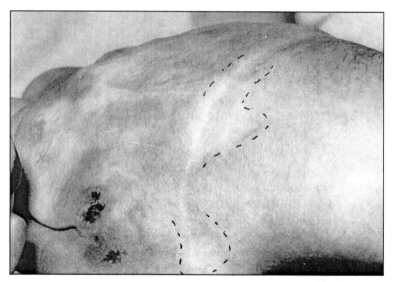

Handcuffs are hardened steel bands that are not flexible and would press into the skin only as far as the surrounding bones would allow. They would not create the indentations seen above. Only a flexible object pressed between the bones would allow for the indentations. The RCMP ignored the indentations above and concentrated on portions of the marks they felt might have been made by handcuffs. Similarly, they ignored the identical marks located on Stonechild's belly. Apparently the RCMP did not consider these very important details.

A simple experiment

One would think that the RCMP would make an attempt to determine if handcuffs could even make the marks depicted on Stonechild's hand in the first place. If they did, or even discussed this, it was not indicated in their notes or reports.

Handcuffs have several features, as revealed in photos provided by Larry Hartwig.

A handcuff consists of a 'single' strand, a 'double' strand and a hinge between the two. The 'single' strand fits in between the 'double' strands so the handcuff can lock in place around a person's wrist.

The bracelet of a handcuff is 5.2 cm in width or 2.04 inches.

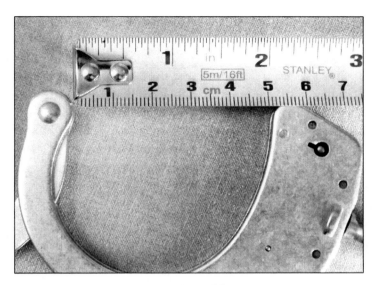

Bracelet width

The mark across the back of Stonechild's hand is relatively uniform, with no appreciable change. It would have had to be made by the "double strand" portion of the handcuff as opposed to either the "single strand" or a combination of the two.

Could handcuffs fit as depicted in the original photographs? We will see with the following experiment. The model was 16 years of age, 5'9" and 140 pounds, roughly the same size as Neil Stonechild at the time of his death. The bracelet could fit around the wrist as depicted below if it were forced onto the wrist. In this case, the wrist was barely able to fit the bracelet.

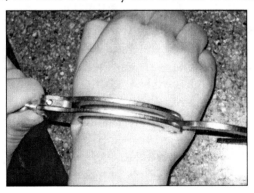

Handcuff in relation to wrist
Bracelet location across back of hand

In this photo, the handcuff was placed in an area on the model's hand which is narrower than the location of the mark on Neil Stonechild's hand. A handcuff would **ABSOLUTELY NOT FIT** across the hand of a person, no matter their size, even if the bones on the thumb, index finger, and pinky finger were squeezed together. In order to fit the bracelet across this area of the hand, bones would have to be broken on either side of the hand (the thumb or pinky finger). Could a handcuff be placed across the hand of the smaller model? Yes, but not with the same orientation as the mark on Stonechild.

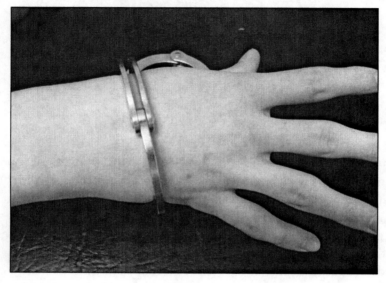

Handcuff placed in approximate location of the mark on Stonechild's hand

The handcuff could be placed on the hand only with this orientation given the structural design of handcuffs and the physiology of the human hand and only with extreme side pressure which caused significant pain for the model. The single strand was just able to engage the ratchet to lock the handcuff into place. Any further tightening would break the bones in the back of the hand. The handcuff could not be placed across the wrist and then pulled farther down the hand without causing very significant injury on the back of the hand from the hinge scraping the tissues on back of the hand.

Let's take a look from another angle.

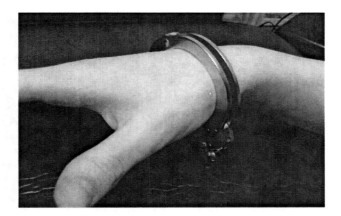

View from another angle

This is the view of the palm of the hand. Note the side-to-side compression and the ratchet teeth in view on the left side of the photo.

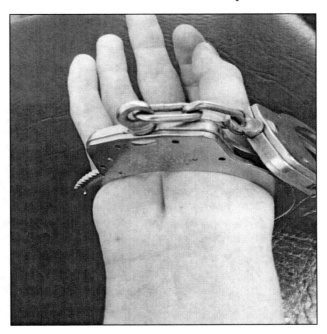

Photo of palm of hand depicting side-to-side compression

View of the back of the hand. Note the gap between the single strand and the back of the hand.

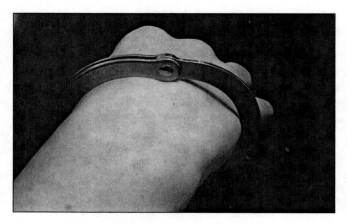

Photo depicting gap between back of hand and handcuff

Note the hinge portion pressing into the back of the hand and the gap by the single strand. If the handcuff were tightened any further, the hinged portion would press into the back of the hand, breaking the bones of the index and middle finger. In addition, the hand was already so compressed that it could not be moved to contact the single strand where the gap was.

Let's look at the marks on the hand after the handcuff is removed.

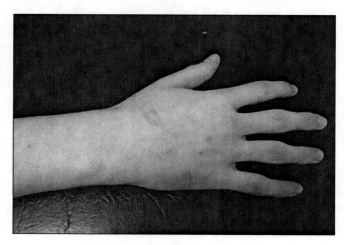

Handcuff mark

In this photo, one can clearly see the double-strand impression at the top of the hand and a clear termination of the mark. Also the single-strand impression at the bottom of the hand, with a clear termination mark and a gap between the two. In comparing the marks to the marks on Neil Stonechild's hand, we can see that the marks are not at all the same.

Close-up photo of the mark five minutes after the handcuff was removed:

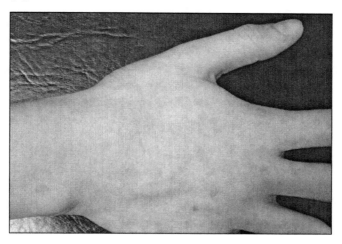

Fade rate of handcuff mark: 10 minutes

IF the marks had been *ante mortem* (as all *medical* experts agreed they were not), fade rate would be the time required for the mark to change from visible (with indentation and skin flushed red) to no longer visible. In the test, above, the "fade rate" was 10 minutes. In his report, Robertson claimed the marks on Stonechild's hand had been made 45 minutes to two hours from the time of death, which would mean that if the marks had been made ante mortem, before death, and the handcuffs removed before death, the marks would have disappeared before he died. This is clearly a *post mortem* mark and therefore could not have been made by handcuffs, given the other, known and well-established evidence that was ignored.

"The problem is," Hartwig concludes, "when you exclude critical evidence, even the impossible becomes possible! But just because something is possible does not make it so, and falls *far* short of the burden of proof *required* in this case."

Stan Goertzen adds, "I believe that Sask Justice and the Provincial Police Commission viewed and dealt with allegations about police more aggressively after the Darrell Night complaint. In my opinion, it became a media and political circus. I believe the Night case was used to justify creating the

Stonechild Inquiry, and the media and political circus had an effect on how things were done during and even after the inquiry. I heard many people refer to the inquiry as the Wild West, where the rules today might not apply tomorrow. In hindsight, I can't say I disagree."

CHAPTER 22 - Child's Play, Four Pigs and the Wild, Wild West: The Stonechild Inquiry (Graphic Photos)

'Gary Robertson, the photogrammetrist, was hired to measure marks that were apparent in the post-mortem photographs of Stonechild's body and, later, to compare these measurements to the measurements of handcuffs used by the Saskatoon Police Service in 1990. As a result of the investigation, the RCMP identified two suspects: Const. Lawrence Hartwig and Const. Brad Senger.'
– Justice David Wright, Final Report of the Commission of Inquiry into Matters Relating to the Death of Neil Stonechild

~ ~ ~

'There have been cases of police brutality in North America, and I've seen my share over the years – I'm working on one now – but we can state that these on Stonechild are not handcuff marks. That the judge chose to believe the photogrammetrist over the other experts is weird!'
– Dr. Valery Rao, chief medical examiner for City of Columbia, Missouri

As folks filed into the Michelangelo Room in a Saskatoon hotel September 8, 2003 for the "Commission of Inquiry into Matters Relating to the Death of Neil Stonechild" in which findings were to have no binding legal effect, many had no idea they were entering, effectively, a murder trial in which the lives of the "villains" would be "strung up," left twisting in legal limbo by the judge, yet, unbelievably, all without any rules! Just like in the wild, wild West.

Upon entering – or, one might say, "upon travelling back to an earlier, lawless time" – attendees at the inquiry were greeted with a poster-sized image of Neil Stonechild's autopsy photo. The photo of a handcuff had been digitally superimposed over the marks on his nose, *and made to appear to fit*. "It was as if Sask Justice was saying, 'We know who did it. We're here to figure out how the police must have done it, because it was impossible!'" said Larry Lockwood. Many believe this is exactly what, in the end, was "figured out" – how the police must have done it.

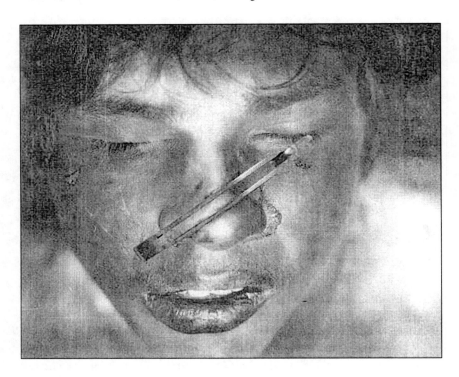

The image, too, was revealed to be not only falsified but impossible, due to the curvature of a handcuff. (The curvature had been disguised by, in the photogrammetrist's word, "Photoshopping": deleting half the handcuff, balancing the remaining half-circle on its two ends, and taking the photo from directly above, so it appeared flat as a hair clip.) Even if, after facts were revealed, people no longer gave credibility to that particular image, the subconscious of many had been permanently seared, as soon as they stepped into the Wild, Wild Inquiry, with the smoking-hot brand: *"Police Did It!"*

"At a normal murder trial, the person who concocted that photo would not have been allowed in as an expert witness," says Stan Goertzen. "Then no one would have seen any of his fabricated images. But they were all allowed in because the inquiry was like the lawless west. Nobody knew what the rules were." It was the exact situation Const. Lockwood had overheard the activist recommending back in 2000: "What is needed now is a commission… *so that the justice system could be bypassed.*"

Police lawyers protested that the image was prejudicial to fairness and it was duly removed, several days later. "It cast a pall on the whole proceeding," says Brad Senger's lawyer, Jay Watson. "It had no business in evidence because there was no evidentiary base for it. But it was spectacular, and got the press going! The inquiry started out bad and got worse."

"That doctored photograph had huge public sway," adds Senger. "It was shown in many newspapers, people concluded that we must have whacked him with handcuffs, and we were done!"

Who would have made the decision to allow displaying that photo? Commission counsel for the inquiry, who made many decisions including those called to testify, was Joel Hesje. A Saskatoon lawyer who grew up a small-town boy, he probably held the RCMP in high regard, much like Larry Hartwig had. And, like Hartwig, when the RCMP provided him with information for the inquiry, Hesje probably accepted whatever they gave him.

The judge hearing testimony and formulating the all-important findings was Saskatonian David Wright. "Why would the Department of Justice appoint someone from Saskatoon?" asks Ed Swayze who, as Regina deputy chief, had followed events closely. "Why not choose someone from another judicial centre or province, so they're not putting a judge on the hot seat locally? Judges are human; people might not talk to him. If it had been a retired judge from another province, would there have been a different decision?"

Fact-finding (not fault-finding) inquiries are established to investigate and report upon a particular event or events, to ensure they are not repeated, explained Ontario Justice Dennis O'Connor in 2007:

"Commonly, they are established in the aftermath of a tragedy or scandal usually with political implications, where the public's confidence or trust in public institutions or officials has been shaken. The normal public institutional responses are seen as inadequate, and governments respond to public pressure by creating an independent, ad hoc credible process to investigate and report on what happened and to make recommendations to prevent a reoccurrence. ...

Unlike criminal or civil trials, inquiries do not need to be conducted within the confines of the fixed rules of practice and procedures. Inquiries are not trials: they are investigations. They do not result in the determination of rights or liabilities [in fact, commissioners are prohibited from making such determinations]; they result in findings of fact and/or recommendations. Subject to what I say below about the need for procedural fairness for those who may be affected by the report of an inquiry, a commissioner has a very broad discretion to craft the rules and procedures necessary to carry out his or her mandate. ...

My second observation about the inquiry process [Justice O'Connor continued] relates to the need to ensure procedural fairness to those who may be adversely affected by the information that emerges during the course of the inquiry or in the report. This is critically important. There is enormous potential for an inquiry, particularly a public inquiry, to seriously damage personal and professional reputations. ...[I]t is essential that commission counsel, in deciding what evidence to call and how to lead it, lean over backwards to be fair and balanced and alert to the potential for unfair damage to reputations."

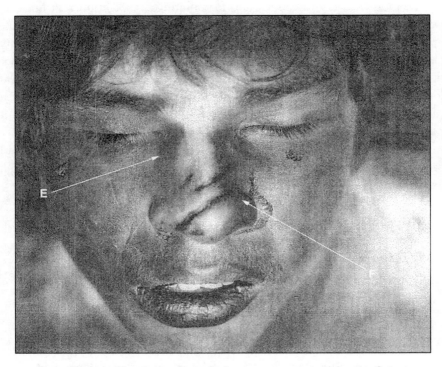

Completely unlike the top line, the bottom scrape extends out of view, wrapping beneath the tip of the nose to one nostril. At top right, the lines spread apart. Fluid beside nose flowed upward, indicating it occurred post mortem from thawed tissue, when the head was positioned back on the autopsy headrest. No blood was found anywhere on the body.

The Stonechild family, Saskatoon Police Service, RCMP, FSIN, retired Sgt. Jarvis, Deputy Chief Wiks, Constables Larry Hartwig and Brad Senger, Gary Pratt and Jason Roy all had standing at the inquiry, their lawyers paid by the provincially-funded commission. Only the City of Saskatoon and Saskatoon Police Association were forced to pay for their own lawyers.

"The old Chinese proverb, 'A photo is worth 1,000 words,' or whatever it is, is actually false," the Ottawa photogrammetrist behind that photo testified before the inquiry. An "expert witness" produced by the RCMP, Gary Robertson continued, "If you don't have any known dimensions in a photograph … I always say it's worth a million lies!"

Sage wisdom, says forensic pathologist Dr. Emma Lew, and Robertson's own photo is a case in point. "In my career, I don't know any of my colleagues who have used a photogrammetric analyst to evaluate lesions on bodies," Dr. Lew told me in an interview. She had received her medical training at the U of S, followed by four years specializing in pathology and another in forensic pathology, for a total 14 years of training, followed by 13 years' experience, as she testified, "looking at real, dead bodies with those very injuries." She was deputy chief medical examiner in Miami-Dade County, Fla, one of the busiest such offices in the world. She had worked high-profile cases including the 1996 Florida Everglades ValuJet crash, which officials called the most challenging crash site they had ever encountered; the swamp infested with "alligators and poisonous snakes."[123] Dr. Lew was not even a paid "police expert," as the commissioner mistakenly wrote about her, but neutral and unpaid. "I often try to help out other agencies, and I'm interested in providing some expertise to help out the Saskatoon community where I grew up and was educated."

In contrast, under cross-examination, Robertson admitted he had lied on his CV. He had a diploma as a mapmaker's technician in which, he said, "there was some photogrammetric classes involved in that bit." He also admitted that he had lied about completing an engineering degree at university. (Nevertheless, for the police hearing two years later, he provided the same CV to legal counsel, and after they pointed out he had been taken to task over it at the inquiry, they blacked out the portion about his engineering degree. The hearing officer then deemed him knowledgeable and proficient enough to be considered an expert at the police hearing.)

Aaron Fox, Hartwig's legal counsel, cross-examined Robertson on whether he was qualified to state opinions regarding human skin:

"Q: In this publication, ... is there anything in there that you've published or printed that deals with identifying marks on human skin, imprints on human skin?

A: Actually, yeah, it does, and that's why we use a lot of these references. ...In that particular chapter in that paper we are doing automated measurements of targeted points and, of course, this is one of the reasons or the ways that we can attain such high accuracies.

Q: Would I see the word 'skin' in here anywhere?

A: No.

Q: No.

A: But it's the same procedure.

Q: The same procedure. I just wouldn't see the word 'skin' anywhere in there.

A: No.

Q: Or 'imprints on skin' anywhere. You referred to some studies and we saw some slides that you did with pigs. How many studies like that have you been involved in, directly, personally involved in?

A: We've been doing the pig skin analysis I guess maybe –

Q: But, sir. Before you answer that, I don't want to know 'we,' I just want to know 'you.' You, how many studies have you been involved in where you implanted a mark on a pig and then made an interpretation of it? How many pigs have you worked on?

A: The first study was -- one was for burn victims on human skin and that was back, I believe, in '85, '84, '85, and then the work that we're doing on - on the skin imprints using pigs I believe was 1995, '96.

Q: So how many pigs did you – we saw three in the slide.

A: I think it was four. We did four.

Q: Four?

A: Yeah.

Q: That's – that's the extent of it, four pigs?

A: Yeah, that's where –

Q: Like, over the years that's what you've worked on?

A: Four pigs."

Lew, who estimated she had analyzed more than 5,000 human bodies to that point in her career, told me she believed Robertson's handcuff theory was an irresponsible leap. "I didn't know anything about photogrammetry until this inquest. My impressions are that it's used to measure land masses and structures from a distance, which is very different from something little such as a lesion on a body." (In addition to the critical fact that there were too few identifiers in autopsy photos to use in determining size of the marks, and RCMP erred in retaking photos of the morgue to establish identifiers. Moreover, the handcuffs Robertson used for his measurements were not even the same as Hartwig and Senger carried.)

"I'm speculating," Lew told me in the post-inquiry interview, "that Robertson said, 'Oh, these two patterns look like handcuffs—they look somewhat parallel, linear, and about the same distance apart. Therefore, they must have been made by handcuffs. But that was done without consideration of the type of injury, the contours of the body, the object used, without the medical knowledge required to evaluate. This non-medical evaluation of an injury has taken the process out of the realm of science and simplified it into child's play, a game. Hence my response during the inquiry of 'Which one of these is not like the others?' (from Sesame Street)."

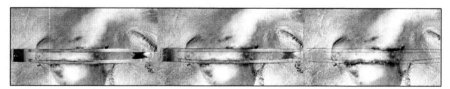

Lines drawn by SPS officers indicate that rails on the photogrammetrist's digitally-overlaid handcuff were manipulated to appear to fit the scratches. **The top rail is straight, the bottom curved.** SPS officers determined that, between the middle of the rails and the joined ends, there is a variance of 1 mm. "You can see the difference in width with your naked eye," said Lockwood. "And on the bottom rail, just right of centre, two sizes appear merged; the left blurry, the right distinct. Robertson's sleight-of-hand was crudely done, but he sold it!"

Fox continued cross-examining Robertson:

"Q: Your report says that 'there is bruising and swelling near the bridge of the nose indicating a possible fracture.'
A: Right and that – there is this particular area on the top of the bridge of the nose. And it was just going by the swelling because we did detect some

swelling, and it was just a comment of the – of the bruising and swelling.

Q: Then why would you put the comment that there is a possible fracture there?

A: Well, I just put it in. It looked – it looked like swelling. I played rugby for maybe 15 years, I've seen some broken noses. I'm not an expert on it, but – –

Q: And you've already agreed you don't have the expertise to make a comment like that.

A: No, I'm not a medical doctor. I wouldn't – I couldn't say for sure if it was broken."

Two medical experts, Saskatoon pathologist Dr. Jack Adolf who performed the 1990 autopsy and Alberta's chief medical examiner Dr. Graeme Dowling who did the 2001 autopsy, had determined the nose was not broken. Both agreed the hand imprint appeared to be the same as the imprints on Stonechild's abdomen: they thought all imprints on Stonechild's body were left by clothing pressing against the skin. Asked if he thought the marks on the hand could have been caused by handcuffs, Dowling replied, "I would not go that far."

Lawyers for the Stonechild family and Jason Roy also seemed less than convinced that the marks were caused by handcuffs, producing industrial "wire ties" as the possible source of the marks. These were entered as an exhibit.

Fox asked Robertson how he made the critical decision that the marks on the hand and nose were made before death (ante mortem) rather than post mortem – the only "expert" to do so:

"A: …One was I contacted several pathologists, including people at forensic conferences, and asked for their input…. Secondly, I have had a doctor working with me, a colleague, for close to 17, 18 years … Dr. Bill Miles …. He has reviewed the work that I've been doing. You know, I -- and because what I do is, I have it reviewed medically. …I do have it checked, and he gave an opinion of the characteristics between an ante mortem and post mortem as well. So we ….

Q: Could you produce that for me?

A: Sure.

Q: Have you produced this to anyone associated with this inquiry prior to now?

A: No, it's just in my files. It's in my pigskin analysis files that we use for our research on pigs.

Q: So you haven't shown this to Commission counsel either?

A: No.

Q: No. This is – I don't see a signature or a letterhead or anything associated with this?

A: Well –

Q: So is that your sort of ante mortem/post mortem file that you've got there?

A: Actually it's from an email. It – because he was busy, he did send me an email and this is the – his actual email. I just extracted from his email.

Q: My question was, is that your sort of ante mortem/post mortem file that you've got there?

A: No, it's just pictures of our pigskin items, what we're using for pigs and letters –

Q Well, what is in there, then? Like, is that your study? Is that the studies we've talked about?

A: No, it's just some correspondence.

Q: Well, would you mind if we took a look at that?

A: Well, I don't know exactly what's in here.

…Q: When did you render your opinion in this matter, Mr. Robertson? What's the date of your report? Your report. The opinion that you gave.

A: I don't know. I think it was, what, 2000 or something. Or three years ago.

Q: 2000?

A: Yeah.

Q Yeah, okay. What you've produced for me is sort of what you rely upon in determining if there's ante mortem or post mortem is an email that was received by you on July 10th, 2003?

A: That's correct.

Q: That would be correct? So you didn't have this email when you rendered this opinion?

A: No.

Q: No. So when you rendered the opinion in 2000, Dr. Miles hadn't looked at this thing and told you these are ante mortem or post mortem; that was your opinion?

A: No, not really, because Bill has heavy –"

After asking three more times, Fox asked the commissioner: "Should I ask the question again, Mr. Commissioner?" Getting the nod, he continued on like a border collie rounding up mountain goats:

"Q: The question I asked you, sir, was that, in your opinion which was rendered in approximately 2000, you stated, 'I also determined that the injuries to his nose and the imprints on his wrist were ante mortem.'
A: I –
Q: That's what you said.
A: And the –
Q: And my question was, did Dr. Miles review the material that you had –
A: No.
Q: -- to assist you in rendering that opinion.
A: Not on the Stonechild. He was reviewing the information that we had on our pigskin –
Q: The only information you've got from Dr. Miles is the general one-page email which you received on July 10th, 2003?
A: Right.
Fox: I wonder if I could mark that as an exhibit, Mr. Commissioner?"

Commissioner Wright then ruled that Robertson would be allowed to testify at the inquiry as an expert witness.

After repeated questioning, Roberson also admitted his measurements of the tiny lines had a margin of error of 25 percent. He was vague on the scale of face to handcuff, which would critically affect the truth of his depiction. (At the later appeal hearing, he admitted he had to *blow up the handcuff* photo to make it appear to fit the marks.) Despite all the holes in his testimony, Robertson concluded: "No, my report says that there was enough identifiers on here to make it consistent with the peerless handcuffs [which Hartwig and Senger had not been using]. I stand by that. There is." (Even though he claimed there were five such identifiers on the nose and five such identifiers on the hand, he admitted under cross examination there were only three in each case. Not enough, even by his standards.)

Drew Plaxton, lawyer for the police association, also drew these admissions from the RCMP's expert witness:

Plaxton: "… through the magic of computer manipulation, you deleted the single-rail portion of the handcuff.

Robertson: Yes, we took a portion of the handcuffs, yes.

Q: And if we look at the handcuffs, I think if we use the magic of real life, looking at those cuffs, if the cuffs were open, there's no way it can be placed across your face without causing damage to your cheek, either high on the cheek or low on the cheek, is that correct?

A: I have no idea. I mean, I haven't – I didn't do the analysis of the impact – or the imprint mark on the nose, just the measurements, so I really can't comment on that.

…Q: Okay, let's take a little experiment here, if you will. Take those handcuffs, please open them up, or close them, and show me how on earth those handcuffs could make a mark similar to what we've seen on Mr. Stonechild's face.

A: [Robertson did not place the cuffs anywhere near his face.] I don't know – he could have – I mean again it would be all hypothetical. It could be – I mean you could have crushed cartilage which would make it flattened out. I mean, there's a whole bunch of assumptions here that I can't make just by looking at these handcuffs.

…Q: And there's a problem now, isn't it? You cut out the particular chunk of the photograph that didn't match the result you wanted to achieve.… Look at those handcuffs; there's two ways they could come into contact with someone's nose. One is convex, the other is concave, right? It's a basically round object. If it goes concave, the edges are going to hit [the cheeks] before the centre portion will hit your nose, right?

A: Right.

Q: And if it goes convex, you have two round objects meeting each other [the handcuff and the bridge of the nose], and there's no way you can get a long line like we see on Neil's face, right?

A: We don't know that and what I'm – you know."

I interviewed retired RCMP Sgt. Ken Bullock. In 2000, as an identification specialist, Bullock had been unable to state that the marks on Stonechild's body were made by handcuffs, so he had contacted Robertson, whom he had hired earlier to work for the RCMP:

"Bullock: I worked in a research section in Ottawa in a branch of the ident services – the equivalent of the American CSI. Gary Robertson had worked with Parks Canada. His specialty was recovering data from

two-dimensional photos. ShapeQuest is a computer application he co-produced which is used by NASA, among others. It's a device used by the military – a scanning densitometer.

Q: Were you happy with his work on the Stonechild case?

A: Yes, he did a good job. I think his evidence was right on the money. I was surprised at the rough time he had on the stand. I don't think the courts were ready for this technology, although it was used back in 1895 to build trusses across the valleys in the mountains for the railroad.

Q: Did you know that he could not demonstrate how he had arrived at some of his data?

A: Yes, and I was surprised; that never happened before. We used Gary Robertson extensively on the Gander crash – we relied on his data. And in the crash of two helicopters at Niagara Falls where several were killed, we were able to establish their exact location using photographs from some of the people in the helicopters. Gary told me he got into a contest with the lawyers at the Saskatoon hearing and had a rough go.

Q: Did you know that he lied about his credentials?

A: I hadn't investigated them. He got the job done. I think if you looked at everyone's credentials closely there would be a lot of red faces. Reading some curriculum vitae is like reading fiction. Gary proved himself with the military and transportation safety. I had a session with Gary after he testified at the Saskatoon hearing – he said it got off the track. He had a lot of court experience, such as cases in California with the Highway Patrol."

Bullock himself may have inadvertently contributed to inaccuracy, as revealed in a letter he had sent Robertson concerning his morgue photos for use in calculating the tiny marks:

Gary – I had the camera set on wide angle with the wide angle adapter in place. … Unfortunately I was using the autofocus. …If it will help I just photo'd the 3DBuilder target, at approx the distance I was working at in the morgue and close enough to almost fill the frame. Don't know if that would help you but it is all I can do. … Ken

Robertson testified he had presented his inaccurately doctored photo of the handcuff on the nose to Regina RCMP Major Crimes in early 2002 (which may have contributed to their apparent tunnel vision about police).

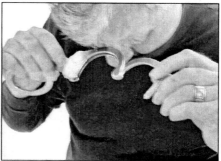

Larry Lockwood illustrated the convex and concave properties of a handcuff; the handcuff would have hit the cheekbones before hitting the nose. Dr. Lew told me: "The only parts of the handcuffs that could have made that type of scratch were not part of the smooth bracelet, but part of the locking device where it has little teeth. Those edges are sharper, and therefore able to make those marks, but they are not the same distance apart as the scratches."

Hesje clearly stated that Roberson was to measure the body marks and take measurements of the handcuffs. He was not to offer any conclusions of what caused the marks. This was explicitly stated by Hesje, yet Wright asked Robertson this question related to the mark on Stonechild's right hand:

> "Wright: What is your sense, just globally speaking, as to whether those marks would be caused by clothing...?"
> Robertson: ...I think it would be very difficult [to say], Your Honour....
> Wright: ... "I'd gather that you are saying that it would be a remote possibility?"
> Robertson: "It would be very remote in my opinion."[24]

With this exchange, Robertson clearly stated that it would be "difficult to say" if the marks were caused by clothing. Then Wright himself makes a statement in the form of a question, asking Robertson for an opinion that **would qualify him as a forensic pathologist.** Robertson's reply would form the basis for several of Wright's conclusions in his Final Report.

Dr. Valery Rao, chief medical examiner for the city of Columbia, Missouri as well as associate professor of pathology, wrote a report based on her study of 44 Stonechild photos, and submitted it in advance of the inquiry. In her opinion, those are not handcuff marks. **She was not called to testify. Commission counsel Joel Hesje was not required to give reasons for his decisions about who he called to testify.**

In an interview at the time, Dr. Rao told me:

"I've been doing this 25 years in a very high-volume place like Miami. I have done many, many cases with handcuff imprints, I have analyzed living and deceased people who have handcuff marks, and Stonechild didn't have anything that resembled a handcuff. I can't even think of a handcuff case that in any way resembled the marks on Stonechild. Using the testimony of somebody like the photogrammetrist, who had only done work on four pigs, is bloody ridiculous!

Nobody goes to people like that photogrammetrist when medical examiners are available who are doing this analysis on a daily basis. The texture of pigs' skin is so different from humans'. The problem is that people like this who get accepted in a court of law one time, then get accepted based on that precedent. Nobody goes to see, 'Wait a minute, let us see what he did that first time around and how acceptable it was in a court of law.' This is an injustice to people who really know these issues! **This may be one of the reasons why an appeal will be granted – on the basis of an unqualified specialist.**

The photogrammetrist should be ashamed of himself! But when you're looking for an expert, you're desperate. You look for anything that will support your point of view. When someone says, 'I can do that!' you don't even ask about their credibility or, 'In how many cases you've done has your view been accepted?'"

This writer has learned of one case in which Gary Robertson had been an expert witness four years before the inquiry, in a 1999 California murder trial. Douglas S. Mouser, 49, was tried for the 1995 strangling murder of his 14-year-old stepdaughter. Mouser was a computer expert who once held top-secret security clearance at the American laboratory responsible for securing the nation's nuclear weapons. The stepdaughter's brother dealt drugs out of the home and she had been spending time with, and courting, two sex offenders. As reported by the American association, Forensic Solutions, described as a "partnership of practicing forensic professionals," there was no evidence of a crime at the residence or of Mouser's involvement in the crime:

"During the entire five month trial, only one piece of associative physical evidence was offered by the prosecution: a mark on her leg examined

by an expert named Gary Robertson (a photogrammetrist). He testified that this mark was identical to the pattern on the seatbelts in Doug Mouser's car, which, he argued, supported the prosecution's theory. However, Mr. Robertson was alone in his opinions.

Every other forensic expert that testified on this issue concluded that Mr. Robertson's interpretations had no legitimate basis, and/or the pattern on her leg was consistent with an underwear mark. This included a defense criminalist, a Department of Justice criminalist testifying for the prosecution, and an expert in photogrammetry with a PhD in engineering who has trained the FBI in image analysis, testifying for the defense. …

It should also be noted that Mr. Robertson did not have a professional CV, and was unable to define the term 'forensic science' when asked to do so by the defence. On Monday, December 20th, 1999, the jury convicted Douglas Mouser of murdering his 14-year-old stepdaughter."[125]

(Mouser could have been out of jail by 2011, but, as of 2015, remains in jail with no chance of parole until 2019 because he refuses to admit guilt.)

Dr. Rao continued:

"The scratches on the nose are brush. You're lying in the brush and you have all these twigs. When the body was taken out of the snow, photos indicated what he was laying on, and that was twigs and brush.

It is a miscarriage of justice. Politically, the case must have been a hot potato! *But we must seek the truth, no matter how it plays out – that is basically what we're after. If the cops come up looking bad, you know what? C'est la vie. You must accept it, these are the facts, move on.* ***But if you haven't got the facts, you've got to try and straighten it out!"***

One of the first lessons pathologists learn is: "Dying changes things," stated Dr. Lew. "Those [initial] pictures taken when he was first discovered at the scene showed two relatively straight linear scratches. They looked thinner and less prominent than the dried out lesions that you're seeing in the morgue. **And that initial photo of the scratches on the nose before the body thawed was not included in the Wright report!**

"**There would be grave miscarriages of justice all over the place if laypeople were able to pronounce that certain wounds were made in a certain way,** simply because they look like it, without consideration of *post mortem* artifacts, including drying of the tissues!"

This fact had not stopped FSIN counsel Silas Halyk asking Gary Horse at the inquiry to pronounce on wounds – and even their cause:

Halyk: "And how obvious or otherwise was it to you that he had cuts on his nose?
Horse: It was obvious. It was, like, you could see them. He was right there, like, I don't know.
Q: Well, like, were they difficult to see?
A: No, they weren't. They were, like, wide. They're uh, good-sized cuts on his face.
… Q: So I mean, would it be obvious to you or to anyone in your mind that there was some foul play here, that something had happened to him before his death?
A: I guess you'd suspect, I don't know, just from seeing what I -- from what I saw."

The commissioner did not intervene.

Examining the only Operation Ferric investigator to take the stand, Jason Roy's counsel Darren Winegarden suggested the hypothetical scenario that police forced Roy to write lies in his first statement (since he did not mention seeing any police). This despite the presence of Dina Sunshine and Roy's girlfriend, Cheryl Antoine, who testified she did not leave Roy alone with the police taking the statement "even for a minute."

Winegarden: "Now just hypothetically speaking, if someone were to try and falsify a statement, to falsify evidence, to force someone to falsify a pure version statement, that would be the most convincing fraud, would that be fair to say, sort of force somebody to use their own hand to make a statement. That would be fairly convincing fraud, would it not?
RCMP Insp. Darrel McFadyen: I wouldn't reference it as fraud. It might be a deceit, yes.
Q: A deceit. So if somebody – if you were to sit someone down, force them to write something in their own hand and then ask them some questions afterwards and make some notes where things were left a little open-ended, that would be the best kind of deceitful statement to make then, would it not?
A: If that was the intention, I suppose, yes.

Q: Okay. Because, you know, clearly if the interview were tape recorded or something like that, then you'd be able to hear the person being forced to be deceitful.
A: Yes."

Former police officer and MP Art Hanger labels this lawyer's technique: "Making an Accusation by Asking Unanswerable Questions," or attempting obfuscation of evidence by suggesting hypothetical scenarios. In a criminal court, such questions never would have been allowed. A Wild, Wild Inquiry, however, does not have the same protections as a criminal court for those viewed as the "accused."

Dr. Lew concluded the marks on Stonechild's hand were *post mortem* and definitely not made by a handcuff, but by the cuff of his jacket pulled over his hand to keep it warm. The weight of his body on his right hand underneath him impressed the fabric into his skin, much like sleeping imprints pyjama fabric.

Dr. Lew's evidence was disregarded because the commissioner ruled her evidence as to the timing of the injuries "unreliable," while he found it extremely unlikely that the marks on the nose could have been caused "fortuitously, by two unrelated, parallel objects." Instead, he accepted the evidence of the photogrammetrist. Commissioner Wright wrote:

"Similarly, I had difficulty with Dr. Lew's characterization of the so-called 'striations' on Neil Stonechild's wrists. The evidence established that he had his sleeves pulled down over his hands to keep them warm. If there was a cuff that might cause marks of some sort, it would not be in relation to his wrist. I refer, of course, to the cuffs that would be on his jacket. I am satisfied that the lumber jacket that he wore likely had button cuffs and would not have contained cuffs of the sort one would see on a windbreaker."

Dr. Lew told me, however, that she had referred to the marks made, not by the lumber jacket, but by *the jacket worn over it*, which had storm cuffs. (The ambulance attendant and officer who took photos at the scene had independently told me the same thing.)

Yet the cuff issue was a central reason the Court of Appeal held as reasonable the Commissioner's findings regarding this evidence. The appellate judge wrote:

"[Senger's] Counsel emphasizes that there was no evidence presented to the Commissioner about the nature of the cuffs on Mr. Stonechild's jacket. This may be so but, in my view, this is not enough to warrant a reassessment of the Commissioner's evaluation of Dr. Lew's evidence. His comment about the cuffs on a lumber jacket was ultimately not the reason why he discounted Dr. Lew's testimony. The real point was that Mr. Stonechild's hands were pulled inside the sleeves of his jacket and that he, that is the Commissioner, could not see the striations which were central to Dr. Lew's opinion. In the end, there is no basis on which the Court, in this proceeding, can second-guess the Commissioner's evaluation of Dr. Lew's testimony."[126]

Wright's report[126] continued: "I would respectfully suggest that Dr. Lew was enhancing her opinion, because of the desire to support her opinion. The enhancement was not justified. Overall, I did not find the evidence of Dr. Lew very helpful."

In the interview with me, Lew acknowledged that relying on medical science alone may not have been of much use to the inquiry: "I understand that there are other factors and other agendas involved here," she said.

Some said Roy should have been prosecuted for perjury. It was established at the inquiry he was lying about when and where he gave his statement which had mentioned nothing about police involvement. He first testified that he gave his statement Dec. 22, 1990, when he "lied for his life" in the police station. Under cross-examination, however, he admitted he actually gave police the statement Dec. 4 in a friend's home, in the presence of friends.

Whether it be a judge, adjudicator, or inquiry commissioner rendering a decision, the primary function to be carried out is a determination of the credibility of each witness. In *F. H. McDougall*, 2008 SCC 53, the Supreme Court clarified the law with respect to the standard of proof in civil cases: nothing more, nothing less than a *balance of probabilities test*. The Court also affirmed that a trial judge must not consider a witness' evidence in isolation, but **should consider the totality of the evidence in the case, and assess the impact of any inconsistencies on questions of credibility and reliability pertaining to the core issues in the case.**

The commissioner not only disbelieved Hartwig and Senger, but believed Jason Roy at certain times and not at others. This is how the commissioner explained some of the glaring discrepancies Roy was caught in during the inquiry (he sometimes took longer than a minute to answer, apparently because he had been caught in a lie):

"*Why then would Roy say he gave a statement on December 20, 1990? In the final analysis, I believe it has to do with Roy's entire involvement with the justice system; his out-of-control life in 1990; and his status as an Aboriginal youth with a criminal record and criminal associates. I have talked elsewhere in this report about the place of Aboriginal people in society and their interaction with the police and the justice system. My earlier impression of these events was that Roy, when faced suddenly with [Const. Louttit finding] the November 30, 1990 statement, one he obviously did not recall, panicked and cast about for some explanation as to why he would give such an account in light of his description of seeing Neil Stonechild in police custody on November 24/25. After considering the matter at some length, I concluded that there was a germ of truth to his repeated avowals that he had given different information to the police about Neil Stonechild and the two constables. Put in its simplest terms, it comes to this: Roy knew that he had given the person who interviewed him (Jarvis) a full account of what happened on November 24/25. When called upon to provide a written statement of the events, he stopped short of implicating the Saskatoon Police Service. His statement that he "blacked out" was a convenient excuse not to reduce to writing the most important events of that night. Whether his decision was prompted by fear or an unwillingness to be involved any further with the police, matters not. What is central to this whole question, and his repeated insistence that the statement he gave did not reflect what he told Jarvis, is the plain proposition that he told the investigating Officer the whole story; a proposition which is supported by other evidence which I will address in the Report. **The fact that ultimately this was not reduced to writing, and that there was no other statement provided, does not, in my respectful view, diminish his account of what happened.** The contents of the November 30 statement are in direct contradiction to what he told the women at the Binning house, what he told Stella Bignell, and what he ultimately told the RCMP....*"

Goertzen's main concern about the commissioner's findings centres on what Goertzen and team of retired officers call the "crucial hour" between 10 and 11 that night, before the officers were paired up for their first dispatch to look for the man in the mustang. The police team writes in their PowerPoint presentation:

> *"Justice Wright believed Jason Roy's story about seeing Neil Stonechild in the back of a police car, bleeding and screaming for his life and asking Jason to help him while Jason was being checked. Justice Wright believed Roy's story to the point that he concluded that the documented times of events were **out of sequence**. This 'theory' had been developed by the RCMP and later used by Justice Wright and [later still at the officers' appeal by] Hearing Officer Silversides, **to conclude that Bruce Genaille was checked sometime between 10:00 and 11:00 p.m. instead of 12:04 a.m. November 25th.***
>
> *Justice Wright heard very little, if any, detailed information about Brad & Larry's working status during the 10 to 11pm time period, and the 10 to 11pm time period was never raised as an issue at the Inquiry. There are several concerns about one of RCMP's 'theories,' and the subsequent conclusions of Justice Wright and Hearing Officer Silversides:*
>
> 1. *Bruce Genaille "must have" been checked before the time his name was queried on CPIC.*
> 2. *That Larry and Brad had time to drive Neil Stonechild to the north end of Saskatoon where his body was found.*
>
> ***When you look at the facts, what Justice Wright described and what was theorized and concluded is not possible. When you look at all of the details of this case, it becomes very apparent that Brad and Larry never had contact with Neil Stonechild.***

The commissioner somehow decided that Hartwig and Senger had gone looking for Stonechild *before they were dispatched to look for him*, during that hour between 10 and 11. Goertzen and team produced a timeline[127] tracking both officers' whereabouts, minute-by-minute, demonstrating why it was not possible.

Stan Goertzen explains:

> *"Commissioner Wright concluded that Brad and Larry had been looking for*

Neil Stonechild sometime between 10:00 - 11:00, or even later, because of a disturbance complaint at the 7-Eleven [which was not recorded and no one, including Roy, was aware of ever occurring], and that they must have checked Bruce Genaille then, but failed to run Genaille's name on the in-car computer until shortly after midnight. The commissioner came to that conclusion because it was the only way Jason Roy's most recent story could even be possible.

There was no testimony that Stonechild and Roy had stopped at the 7-Eleven except for what Roy said: that they stopped in and just stood inside the 7-Eleven for about five minutes to warm up after they left Binning's, and before they got to Snowberry Downs.

I had two young men retrace the route that Roy later described as the one he and Neil took that night, after leaving the party at Binning's house with the intent of doing a B & E to find more liquor," Goertzen continues:

To test the commissioner's conclusion, let's **walk backward** *through this important period of time, starting with what we know: Neil Stonechild being thrown out of Snowberry Downs apartment by Trent Ewart at, or just before, 11:49pm.*

11:49: Trent Ewart tells police communications that Neil Stonechild won't leave (If Neil rang the buzzers on that apartment for 5 minutes, that takes the time back to 11:44).

11:44: Neil starts buzzing to gain access to Snowberry Downs.

11:40: Neil and Jason Roy argue near the tennis courts at Snowberry Downs about looking for Neil's ex-girlfriend, after trying to get into 2 apartment complexes.

11:30-11:40: Neil and Jason try unsuccessfully to locate Jason's ex-girlfriend in the first two apartment complexes, before going to the third and last apartment complex at that location.
11:38-11:40: Neil and Jason leave the 7-Eleven after warming up for about 5 minutes and walk across the street to Snowberry Downs.

11:35-11:40: Neil and Jason stand inside the 711 to warm up before they continue to the apartments across the street.

11:30-11:35: It takes just over 4 minutes for a male the same size as Neil to walk from the Binning party home to the 7-Eleven. Jason said they walked quickly because it was cold.

11:30: Neil Stonechild and Jason Roy leave the party at the Binning residence with the intent of doing a B & E to look for money or liquor.

*Given the time parameters above, [Goertzen concludes], it is quite possible and likely that **Neil and Jason never went into that 7-Eleven until about 11:30pm, completely contrary to what Justice Wright arrived at in his decision, that Stonechild and Roy created an incident at 7-Eleven which Hartwig and Senger somehow found out about and went looking for Stonechild before they were dispatched to look for him**. Remember that Larry and Brad weren't working together from 10:00-10:45 and then they had a 13-minute drive to their first call on Tache Crescent, where they would arrive at 10:59 pm. Again making it impossible for them to have been looking for Neil prior to being dispatched to Snowberry Downs, as Justice Wright concluded.*

"I believe Justice Wright's got it wrong in his decision when he tries to explain and support Jason Roy's most recent story, negating the evidence of Neil's cousin, Bruce Genaille," says Goertzen, continuing:

"Bruce Genaille was checked a couple minutes after Jason Roy (alias Tracy Horse) at 12:04 a.m. and about a block closer to Snowberry Downs. When Bruce was checked and Cst Hartwig and Cst Senger took his ID (most likely so that they could run his name for warrants or a description), Genaille testified clearly and emphatically that there was no one in the back of that police car.

If you believe Bruce Genaille when he says his cousin Neil wasn't in the back of that police car; then Jason Roy's story about seeing Neil in the back of that same police car, a block away, a mere minute of driving time from where Bruce Genaille was checked, has to be a complete fabrication, because Neil didn't just disappear!

All this, while a male matching Neil's description is chased away after hiding near a private residence on O'Regan Crescent about 3 blocks away."

"What do the facts tell us?" Goertzen asks. "Did Justice Wright get it wrong when he chose to believe Jason Roy, in spite of, and contrary to, documented evidence and the testimony of Neil's own cousin that Neil was not in that car? **Wright echoes [RCMP Sgt.] Warner's summary,"** Goertzen concludes, **"but if you follow the facts, it couldn't have happened, and the whole house of cards comes tumbling down."**

Dave Scott gave testimony at the inquiry and was left demanding, "What in the world is going on here?" He explains, "Hesje had interviewed me before the Stonechild Inquiry and kept turning the recorder off and on! After giving evidence, I phoned him and demanded [unsuccessfully] that he recall me the next day, as I suddenly realized what they were up to. It still is the WILD WEST!"

Having been lassoed, staked and burnt at the inquiry, Scott wrote in restrained fury to Hesje:

"Dear Sir,

After careful reflection of my recent witnessing at the Stonechild Inquiry, I felt it important to respond. This only for the reason that I am deeply concerned with what is happening to any proper process of a Commission that is mandated to protect the truth and integrity of a competent and able justice system.

*At first I thought I should simply walk away like everyone else and breathe a sigh of relief, thinking that all is finally over. Then I realized that after 35 years, **I had now lost the trust and confidence in the very justice system that I had sworn to protect and uphold.** Therefore, I thought perhaps expressing my feelings is needed in the hope it may encourage some principled people in law to abide by the belief that **integrity and honesty is a complete must, no matter the cost.***

*…Does this mean none of us did, or would, receive any proper and fair consideration defending our reputation against the hurtful intentions of others? Are inquiry questions of other witnesses being based on as much poorly investigated and false information as mine? What in the world is going on here? **This is absolute cruelty to expose innocent people to such harsh lies and untruthful allegations! How will the public ever***

gain any appreciation or support for a justice process driven by such abuse!

Some biased media and mean-spirited politics have disturbed many, many people in our community over this very unfortunate death and other events in our community. So much so, that **the belief is that some people have a vested interest in seeing this kind of tension between police and Aboriginal people. In addition to these serious concerns, do we now have a Commission whose principles and integrity are in disrepute because of an inability to act fairly and responsibly?**
Yours truly,
Dave Scott, Police Chief (retired)"

Today Scott says, "Colleen and I decided to not mail the letter. In hindsight, after now becoming aware of what really happened, it not only should have been mailed, but I should have returned to the inquiry and demanded publicly to be recalled! I regret giving up."

CHAPTER 23 - Commissioner
David Wright's Findings

'Could the high-profile Commission have been high-jacked by special interests and self-serving participants? The evidence exposed in When Police become Prey demands the appropriate verdict. It cries out for justice!'
–MP Art Hanger, retired

Justice Wright's findings in his Stonechild Inquiry Report, October 2004:

- **The commissioner concludes that the intoxicated Stonechild and Jason Roy must have caused a disturbance at a 7-Eleven store soon after 11 p.m., although there was absolutely no evidence discussed or presented that such a "phantom call" ever occurred.**

[Roy's testimony at the inquiry:
"Q: Okay, and the purpose of going to the 7-Eleven was to warm up.
A That's right.
Q You didn't have any money to buy anything at that point so it's mainly just to get in there, get out of the cold, to get warmed up for a bit?
A That's right."]

- **The commissioner concludes, without any evidence to support it, that Hartwig and Senger must have (somehow) learned that Stonechild had created a disturbance at 7-Eleven and then stopped Genaille shortly after 11 p.m., looking for Stonechild before they were dispatched to look for him.** [This despite the fact that Hartwig and Senger's notes, as well as Saskatoon Police Service dispatch records, show they took 12 "back-to-back" calls that night and had no time to do anything they were not dispatched to do.]

- **The commissioner concludes they must have held onto Genaille's name and not checked it with CPIC until an hour later.** [Police officers say they always "CPIC suspicious persons" when they encounter them, so they can make an arrest if there is a warrant out for them. Once released, the person may be "somewhat difficult" to track down.]

- **The commissioner concludes the constables must have encountered Stonechild at Snowberry Downs shortly after 11:51 p.m. and taken him into custody without mentioning it to anyone, and then stopped to talk to Jason Roy who says he observed Stonechild in the back of the vehicle. Roy gives the false name of Tracy Horse to police and says that Stonechild, handcuffed and bloodied in the back of the car, screams, "Jay, help me, they're going to kill me!"**

- [The judge ignores the fact that, if that were true—that someone who gave his name as "Tracy" was now being addressed by his friend as "Jay" – the police would have investigated that incongruency. Instead, they released "Tracy," which indicates they could not have had Stonechild in custody or they would have arrested Roy for obstructing police by giving a false name. Hartwig and Senger continue to search for Stonechild and come upon Genaille. Hartwig *duly notes Genaille in the proper chronological order in his notebook*, thereby casting into question the commissioner's allegation that they had encountered Genaille earlier. A careful evaluation of the timeline proves this finding impossible.]

- **The commissioner notes the time between the Horse CPIC (11:56) and the clearance of the Ewart complaint (12:17) was 21 minutes, and then officers took an additional six minutes to arrive at O'Regan Crescent. "What happened in this 27-minute interval? Where were Hartwig and Senger and what were they doing?" the commissioner demands.**

- [Wright has explained away their 12:04 CPIC re: Bruce Genaille by claiming, on the basis of no evidence whatsoever, that they didn't CPIC him <u>until an hour after encountering him</u>. Genaille testified the officers talked to him for about 10 minutes, which, if the officers had CPICed him *at the time*, according to SPS protocol, would have kept them busy right though until 12:14. They could not have driven Stonechild very far in nine minutes and still made it back to O'Regan. In fact, they couldn't have driven Stonechild very far in Wright's alleged 27 minutes and still made it back to O'Regan, a few blocks away. (The RCMP, the Commissioner, and everyone else sitting in judgment also ignored the fact that Hartwig and Senger attended the scene and spoke with Ewart. The only time this could have occurred is between the Genaille street check and the time they cleared the call.)]

- **The commissioner concludes that he finds "Stonechild was probably last seen in the custody of the two officers," and adds, "I am satisfied that Const. Hartwig and Const. Senger had adequate time between the Snowberry Downs dispatch and O'Regan Crescent dispatch to transport Stonechild to the northwest industrial area of Saskatoon." (A declaration that Jason Roy told the truth, Hartwig and Senger lied, and are dirty cops.)**

Larry Hartwig analyzes these findings:

"David Wright's role and mandate, clearly set by the Terms of Reference, was to make findings and recommendations with respect to the administration of justice *in the Province of Saskatchewan. There was no direction to make findings as to how Stonechild died.* [Ironically, on the other hand, RCMP were expected to determine how Stonechild died and, in 18 months, could not!]
*"Wright was to act within the parameters set for the inquiry and within the powers granted to provincial legislature. He was to understand that the inquiry does not provide the evidentiary and procedural safeguards that would prevail as a trial. He was to understand the rights of the individual and to avoid any findings that may appear to the public as determinations of legal liability. **He was to avoid findings that were, in effect, a substitute for a police investigation and a trial.***
"What David Wright established by his 'findings' [Hartwig continues] *is that real evidence does not carry as much weight as hearsay evidence. **He also established that repeated claims of police misconduct, even if***

there is, in my opinion, no evidence to support such allegations, are enough to make an adverse finding of misconduct.

"*I cannot understand how David Wright could have made the conclusions he did, which were essentially the errant, untested assumptions made by the RCMP investigators who were excluded from testifying. This is a free-for-all where anyone can say anything about the police, and those acting on behalf of Sask Justice support it! Such actions by those acting on behalf of "justice" threaten the safety and security of us all.*"

Brad Senger's biggest question about the inquiry: "*Why were the RCMP investigators not called to testify?* They spent 18 months investigating, but were never cross-examined on their notes, information they gathered, how they came to their conclusions, where they dug out the information, and what other experts they considered using but did not use – because they did not give the answer the RCMP wanted." Senger urges: "We must have rules of evidence for inquiries! They are being treated as a court, so they should have the same rules as a court: no hearsay, no opinions presented as though they were fact, and the only experts who can testify must be proven and tested."

Larry Hartwig adds, "When you look at the way the commissioner cherry-picked his evidence, his qualification of Robertson as a forensic expert vs. his rejection of the forensic experts' evidence, his recognition that portions of the RCMP and the commission counsel's evidence was potentially corrupt, yet none of these people were called to testify and have their evidence challenged, it paints a clear picture: *someone was going to pay for a freezing death.* They couldn't accomplish this through any kind of trial where the rules of evidence and normal protections under the law apply. They used a public inquiry where we would have no right to call evidence or defend ourselves. They used a public inquiry where we would have little recourse under the law to refute the findings, and where there wasn't the political integrity or will to refute the commissioner's findings."

"The record leaves upon my mind the impression that the horror of the [situation] demanded a victim, and that as a result thereof, the defendant was bound as a smoking sacrifice upon the altar of conjecture and suspicion," wrote American Senator Sam J. Ervin about a different case with many similarities to Stonechild's, in this writer's opinion. "It is contended that the facts and circumstances are so slight in probative value that in themselves and standing alone they would not amount to evidence, but when taken in combination they constitute a rope of great strength. **I do not concur in this reasoning. Unless the principles of mathematics have been recently changed, adding a column of zeros together produces zero; neither can a multitude of legal zeros beget a legal entity."**[128]

Others say Wright seriously overreached his mandate since he was not supposed to make findings of guilt, merely recommendations for preventing such a situation recurring. With the stroke of his pen, he derailed two men's lives – their reputations in the community, their careers as they approached middle age at 40 and 45, their financial health and in Hartwig's case, his physical and psychological health.

Yet they were left twisting in legal limbo since the law offers no recourse for refuting the findings of a public inquiry. The commissioner was well aware of this danger, having noted in his report: "Of equal importance, if no charge is subsequently laid, a person found responsible by the commissioner *would have no recourse to clear his or her name.*" In other words, not found guilty in a court of law, but guilty nonetheless in public perception; something one might expect only in the wild, wild west when anarchy reigned.

Fall-out from the inquiry? First, the officers, with 29 years' impeccable service between them were fired for not writing in their notebooks that they had Stonechild in their custody. **They appealed to the Saskatchewan Police Commission.** A five-month hearing under the Police Act upheld the chief's decision to fire them.

They applied to the Saskatchewan Court of Appeal to throw out the result of the inquiry on the basis it was outside the scope of the investigation for the commissioner to decide whether or not the officers had Stonechild in their custody. In addition, Hartwig's lawyer asserted that Roy's testimony about seeing Stonechild in the back of a police cruiser on the last night he was seen alive was not only *"erroneous, perverse, capricious and made without regard for the material before the inquiry,"* but was also "completely contrary to the evidence presented at the inquiry." Appellate court Justices Richards, Klebuc and Hunter ruled that Justice Wright did not have to come to the conclusion he did, but they felt they have to give deference to his findings.

The appellate judges cited portions of the Commissioner's finding which state he considered Roy's testimony credible, and also that there was corroborating evidence.

"The Commissioner wrote as follows at p. 194 of his report:

... There were a number of errors and inconsistencies in Roy's evidence,

but, as I have noted, most can be explained by the disorienting lifestyle he was leading at the time. However, as I stated in my review of the evidence, I have found that the core of Roy's testimony – that he was stopped by the police on November 24/25, 1990, and that he observed Stonechild in the back of a police car – to be credible and corroborated by other evidence. Further, Roy's evidence of his encounter with the officers stands uncontradicted by the evidence of Cst. Hartwig and Cst. Senger who maintained throughout their testimony that they had no recollection of stopping Roy and no memory of the 25-plus minutes they spent on a dispatch call involving Stonechild on November 24/25, 1990, notwithstanding the fact that Stonechild turned up dead on November 29, 1990."[129]

Finally, the former officers sought to have their case heard by the Supreme Court. Although that court previously had heard cases of alleged inquiry injustice, this, too, was denied them.

Is it possible that the justice system has become race-based and biased? "I saw the two RCMP officers who conducted the investigation, Sgt. Jack Warner and Staff Sgt. Ken Lyons, leave the inquiry and go for a drink with Stonechild's mother Stella Bignell and her lawyers Donald Worme and Gregory Curtis, as well as Jason Roy's lawyer Darren Winegarden, and the lawyer for the FSIN, Catherine Knox," says Bernie Eiswirth, executive officer for the Saskatchewan Federation of Police Officers. "They went for a drink at the Radisson Hotel lounge. The RCMP investigators weren't trying to hide the fact that they were very buddy-buddy and had close ties with the family throughout the investigation. During the inquiry they talked a lot, and at the press conference Oct. 26, 2004, Stella thanked Cpl. Jack Warner who conducted the RCMP investigation. *It was clear that the RCMP were advocates on behalf of the family and not investigating as impartial fact-finders. They never questioned Roy's veracity.*"

A **public inquiry is intended to end a moral panic,** answering a community's questions and reducing social tension. Did that occur here? Not according to Aboriginal social worker Melvin McGhee. He said at the time that if anything was to blame for rising tensions between police and Natives, it was the unfair portrayals of Hartwig and Senger perpetuated by some media and reaffirmed by the inquiry. "I believe with all my heart that Larry and Brad have been hung out to dry," McGhee told me. "They were scapegoats for this tragedy. The justice system should stand beside them and find the facts; instead they were *breaking down the bridges* that had been built between the Aboriginal and police communities."

Saskatoon bus driver Rob Houston says he heard "lots of talk on the bus about the inquiry and police being set up as political fall guys. People said this was going to make them more racist. Lots of people were reading inquiry transcripts on the internet rather than the newspaper. Jason Roy admitted he made up stuff, lied, added details that couldn't possibly be true. Yet Wright said his testimony was sincere, and chose to disbelieve the police. Jason Roy says he saw Stonechild in a police car. Moments later, another witness said he was not. Where did he go? The other guy had no reason to lie. I was astounded! There's no way they should have been able to put the blame on police. But the same thing is happening with police services right across the country. Special interest groups are looking at an easy target; police can't fight back because of the Provincial Police Act.

"The moment I get my pension," Houston says, "I'm gone from this province. Judges here are unbelievable! I'm thoroughly disgusted. I've been here all my life, but there's no use living here if someone can ignore evidence and run a trial by innuendo and assumption. They could do this to anyone! Under the Charter of Rights, we're all supposed to be treated equally!"

Retired MP Art Hanger agrees. "The commissioned inquiry appears to have created an environment of suspicion, deceit, and fear that have fostered new levels of racial tension and hatred. Let's not forget the officers and their families whose lives were literally ripped away from them and were rendered helpless by the State; unable to defend themselves, unable to counter false accusation through the media, and unable to find an advocate to speak on their behalf. Were the political cards so stacked against them that the rule of law was subverted? Matters past can never be completely righted but I do pray that healing comes to the Hartwig and Senger families, and that their integrity be restored. Honest citizens would want it so."

The inquiry did not improve relations between police and the justice system, as David Haye, president of the Saskatchewan Federation of Police Officers wrote to Justice Minister Frank Quennell. "The ability of our members to provide policing services throughout the province has been undermined by the Commissioner through his publication of a finding based on a standard less than that of a 'balance of probabilities' as found in the Police Act or civil law. How do we persuade our members that they continue to provide quality police service to their communities when they doubt that they will be fairly treated when an allegation is made about their conduct? …[At a meeting with police elected representatives on Oct. 26, 2004, Deputy Minister of Justice Doug] Moen reportedly commented that there was no way that those two officers (Csts Senger and Hartwig) could ever police in Saskatoon again. From this comment the Federation draws the inference that Mr. Moen believes, and thus the Justice Department believes, that the members have done something wrong. They are assessing blame and assigning wrongdoing without a trial, without a hearing and frankly without any evidence that would stand up in any credible review of what occurred."

Robert Marshall, Winnipeg police detective turned columnist, summarized the inquiry this way: **"It was a firestorm of political correctness, more diversionary than useful. It satisfied a political need as it served up a pound of blue flesh and filled legal pockets while race relations in the City of Bridges continued on in crisis-mode."**[130]

This is the very definition of moral panic, unresolvable as long as the issue at the centre of the storm is taboo, banned from discussion. Even in a nine-month, $2-million public inquiry. Is that, then, the legal equivalent of running in circles and squawking?

But surely the inquiry should have given the mother some closure? Mrs. Bignell told me she was not at all happy with the outcome. She refused to make the audacious leap made by many, from the judge's finding that "Stonechild was probably last seen in the custody of the two officers," to assuming Hartwig and Senger must be responsible for his death. "I wanted the inquiry to find out who took my son out there," she said. "And yet, after all this time, we still do not know! Justice has not been served."[131]

As for Larry Hartwig:

"When David Wright handed down his findings essentially blaming me for Neil's death, that is when my life really fell apart. I was sick in bed for about eight months. I had to take medication to keep me alive. My family income was cut by two-thirds and my wife had to work full-time to support me and our children. I had no benefits or income. I had lost my reputation, honour and my family history past and future. I was a 'dirty cop' who got away with murder. I had no way out other than suicide, but my faith in God prevented me from doing that. But in time I even lost that, and felt that suicide was inevitable.

My wife became my primary care giver and remains so to this day.

Although she states I am not the man she married, she still sticks by me. She is an absolute saint. I owe my life to her and to those who have supported me all these years. Although currently employed and thankfully so, I am unable to find a career I can find satisfaction in and dedicate my life to. To this day, I have not had a single job interview and am prevented from working in the city I so diligently served.

For me, there is no way out. No one wants to listen. Journalists have told the story, people have made up their minds and put this behind them. As one journalist told me, 'No one wants to rip the bandage on this one!' The only thing is, you can't put a bandage over the cancer of corruption. You can't continue to cover something up and sacrifice everything our justice system is supposed to stand for.

The truth, on the other hand, is like water. It will find its way around any object put in its path. Now I break my silence and heads will roll. If it be mine as well, so be it. I will tell my story and expose the corruption that exists in our justice system surrounding this case."

CHAPTER 24 - What was Roy Really Remembering?

'Guilt can do funny things to your memory sometimes.'
– Television drama, 'The Guardian'

When I interviewed Jason Roy, I found him personable. He appeared depressed, but was helpful and humorous getting the tape recorder microphone positioned correctly, and earnest and interested in debating clues in the Stonechild case. Until I brought up the wrong clue.

Jason Roy testifying at Stonechild Inquiry. (CP PHOTO/Saskatoon *StarPhoenix*- Gord Waldner)

I wanted to understand what had made the judge believe Roy's testimony over that of two officers described by their police chaplain Rick Lane as "two of the cleanest people in lifestyle and attitudes I've ever had the privilege of working with." The commissioner had written: "I had ample opportunity to observe [Roy] during his testimony. He struck me as sincere and thoughtful and as still deeply affected by the death of his friend and what followed. While Roy's testimony contained errors and contradictions [the commissioner listed at least six of them], this does not prevent me from finding credible his testimony related to what he observed on the evening of November 24th and the morning of November 25, 1990."

I wanted to know what would have made the commissioner say, in the face of those many glaring errors and contradictions, *He seemed sincere*?

I met Roy in a Saskatoon restaurant on November 12, 2008, long after the storm of inquiry and inquests had died down. He told me that after spending an astonishing nine years of his life in jail, now, at age 33, he was settled down and working in a warehouse. He opened by saying he felt he had been brought into this world for a purpose, "to witness what I witnessed. I don't want to sound arrogant in any kind of way," he said, "because, it's just that, like, the way that the whole course of the events and everything happened, it had to have happened for a reason. Why it happened is because of, uh, the injustices that have happened to the Native people for however long they've been going on. And, um, it happened to bring out all the pain and suffering that's happened to the Native people—not only Native people, but people of any kind of ethnicity or colour in this country. It's not me needing to correct them; it's me being a part of a big plan."

I asked him what sort of injustices needed correcting.

JR: Um, the injustices. Well, Native people being Native people, it's an injustice in itself.
Q: How is that an injustice?
JR: This happened because the country, Saskatoon, the country, the world was needing to know of the inequalities that are out there, the inequalities that, that, and the lopsidedness of our society.
Q: Okay. What sort of injustice and inequalities have you yourself seen against Native people?
JR: Well the biggest one in my life is the Neil Stonechild story. That's the biggest one I've seen, but I've seen lots of things happening all the time. I still see them. You know, it's just the off-handed look of a clerk at a store or something like that, if you walk into a store and, you know, you're automatically assumed to be a thief of some kind.
Q: What is your ancestry?

Jason explained that when his Cree mother was pregnant with him, she discovered that his white father was married with kids. "She told him just to walk away and never bother us again, and that's what he did." When Jason was six weeks old, his mother met a Métis man who, he said, had been a good father to him.
During the inquiry, Jason had revealed a little more:

Aaron Fox: "And [in 1990], did you have an alcohol abuse problem?
A: Yes, I did.
Q: Drug abuse problem?
A: Yes.
Q: And can you tell me sort of when your alcohol problems started?
A: Before I was born.

Q: Before you were born. and can you explain to me what you mean by that, in the sense of before you were born?

A: I was born into an alcoholic family.

Q: Okay, and do you suffer from fetal alcohol syndrome?

A: I'm not going to say that I do. I've never been diagnosed as that.

Q: Have you ever checked to see if -- if that was a syndrome that you suffer from? Like has that ever been checked?

A: No.

In his interview with me, Jason continued: "I've lived here my whole life, and I've lived in the hood and I've grown up Native my entire life. And their problems are my problems, you know, and that just sounds, that just sounds arrogant, just not me to say it. It's our problems; that's a better way to put it."

JR: I didn't make this happen or want this to happen, or have any, any insight as to what was gonna go on." [An unusual thing to say: "I didn't make this happen." It suggests the incident was manufactured. Yet he did make the multi-million dollar Stonechild investigation and inquiry happen. Single-handedly. With a story about police that was far-fetched and constantly changing. Was he feeling guilty about that?] *You know, like I lived through the experience of Neil being taken.* [Interesting that he didn't say "murdered."] *And I lived through the inquiry, and just continued to just be, you know, like, just be and be myself, you know, and work and make a living for myself. Like I don't have any agenda to try and, uh, be an activist of any kind, you know, take it on in any kind of a serious role. You know, like, my experience is enough in itself to, like, for people to, you know, that don't want to listen to what I have to say about things when it comes to justices and injustices, you know, like, I've just been given a gift.*

Q: OK, but I just had a thought. Did you feel that you wanted to correct the problems before the Stonechild event?

JR: Absolutely. Yeah, I did.

Q: But um, I was wondering, and correct me if I'm wrong, I was just wondering if your biological father made you have some anger toward white people, 'cause your Métis father is wonderful, your Native mother is wonderful; they've obviously stayed with you...

JR: No. No. No, he has no relevance as to how I feel about the race, the racial relations that I have with the world. I guess what you're looking for is my — you might get the impression that I have a racist bone in me, a racist side of, of my existence or whatever. But it's not so much that; it's just that, you know I, I have a serious dislike for the uniform, and not, not all police officers are white, you know, **but, uh, the people that are involved with all these freezing deaths were, you know, were probably white.** [I didn't bring up the fact that no one had been found involved in any freezing deaths except, in an out-of-court forum, Hartwig and Senger, and only because of what Jason himself had testified.]

Q: Why do you have a serious dislike for people in uniform?

JR: Well, besides the obvious, uh, they're very [long pause]—I've just seen a very lot of abuse of, abuse of authority.

Q: Okay. Can you give me an example?

JR: Give you an example...

Q: Yeah.

JR: I can't think of anything right offhand, no.

Q: Okay. I'm just going to bring this up, and you're not going to be pleased with me, but you know what? It is easy to blame things on racism, even when it isn't...

JR: And, yeah, you're absolutely right, you know, because of the way society is, it makes it very easy for people to blame racism for, you know, even just very simple, honest arguments that, that don't have any racist tendencies behind them...

Q: Yeah, yeah.

JR: ... you know, but it's easy to do that because it's, it's the predominant thing for a person of non-white ancestry to, to see as an excuse for whatever behavior happens."

I asked him what kind of person Neil Stonechild was. "Always, always smiling, he was always smiling. But if you pissed these guys off, man, if you piss them off, just like, just like me or anybody else like me, any of us, we could be vicious if we wanted to be."

Like others, I sensed he carried a lot of guilt about Neil's death. Jason had said he tried to convince Neil not to go out that freezing night to find Lucille:

"JR: But I couldn't talk him outta wanting to go. And so, finally I just resigned myself to the fact that he was gonna go whether I liked it or not. And I didn't want him to go, go alone. And so we got suited up and dressed up as warm

as we could on that day with what we had, and we headed out into the night.

Q: You know what? You could have let him go alone to the apartment to find Lucille. You know, the feeling I'm getting – correct me if I'm wrong – is that you're feeling guilty about it.

JR: Oh, yeah. I have since it happened.

Q: And I mean, you could have let him go alone--

JR: Eh--

Q: --you know?

JR --Whoooooooooooooooooo [long sigh].

Q: If you'd let him go alone, would that have helped your guilty conscience?

JR: It woulda been worse.

Q: Well, that's just it! That's my point!

JR: Well I'm not really, I'm more proud than feeling guilty. I'm more proud of what I did and what I went through, than guilty. And that's what kind of makes it okay.

Q: And you're proud of what you did in terms of standing up and testifying against the police?

JR: Yep."

I wondered if journalists had given Jason the perfect opportunity to alleviate that terrible guilt, to "make it okay," when they made connections between the Night incident and the freezing deaths around that time. All of them blaming people in uniform.

Jason talked about having attended an event the evening before our interview at which the Stonechild death was discussed:

"You shoulda heard the people. Like, I'm pretty reclusive now, since the inquiry's been over. I've been fairly reclusive. And last night when I went to this showing and, like, not a lot of people recognized me. Like, people who knew me, knew who I was or whatever, they'd say hi, but then, the majority of the people that were in there didn't know who I was. But once I got up and had to announce my name on the microphone, eh, you could just, you could hear a pin drop in that place. I was kinda surprised at that...

Q: Well I don't think your picture was flashed around, but your name sure was.

JR: *In that book, I asked for my picture not to be in there.* [The book, Starlight Tour, Neil Stonechild's Last, Lonely Night, in which Roy had featured largely.]

Q: *I didn't feel they were very flattering to you in that book.*

JR: *No, they weren't.*

Q: *Why not?*

JR: *I guess they just got a certain impression of me and rode with it. Like I'm a very, uh, I don't know how to summarize who I am, or how I am, but I'm a very, I can be aggressive, but I'm passive at the same time. Like, I don't take no shit from nobody. And, I don't know, I have, uh, I've spent about nine years in jail. So it's made me a very angry person. You know, along with this, along with this situation with the cops and stuff like that, I'm an angry person inside, I'm a very angry person. A lot of disgust to the world, to certain aspects of this world. And I let it show; I kinda wear my heart on my sleeve sometimes. I dunno."* ...

Q: *Ok, so if someone were to ask you why people believed you, what made them believe you?*

JR: *Well, I think that, um, they couldn't ignore my story anymore, because of the other guys that this kinda thing was happening to. They couldn't ignore the fact that, you know, there's, uh, there's something going on here, there's some kind of a pattern and that, you know, every case had to be looked into and couldn't be ignored anymore. You know, I don't think there was so much believing at the time, because it's a very, uh, it's a very wild story, for anybody to hear, and, ya know I bet that right up until the day that the findings for the inquiry, ya know, there was a lot of speculation about me, ya know, there was a lot of doubters. I had doubters in my own family. There was people that doubted what I had to say.*

Q: *Why?*

JR: *I dunno why they doubted me. You know, they didn't come and say things to me outright, but, you know, like, um, people were embarrassed of, people thought that I was gonna ruin our name here in the city. Like, my parents and my brothers, my one brother anyway, they've worked a long, long, long time in their life to build up the reputation that they have in our community. They felt that I was gonna tarnish that in some way.*

Q: *How did they think you might tarnish it?*

JR: *That the findings for the inquiry would come out, and the judge'd rule that he did not believe a word I said.*

Q: I see.

JR: And that would, ya know, make me a liar.

Q: But instead of that, you're a hero.

JR: Yep. Right up until the day the findings came out, in everybody's eyes I was just that guy that said that he saw Neil in the back of a cop car. And then after that, I was the guy that saw Neil in the back of the car, not just said it. But, you know, like, there was a lot of people in a lot of organizations and things in society that took into consideration what I had to say."

In the later Hearing under the Police Act, Roy had also been confident, even emotional, in recounting his memory of Stonechild in a police car. The commissioner said he believed his testimony partly because Roy stuck him as "sincere," despite "errors and contradictions." Yet a 1951 BC case, *Faryna v. Chorny*,[132] had determined:

> *"The credibility of interested witnesses, particularly in cases concerning a conflict of testimony, cannot be gauged solely by whether the demeanor of a particular witness carried conviction of the truth.*
>
> *A court of appeal must be satisfied that the trial judge's finding of credibility was based, not on one element only, to the exclusion of others, but on the fact that it was based on all the elements by which it can be tested in the particular case.*
>
> *For a trial judge to say 'I believe him because I judge him to be telling the truth' is to come to a conclusion on a consideration of only half the problem: and it may be self-direction of a dangerous kind.* **He should go further and say that the testimony of a witness whom he believes is in accordance with the preponderance of probabilities in the case and he should also state his reasons for that conclusion."**

From my years of investigation, I was confident Stonechild had not been in Hartwig and Senger's car. So what was Roy remembering in such a convincing way? Many believe he made up this story based on his conclusions that the police must have picked him up, must have beaten him up, must have dropped him off where he died. All logical conclusions, based on his paradigm of police officers. None of it supported by the evidence.

Under a Freedom of Information request, I had learned that on July 7,

2005, during Hartwig and Senger's Police Act Hearing in which they were fighting their shameful dismissal, a witness came forward to police. This witness had information that the portion of Jason Roy's allegation where he claimed Neil yelled, "They are going to kill me!" was not referring to police at all. This witness stated that a named (but redacted) person (possibly Jason Roy) had told him or her in early 1991, while a young offender in this person's care, a far different version of events than was provided at the Hartwig and Senger Police Act hearing. **This person said the allegation where Neil allegedly yelled, "They are going to kill me," was referring to a group of boys with whom Neil was in a fight at a pool hall.**

Acting SPS Police Chief Keith Atkinson recorded the information and forwarded it to RCMP Chief Supt. McFadyen and Staff Sgt. Lyons to have a "competent investigator" investigate it. The SPS would have realized this was new information that might have established that Jason Roy's allegation was a hoax. The RCMP were notified but not the officers, their lawyers, or police association. Certainly the public has not heard about it until now. There has been no action by the RCMP in this regard and the information continues to be treated as confidential. This is potentially another RCMP act of Criminal Mischief and perjury.

Retired SPS Sgt. Darrell Connell wrote about the memory he believes Roy was relying upon:

"Before I get to the incident, I should say I had been a police officer for the city of Saskatoon since July 1981. In late 1982 or early 1983, I started to work a part-time second job at Kilburn Hall [young offender closed-custody facility; juvenile jail], so I got to know all the young offenders back then. It was a good thing, because I would go to calls where a young person would be dealing with the police and would give a false name. I would pull up and identify them, much to their dismay.

I can't remember the exact date; I did not take notes of this incident since I was only backing-up the officers dealing with the issue, but I moonlighted at Kilburn Hall until November 1990 after my wife graduated from nursing college, so I know this incident occurred just before then, either late 1989 or very early 1990 [Stonechild died in November 1990].

It was dark out – late evening or after midnight. I remember going to check on a patrol car dealing with a situation. As I always did when not busy myself, I drove to the area where the police car was, so in case they requested assistance, I would be a lot closer.

In this particular incident, I remember getting close to the police car and

I observed Jason Roy walking along the sidewalk in a South to North direction, right against the wall. He was walking slowly and was about 20 to 30 yards away, and he appeared to be trying to look at the person in the back of the police car. I recognized him as Jason Roy at the time. I then drove up to the driver's door of the police car. They had a young male person in the back seat and he had a fair amount of blood on his face. It was either Neil or Jake Stonechild. He was screaming things like, 'They were going to kill me, Jay!' and I believed this was all directed at Jason Roy, as he used the name 'Jay.' Jason was by then quite a bit closer to the patrol car that Neil or Jake was in. I came to the conclusion at that time that Jason had run away when that person was getting beaten up.

I can't remember why I thought it was one of the Stonechilds, but it was either because the officers in the car told me who it was or I recognized him myself from working at Kilburn Hall. The reason I remember it at all was because, when Jason Roy told the Stonechild Inquiry that he saw Neil Stonechild in the back seat of the patrol car screaming, 'They're gonna kill me, Jay!' it was identical to what happened when Neil or Jake got beaten up earlier. **I believe Jason transposed the real situation onto the one he was lying about.** *Later on, I did try to see if anyone dealt with Neil or Jake Stonechild after he got beat up, but was unsuccessful in locating the two police officers. I came to the belief that they either didn't charge him, or took him to the hospital and didn't leave a report.*

The things I am positive about was Jason Roy and his actions, and Neil or Jake Stonechild being bloodied in the back of a police car and yelling, 'They were going to kill me, Jay!'

One of several things that really bothered me at the time of the inquiry was, I knew that when young offenders got arrested, they would brag about it because it was a status symbol. Being arrested was not anything to be ashamed of. Jason Roy supposedly saw Neil in the back of the police car screaming, 'They're going to kill me, Jay!' If so, he would have rushed home to tell Neil's family immediately that Neil got arrested and he would also have told all their friends. So why did Jason Roy wait a long time before telling that story about Neil being arrested? Because it never happened.

The next part that bothered me was that when Neil's body was found, it was not covered in blood, as Jason Roy claimed when he was in the back of the police car. If the police had beaten him up, as Jason Roy claimed, where would they have taken him to wash his face and clothes and then dry the clothes before setting him off to freeze to death? But in the situation where I saw Neil in the back of the police car, he was covered in blood and screaming at Jason Roy, calling him Jay. Funny coincidence, to say the least, and that happened within months of the incident I believe he fabricated.

The last thing is: when Jason Roy gave the false name of Tracy Lee Horse and was CPIC'd and under that name he came back negative. But he claims that Neil was screaming, 'They're gonna kill me, Jay!' There isn't a police officer alive who wouldn't have picked up on the name of JAY after giving his name as Tracy Horse. He would have been arrested immediately to find out who he really was, through photographs or fingerprints, and then an obstruction charge would have been laid. Once again, identical to the situation I attended!"

I wanted to ask Jason Roy about the officer's allegation:

"Q: You know, what comes across very clearly is your memory of seeing Neil in a police car. You're very confident about that, aren't you?

JR: Very. There's nothing in this world that'll ever change that.

Q: Um hm, um hm. Now, don't get mad, just take a deep breath. Um. Do you remember Neil being in a police car after he was beaten up by some people in a pool hall?

JR: I don't know anything about that at all! [No confusion; no clarifying questions; immediate understanding of what I was referring to, and denial.]

Q: You don't remember that?

JR: No, that's, that's, I don't know anything about that at all!

Q: Because, um, somebody has told me that he was there one time when either Neil or Jake Stonechild was beaten up. The police had been called and had taken him into the back seat of their car to, to help him because he, he was beaten up, and was bleeding ...

JR: Yeah, I see, I see where you're trying to go with this and I, and you know, you want to know if I, if I'm mistaken of the time...

Q: Yeah exactly, exactly.

JR: ...and there's nothing in my life that's ever happened that's remotely similar to the situation that I had with Neil that night!

Q: Mm hm, mm hm. Well, um, I'm just wondering because it just struck me: I wonder if it's possible that, that that's what you're remembering because (Roy laughs) you know, I, I feel very confident that you are remembering something, you're very sincere about it and very relaxed about it, you know and you, you remember seeing that, but I'm just wondering, is it possible?

JR: No.

Q: Because, um, you don't remember that having happened, eh?

JR: No, I don't remember it happening 'cause it never happened in my sight, I mean to me in my experience and in my life, seeing Neil in the back of a police car bleeding [sic]. I don't like that. I don't like that insinuation or anything like that, that I could be just mustering up some memories of some other thing to make some other thing better!

Q: Yeah, okay, well that's good. I just had to run it by you because this fellow told me about that, he was there and he said, um, that you were there and he said, 'I wonder if Jason is remembering...'

JR: Are you working for the police? You're, you're starting to sound like it! [Why would he mention police? I hadn't told him that the person describing that situation was a police officer. Unless he knew that police had been involved in the pool hall incident described? Jason certainly reacted with a sudden high level of suspicion and defensiveness.]

Q: No. Now what other questions have I got on my list?

JR: Yeah, I think we're just about done here.

Q: Okay. Great! Well, thank you very much...

JR: I sure hope you don't misrepresent me in anything that I said.

Q: I won't misrepresent you. I will quote you absolutely accurately.

JR: Because it just feels like now that, now that you've got my story, that I'm not, I'm of no use to you. Your attitude and your behaviour toward me has just changed a bit.

Q: I didn't know that I did that. How did it change?

JR: You're just coming across as, as, as all of the other people that I've come across in my life that uh, okay, they want their story, they get their story and then, then they're not that same people they were the hour or two before I met them!

Q: Jason, I'm going to tell you something and that is that, um, I really think you did everything in your power with Neil Stonechild that night and I feel like you're, you know, feeling badly and I do not believe anybody could've done any more than you did and I'm saying that from the bottom of my heart! I'll tell you, I was so, at that time when I was at the hearing,

I had a son that wasn't that much older than Neil was, you know in those pictures and it just, it, it really did affect me. And what I said to myself then was: 'We've got to stop things like this happening you know, um, guys getting drunk and ending up freezing to death.' I, I honestly do not know what happened to Neil that night. I would really, really like to know.
JR: Hey! Could you say that again?
Q: I said I don't know what happened to Neil that night.
JR: I just told you what happened to him!
Q: No, no, no. You don't know that the police took him out there. Nobody knows that.
JR: Okay. [Jason Roy does not claim police took Neil to the field.]
Q: But I'll tell you, I have talked to Larry Hartwig and Brad Senger and you know, they said: 'We were working together that night for the first time. Why would we do something like that when we didn't know each other and couldn't trust each other to, to keep quiet about it? You don't do that with a total stranger.'
Before Neil, they were dispatched to look for somebody else. They found him, he was Aboriginal, they drove him home. Then they were dispatched to look for Neil. They said they couldn't find Neil and they went, um, hang on, then they talked to you. Then they said, uh, they came out of an alleyway, and there was a median in the middle of the road. They said they did a U-turn around the median and they interviewed somebody a block away on the other side of the street from you.
JR: Bruce Genaille.
*Q: Bruce Genaille. Genaille was Neil's cousin, and he stood beside the police car for ten minutes and said there was nobody in the back of the car. So I am just trying to figure out what the heck happened. Where did Stonechild go in that block or block-and-a-*half between your seeing him and Bruce not seeing him? *[No response.]*
And how did he get out to the field? If the police didn't drive him, some people have speculated that he could've walked out there. I do not believe that at all! How in the heck could he have gotten out there if it wasn't the police? Could it have been, um, Gary Pratt? Why don't you think it was Gary Pratt?
JR: That's not the way things worked then. That's not the way things work.
Q: Could he have taken a taxi and not had the money and a taxi dropped him off just because they were mad at him?

JR: I don't know. I guess nobody will ever know, eh, unless the, until the people admit to it. [Here Roy repeats that he does not assume police did it.]

Q: Well, it is a big mystery. Maybe we will never, ever know. But you know, Brad Senger said to me, 'You know it just defies common sense. I was still on probation with the Police Service and if I'd done anything wrong, they could kick me out without a reason, just kick me out and I'd be finished.' He said, 'All my life I wanted to be a cop,' and he said, 'Why would I jeopardize that long-held dream by doing something stupid? What benefit would we get from, from leaving a guy out where he could freeze to death?'

JR: Well, you know, like this has been happening since the seventies, the sixties, and you know like, the police they have their, they have their own society. They have their own little world that they live in, you know and I, I can only speculate, I don't know, I don't know how they live but you know, just like us on the street, we have a code that we live by. And either you follow it or you don't, you know, either you're with it or you're not, you know and, you know, like maybe they're, maybe they were just trying to, you know like, 'cause other cops have done it to other people. You know, they figure I don't know, I don't even, I'm not even going to go on record with this thing saying anything about what the, what the motives were behind what they did.

Q: I know but I, I met them, they're really decent people.

JR: To me, to me they're dirty pigs and that's all they'll ever be!

Q: That's how I started out when I first started doing this. My first article...

JR: I'm just getting, I'm just getting mad, you know! I'm just getting mad!

Q: My first article that I ever wrote, the cover said 'Racist Cops.' That's where I came from.

JR: I didn't come here to get mad. You know like, f---! They're dirty pigs and that's all there is to it and I want to, I'm done here, I want to go home! I think that's, you know, I'm pissed off now!"

(end audio)

CHAPTER 25 - Tunnel Vision or Repression of Evidence? By Whom? RCMP or Sask Justice?

'Why wasn't I asked to testify at the Stonechild Inquiry? I think I knew too much.'
– Saskatoon ambulance attendant

"If I had been asked to testify," says the ambulance attendant who picked up Neil Stonechild's remains, "my testimony would have collaborated Dr. Emma Lew's and contradicted the photogrammetrist, the only person who claimed those were handcuff marks. There would have been justice. But because facts were excluded, justice did not have a chance to be done."

The RCMP officer's interview with "Smyth" was not even mentioned in the RCMP investigative report. That interview, "Smyth" claims, included his recollection that the marks on the hands matched the storm cuffs on the jacket, and there was only "one little mark on the nose that could have been caused by sagebrush or any of the vegetation there."

"Those [initial] scene pictures showed two relatively straight linear scratches," Dr. Lew told me. "They looked thinner and less prominent than the dried out lesions that you're seeing in the morgue. *And that initial photo of the scratches on the nose before the body thawed was not included in the Wright report."*

The RCMP summarized an interview with Jason Roy:

"Other observations which ROY made at the time were that STONECHILD was handcuffed and had an injury to his face which was bleeding."

Yet Roy's actual words were: "gushing blood." Did the RCMP repress those words because none of the medical or police officials who dealt with Stonechild's body saw any evidence of blood on his body, his clothes or the snow?

Why would Lyons fail to mention that RCMP Cpl. Nick Hartle was present during some of Larry Hartwig's interview? Why did Hartle report something significantly different than Lyons – Hartwig "denied any wrongdoing whatsoever" and stated "he had never hurt, assaulted, or dropped off anyone, ever." Why were Hartle's notes excluded from the RCMP's final report?

What about the information I obtained under FOI legislation that on July 7, 2005, a witness came forward with information that Jason Roy's allegation about Neil allegedly yelling, "They are going to kill me," was referring not to Hartwig and Senger, but to a group of boys with whom Neil was in a fight at a pool hall? SPS gave that information to the RCMP and it was never heard of again.

What about Darlene Nadeau, also not called to testify, who had described the person hiding in her yard a few blocks from Snowberry Downs on the night Stonechild went missing? If someone matching Neil Stonechild's description had been hiding in her yard at 11:56 p.m., then it was far less likely Stonechild could have been bleeding in a police car three blocks away at 11:56 p.m., as Jason Roy later claimed. With no idea that the RCMP were trying to determine if she might have seen Stonechild, an Aboriginal person, she had told Sgt. Lyons:

"...from what I can remember, he may or may not have been Native. If the police had interviewed me that night, my impression probably would have been that he was Native. Uh... but he may not have been. The reason why I'm saying that is 'cause I...he... wasn't blond-haired and he was definitely dark-haired, either dark brown or black. It was straight. It was past shoulder-length. Uh...from what I remember seeing, he either had a really light jacket on...I believe it was a blue jean jacket or something like that, you may not have been able to easily distinguish. He wasn't dressed for the winter. ...The feeling I have strong is that it was not appropriate wear for the winter, but it was a jacket of some type. Open because I...closing my eyes I see a difference between the colour of his shirt and his jacket, you know... like there was a distinction there... [When found, Stonechild, with hair past shoulder-length, was wearing a blue jacket over a red lumberjack shirt, blue jeans and runners.]. Uh... either khaki canvas or blue jeans and running shoes."

This is how someone within Operation Ferric summarized that description:

"person believed to be native (unsure) wearing a jean jacket or light coat and looking cold."

Would anyone reading those 16 generic words believe there was anything useful to be gained by reading Nadeau's interview? Does that explain the fact that no one in either the justice system or the Stonechild Inquiry raised concerns about numerous glaring errors in RCMP material – because they read the summaries but not the interviews?

Disclosure provisions have been in common-law for 800 years, since the signing of the *Magna Carta* in 1215. The Magna Carta also established as law that "No free man shall be taken or imprsoned [sic] or deprived or outlawed or exiled or *in any way ruined*, nor will we go or send against him, *except by the lawful judgment of his peers or by the law of the land.*" In the Hartwig/Senger case, that 800 year-old law was also ignored.

At what point do RCMP investigator "errors" become immoral or nefarious, if they lead to innocent people suffering?

Stan Goertzen comments:

"I don't believe that Lyons was corrupt. I believe he took the easy way out and simply accepted Warner's hypothesis as to what might have happened to Neil Stonechild. I believe Warner, Lyons and other RCMP investigators simply went through the motions once they developed this tunnel vision approach to investigating and interviewing witnesses. In my opinion, Lyons and Warner should have put a lot more effort into picking the fly shit out of the pepper [separating relevant from irrelevant information]. But what may be nefarious is their summaries, which did not contain important exculpatory information from other sources. I believe that a lot of information was missed or misrepresented in investigative summaries or reports to Commission Counsel Hesje, as a result of what I believe was tunnel vision on the part of Warner and Lyons. And even worse, these same RCMP investigators were never required to testify at the inquiry."

RCMP Sgt. Colin Crocker agrees:

"I think Regina RCMP Major Crimes did a lot of work, but they may have had blinders on because they took the word of the FSIN investigator, made it gospel and focused on two guys only. The FSIN seemed really down on the SPS and RCMP. Their philosophy seemed to be: if they got an officer down, good for them!"

Soon after the Stonechild Inquiry concluded by echoing Warner's report, an informal complaint was lodged by the Saskatoon police association that Warner had withheld important information from the investigation file. However, before a formal complaint could be filed against him for this serious breach, Warner retired suddenly from the Mounties and went to work – as a special investigator for the FSIN. "I was troubled with the thought that any evidence that was contrary to the findings of the Stonechild Inquiry report might have been excluded from an open police file," Goertzen says. **"This concerned me because, if it was the result of neglect or laziness, that was troubling, and if it was withheld from the file intentionally, then it was potentially a much more serious matter."**

At the time of the Stonechild Inquiry, the banker provided RCMP with his information about seeing a man matching Stonechild's description – "I'm sure it was him!" – walking under his own power, shivering, toward the location, 12 blocks away, where his body was found.

But the banker might as well not have bothered. The RCMP obtained his statement at the beginning of the inquiry and advised counsel for the inquiry, Joel Hesje. While Hesje may have claimed to have disclosed it to all parties, why did he not send lawyers an update containing only the banker's new information, rather than sandwich it in amongst all previous material? Most troubling, though: why didn't Hesje call this banker to testify, with what was obviously important, pertinent information? What harm would it have done?

Dave Scott comments:

"The investigating RCMP fell into a trap: they formed in their minds a hypothesis which would give them tunnel vision so they would force the pieces of the puzzle to fit.

I'm concerned hearing about an ambulance attendant not called to give evidence. The information from the bank manager should have been made public but was buried during the inquiry. In other words, it was hidden.

This was manipulation of evidence. *The very people who investigated were not required to give their evidence at the inquiry. I am suspect as to why. When have we ever seen such damning allegations made, publicly attracting national and international attention, and investigators are not brought forward to provide their findings publicly so that they could be scrutinized and challenged. It's unheard of. I've never – I can't even*

imagine such a betrayal! Inexpert testimony, dishonest witnesses, physical evidence distorted – meaning handcuff allegations, three key witnesses and investigators not being called to give evidence!
The RCMP became politicized, and they looked at a political answer, political resolution, a political means of maintaining law and order, rather than using due process of law."

In advance of the inquiry, Dr. Valery Rao, chief medical examiner for the city of Columbia, Missouri, had written a report submitted to the inquiry based on her study of 44 Stonechild photos. In her opinion, those were not handcuff marks. Commission Counsel Joel Hesje did not call her to testify. In a later interview Dr. Rao told me, "But when you're looking for an expert, you're desperate. You look for anything that will support your point of view." But Commission Counsel is not supposed to have a point of view that he or she wants to support. Hesje was supposed to be neutral. At what point do Sask Justice errors become nefarious?

Bob Stenhouse is an Alberta RCMP Staff Sergeant who resigned in 2002 under threat of dismissal for whistle-blowing by leaking RCMP information to outside sources. In a 2005 interview with me, he said: "It wouldn't surprise me if RCMP investigators got the wrong men in the Stonechild Investigation. We're trained to look at all the evidence, but *we tend to think our job is to get a conviction* rather than simply to gather evidence. If it's in your mindset that you must get a conviction, you can compromise on the truth and thoroughness by only collecting evidence that strengthens your own theory. *This has been happening across Canada for years and years."*

This was my interview with Sask. Justice Minister Frank Quennell a month after the release of the Inquiry Report:

How much does public outrage influence the way decisions go in an inquiry?

"Judge Wright who was the commissioner in the inquiry was a Queen's Court Judge when I graduated in 1985. It is his job to make decisions based upon the evidence before him, and not to make political decisions. I don't believe public outrage would affect him. He's not only a judge of considerable experience but also a person of judicious temperament."

Do Saskatchewan courts have different standards for Aboriginal and white people?

"Courts and judges of Saskatchewan strive to treat people as equal before the law, and the judges who have been appointed by the provincial government to the provincial court or to superior courts by the federal government achieve that goal."

Is there any pressure on judges to produce a certain outcome to an inquiry?

"Certainly not. The commissioner to the Stonechild Inquiry was appointed by the government. Terms of reference were set out. There was absolutely no interference or communication between the justice department and Commissioner Wright while the inquiry was being conducted. Commissioner Wright would not accept communication from me until after the report released, and I did not try to communicate with him until after the report was released, at which time I called and thanked him for his work."

Is a parallel Aboriginal, or two-tier, justice system a possibility?

"You'd have to talk to the vice chief, Lawrence Joseph of the Federation of Saskatchewan Indian Nations to get their position on their response to either the Inquiry into the Death of Neil Stonechild or the Commission on Justice Reform and First Nations and Métis People. I don't have the same view as Vice Chief Joseph on every point as to how we should proceed, but I don't think he would describe it as a two-tier system."

How do you differ from him?

"I believe that we can in Saskatchewan make changes to our justice system, to our relationships between police and aboriginal people such that the justice system is seen as fair and equitable by everybody, and that every citizen in Sask can have confidence in it. I think there is common agreement that we need to have a police force that is representational of the population, that there are more Aboriginal peace officers, that it would be appropriate to have more Aboriginal judges, and Aboriginal prosecutors.

That recommendation came out of the Justice Reform Commission, and is one that many people in Saskatchewan would agree with, including the FSIN."

Are you considering replacing the Saskatoon police with RCMP?

"There's been some discussion by some commentators about that idea, which I think is quite premature, following release of the Stonechild Inquiry Report. I have asked the local Saskatoon Police Commission to come up with a plan to ensure that there's confidence in the local police force. I'm having that plan's development and implementation reviewed by our provincial Police Commission. It has met over the past couple of days with the local commission, so that work is underway now. I believe local leadership in the police and city council are on the commission. That local commission should have an opportunity to make changes and respond constructively to Justice Wright's report."

So you think that justice is alive and well in the province of Saskatchewan?

"I think that the justice system in Saskatchewan serves the people of Saskatchewan very well."
In the end, it does not matter whether motives were unconscious (tunnel vision) or deliberate (corruption). The fact is, in this case, the justice system – RCMP and Sask Justice – failed to produce justice.

Retired Calgary police officer and MP Art Hanger observes:

"To my mind, what happened in Saskatoon was not locally-driven, but more broad-based – this is Canada we're talking about! *From Caledonia to the West Coast, the same rhetoric is being used. The federal justice department drafts legislation for various departments, and when you place people of a certain mind-set in the justice department, that's what's going to get churned out. This involved the whole bureaucracy, yet the bureaucrats' agenda is not for the good of the country. It is for themselves.*
As for the RCMP? They were trying to destroy the Saskatoon Police Service and they received their marching orders from Ottawa. The bureaucrats

were supporting the Native Indian movement, just as they have elsewhere in the country. The RCMP is too close to the political agenda in Ottawa and must appease Aboriginal people at every turn. In order to pay for the sins of our forefathers, we must coddle them. This agenda has been adopted deep in the bureaucracy, and it has tainted the RCMP.

Normally, in a trial where the court was to hear all evidence, say in some major crime, a defence lawyer would, and could in this case, create a reasonable doubt in front of a judge or jury. A reasonable doubt is all a judge would have to weigh regarding factual evidence; the verdict for Hartwig and Senger then would be: 'Not guilty.' In this case, there would have been insufficient evidence to convict. There is no question the two accounts are so close together, in both time and space, that doubt could be cast on the RCMP account that Stonechild was in a police car at that time. Personally I believe, from the evidence here, there is enough doubt to exonerate the officers. That is what should be done."

CHAPTER 26 - How did Neil Stonechild get out to that Field – and Why? My Theory

'He was really in love with a girl named Lucille....'

– Julie Binning

"What is so tragic about this whole thing," states Sgt. Ernie Louttit, "is how promising a lad Neil was. Brushes with the law aside, he was a bright, happy kid and loved by his family and I think on a personal note it just – I joined here when I was seventeen. My mom was very much like his mom, Mrs. Bignell, and I think that's where my emotional connection came in. You know, seventeen is a time of promise and hope and even if you have a scrape with the law, it's not irreversible. As far as tragedies go, that was an absolute tragedy. As far as us knowing how he came to be out in that field, I don't know if we'll ever know with any degree of certainty, ever."

Not with any certainty, perhaps. But having pored over the cold, hard facts and interviewed countless people, I have formed a theory on how Neil Stonechild got out to that field – and why.

I started my research with the belief that someone – whether police or criminals – had to have driven him the six km (3.7 miles) out there. No one, I thought, could walk that far in that cold. I have since interviewed the woman who saw someone closely matching Stonechild's description being chased from his hiding place a few blocks from Snowberry Downs, seven minutes after Stonechild's last reported sighting there. As she and I were driving north from that hiding place, I asked, "If you were going to walk from O'Regan Crescent to the Hitachi building in the north end of the city, how would you do it?" She replied, "He could have come across these fields to the left of us because back in 1990, a lot of that newer area, Westview, wasn't there. That was all open fields back then. It would have been a shorter distance then, because it would have been cross-country."

I have interviewed the second independent, unbiased source, also not called to testify, the banker who tried to alert authorities to his sighting of Stonechild ("I'm sure it was him!") late on the night he went missing, staggering on the 51st Street overpass toward the location his body was later found, 12 blocks away.

I have learned from the ambulance attendant (again, not called to testify) that the body had frostbite on the cheeks. This indicates Stonechild had been out in the cold an extended length of time before he died since, after death, skin cannot be injured by the cold.

I have learned there were no defensive wounds on the body, which he might have got by struggling with someone who dropped him off against his will.

And I have learned that Stonechild's Saulteaux heritage, which included renowned Canadian marathoner Paul Acoose, was known for outstanding running and walking abilities.[133] Author Barbara Zieman writes: "Outstanding as [Paul Acoose's] speed and endurance may have seemed, young Paul was simply following Indian tradition. ...Indian 'work running,' ceremonial running and inter-tribal competitive running games never ceased to amaze outsiders."[134] So perhaps the former wrestling champion Stonechild was capable of walking the six km under those conditions, seemingly impossible in my Caucasian experience.

I talked to a former street kid who knew Stonechild who said, "Neil could have walked, definitely. We walked everywhere. The money that we had, we kept for booze or dope; we didn't spend it on transport. We walked right from one end of the city to the other. That was nothin' to us kids. We could have done it drunk – I've done it. We wore hardly nothing. Just regular clothes that you'd wear in the summertime; jeans and a shirt. Then we'd usually have like a jean jacket and a lumberjack jacket and runners. It was like we were immune to the weather. I'm not like that now. I think it was conditioning from the time we were little; we didn't wear much, so the body conditions itself to heat itself better. We never wore stuff like a hat or gloves, never! We didn't want to look stupid, eh? We had a style to keep!"

I have interviewed Jason Roy who said that Neil was "still raw" from his forced break-up with Lucille Neetz, after learning they were very closely related. Neil "just hated that [break-up] so much because he really loved her and he really cared for her and he was just torn apart that he couldn't be with her." Even Neil's new girlfriend at the time, Julie Binning, told the RCMP 10 years later: "[Neil and I] had been kind of going out a little. But he was really in love with a girl named Lucille...."

I learned about 18-year-old John Webb who, the same week Stonechild disappeared in 1990, walked out of a farmhouse 100 km east of Saskatoon and was later found frozen to death with no shoes on, part of his shirt undone, superficial lacerations on his face and a deeper laceration over the bridge of his nose. Why? He had left the house "quite drunk" following an argument with his girlfriend.

On the last night Neil was seen alive, he so desperately wanted to see Lucille that he single-mindedly managed to gain entrance, first to the locked apartment building, and then, with 180 suites to chose from, to the very suite in which Lucille was babysitting. (Trent Ewart would tell RCMP: "When I arrived home, while I was taking off my shoes, somebody walked into the apartment and I pushed him out and locked the door and Lucille told me that it was her ex-boyfriend, Neil Stonechild, and that she was scared of him and thought he was violent and he was drunk." Finally, Roy reported that, on the bus earlier that day, Neil was "just fuming" because he "didn't like the fact of seeing [Lucille and Gary] together."

Knowing those facts, I conclude:

The evidence suggests that on that night, having been forcefully evicted from the apartment in which Gary was together with Lucille – and she was afraid of him! – Neil finally grasped the painful reality. *He would never be together with the girl he loved.* Already suffering from many troubles in his life: abusing alcohol, serving a sentence in a group detention home from which he was AWOL, doing B & Es for money, he now had been "torn apart" and kicked out into the freezing cold alone, with the cops after him. (Ten years later, Lucille would tell a reporter: "I still have some regrets about that to this day.")[135]

I believe that in his aching, despairing, depressed and inebriated state, the emotional youth set off walking blindly, just to get away – anywhere! *I believe it was heartbreak that motivated the distraught 17-year-old to walk and keep on walking into that black, bitter morning, never recognizing that his brain was fogging over with hypothermia until, tragically, it was too late to reach help.*

Information learned later seemed heart-rending corroboration. When Neil's body was found, he had no money in his pockets, and no ID. The only items he carried were a vial of "Hero" cologne, a bus ticket and a few photos, including the tattered image of a girl. The symmetry of her beauty was a haunting echo of his own. Lucille Neetz.

When I outlined my theory to Neil's cousin, Lorraine Stonechild, she replied thoughtfully, "He could have been walking off his pain."

Whether my "heart-broken" theory is correct or not, what matters is that police had nothing whatsoever to do with Stonechild's death.

When I outlined my theory to Stan Goertzen, he wrote:

"I believe that Justice Wright got it wrong in his findings, when he changed the sequence of time when Bruce Genaille was checked (CPIC showed it was after midnight) and used an undocumented call to a 7-Eleven store (not documented anywhere in Communication computer records or by any staff from that 7-Eleven store) to make his decision fit Jason Roy's ever-changing story.

I believe that when the facts are looked at without prejudice, they still tell a tragic story, but a different story.

The facts tell me that Neil Stonechild lived a high-risk lifestyle and that after an evening of drinking and partying, he made poor decisions that ultimately resulted in his freezing death. **The facts clearly show me that it was impossible for Brad or Larry to have had contact with Neil that night.**

Neil's tragic death should have been investigated more completely by the Saskatoon Police Service when his frozen body was discovered. I believe a more complete investigation by Major Crimes officers would have cleared this matter up at the time.

In my opinion, it's also tragic that RCMP Investigator Warner didn't do a better job. I would have liked to see him explain his prowess at the inquiry.

It is a tragedy that two innocent people and their families continue to live with the stigma of an unproven allegation by one person with a hatred for the police and the resulting witch-hunt that occurred."

Dave Scott has called the Hartwig and Senger case "the biggest injustice this province has ever seen!" The question now becomes: **in the interests of justice for Saskatchewan and Canada as a whole, who will dare correct the biggest injustice this province has ever seen?**

EPILOGUE: Lessons Learned from Saskatchewan's Legal Travesties

'What's happened in Saskatoon has the potential to break down barriers that we as a democracy and as a province champion. We say we want everything to be fair and proper and good, but if we follow the course we're on right now, how easy would it be then to persecute an unpopular minority? It's so fundamental that we should all be stepping back to take a look at it.'
– Sgt. Ernie Louttit

Earlier I wrote: When Police Become Prey documents my journey of discovery into the land of myth, followed by efforts to learn how the snow-job – the disastrous lie that Saskatoon police were causing Aboriginal freezing deaths – could have been foisted upon the intelligent peoples of my home province.

What I learned was this: the people have not been snowed. They have been cowed. Silenced. Gagged. Most citizens, Aboriginal and White, are not "myth-informed." They know exactly what is going on – freezing deaths are the result of high-risk lifestyles.

My observation is backed by the 2004 CTV Saskatoon poll asking: "Do you think [former Constables] Dan Hatchen & Ken Munson should have their convictions overturned?" to which 73 percent of respondents answered YES. My observation is supported by the fact that sales of *The StarPhoenix*, following a decade-long decline, rose 1.3 percent during the explosion of "Starlight Tour" articles in 2000, followed by large drops in sales in years following, despite on-going coverage of trial, inquests and the Stonechild Inquiry. My observation is backed by Brad Senger revealing, "Perhaps I'm naïve or just lucky, but 90 to 95 percent of the people I meet understand that a bad thing happened to me, and I have never had anyone say: 'You're the one that killed that native kid!' Among those I work with, most soon realize that's not what I'm about."

My observation is also backed by emails received, such as this from a self-described "ordinary citizen":

"Both the Native and non-Native population suffer greatly, due to political correctness that blames racism, rather than face their responsibility, condoning a criminal/substance abuse subculture."

The people have been scared silent. Shouted down. Bullied by fears of the ugly label so easily tossed off, so difficult to defend against: "Racist!" Native people say their own community tries to stifle their support of police by calling them "Apple" (red on the outside, white on the inside). Saskatchewan people have been trained to whisper. Again and again, while checking over their shoulders, they have muttered to me, "It's great that you're exposing the facts! Keep it up!" Yet they don't dare attach their names to the project.

Isn't it a shame that people are not all of one pigment? Then we could discuss issues openly, and no one could use allegations of intolerance and discrimination to muzzle anyone else. Since we are not superficially identical, we must relearn tolerance; tolerance of free speech. Tolerance of discussion about cold, hard proven facts, however painful. And brave in working together to transform painful facts.

Thoughts:

1. People working within the justice system must deal with the fact that they or their children have had run-ins with police, and not take it out on that officer or the next encountered. This author was told by a former SPS officer that a lawyer prominent in cases against police was arrested, and later convicted, for Impaired Driving. He told the arresting SPS officer, between spitting and swearing: *"You're nothing but a White piece of shit and one day I will have your job!"* And he did. For reasons of legal confidentiality, I have not revealed known facts about others working within the justice system. What I can say is this: "Clean up your own acts and you will have no need to be vengeful."

2. Readers should know that several SPS officers are married to nurses who have had to care for the very people – or their relatives – who have ruined officers' lives. These nurses helped the patients without ever revealing they were married to police officers. *One nurse dealt directly with the man whose lone allegation had torn apart her own husband and the life they had built together.* "While treating his relative, I had to talk daily to Jason Roy who was patient advocate," Sandy Hartwig

explains. "I had to pretend I wasn't who I was. One day I was down on my knees, milking blood clots out of his relative's catheter tubing while Jason stood there talking about the role he played in my husband's firing. Luckily I had my back turned to him as I felt myself pale for a moment, but was able to refocus and not show my true feelings [and thus go on milking blood clots]. I try to put the inquiry on the back burner. Yes, it happened and yes, it has had a tragic impact on our family. I don't think about it every day like I feel Larry has, but it is encounters like these that stir up toxic memories. I do a lot of venting to Larry after work some days, let me tell you!"

3. Saskatchewanites are fierce in defence of the underdog. Is it possible we tend to identify with the victim? If so, is that because so many are descended from immigrants who fled persecution that, when faced with alleged injustice, we tend toward knee-jerk reactions. This can lead to Noble Cause Corruption: get the bad guy by whatever means possible; the end will justify the means. The lesson required is this: before reacting, make certain you know who is the genuine underdog, as well as the top dog merely cultivating the appearance of victim. For those in the legal system: rise above prejudgment and *follow the dictates of the evidence.*

4. Public Inquiries must either be discontinued or have their rules stringently enforced. Judges are neither to assign blame nor leave the impression of having assigned blame.

5. Canadians are terribly politically-correct. We must overcome this and learn to treat everyone equally. No one is automatically to be believed simply because they are of a certain profession, age or pigment. *Particularly* if they have a long criminal record and a story that keeps changing to deal with emerging evidence.

6. All RCMP, police and justice officials in this country must be trained in characteristics peculiar to hypothermic deaths. After freezing and thawing, things appear markedly different than what they are.

7. If you are a reporter, write for the long-term, not for the excited, morally-panicked short-term. You will look less foolish if your reporting stands the test of time.

8. A Saskatonian's allegation deserves study and remedy: "The media whipped the city into a frenzied witch-hunt. The media is no longer interested in just reporting the news; they want to *make* the news."

9. Friends and families of those drinking or drugging to excess must be educated to look after them, rather than, when misadventure occurs, salving consciences by blaming someone completely uninvolved.

10. Puffery is for birds. When this journalist spoke to one newspaper editor, several law professors and some elected officials in Saskatchewan, as well as one Toronto-based NFB official, attempting to provide them with objective evidence supporting the four fired officers, right before my eyes these self-proclaimed moral authorities puffed up like fowl and tried to stare me down. They actually appeared to increase in size! They went silent and one shook, as if to say, "How dare you question me?" When they spoke, it was with disgust. It was hard not to laugh. Is this how they scare people silent? Are they unaccustomed to challenges? Does truth frighten so greatly that they dare not debate, therefore attempt intimidation? They must be taught that, in most of the developed world, reason and free speech prevail over bullying and self-inflation.

Bottom line: "Bias, conflict of interest, political interference and calculated manipulation have raised concerns with Saskatchewan Justice," states former Saskatoon Police Chief Dave Scott. "Federal justice officials must review the actions of Saskatchewan Justice to ensure citizens and their police officers receive unbiased and fair justice instead of betrayal."

AFTERWORD: 'Was the Stonechild Inquiry an Impartial Process?' by Judge Wallace Craig (retired)

'I had anticipated that the commissioner had, as a finding of fact, clearly determined, first and foremost, the credibility of each witness....'
– The Honourable Wallace Craig

After reading *When Police become Prey*, I scrutinized Commissioner Wright's 2004 report [writes retired Judge Craig]. It is a very lengthy compilation of extracts of testimony and documentary evidence, together with his findings and recommendations. Keeping in mind that the usual rules of evidence are somewhat less-rigidly applied in an inquiry, nevertheless I had anticipated that the Commissioner had, as a finding of fact, clearly determined, first and foremost, the credibility of each witness, and that he had done so before making judicial determinations on the admissibility and cogency of the evidence of each witness.

Jason Roy was the key witness in the inquiry. It is significant that the Commissioner accepted one aspect of Jason Roy's testimony *which was the tipping point in the Report.* Although the Commissioner found Roy's testimony rife with inconsistencies, he concluded that Roy's evidence – that he saw Neil Stonechild in a police car in the custody of Officers Hartwig and Senger – was determinative, and that testimony of officers Hartwig and Senger was untenable.

To me [Judge Craig continues], it is obvious that Roy's assertion became the cornerstone of the Report of the Inquiry.

Despite its inconsistency, Commissioner Wright ruled that Roy's evidence provided a "germ of truth" to his claim that he saw Stonechild seated in a police car with Constables Hartwig and Senger. That "germ of truth" became the basis for remarkable postulations by the Commissioner, which sealed the fate of the officers, that:

a. he found that Stonechild was probably last seen in the officers' custody,
b. the officers would have had enough time to transport him to the location he was later found frozen, and

c. the marks were consistent with handcuffs.

From these findings, one might infer the officers transported Stonechild to the outskirts of Saskatoon and left him to fend for himself in the grip of life-threatening cold weather.

Without the cornerstone of Jason Roy's evidence, all of the Commissioner's inferential conclusions seem insupportable.

At page 49 of the Commissioner's Report, he writes:

"In the final analysis, I do not need to rely solely on Roy's account of what happened to reach the conclusions I do. However, I want to make some comments about Roy's presentation as a witness. I had ample opportunity to observe him during his testimony. He struck me as sincere and thoughtful and as still deeply affected by the death of his friend and what followed.

While Roy's testimony contained errors and contradictions, this does not prevent me from finding credible his testimony relating to what he observed on the evening of November 24th and the morning of November 25th, 1990. I am reminded of the words of Ontario Court of Appeal, affirmed by the Supreme Court of Canada in R. Abdallah:

'There is evidence on which a jury or judge, properly instructed and acting reasonably, could have convicted. Even with the prior inconsistent statements and the inadequate explanations for them, in these circumstances it was open to the trial judge to accept all, some, or none of the complainants' evidence. Having accepted some of it, it was open for him to convict, as he did, on all three counts.'

It is necessary for me to make these observations about his credibility [Commissioner Wright continues,] because I might otherwise give the impression that I am depending on other persons' evidence to support him as credible. That is not the case. The existence of corroborating evidence does, of course make my task a good deal easier. ***I conclude by commending Jason Roy for his tenacity in pursuing this matter over many years."*** (Emphasis added.)

By praising Jason Roy for his "tenacity," [retired Judge Craig continues,] the Commissioner exuded empathy and, in the least, identified himself mentally with Roy. On this point, readers may wish to examine the Report of the INQUIRY[136] to see for themselves whether the Commissioner had a similar empathy for Saskatoon police officers Larry Hartwig and Brad Senger. They are police officers whose duties can be traced back to the first municipal police force: the London Bobbies of Sir Robert Peel. Peel famously said: "The Police are the Public and the Public are the Police." Without them, we would live in anarchy.

Readers must be mindful of the black-and-white distinction between lawyering and judging [retired Judge Craig concludes]. To be successful, and to secure the proper interests of clients involved in civil or criminal litigation, a trial lawyer must be an activist (never a mercenary). Immediately upon leaving the practice of law, a neophyte judge begins a difficult transformation from activist in the adversarial process, to pacifist sitting above the fray, struggling to be neutral and impartial, no matter how difficult it may become to endure the cut-and-thrust of counsel. Steadfastly remaining impartial, and appearing to do so, while giving both sides a fair opportunity to make their case, a judge then strives to deliver a judgment that, hopefully, will result in the losing litigant saying, "Well, at least the old beak gave me a fair hearing!"

To me, there is a similarity between a judge struggling to be impartial and a high-wire artist balancing on a thin wire. It is an analogy the reader might wish to apply to Commissioner Wright and his exhaustive Report.

Walking the high wire requires the absolute concentration of the high-wire artist. To remain well-balanced as he walks the tightrope, the high-wire artist maintains his balance using a balancing-pole of flexible metal to keep him on the straight and narrow wire. In a trial, a judge must walk a straight and narrow line from start to finish, even-handedly neutral, carrying the balancing-pole of absolute impartiality. **Without impartiality, injustice prevails.**

I found McLean's book to be a "true life whodunit!" Was the hypothermic death of Neil Stonechild accidental? Did the aftermath of his death result in a sensational tabloid witch-hunt of members of the Saskatoon Police Service? Was the Commission of Inquiry an impartial process?

YOU BE THE JUDGE!

– Wallace Gilby Craig served 26 years as judge in Vancouver's Provincial Criminal Court, followed by six years as adjudicator with the federal Human Rights Tribunal

Endnotes

1. Larry Lockwood, "Time to move beyond hateful remarks," Saskatoon *StarPhoenix*, Dec. 18, 2002, A14.
2. Larry Lockwood, "McNab Park proves community policing works," *StarPhoenix*, Dec. 4 and 5, 2003, A15.
3. C. Stuart Houston, *R. G. Ferguson: Crusader against Tuberculosis* (Toronto: Hannah/Dundurn Press, 1991) 122.
4. Houston, 31.
5. R.G. Ferguson, MD, *Studies in Tuberculosis* (Toronto: University of Toronto Press, 1955) 82.
6. Hugh Dempsey, *Crowfoot, Chief of the Blackfeet* (Norman: University of Oklahoma Press, 1972) 181.
7. R.G. Ferguson, MD, "Tuberculosis among the Indians of the Great Canadian Plains, Preliminary Report of an Investigation being carried out by the National Research Council of Canada," paper delivered to the National Association for the Prevention of Tuberculosis in London, England, Oct. 15, 1928, 19.
8. *Crowfoot*, 129.
9. *Studies in Tuberculosis*, 82.
10. FSIN leader Lawrence Joseph filmed by National Film Board speaking to Aboriginal talking circle, June 19, 2001. Material obtained under freedom of information legislation.
11. Les MacPherson, "How many other frozen bodies will turn up?" *StarPhoenix*, Feb. 17, 2000, A3.
12. Chris Tyrone Ross, "Year starts with an 'uproar' in the Aboriginal Community," *Saskatchewan Sage*, March 13, 2000, 4.
13. Shannon Boklaschuk, "Mother doesn't blame police for son's death," *StarPhoenix*, A7.
14. Jason Warick, "Did Wegner coroner's inquest hear the whole story?" *StarPhoenix*, Feb. 16, 2002, E1.
15. "City Briefs," *StarPhoenix*, Dec. 1, 1990.
16. At that hearing, Roy would be asked about his last criminal conviction. He testified: "I would probably say '96." When it was suggested the year it had actually been 2003, a year before the hearing, he agreed. He stated the crime was unlawfully in a dwelling, when it was actually mischief by willful damage over $5000. His sentence for intentionally doing more than $5,000 damage? Absolute discharge.

17. Information obtained under Access to Information legislation.
18. Randy Burton, "Welcome to Theatre of the Absurd," *StarPhoenix*, Feb 8, 2001, A2.
19. www.fsin.com/index.php/commission (Retrieved April 2013).
20. Leslie Perreaux, "Private Eyes to Shadow Task Force: FSIN hires own team to check up on RCMP," *StarPhoenix*, March 22, 2000, A1/FRONT.
21. "In the age of the Internet, virtual mobbing is the inevitable Doppelgänger of moral panic," writes political scientist Tom Flanagan. "Whether verified or not, stories of outrage rocket around the world at the speed of light. People make sense of them by fitting them into pre-existing frameworks of evil and threat. No time for research or reflection when the social order is threatened on all sides by folk devils – child pornographers, drug dealers, and jihadis in the imagination of the right; racists, big corporations, and the oil sands in the imagination of the left. Even if the law no longer allows us to stone those folk devils, we can metaphorically do the equivalent by online denunciation." *Persona Non Grata: New Technology and the Threat to Freedom of Speech* (Toronto: Random House Canada, 2014).
22. Jason Warick, "Allegations of police abuse put Saskatoon on Amnesty list," *StarPhoenix*, May 31, 2001, A1/FRONT.
23. Julian Branch, "Aboriginal group says police should have been charged with attempted murder," Canadian Press Newswire, May 15, 2000.
24. Documents obtained under access to information legislation.
25. See documents: www.whenpolicebecomeprey.com/commission
26. Scott Edmunds, "Axworthy asks for help: Ottawa urged to intervene in Saskatchewan's native question," *StarPhoenix*, March 2, A1/FRONT.
27. Candis McLean, "What's wrong with the Mounties? The RCMP are hobbled by growing political interference, an expert veteran concludes," *The Report* Newsmagazine, Dec. 20, 1999, 27.
28. Robert Marshall, "A Firestorm of Political Correctness: Why alleged Starlight Tours ruined careers without a nickel's worth of evidence," Winnipeg *Free Press*, Feb. 12, 2011, H11.
29. Les MacPherson, "MLA found man's frozen body," *StarPhoenix*, Feb. 19, 2000, A3.
30. Michele Mandel, "Aliens in own land," Toronto *Sun*, Feb. 20, 2000, 4
31. "Canada AM with Valerie Pringle," CTV, May 12, 2000.

32. Chris Tyrone Ross, "Year Starts with an 'Uproar' in the Aboriginal Community," *Saskatchewan Sage*, March 13, 2000. www.ammsa.com/publications/saskatchewan-sage/year-starts-uproar-aboriginal-community

33. Stanley Cohen, *Folk Devils and Moral Panics* (London: MacGibbon & Kee Ltd., 1972) 9.

34. Erich Goode and Nachman Ben-Yehuda, *Moral Panics: The Social Construction of Deviance* (Oxford: Blackwell Publishers Inc., 1994) 31.

35. Goode and Ben-Yehuda, 111.

36. "Report of the Working Group on the Prevention of Miscarriages of Justice," 2004. www.justice.gc.ca/eng/rp-pr/cj-jp/ccr-rc/pmj-pej/sum-som.html. Retrieved March 2012.

37. Kenneth Thompson, *Moral Panics* (London and New York: Routledge, 1998), 17.

38. Thompson, introduction.

39. Thompson, 141.

40. Another example is the case of six-year-old JonBenét Ramsey of Boulder, Colorado, murdered in her home Christmas night, 1996. Initially, police could not find her body. "The world media was quick to sensationalize our tragedy and led a tabloid-fuelled frenzy that sought our conviction for the murder of our child," wrote her father, John Ramsey, of his trial in the court of public opinion. In addition, the police department was determined on its suspects; investigators placed their bet early and would not deviate, regardless of the lack of evidence: there was no physical evidence implicating the parents, no motive, no signs of past aggression or physical neglect. The fact that there was not enough evidence to charge anyone did not stop the media circus. A repairman attempted to tap the parents' phone; a reporter knelt beside Ramsay in church, seeking a quote as he took Communion. Year after year, the little girl's face was plastered on magazines continent-wide. Files released years later indicated that a grand jury had been prepared to indict the couple for child abuse resulting in death, but one man, the district attorney, had the fortitude to stand up to pressure and say: "We do not have enough evidence to lay a charge."

    Twelve years later, advances in DNA technology cleared the parents. In a July 2008 letter, the district attorney wrote Ramsay: "To the extent that we may have contributed in any way to the public perception that you might have been involved in this crime, I am deeply sorry. No innocent person should have to endure such an extensive trial in the court of public opinion, especially when public officials have not had sufficient evidence to initiate a trial in a court of law." *The Other Side of Suffering: The Father of JonBenét Ramsey Tells the Story of his Journey from Grief to Grace* (New York: Faith Words, 2012).

41. Const. Mathew Bradford, "Replace The *StarPhoenix* with *Leader Post* reporters," *StarPhoenix*, Mar. 23, 2006, A11.

42. After declining an industry-standard 10% between 1990 and 1999, The *StarPhoenix*'s "total copies sold" increased an average 4,500/week (1.3%) in 2000 (from 361,877/week in 1999, to 366,382 in 2000). In 2001, that number dropped to a pre-"starlight tour" level of 359,756, and continued steadily downward to 330,455 by 2005. (Circulation data from the Canadian Newspapers Association.)

43. Thompson, 15.

44. Marion Starkey, *The Devil in Massachusetts: A Modern Enquiry into the Salem Witch Trials* (New York: A. A. Knopf, 1949).

45. Douglas Starr, "The Interview: Do police interrogation techniques produce false confessions?" *The New Yorker*, Dec. 9, 2013, 42-49.

46. Douglas Starr, "The Interview: Do police interrogation techniques produce false confessions?" *The New Yorker*, Dec. 9, 2013, 42-49.

47. Douglas Quan, "Judge deems interrogation method 'oppressive'; Ruling says widely used Reid Technique infringes on rights," Vancouver *Sun*, Sept. 11, 2012, B4.

48. Suzanne Reber and Robert Renaud, Starlight Tour: *The Last, Lonely Night of Neil Stonechild* (Toronto: Random House, 2005) 227.

49. *Starlight Tour*, 227-8. Given the fact that the "union rep" myth could so easily be disproven, what other information in the book did the authors fabricate not so easily fact-checked? For example, they wrote, p. 404: "Dave Scott did not agree to be interviewed for Starlight Tour." Scott responds, "Another mistruth!"

50. Nick Brune, Dave Calverley and Alastair Sweeny. *History of Canada Online* (Northern Blue Publishing). www.canadachannel.ca/HCO/ Retrieved February, 2010.

51. www.flickr.com/photos/rhcask/3145156071/. Retrieved February, 2010.

52. "The Dakota alliance, which included even the [western branches of the Dakota nation], held an extensive area west of the Great Lakes against the

Americans as well as against the Indians of the south and west who were sympathetic to [the American] cause." Dietz, Alexander, *Wapahaska: The Early History of the Whitecap Band* www.Whitecapdakota.com. (Retrieved August, 2010.)

53. Richard G. St-Pierre, "History, Use and Economic Importance of the Saskatoon" www.prairie-elements.ca/saskatoon/1.2-history.pdf 1. (Retrieved February, 2011.)

54. Richard St-Pierre, 2.

55. www.ducklake.ca

56. www.Whitecapdakota.com/culture/history_culture.php (retrieved February, 2011).

57. www.fnmr.gov.sk.ca/community/maps/firstnations

58. www.fcpp.org/publication.php/2491

59. A. C. Cairns, *Citizens Plus: Aboriginal Peoples and the Canadian State* (Vancouver and Toronto: UBC Press, 2000) 6, 115, 211.

60. gismap.usask.ca/website/Web_atlas/AOUAP/

61. *Populace*, City of Saskatoon, Spring, 2001.

62. Joseph Quesnel, "On-Reserve Folks Need Change," Frontier Centre for Public Policy. www.fcpp.org/publication.php/2455

63. P.D. Smith, *City: A Guidebook for the Urban Age* (London: Bloomsbury; 2012).

64. The Aboriginal community is growing at six times the national average. (Calvin Helin, *Dances with Dependency: Out of Poverty through Self-reliance*, (Vancouver: Orca Spirit Publishing, 2006).

65. Robert Lunney, *Parting Shots; My Passion for Policing* (Edmonton: Robert Lunney Associates, 2012) 193.

66. Murry Mandryk, "Rob Norris' Big First Nations Challenge," Regina *Leader Post*, June 5, 2012, A6.

67. In Manitoba, although they then formed only two percent of the population, Aboriginal people made up thirty to 45 percent of victims. C. Stuart Houston, *R. G. Ferguson: Crusader against Tuberculosis* (Toronto: Hannah/Dundurn Press, 1991) 31.

68. In 2014, the Harper government would cut and cap at $500,000 annually the core funding for regional First Nation political organizations.

69. www.fsin.com/images/stories/fsindownloads/communications/Annual_Reports/2011-2012_FSIN_Annual_Report_8MB.pdf, 65.

70. Murray Mandryk, Regina *Leader Post*, Sept. 19, 2011. (fnbc.info/finding-fix-fsin); retrieved May 1, 2012.)

71. Doug Cuthand, "SIGA destined to become Crown corporation," *StarPhoenix*, Dec. 29, 2000, A13.

72. www4.hrsdc.gc.ca/.3ndic.1t.4r@-eng.jsp?iid=36

73. www.climate.weatheroffice.gc.ca/climate_normals

74. According to Statistics Canada, in 2000 the Canadian population was about 30,750,000; Saskatchewan's was 1,023,636 (3.3%). The country suffered 92 freezing deaths; Saskatchewan 18 (20%). Statistics Canada. Table 102-0540 - Deaths, by cause, and Saskatchewan Dept. of Health.

75. Joanne Paulson, "Sunny Saturday great day to party," *StarPhoenix*, May 27, 1996, B8.

76. Saskatoon city archivist Jeff O'Brien, in a speech at centennial celebration of Saskatoon Forestry Farm, May 26, 2013.

77. Twila Reddekopp, SaskBusiness, Dec. 1, 2010. www.thefreelibrary.com//printPrintArticle.aspx?id=246017203 (retrieved March 2011).

78. web.archive.org/web/20080219160730/www40.statcan.ca/l01/cst01/Legal04b.htm

79. Ken MacQueen with Patricia Treble, "The Rankings: Canada's Most Dangerous Cities, *Maclean's*, March 5, 2009 www2.macleans.ca/2009/03/05/the-most-dangerous-cities-in-canada/

80. www.statcan.gc.ca/daily-quotidien/080717/dq080717b-eng.htm

81. Canadian Centre for Justice Statistics based on CANSIM table www5.statcan.gc.ca/cansim/a26?lang=eng&retrLang=eng&id=2520051&tabMode=dataTable&srchLan=-1&p1=-1&p2=9

82. Statistics Canada. Table 252-0013 - Crime statistics, by detailed offenses, annual (number unless otherwise noted) CANSIM (database). www5.statcan.gc.ca/cansim/a05?lang=eng&id=1020540 (retrieved: February 2011).

83. Zack O'Malley Greenburg, Forbes Staff, "America's most dangerous cities," April 23, 2009. www.forbes.com/2009/04/23/most-dangerous-cities-lifestyle-real-estate-dangerous-american-cities.html (retrieved: February 2011). © 2009 Forbes LLC. Used with permission.

84. Lori Coolican, "Mother sues cops over son's death," *StarPhoenix*, February 26, 2001, A1/FRONT.

85. Ryan Holiday, *Trust Me, I'm Lying: Confessions of a Media Manipulator* (New York: Portfolio/Penguin, 2012) 73.

86. Lori Coolican, "Women who say cops held Wegner feared retaliation," *StarPhoenix*, Jan. 25, 2002, A1/FRONT.

87. Rod Nickel, "Stonechild's mom issues ultimatum: Police commission given Oct. deadline to settle with family," *StarPhoenix*, July 27, 2005, A3.

88. Julie Saccone, "Stonechild lawsuit baseless: Hartwig, Senger lawyers," *StarPhoenix*, Nov. 2, 2005, A8.

89. Darren Bernhardt, "Stonechild suit expires: Mom of teen who froze to death surprised lawsuit against police not acted on," *StarPhoenix*, May 4, 2006, A3.

90. Christy Blatchford, "Former officers in no-win situation: 'I have many aboriginal friends,' inquest into death of native man told," *National Post*, Nov. 3, 2001, A4.

91. Ann Harvey, "First Nations must do more for members," Canadian Press Newswire, Oct. 21, 1998.

92. Tom Kizzia and Tataboline Brant, Associated Press, "For visiting villagers, a trip to town was their last," Anchorage *Daily News*, November 13, 2005. Used with permission of Associated Press ©2015. All rights reserved.

93. www.rehab-international.org/blog/new-study-finds-nearly-12-percent-of-native-americans-die-due-to-alcohol-abuse-and-addiction

94. Jason Warick, "FSIN angers Mounties: Strongly-worded letter sent to FSIN headquarters," *StarPhoenix*, Feb. 22, 2002, A1/FRONT.

95. Patrick Barbar, "Wegner inquiry credibility at stake," *StarPhoenix*, Feb. 4, 2002, A8.

96. Jason Warick, "Bombshell suspends inquiry: New information could spark criminal probe: Wegner lawyer" *StarPhoenix*, Jan. 24, 2002, A1/FRONT.

97. www.climate.weather.gc.ca/climateData/hourlydata_e.html?timeframe=1&Prov=SASK&StationID=3328&hlyRange=1953-01-01|2012-03-20&Year=1990&Month=11&Day=25

98. www.justice.gov.sk.ca/stonechild/transcripts/STONECHILD-14.pdf p. 2579.

99. Leslie Perreaux, "Decade-old death resurfaces," *StarPhoenix*, Feb. 22, 2000, A1/FRONT.

100. www.google.ca/maps/@52.145031,-106.720297,3a,75y,103.86h,87.69tdata=!3m4!1e1!3m21s_-tMy1-6spCiegwgMBYaVg!2e0!6m1!1e1

101. The police called to the scene of Stonechild's death estimated his age at 30. One of Neil's long-time associates also told me: "Neil looked older than his age because of abusing drugs and alcohol since about the age of 13."

102. www.justice.gov.sk.ca/stonechild/transcripts/STONECHILD-8.pdf 1454.

103. The Ministry of Justice consents to the reproduction and publication of any police photos which were entered as exhibits in the Stonechild inquiry proceedings.

104. Dave Brown, "Freezing to death, or surviving," Ottawa *Citizen*, Jan. 19, 2013, E8.

105. A number of investigative reports can be viewed beginning at Appendix L: www.justice.gov.sk.ca/stonechild/finalreport/Stonechild.pdf

106. www.justice.gov.sk.ca/stonechild/transcripts STONECHILD-14.pdf, 2571

107. Betty Ann Adam, "Mom saw bruising: Stonechild inquiry hears tearful testimony during first day," *StarPhoenix*, Sept. 9, 2003, A1/FRONT.

108. Terry Craig, "Family suspects foul play," *StarPhoenix*, Mar. 4, 1991, A1/FRONT.

109. Hitler continued, "Even though the facts which prove this to be [a lie] may be brought clearly to their minds, they will still doubt and waver and will continue to think that there may be some other explanation. For the grossly impudent lie always leaves traces behind it, even after it has been nailed down, a fact which is known to all expert liars in this world and to all who conspire together in the act of lying." – Adolf Hitler, *Mein Kampf*, vol 1, chapter X.

110. Transcript of "CBC News investigation into the death of Lawrence Wagner [sic]" by Brookes Decillia, "The World at Six," April 18, 2003.

111. Ann Harvey, "Get all the facts, chief," *Yorkton This Week and Enterprise,* May 16, 2007, A4.

112. www.ammsa.com/publications/windspeaker/saskatoon-police-chief-admits-starlight-cruises-are-not-new Retrieved May 2015.

113. www.ammsa.com/publications/saskatchewan-sage/year-starts-uproar-aboriginal-community Retrieved May 2015.

114. Tannis Fowler, "Probe into aboriginal deaths frustrates FSIN," *StarPhoenix*, June 29, 2001, A3.

115. Interview as feature alongside the movie, *High Crimes.*

116. www.canlii.org/en/sk/skca/doc/2008/2008skca81/2008skca81.html?search UrlHash=AAAAAQAGU2VuZ2VyAAAAAAE&resultIndex=1

117. *Starlight Tour,* 393.

118. SPS file 99-18290.

119. Brian Stewart, *Starlight Tours*, CBC television, "The National," Mar 7, 2000.

120. See statement: www.whenpolicebecomeprey.com/statement

121. Public Inquiry, p. 6172-6174, www.justice.gov.sk.ca/stonechild/transcripts/STONECHILD-32.pdf.

122. Lori Coolican, "Martensville Scandal: Trial and Error," *StarPhoenix*, June 24, 2006, E1.

123. Mireya Navarro, "Search called off for survivors of crash in Everglades," New York *Times*.

124. www.justice.gov.sk.ca/stonechild/transcripts/STONECHILD-23.pdf

125. www.corpus-delicti.com/mouser.html

126. Hartwig v. Commission of Inquiry into matters relating to the death of Neil Stonechild, 2008 SKCA 81, paras. 88-89: www.canlii.org/en/sk/skca/doc/2008/2008skca81/2008skca81.html?searchUrlHash=AAAAAQAGU2VuZ2VyAAAAAAE&resultIndex=1.

127. www.whenpolicebecomeprey.com/timeline .

128. Sam. J. Ervin, Jr. *Humor of a Country Lawyer*, Wilmington: University of North Carolina Press, 1983, 47.

129. See Hartwig v. Commission of Inquiry into matters relating to the death of Neil Stonechild, 2008 SKCA 81, paras. 78-83 - www.canlii.org/en/sk/skca/doc/2008/2008skca81/2008skca81.html?searchUrlHash=AAAAAQAGU2VuZ2VyAAAAAAE&resultIndex=1

130. Robert Marshall, "A Firestorm of Political Correctness: Why alleged Starlight Tours ruined careers without a nickel's worth of evidence," Winnipeg *Free Press*, Feb. 12, 2011, H11.

131. Parts of this chapter were published in my article in the Dec. 20, 2004 issue of *The Western Standard*, "Case (not) Closed," 31.

132. *Faryna v. Chorny*, BCCA, WWR, 171.

133. "Until his late-70s, Paul Acoose walked everywhere, including regular treks of 10 km or more to visit friends and family." Jason Warick, Canwest News Service, "Across the finish line: Legacy of Paul Acoose runs through Sask. Reserve community," March 28, 2010. www.kelowna.com/forums/topic/across-the-finish-line-legacy-of-paul-acoose-runs-through-sask-reserve-community Retrieved May 2015.

134. Barbara Zieman, "Run for Acoose," *Saskatchewan Indian*, Sept. 1982, v12 n07 p60. Retrieved May 2015.

135. Leslie Perreaux, "Decade-old death resurfaces," *StarPhoenix*, Feb. 22, 2000, A1/FRONT.

136. www.justice.gov.sk.ca/stonechild/finalreport/default.shtml

Author Biography

Launching her career with a regular column in the Yorkton *Enterprise* at the age of 16, Candis McLean earned a BA and MA in English from the University of Saskatchewan before moving with her geologist husband to Calgary. There she worked in print and radio, winning the Canadian Radio and Television News Directors award for outstanding work in the documentary field. Her proudest moment came in 2004 when her cover story about forgotten victims of tainted blood transfusions was placed on the desk of every MP, and a parliamentary committee later unanimously voted to open the compensation fund to *all* victims. "[Your article] put a face to the plight of the victims," wrote a spokesperson with the Canadian Hemophilia Society, "and created a blueprint on how the government could move forward."

In 2005, Candis teamed up with son, Stuart, to produce a film documentary, *When Police Become Prey: What Lies Behind "Starlight Tours."* After screenings in Canadian centres, their film won the coveted award, "Audience Choice for Best Documentary," at the 2010 New Hope Film Festival in Pennsylvania. Pursuing her interest in Aboriginal peoples, she worked with Vancouver lawyer Calvin Helin on his book *Dances with Dependency: Indigenous Success through Self-reliance*, which became an international best-seller. Her hope is that this book, *WHEN POLICE BECOME PREY: The Cold, Hard Facts of Neil Stonechild's Freezing Death*, puts a face to the plight of police victims of racist "justice," and creates a blueprint on how government can move forward.

More to Come

Book 2

WHEN POLICE BECOME PREY: CHIEF DAVE SCOTT AND THE CRISIS IN POLITICALLY-CORRECT JUSTICE

International award-winning former Saskatoon Police Chief Scott describes the dramatic years leading up to allegations of police conducting 'Starlight Tours.' His files include breath-taking pursuits of allegations against doctors, lawyers and a deputy chief. 'When I look back at that case over several decades,' Scott says of one, 'I see why many citizens of our nation began to distrust our justice system. When there is no reason for any reasonable person to question the guilt of an individual, yet the justice system intervenes for whatever reason to allow the person to walk free – it really drives people nuts! Up until that time I had never lost a major criminal case, and I don't think I lost that one. The people lost that one! What I realize now is that the justice system had begun to protect the criminal and not the public.' Scott discusses the urgent need for police and leaders to be forward thinkers about twenty-first century realities: public protection and ways to select, train, prepare and support police officers.

(Read more: www.WhenPoliceBecomePrey.com/Crisis)

Book 3

WHEN POLICE BECOME PREY: DARRELL NIGHT WALKED AND JUSTICE DIED

Armed with new evidence, we unravel the web of contradictions surrounding allegations of police abuse in so-called 'Starlight Tours.' Have Canadian police dropped off Native people in areas where they froze to death, as headlines around the world proclaimed? Two fired constables speak out for the first time publicly about what actually occurred that early morning when they dropped off Darrell Night – in the ride that rocked their lives. Night arrived home safely. But the tragic coincidence of two Native men later found frozen to death in the city's west-end sparked activist and media outrage. The officers were publicly condemned before anyone listened to their side of the story. Even the justice system seemed to bow to activist pressure. The officers were sent to prison where their murder was plotted. Learn the other side of the story – and implications for justice systems worldwide. When Police become Prey, will justice be served? Or will justice turn political, and truth be silenced.

(Read more: www.WhenPoliceBecomePrey.com/NightWalked)

Film Documentary

WHEN POLICE BECOME PREY: WHAT *LIES* BEHIND STARLIGHT TOURS

Following an idealistic dream of working with the Aboriginal people he had read so much about, a British Bobbie moved to Canada. For 18 years Constable Ken Munson worked in the Saskatoon's west end, winning commendations for life-saving work. All that came to an end when sensational allegations were broadcast around the world that he and his partner were racists responsible for freezing deaths of two Aboriginal men in what the media dubbed 'Starlight Tours.' In this documentary, the two officers break their silence about what occurred in their police cruiser that early morning in January 2000, when they dropped off Darrell Night near the outskirts of the city. Is political correctness overtaking the justice system in the western world? What role do media play in court decisions? Are we losing colour-blind justice? Could the justice system treat you the same way?

(Read more: www.WhenPoliceBecomePrey.com/Documentary)

Follow me on Twitter @policeprey

CPSIA information can be obtained at www.ICGtesting.com
Printed in the USA
LVOW08s1532301215

468277LV00010B/82/P